P9-EEP-934

SOMETHING ABOUT THE AUTHOR

ISSN 0276-816X

SOMETHING ABOUT THE AUTHOR

Facts and Pictures about Authors and Illustrators of Books for Young People

EDITED BY

ANNE COMMIRE

VOLUME 61

Gale Research Inc. • DETROIT • NEW YORK • LONDON

Managing Editor: Anne Commire

Editors: Agnes Garrett, Helga P. McCue

Associate Editors: Elisa Ann Ferraro, Eunice L. Petrini

Assistant Editors: Marc Caplan, Linda Shedd

Sketchwriters: Catherine Coray, Cathy Courtney,
Johanna Cypis, Marguerite Feitlowitz, Mimi H. Hutson, Deborah Klezmer, Dieter Miller

Researcher: Catherine Ruello

Editorial Assistants: Joanne J. Ferraro, Marja T. Hiltunen, June Lee, Susan Pfanner

Production Manager: Mary Beth Trimper

External Production Assistant: Marilyn Jackman

Production Supervisor: Laura Bryant

Internal Production Associate: Louise Gagné

Art Director: Arthur Chartow

Keyliner: C. J. Jonik

Special acknowledgment is due to the members of the *Something about the Author Autobiography Series* staff who assisted in the preparation of this volume.

Library of Congress Catalog Card Number 72-27107

ISBN 0-8103-2271-4
ISSN 0276-816X

Printed in the United States

Published simultaneously in the United Kingdom
by Gale Research International Limited
(An affiliated company of Gale Research Inc.)

Contents

A

B

C

D

E

F

G

H

K

L

M

N

O

P

R

S

T

U

V

W

Z

Introduction

As the only annually published ongoing reference series that deals with the lives and works of authors and illustrators of children's books, *Something about the Author (SATA)* is a unique source of information. The *SATA* series includes not only well-known authors and illustrators whose books are most widely read, but also those less prominent people whose works are just coming to be recognized. *SATA* is often the only readily available information source for less well-known writers or artists. You'll find *SATA* informative and entertaining whether you are:

—a student in junior high school (or perhaps one to two grades higher or lower) who needs information for a book report or some other assignment for an English class;

—a children's librarian who is searching for the answer to yet another question from a young reader or collecting background material to use for a story hour;

—an English teacher who is drawing up an assignment for your students or gathering information for a book talk;

—a student in a college of education or library science who is studying children's literature and reference sources in the field;

—a parent who is looking for a new way to interest your child in reading something more than the school curriculum prescribes;

—an adult who enjoys children's literature for its own sake, knowing that a good children's book has no age limits.

Scope

In *SATA* you will find detailed information about authors and illustrators who span the full time range of children's literature, from early figures like John Newbery and L. Frank Baum to contemporary figures like Judy Blume and Richard Peck. Authors in the series represent primarily English-speaking countries, particularly the United States, Canada, and the United Kingdom. Also included, however, are authors from around the world whose works are available in English translation, for example: from France, Jean and Laurent De Brunhoff; from Italy, Emanuele Luzzati; from the Netherlands, Jaap ter Haar; from Germany, James Krüss; from Norway, Babbis Friis-Baastad; from Japan, Toshiko Kanzawa; from the Soviet Union, Kornei Chukovsky; from Switzerland, Alois Carigiet, to name only a few. Also appearing in *SATA* are Newbery medalists from Hendrik Van Loon (1922) to Lois Lowry (1990). The writings represented in *SATA* include those created intentionally for children and young adults as well as those written for a general audience and known to interest younger readers. These writings cover the spectrum from picture books, humor, folk and fairy tales, animal stories, mystery and adventure, science fiction and fantasy, historical fiction, poetry and nonsense verse, to drama, biography, and nonfiction.

Information Features

In *SATA* you will find full-length entries that are being presented in the series for the first time. This volume, for example, marks the first full-length appearance of Babette Cole, Michael Ende, Lilian Obligado, E. C. Segar, and Piero Ventura.

Obituaries have been included in *SATA* since Volume 20. An Obituary is intended not only as a death notice but also as a concise view of a person's life and work. Obituaries may appear for persons who have entries in earlier *SATA* volumes, as well as for people who have not yet appeared in the series. In this volume Obituaries mark the recent deaths of Sylvia Cassedy, Kathleen Mary Lines, Charles Mercer, and Katharine James Savage.

Revised Entries

Since Volume 25, each *SATA* volume also includes newly revised and updated entries for a selection of *SATA* listees (usually four to six) who remain of interest to today's readers and who have been active enough to require extensive revision of their earlier biographies. For example, when Beverly Cleary first appeared in *SATA* Volume 2, she was the author of twenty-one books for children and young adults and the recipient of numerous awards. By the time her updated sketch appeared in Volume 43 (a span of fifteen years), this creator of the indefatigable Ramona Quimby and other memorable characters had produced a dozen new titles and garnered nearly fifty additional awards, including the 1984 Newbery Medal.

The entry for a given biographee may be revised as often as there is substantial new information to provide. In this volume, look for revised entries on Anthony Browne, Eloise Greenfield, and Marijane Meaker.

Illustrations

While the textual information in *SATA* is its primary reason for existing, photographs and illustrations not only enliven the text but are an integral part of the information that *SATA* provides. Illustrations and text are wedded in such a special way in children's literature that artists and their works naturally occupy a prominent place among *SATA*'s listees. The illustrators that you'll find in the series include such past masters of children's book illustration as Randolph Caldecott, Walter Crane, Arthur Rackham, and Ernest H. Shepard, as well as such noted contemporary artists as Maurice Sendak, Edward Gorey, Tomie de Paola, and Margot Zemach. There are Caldecott medalists from Dorothy Lathrop (the first recipient in 1938) to Ed Young (the latest winner in 1990); cartoonists like Charles Schulz ("Peanuts"), Walt Kelly ("Pogo"), Hank Ketcham ("Dennis the Menace"), and Georges Rémi ("Tintin"); photographers like Jill Krementz, Tana Hoban, Bruce McMillan, and Bruce Curtis; and filmmakers like Walt Disney, Alfred Hitchcock, and Steven Spielberg.

In more than a dozen years of recording the metamorphosis of children's literature from the printed page to other media, *SATA* has become something of a repository of photographs that are unique in themselves and exist nowhere else as a group, particularly many of the classics of motion picture and stage history and photographs that have been specially loaned to us from private collections.

Index Policy

In response to suggestions from librarians, *SATA* indexes no longer appear in each volume but are included in each alternate (odd-numbered) volume of the series, beginning with Volume 58.

SATA continues to include two indexes that cumulate with each alternate volume: the **Illustrations Index,** arranged by the name of the illustrator, gives the number of the volume and page where the illustrator's work appears in the current volume as well as all preceding volumes in the series; the **Author Index** gives the number of the volume in which a person's Biographical Sketch, Brief Entry, or Obituary appears in the current volume as well as all preceding volumes in the series.

These indexes also include references to authors and illustrators who appear in *Yesterday's Authors of Books for Children* (described in detail below). Beginning with Volume 36, the *SATA* Author Index provides cross-references to authors who are included in Gale's *Children's Literature Review.* Starting with Volume 42, you will also find cross-references to authors who are included in the *Something about the Author Autobiography Series* (described in detail below).

What a *SATA* Entry Provides

Whether you're already familiar with the *SATA* series or just getting acquainted, you will want to be aware of the kind of information that an entry provides. In every *SATA* entry the editors attempt to give as complete a picture of the person's life and work as possible. In some cases that full range of information may simply be unavailable, or a biographee may choose not to reveal complete personal details. The information that the editors attempt to provide in every entry is arranged in the following categories:

1. The "head" of the entry gives

—the most complete form of the name,
—any part of the name not commonly used, included in parentheses,
—birth and death dates, if known; a (?) indicates a discrepancy in published sources,
—pseudonyms or name variants under which the person has had books published or is publicly known, in parentheses in the second line.

2. "Personal" section gives

—date and place of birth and death,
—parents' names and occupations,
—name of spouse, date of marriage, and names of children,
—educational institutions attended, degrees received, and dates,
—religious and political affiliations,
—agent's name and address,
—home and/or office address.

3. "Career" section gives

—name of employer, position, and dates for each career post,
—military service,
—memberships,
—awards and honors.

4. "Writings" section gives

—title, first publisher and date of publication, and illustration information for each book written; revised editions and other significant editions for books with particularly long publishing histories; genre, when known.

5. "Adaptations" section gives

—title, major performers, producer, and date of all known reworkings of an author's material in another medium, like movies, filmstrips, television, recordings, plays, etc.

6. "Sidelights" section gives

—commentary on the life or work of the biographee either directly from the person (and often written specifically for the *SATA* entry), or gathered from biographies, diaries, letters, interviews, or other published sources.

7. "For More Information See" section gives

—books, feature articles, films, plays, and reviews in which the biographee's life or work has been treated.

How a *SATA* Entry Is Compiled

A *SATA* entry progresses through a series of steps. If the biographee is living, the *SATA* editors try to secure information directly from him or her through a questionnaire. From the information that the biographee supplies, the editors prepare an entry, filling in any essential missing details with research. The author or illustrator is then sent a copy of the entry to check for accuracy and completeness.

If the biographee is deceased or cannot be reached by questionnaire, the *SATA* editors examine a wide variety of published sources to gather information for an entry. Biographical sources are searched with the aid of Gale's *Biography and Genealogy Master Index*. Bibliographic sources like the *National Union Catalog*, the *Cumulative Book Index*, *American Book Publishing Record*, and the *British Museum Catalogue* are consulted, as are book reviews, feature articles, published interviews, and material sometimes obtained from the biographee's family, publishers, agent, or other associates.

For each entry presented in *SATA*, the editors also attempt to locate a photograph of the biographee as well as representative illustrations from his or her books. After surveying the available books which the biographee has written and/or illustrated, and then making a selection of appropriate photographs and illustrations, the editors request permission of the current copyright holders to reprint the material. In the case of older books for which the copyright may have passed through several hands, even locating the current copyright holder is often a long and involved process.

We invite you to examine the entire *SATA* series, starting with this volume. Described below are some of the people in Volume 61 that you may find particularly interesting.

Highlights of This Volume

ANTHONY BROWNE......showed an early interest in drawing. He would watch his father draw soldiers and battle scenes for the amusement of his sons who would join the activity. "Both he and my brother would draw...a soldier...with all details of uniform and gun. I, on the other hand, would draw battle scenes with jokes thrown in." With his degree from art school, Browne worked brief stints as a medical illustrator, teacher, and illustrator of greeting cards. This last position opened doors to publishing for him as both author and illustrator of children's books. "*Gorilla* had its roots in a card I'd done....It was a picture of a great big male gorilla holding a teddy bear. I think the image goes back to my father, who in some ways was like a gorilla, big and potentially aggressive during his pub days. I spent a lot of time at a zoo near Canterbury. The story, of course, hinges on a mixture of a big powerful gorilla and a small vulnerable girl (who had metamorphosed from the original teddy bear)." Browne's illustration earned him the coveted Kate Greenaway Medal. "No one realized [it] was going to be a runaway success. We all thought it was good work, felt hopeful and that was it....The Kate Greenaway Medal was a thrill...."

BABETTE COLE......was born in the Channel Islands where she spent most of her time exploring the island with her pony, Promise. Although her family was Protestant, she attended a convent school "where it was instilled in me to be honest and good, lest a large finger would come forth from the sky and squash me like an ant. So I was very good and always told the truth. As I got older, however, I became more devious." Now the illustrator of more than thirty children's books and the recipient of a Kate Greenaway Medal for *Prince Cinders,* Cole's talents were not always so highly regarded. "[In art school,] they didn't appreciate my sculptures....I was asked to 'make something sensuous,' so I made this lovely little black bottom that you could hold in your hand. It was made of highly polished black resin. But nobody liked it. The other students had made these enormous pieces with girders....'You don't take this seriously, do you?' they would ask, and I would respond, 'No. That's the point.'"

MICHAEL ENDE......is best known for his *Die unendliche Geschichte*, published in America as *The Neverending Story*. "In every person there is a child who wants to play...beauty can exist only in free play...the wondrous is always beautiful; only the wondrous is beautiful....The child that I used to be is still alive in me today, and there is no abyss of adulthood separating me from him. Basically, I feel that I am the same person now that I was then...a child who never loses its ability to wonder, to question, to feel excitement, who is vulnerable and exposed, who suffers, seeks comfort, senses hope...and who embodies our future until our dying day....It is for this child in me, and in all of us, that I tell my stories....To write a fantasy is to embark on a journey to an unknown destination. It is just like starting *The Neverending Story*."

ELOISE GREENFIELD......was growing up in Washington in the 1930s and 40s, when blacks "could sit anywhere [on the streetcars,] but we couldn't sit down at the drugstore soda fountains. We could shop downtown, but we might have to stand at the counter while the saleswoman waited on all the whites first, even if they had come in last, or we might not get waited on at all....There were a lot of things we couldn't do and places we couldn't go. Washington was a city for white people. But inside that city, there was another city. It didn't have a name and it wasn't all in one area, but it was where black people lived....There was always, in my Washington, a sense of people trying to make things better." Greenfield sees her writing as a way to help build a large body of literature "in which Black children can see themselves and their lives and history reflected....At the right time, in the right circumstances, falling on the right mind, a word may take effect."

MARIJANE MEAKER......was seventeen when she adopted her first pseudonym and just out of college when she became her own literary agent. "My pseudonyms were my clients....I visited editors and talked about Laura Winston (who wrote slicks for women's magazines), Mamie Stone (who wrote confessions), Edgar Stone, her 'husband' (who wrote detective stories), and Winslow Albert (who wrote articles)....They were all me." Having written many tales of murder and suspense, Meaker took on yet another persona: writer of books for young people. "Miraculously, as I sat down to make notes for...stories, things that happened to me long ago came back clear as a bell, and ringing, and making me smile and shake my head as I realized I had stories in me about *me*—no longer disguised as a homicidal maniac, or a twisted criminal bent on a scam, but as the small-town kid I'd been, so typically American and middle class and yes, vulnerable, but not as tragic and complicated as I used to imagine....So I had a new identity for myself in middle age: M. E. Kerr."

E. C. SEGAR......ran his first episode of "Thimble Theatre" in the *New York Journal* in 1919. The strip featured a cast of characters known as the Oyl family: Castor Oyl and Ma Oyl, Olive Oyl, and her beau, Ham Gravy. A full ten years passed after that first episode before Castor Oyl and Ham Gravy found themselves in need of a sailor. Bud Sagendorf, Segar's assistant and successor, recalled the scene: "As logical adventurers would, they searched the waterfront. Seafaring jobs must have been plentiful, for they found only one man in need of employment—a strange-looking character with a jutting chin and one eye. After assuring himself that this odd figure was indeed a sailor, Castor hired him on the spot....Readers of 'Thimble Theatre' that day could not know they had witnessed the birth of a legend and folk hero." On January 1, 1929, Popeye was born, and by 1932 his promotion of spinach had increased U.S. consumption of the vegetable by thirty-three percent.

These are only a few of the authors and illustrators that you'll find in this volume. We hope you find all the entries in *SATA* both interesting and useful.

Yesterday's Authors of Books for Children

In a two-volume companion set to *SATA, Yesterday's Authors of Books for Children (YABC)* focuses on early authors and illustrators, from the beginnings of children's literature through 1960, whose books are still being read by children today. Here you will find "old favorites" like Hans Christian Andersen, J. M. Barrie, Kenneth Grahame, Betty MacDonald, A. A. Milne, Beatrix Potter, Samuel Clemens, Kate Greenaway, Rudyard Kipling, Robert Louis Stevenson, and many more.

Similar in format to *SATA, YABC* features bio-bibliographical entries that are divided into information categories such as Personal, Career, Writings, and Sidelights. The entries are further enhanced by book illustrations, author photos, movie stills, and many rare old photographs.

In Volume 2 you will find cumulative indexes to the authors and to the illustrations that appear in *YABC.* These listings can also be located in the *SATA* cumulative indexes.

By exploring both volumes of *YABC,* you will discover a special group of more than seventy authors and illustrators who represent some of the best in children's literature—individuals whose timeless works continue to delight children and adults of all ages. Other authors and illustrators from early children's literature are listed in *SATA,* starting with Volume 15.

Something about the Author Autobiography Series

You can complement the information in *SATA* with the *Something about the Author Autobiography Series (SAAS),* which provides autobiographical essays written by important current authors and illustrators of books for children and young adults. In every volume of *SAAS* you will find about twenty specially commissioned autobiographies, each accompanied by a selection of personal photographs supplied by the authors. The wide range of contemporary writers and artists who describe their lives and interests in the *Autobiography Series* includes Joan Aiken, Betsy Byars, Leonard Everett Fisher, Milton Meltzer, Maia Wojciechowska, and Jane Yolen, among others. Though the information presented in the autobiographies is as varied and unique as the authors, you can learn about the people and events that influenced these writers' early lives, how they began their careers, what problems they faced in becoming established in their professions, what prompted them to write or illustrate particular books, what they now find most challenging or rewarding in their lives, and what advice they may have for young people interested in following in their footsteps, among many other subjects.

Autobiographies included in the *SATA Autobiography Series* can be located through both the *SATA* cumulative index and the *SAAS* cumulative index, which lists not only the authors' names but also the subjects mentioned in their essays, such as titles of works and geographical and personal names.

The *SATA Autobiography Series* gives you the opportunity to view "close up" some of the fascinating people who are included in the *SATA* parent series. The combined *SATA* series makes available to you an unequaled range of comprehensive and in-depth information about the authors and illustrators of young people's literature.

Please write and tell us if we can make *SATA* even more helpful to you.

Acknowledgments

Grateful acknowledgment is made to the following publishers, authors, and artists for their kind permission to reproduce copyrighted material.

HARRY N. ABRAMS, INC. Illustration by Ivan Bilibin from *Sister Fox and the Wolf* by Alexander Pushkin./ Sidelight excerpts from *Ivan Bilibin* by Sergei Golynets. Translation by Glenys Ann Kozlov. Both reprinted by permission of Harry N. Abrams, Inc.

ANDREWS, McMEEL & PARKER. Illustrations by Jules Feiffer from *Ronald Reagan in Movie America: A Jules Feiffer Production* by Jules Feiffer. Copyright © 1988 by Jules Feiffer./ Illustrations by Jules Feiffer from *Feiffer's Children* by Jules Feiffer. Copyright © 1986 by Jules Feiffer./ Illustration by Jules Feiffer from *Feiffer's Children, Including "Munro"* by Jules Feiffer. Copyright © 1959 by Jules Feiffer. All reprinted by permission of Andrews, McMeel & Parker.

ATHENEUM PUBLISHERS. Jacket illustration by Phyllis Tarlow from *Brad's Box* by Mary Alexander Walker. Cover illustration copyright © 1988 by Phyllis Tarlow. Reprinted by permission of Atheneum Publishers.

AURORA ART PUBLISHERS. Sidelight excerpts from *Ivan Bilibin* by Sergei Golynets. Translation by Glenys Ann Kozlov./ Illustration by Ivan Bilibin from *The Feather of Finist the Falcon.* Copyright © 1981 by Aurora Art Publishers. Both reprinted by permission of Aurora Art Publishers.

CAROLRHODA BOOKS, INC. Illustration by Jim LaMarche from *A Matter of Pride* by Emily Crofford. Copyright © 1981 by Carolrhoda Books, Inc./ Illustration by Jo Esco from *Becky* by Karen Hirsch. Text copyright © 1981 by Carolrhoda Books, Inc. Illustrations copyright © 1981 by Jo Esco. Both reprinted by permission of Carolrhoda Books, Inc.

CHILDREN'S PRESS. Illustration by Lois Axeman from *Katie Did It* by Becky Bring McDaniel. Copyright © 1983 by Regensteiner Publishing Enterprises, Inc. Reprinted by permission of Children's Press.

COLLINS-PICTURE LIONS. Illustration by Babette Cole from *Princess Smartypants* by Babette Cole. Copyright © 1986 by Babette Cole. Reprinted by permission of Collins-Picture Lions.

THOMAS Y. CROWELL, INC. Jacket illustration by Moneta Barnett from *Sister* by Eloise Greenfield. Copyright © 1974 by Eloise Greenfield./ Illustration by Moneta Barnett from *Me and Neesie* by Eloise Greenfield. Illustration copyright © 1975 by Moneta Barnett./ Illustrations by Jerry Pinkney and Sidelight excerpts from *Childtimes: A Three-Generation Memoir* by Eloise Greenfield and Lessie Jones Little. Copyright © 1979 by Eloise Greenfield and Lessie Jones Little./ Illustration by Diane and Leo Dillon from *Honey, I Love and Other Poems* by Eloise Greenfield. Text copyright © 1978 by Eloise Greenfield. Illustrations copyright © 1978 by Diane and Leo Dillon. All reprinted by permission of Thomas Y. Crowell, Inc.

DELL PUBLISHING CO., INC. Jacket illustration by Mark Gerber from *The Question Box* by Roberta Hughey. Text copyright © 1984 by Roberta Hughey. Jacket illustration copyright © 1984 by Mark Gerber./ Jacket illustration by Dan Brown from *Dance a Step Closer* by Mary E. Ryan. Text copyright © 1984 by Mary E. Ryan. Jacket illustration copyright © 1984 by Dan Brown. Both reprinted by permission of Dell Publishing Co., Inc.

ANDRE DEUTSCH LTD. Sidelight excerpts from *Conversations with Henry Brandon* by Henry Brandon. Reprinted by permission of Andre Deutsch Ltd.

DIAL BOOKS FOR YOUNG READERS. Sidelight excerpts from *The Great Comic Book Heroes,* compiled by Jules Feiffer./ Illustrations by Tom Feelings from *Daydreamers* by Eloise Greenfield. Text copyright © 1981 by Eloise Greenfield. Illustrations copyright © 1981 by Tom Feelings. All reprinted by permission of Dial Books For Young Readers.

DOUBLEDAY & CO., INC. Illustration by Jennifer Emry-Perrott from *A Tale of Three Leopards* by Betty Dinneen. Text copyright © 1980 by Betty Dinneen. Illustrations copyright © 1980 by Jennifer Emry-Perrott./ Jacket art design by Richard Mantel from *The Neverending Story* by Michael Ende. Translated from the German by Ralph Manheim. Copyright © 1979 by K. Thienemanns Verlag. Translation copyright © 1983 by Doubleday & Co., Inc./ Jacket illustration by Fred Marcellino from *Momo* by Michael Ende. Copyright © 1973 by K. Thienemanns Verlag. New English language translation copyright © 1984 by Doubleday & Co., Inc./ Sidelight excerpts from *Sudden Endings* by M. J. Meaker./ Illustration by Lilian Obligado from *Lassie Come-Home* by Eric Knight. Text copyright 1940 by Jere Knight. Illustrations copyright © 1964 by Nelson Doubleday, Inc. All reprinted by permission of Doubleday & Co., Inc.

E. P. DUTTON. Illustration by Penrod Scofield from *Isaac Bashevis Singer: The Story of a Storyteller* by Paul Kresh. Text copyright © 1984 by Paul Kresh. Illustrations copyright © 1984 by Penrod Scofield./ Jacket illustration by Eric Jon Nones from *Have a Heart, Cupid Delaney* by Ellen Leroe. Copyright © 1986 by Ellen W. Leroe./ Photograph from *Across the Bridge to China* by Gwenn Boardman Petersen. Copyright © 1979 by Gwenn Boardman Petersen. All reprinted by permission of E. P. Dutton.

EDITIONS ALBIN MICHAEL. Sidelight excerpts from *Pushkin: A Biography* by Henry Troyat. Reprinted by permission of Editions Albin Michael.

FABER & FABER LTD. Illustration by Alan Baker from *Wordspells,* compiled by Judith Nicholls. Text copyright © 1988 by Judith Nicholls. Illustrations copyright © 1988 by Alan Baker. Reprinted by permission of Faber & Faber Ltd.

FANTAGRAPHICS BOOKS. Illustration by Jules Feiffer from *Feiffer: The Collected Works, Volume One* by Jules Feiffer. Copyright © 1989 by Jules Feiffer./ Illustration from *The Complete E. C. Segar, Popeye: Volume Two, Sundays, 1932-1934,* edited and introduced by Rick Marschall. Copyright © by King Features Syndicate. Both reprinted by permission of Fantagraphics Books.

PHILIPP FELDHEIM, INC. Illustration by Bina Gewirtz from *Savta Simcha and the Seven Splendid Gifts* by Yaffa Ganz. Copyright © 1987 by Yaffa Ganz. Reprinted by permission of Philipp Feldheim, Inc.

HAMISH HAMILTON LTD. Illustration by Anthony Browne from *A Bear-y Tale* by Anthony Browne. Copyright © 1989 by Anthony Browne and Hamish Hamilton Ltd./ Illustration by Babette Cole from *King Change-a-Lot* by Babette Cole. Copyright © 1988 by Babette Cole./ Illustration by Babette Cole from *Prince Cinders* by Babette Cole. Copyright © 1987 by Babette Cole. All reprinted by permission of Hamish Hamilton Ltd.

HARPER & ROW, PUBLISHERS, INC. Illustration by Al Capp from *The Hardhat's Bedtime Story Book* by Al Capp. Copyright © 1970, 1971 by New York News, Inc./ Illustration by Ellen Eagle from *Someday with My Father* by Helen E. Buckley. Text copyright © 1985 by Helen E. Buckley. Illustrations copyright © 1985 by Ellen Eagle./ Illustration by Carole Byard from *Africa Dream* by Eloise Greenfield. Text copyright © 1977 by Eloise Greenfield. Illustrations copyright © 1977 by Carole Byard./ Jacket illustration by Jay J. Smith from *Dinky Hocker Shoots Smack!* by M. E. Kerr. Copyright © 1972 by M. E. Kerr./ Jacket illustration by Fred Marcellino from *I'll Love You When You're More Like Me* by M. E. Kerr. Copyright © 1977 by M. E. Kerr./ Jacket illustration by Leslie Bauman from *Is That You, Miss Blue?* by M. E. Kerr. Copyright © 1975 by M. E. Kerr./ Jacket illustration by Fred Marcellino from *Gentlehands* by M. E. Kerr. Copyright © 1978 by M. E. Kerr./ Jacket illustration by Andrew Rhodes from *Fell* by M. E. Kerr. Text copyright © 1987 by M. E. Kerr. Jacket illustration copyright © 1987 by Andrew Rhodes and Harper & Row, Publishers Inc./ Jacket illustration by Andrew Rhodes from *Night Kites* by M. E. Kerr. Text copyright © 1986 by M. E. Kerr. Jacket illustration copyright © 1986 by Andrew Rhodes and Harper & Row, Publishers Inc./ Jacket illustration by Peter Clemens from *If I Love You, Am I Trapped Forever?* by M. E. Kerr. Copyright © 1973 by M. E. Kerr./ Jacket illustration from *What I Really Think of You* by M. E. Kerr./ Sidelight excerpts from *Me, Me, Me, Me, Me: Not a Novel* by M. E. Kerr. All reprinted by permission of Harper & Row, Publishers, Inc.

WILLIAM HEINEMANN LTD. Illustration by Babette Cole from *Three Cheers for Errol!* by Babette Cole. Copyright © 1988 by Babette Cole. Reprinted by permission of William Heinemann Ltd.

HOLIDAY HOUSE, INC. Illustration by Lilian Obligado from *One Terrific Thanksgiving* by Marjorie Weinman Sharmat. Text copyright © 1985 by Marjorie Weinman Sharmat. Illustrations copyright © 1985 by Lilian Obligado. Reprinted by permission of Holiday House, Inc.

HENRY HOLT & CO. Jacket illustration by Eric Jon Nones from *The Last Goodie* by Stephen Schwandt. Copyright © 1985 by Stephen Schwandt. Reprinted by permission of Henry Holt & Co.

THE HORN BOOK, INC. Sidelight excerpts from *Illustrators of Children's Books: 1957-1966*, compiled by Lee Kingman and others. Copyright © 1968 by The Horn Book, Inc. Reprinted by permission of The Horn Book, Inc.

HOUGHTON MIFFLIN CO. Jacket illustration by Eric Velasquez from *The Bronze King* by Suzy McKee Charnas. Text copyright © 1985 by Suzy McKee Charnas. Jacket illustration copyright © 1985 by Eric Velasquez./ Jacket photograph by Thomas N. Bethell from *A Thousand Days: John F. Kennedy in the White House* by Arthur M. Schlesinger, Jr. Copyright © 1965 by Arthur M. Schlesinger, Jr./ Photograph by Paul Slade. Jacket design by Louise Noble from *Robert Kennedy and His Times* by Arthur M. Schlesinger, Jr. Text copyright © 1978 by Arthur M. Schlesinger, Jr. Photograph copyright © 1978 by Paul Slade./ Cover illustration by Jasper Johns, photographed by Geoffrey Clements from *The Cycles of American History* by Arthur M. Schlesinger, Jr. Text copyright © 1986 by Arthur M. Schlesinger, Jr. Cover design copyright © 1986 by Robert Anthony, Inc. Cover illustration copyright © 1986 by V.A.G.A. All reprinted by permission of Houghton Mifflin Co.

INTERNATIONAL POLYGONICS LTD. Cover illustration by Roger Roth from *Rose's Last Summer* by Margaret Millar. Copyright 1952, © 1980 by Margaret Millar Survivor's Trust. Cover illustration copyright © 1985 by International Polygonics Ltd. Reprinted by permission of International Polygonics Ltd.

JIFFY PRINTERS. Sidelight excerpts from *Early Memories of Chester, Illinois* by Jessie Lee Huffstutler. Reprinted by permission of Jiffy Printers.

KITCHEN SINK PRESS, INC. Photograph of Catherine and Al Capp at Seabrook Beach, New Hampshire./ Illustrations by Al Capp from *Li'l Abner Dailies, Volume One: 1934-1936* by Al Capp. Copyright © 1990 by Capp Enterprises, Inc./ Illustrations by Al Capp from *Li'l Abner Dailies, Volume Three: 1937* by Al Capp. Copyright © 1988 by Kitchen Sink Press, Inc. All reprinted by permission of Kitchen Sink Press, Inc.

ALFRED A. KNOPF, INC. Illustration by Anthony Browne from *I Like Books* by Anthony Browne. Copyright © 1988 by Anthony Browne./ Illustration by Anthony Browne from *Willy the Wimp* by Anthony Browne. Copyright © 1984 by Anthony Browne./ Illustration by Anthony Browne from *Alice's Adventures in Wonderland* by Lewis Carroll. Illustrations copyright © 1988 by Anthony Browne./ Illustration by Anthony Browne from *Willy the Champ* by Anthony Browne. Copyright © by Anthony Browne./ Illustration by Jules Feiffer from *The Phantom Tollbooth* by Norton Juster. All reprinted by permission of Alfred A. Knopf, Inc.

THE LIBRARY OF CONGRESS. Illustration from *The Department of Justice* by Lynne Dunn. Introduction by Arthur M. Schlesinger, Jr. Copyright © 1989 by Chelsea House Publishers. Reprinted by permission of The Library of Congress.

J. B. LIPPINCOTT CO. Illustration by James Calvin from *Talk about a Family* by Eloise Greenfield. Text copyright © 1978 by Eloise Greenfield. Illustrations copyright © 1978 by James Calvin. Reprinted by permission of J. B. Lippincott Co.

LITTLE, BROWN & CO., INC. Illustration by Richard Brown from *Egg-Drop Day* by Harriet Ziefert. Text copyright © 1988 by Harriet Ziefert. Illustrations copyright © 1988 by Richard Brown. Reprinted by permission of Little, Brown & Co., Inc.

LITTLE MAMMOTH. Illustration by Anthony Browne from *Gorilla* by Anthony Browne. Copyright © 1983 by Anthony Browne. Reprinted by permission of Little Mammoth.

MAIN LINE BOOK PUBLISHERS. Illustration from *Pope John Paul II* by Timothy Walch. Introductory essay on leadership by Arthur M. Schlesinger, Jr. Copyright © 1989 by Chelsea House Publishers. Reprinted by permission of Main Line Book Publishers.

JULIAN MESSNER. Illustration from *Robotics* by Stuart and Donna Paltrowitz. Copyright © 1983 by Stuart Paltrowitz and Donna Paltrowitz. Reprinted by permission of Julian Messner.

MONDADORI INFOMATICA. Illustration by Luca Novelli from *My First Book about Computers* by Luca Novelli. Translation by Laura Parma-Veigel. Copyright © 1983 by Arnoldo Mondadori Editore. Copyright © 1986 by Microsoft Press. Reprinted by permission of Mondadori Infomatica.

WILLIAM MORROW & CO., INC. Illustration by Toni Goffe from *Stamp Your Feet Action Rhymes,* compiled by Sarah Hayes. Text copyright © 1988 by Sarah Hayes. Illustrations copyright © 1988 by Toni Goffe./ Illustration by Toni Goffe from *Joe Giant's Missing Boot* by Toni Goffe./ Illustration by Toni Goffe from *Clap Your Hands: Finger Rhymes,* compiled by Sarah Hayes. Copyright © 1988 by Sarah Hayes. Illustrations copyright © 1988 by Toni Goffe./ Illustration by Susan Varley from *The Monster Bed* by Jeanne Willis. Text copyright © 1986 by Jeanne Willis. Illustrations copyright © 1986 by Susan Varley. All reprinted by permission of William Morrow & Co., Inc.

NAL BOOKS. Illustration by Tim Hildebrandt from *Fang, the Gnome* by Michael Greatrex Coney. Copyright © 1988 by Michael Coney. Reprinted by permission of NAL Books.

OXFORD UNIVERSITY PRESS, INC. Illustration by Jane Cope from *Glubbslyme* by Jacqueline Wilson. Copyright © 1987 by Jacqueline Wilson. Reprinted by permission of Oxford University Press, Inc.

PELICAN PUBLISHING CO., INC. Illustration by Al Capp from *Great Cartoonists and Their Art* by Art Wood. Copyright © 1987 by Art Wood. Reprinted by permission of Pelican Publishing Co., Inc.

PENGUIN BOOKS. Illustration from *Little Murders* by Jules Feiffer. Copyright © 1968 by Jules Feiffer. Reprinted by permission of Penguin Books.

PHILOMEL BOOKS. Illustration by Carole Byard from *Grandmama's Joy* by Eloise Greenfield. Text copyright © 1980 by Eloise Greenfield. Illustrations copyright by Carole Byard. Reprinted by permission of Philomel Books.

PLEASANT CO. Illustration by Renee Graef from *Meet Kirsten* by Janet Shaw. Copyright © 1986 by Pleasant Co. Reprinted by permission of Pleasant Co.

PROGRESS PUBLISHERS. Illustration by B. Dekhteryov from *The Fisherman and the Goldfish* by Alexander Pushkin. Reprinted by permission of Progress Publishers.

PUFFIN BOOKS. Cover illustration by Derek James from *The Crazies and Sam* by Judy K. Morris. Copyright © 1983 by Judy K. Morris and Viking Penguin, Inc./ Illustration by Lilian Obligado from *Faint Frogs Feeling Feverish and Other Terrifically Tantalizing Tongue Twisters* by Lilian Obligado. Copyright © 1983 by Lilian Obligado de Vajay. Both reprinted by permission of Puffin Books.

THE PUTNAM PUBLISHING GROUP, INC. Illustration by Pat Cummings from *Good News: Formerly "Bubbles"* by Eloise Greenfield. Text copyright © 1972 by Eloise G. Greenfield. Illustrations copyright © 1977 by Pat Cummings./ Illustration by Piero Ventura from *Great Composers* by Piero Ventura. Copyright © 1988 by Arnoldo Mondadori Editore. English translation copyright © 1989 by Arnoldo Mondadori Editore./ Illustration by Piero Ventura from *Great Painters* by Piero Ventura. Copyright © 1984 by Arnoldo Mondadori Editore. English translation copyright © 1984 by Arnoldo Mondadori Editore./ Sidelight excerpts from the Introduction to *There Once Was a Time* by Piero Ventura. Copyright © 1986, 1987 by Arnoldo Mondadori Editore. All reprinted by permission of The Putnam Publishing Group.

RADUGA PUBLISHERS. Illustration by Vladimir Konashevich from *Alexander Pushkin Tales* by Alexander Pushkin. Copyright © 1985 by Raduga Publishers. Reprinted by permission of Raduga Publishers.

ROUNDTABLE PRESS, INC. Illustration by Al Capp from *America's Great Comic-Strip Artists* by Richard Marschall. Copyright © 1989 by Cross River Press Ltd. Reprinted by permission of Roundtable Press, Inc.

VIKING PENGUIN, INC. Illustration by Anthony Browne from *The Visitors Who Came to Stay* by Annalena McAfee./ Illustration by Lilian Obligado from *A Dog Called Scholar* by Anne H. White. Copyright © 1963 by Anne H. White./ Illustration by Lilian Obligado from *Pickles and Jake* by Janet Chenery. Text copyright © 1975 by Janet Dai Chenery. Illustrations copyright © 1975 by Lilian Obligado de Vajay./ Illustration by Boris Zvorykin from *Boris Godounov* by Alexander Pushkin. Copyright © 1982 by Viking Penguin, Inc. Reprinted by permission of Viking Penguin, Inc.

WAYLAND/SILVER BURDETT. Photograph by Roland Weber from *The St. Lawrence* by Honor Leigh Winks and Robin W. Winks. Copyright © 1980 by Wayland Publishers Ltd. Reprinted by permission of Wayland/Silver Burdett.

WORKMAN PUBLISHING CO., INC. Illustrations by E. C. Segar and Sidelight excerpts from *Popeye: The First Fifty Years* by Bud Sagendorf. Copyright © 1979 by King Features Syndicate, Inc. and Workman Publishing Co., Inc. Reprinted by permission of Workman Publishing Co., Inc.

Sidelight excerpts from an article "Conversation with Arthur M. Schlesinger, Jr.: The Use of Oral History" by Lynn A. Bonfield in *American Archivist*, fall, 1980. Reprinted by permission of *American Archivist.*/ Illustration by Margot Apple from *The Blueberry Bears* by Eleanor Lapp. Text copyright © 1983 by Eleanor Lapp. Illustrations copyright © 1983 by Margot Apple. Reprinted by permission of Margot Apple./ Illustration by Juan Barberis from *The Call of the Wild* by Jack London. Adapted by Lillian Nordlicht. Copyright © 1980 by Raintree Publishers, Inc. Reprinted by permission of Juan Barberis./ Sidelight excerpts from an article "20th IBBY Congress in Tokyo," by Michael Ende in *Bookbird*, numbers 3 and 4, September 15/October 15, 1986. Reprinted by permission of *Bookbird.*/ Sidelight excerpts *From Dogpatch to Slobbovia: The (Gasp!!) World of Li'l Abner* by David Manning and Al Capp. Reprinted by permission of Boston University School of Communications./ Sidelight excerpts from an article "Popeye," by E. C. Segar in *Cartoonist Profile,* March, 1972. Reprinted by permission of *Cartoonist Profile.*/ Self-portrait of Al Capp in *Chicago Tribune*. Reprinted by permission of Chicago Tribune-New York News Syndicate, Inc./ Sidelight excerpts from an article "Say Something about the Status Quo: 'Al Capp, Master Satirist of the Comics,'" by Rick Marschall in *Classic Comics Library*, April, 1986. Reprinted by permission of *Classic Comics Library.*

Sidelight excerpts from an article "Memories of a Pro Bono Cartoonist," by Gary Groth in *Comics Journal*, August, 1988. Reprinted by permission of *Comics Journal.*/ Sidelight excerpts from an article "Jules Feiffer, Cartoonist—Playwright" by Christopher Durang in *Dramatist Quarterly*, winter, 1987. Reprinted by permission of *Dramatists Quarterly.*/ Sidelight excerpts from an article "Something to Shout About," by Eloise Greenfield in *Horn Book Magazine*, December, 1975. Reprinted by permission of Eloise Greenfield./ Sidelight excerpts from an article "Every Culture Needs a Myth: Ende" by Ulrike Meier in *Japan Times,* August 26, 1986. Reprinted by permission of *Japan Times.*/ Sidelight excerpts from an article "Profile: Eloise Greenfield," by Rosalie Black Kiah in *Language Arts,* September, 1980. Reprinted by permission of *Language Arts.*/ Sidelight excerpts from an article "'It's Hideously True' Creator of Li'l Abner Tells Why His Hero Is (Sob!) Wed" by Al Capp in *Life* Magazine, March 31, 1952. Reprinted by permission of *Life* Magazine./ Sidelight excerpts from an article "My Well-Balanced Life on a Wooden Leg" by Al Capp in *Life* Magazine, May 23, 1960. Reprinted by permission of *Life* Magazine./ Sidelight excerpts from *Pushkin: A Biography* by David Magarshack. Reprinted by permission of Elsie Magarshack./ Sidelight excerpts from an article "Profiles: Ooff!!! (Sob!!) Eep!!! (Gulp!!) Zowie!!! II," by J. Kahn, Jr. in *New Yorker*, December 6, 1947. Reprinted by permission of *New Yorker.*

Sidelight excerpts from an article "In Writing 'Grown-Ups,' Jules Feiffer Found He Really Liked His Parents," by Michiko Kakutani in *New York Times*, December 15, 1981. Reprinted by permission of *New York Times.*/ Sidelight excerpts from an article "Jules Feiffer," by Roy Newquist in *Counterpoint*, 1964. Reprinted by permission of Rand McNally & Co./ Sidelight excerpts from an article "Recap on Al Capp," by William Furlong in *Saturday Evening Post*, winter, 1971. Reprinted by permission of *Saturday Evening Post.*/ Sidelight excerpts from an article "Conversations," by Marian Christy in *St. Louis Post Dispatch,* November 3, 1985. Reprinted by permission of *St. Louis Post Dispatch.*/ Sidelight excerpts from an article "Spellbinding Storytellers Spin Their Tales on WQXR-AM," in *Talk Radio Guide,* February, 1990. Reprinted by permission of *Talk Radio Guide.*/ Illustration by Al Capp and photograph of Al Capp on the cover of *Time* magazine. Reprinted by permission of Time, Inc./ Illustration by Jennie Williams from *My Brother Is Afraid of Just about Everything* by Lois Osborn. Text copyright © 1982 by Lois Osborn. Illustrations copyright © 1982 by Jennie Williams. Reprinted by permission of Jennie Williams.

PHOTOGRAPH CREDITS

Bruce Bond: R. Kimlin Johnson; Suzy McKee Charnas: copyright © 1985 by Stephen Charnas; Babette Cole (in front of Ivy Cottage): Cathy Courtney; Michael G. Coney: Memory Lane Photography; Ellen Eagle: Gordon Leavitt; Yaffa Ganz: copyright © by Karen Benzian; Toni Goffe: Tim Goffe; Marijane Meaker: Zoe Kamitses; Jeanette Mines: Ebert (Oak Park); Mildred Morningstar: Olan Mills; Stephen Schwandt: copyright © 1988 by Karen Schwandt; E. C. Segar: Marie Segar Clausen; Janet Shaw: Bob McCleary; Alan Sillitoe: copyright © 1990 by D. Sillitoe.

Appreciation also to the Perfoming Arts Research Center of the New York Public Library at Lincoln Center for permission to reprint the theater still from "Li'l Abner."

SOMETHING ABOUT THE AUTHOR

ABBOTT, R(obert) Tucker 1919-

PERSONAL: Born September 28, 1919, in Watertown, Mass.; son of Charles Matthew (a paint manufacturer) and Frances (a homemaker; maiden name, Tucker) Abbott; married Mary M. Sisler, February 18, 1946 (died, 1964); married Sue Sweeney Darwin, January 8, 1966 (died, 1976); married Cecelia White (a fashion coordinator), May 13, 1977; children: (first marriage) Robert Tucker, Jr., Carolyn Tucker, Cynthia Douglas. *Education:* Harvard University, B.S., 1946; George Washington University, M.S., 1953, Ph.D., 1955. *Politics:* Independent. *Religion:* Episcopalian. *Home:* 2208 South Colonial Dr., Melbourne, Fla. 32901. *Agent:* Gloria Mosesson, Suite 3501, 20 Exchange Place, New York, N.Y. 10005. *Office:* American Malacologists, P.O. Box 2255, Melbourne, Fla. 32902.

CAREER: U.S. National Museum, Washington, D.C., assistant curator, division of mollusks, 1946-49, associate curator, 1949-54; Academy of Natural Sciences of Philadelphia, Philadelphia, Pa., research scientist and holder of Pilsbry Chair, 1954-69; Delaware Museum of Natural History, Greenville, Del., assistant director (malacology), 1969-78. President, American Malacologists, Inc., Melbourne, Fla.; founding director, Shell Museum and Educational Foundation, Sanibel Island, Fla. Adjunct professor, University of Delaware, 1976-78. Member of ten scientific expeditions in search of marine life, in the Philippines, Zanzibar, Thailand, Australia, the Marianas, Hawaii, Bermuda, West Indies, Fiji, and Samoa. Member of board of directors, Natural Sciences Foundation, 1956-63; member of board of trustees, Bermuda Biological Station, 1970-80. *Military service:* U.S. Navy Reserve, 1942-46; became lieutenant.

MEMBER: American Association for the Advancement of Science (fellow; life member), American Malacological Union (life member; president, 1956-57), Society of Systematic Zoology (secretary, 1960-62), Australian Malacological Society (patron, 1960—), Philadelphia Shell Club (founder; president, 1955-57), American Society of Journalists and Authors, Sons of the American Revolution, Harvard Club, Explorers Club (New York). *Awards, honors:* Smithsonian Award for Outstanding Service, 1954; Dugan Award in Aquatic Science from the American Littoral Society, 1978.

WRITINGS:

Handbook of Medically Important Mollusks of the Orient and Western Pacific, Museum of Comparative Zoology, Harvard University, 1948.

(Contributor) *A Manual of Tropical Medicine,* Saunders, 1954.

American Seashells, Van Nostrand, 1954, 2nd edition, 1978.

Introducing Sea Shells: A Colorful Guide for the Beginning Collector, Van Nostrand, 1955.

Shells, National Audubon Society, 1958.

The Marine Mollusks of Grand Cayman Island, British West Indies (monograph), Academy of Natural Sciences (Philadelphia), 1958.

The Genus Strombus in the Indo-Pacific, Academy of Natural Sciences, 1960.

How to Know the American Marine Shells, Signet, 1961.

(With Germaine L. Warmke) *Caribbean Seashells,* Livingston, 1961.

Sea Shells of the World, Golden Press, 1962, revised edition (illustrated by George F. Sandstrom and Marita Sandstrom), 1985.

(With R. J. L. Wagner) *Van Nostrand's Standard Catalog of Shells,* Van Nostrand, 1964, 3rd edition, 1978.

Shells, Doubleday, 1966.

Quiz Me: Seashells (Braille), Twin Vision, 1967.

Venom Apparatus and Geographical Distribution of Conus Gloriamaris (pamphlet), Academy of Natural Sciences, 1967.

R. TUCKER ABBOTT

Seashells of North America: A Guide to Field Identification (illustrated by G. F. Sandstrom), Golden Press, 1968.

(With Hugh Stix and Marguerite Stix) *The Shell: Five Hundred Years of Inspired Design,* Abrams, 1968.

(Editor) *Swainson's Exotic Conchology,* Delaware Museum of Natural History and Van Nostrand, 1968.

Kingdom of the Seashell, Crown, 1972.

Shells in Color (illustrated by K. B. Sandved), Viking, 1973.

American Malacologists, American Malacologists, 1973, supplement, 1975.

Seashells, Bantam, 1976.

(With S. Peter Dance) *Compendium of Seashells,* Dutton, 1982, revised edition, American Malacologists, 1986.

Collectible Florida Shells, American Malacologists, 1984.

Collectible Shells of Southeastern U.S., Bahamas, and Caribbean, American Malacologists, 1984.

Register of American Malacologists, American Malacologists, 1987.

Compendium of Land Shells, American Malacologists, 1989.

Shells, Portland House, 1989.

Writer of reports on mollusks issued by Museum of Comparative Zoology, Harvard University, Smithsonian Institution, and Raffles Museum, Singapore. Contributor to *World Book Encyclopedia, Encyclopedia Americana, Grolier's Encyclopedia,* and other encyclopedias. Contributor to *Natural History, Science Digest, Palm Beach Life, Sojourn, Mariner's Guide to Oceanography, Nautilus, Golden Years* and *Science Counselor*. Editor-in-chief, *Indo-Pacific Mollusca,* 1959-76, and *Nautilus,* 1970-86.

ADAPTATIONS:

"Seashells of North America" (cassette), American Malacologists, 1987.

"Exploring Collectible Shells" (cassette), American Malacologists, 1987.

WORK IN PROGRESS: American Sheashells, 7,000 species, 3rd edition; *Seashells, Canadian Nature Guides,* and gallery books, for W. H. Smith; *The Pocket Guide to Seashells of the Northern Hemisphere,* for Dragon's World (London); *Seashells of Southeast Asia,* for Graham Brash (Singapore).

SIDELIGHTS: "Science books can be frighteningly complicated. I know, because I could hardly get through my college texts on genetics, bio-statistics, and evolutionary cladistics. In the beginning, I didn't even know what some of the words meant!

"This all made me determined to translate my favorite science, conchology, into illustrations and languages that would truly interest and inspire beginners, both young and old.

"Two things helped. I was a rotten student from the start, mainly because I had spent all my youthful spare time romping through the woods or up and down the seashore looking for and collecting weird insects, mysterious plants, and beautiful seashells. Being poor in grades, I had to work hard at my studies and I appreciated the simpler explanations of problems.

"Secondly, I believe I inherited a desire, nay, an urge, to write. If musical genius can run through family lines, as geneticists tell us, why not also the ability and desire to write? Sometime after I had served as editor of our high school annual and had written a few stories, I learned with surprise that my great-granduncles, Jacob Abbot (one 't') and John Stevens Cabot Abbott (two 't's') wrote over 200 books for children and many histories for adults during the mid-1800s.

"I was schooled and practiced in the biological sciences, first at Harvard under the tutelage of Dr. William J. Clench, and later, was a research malacologist (or conchologist) at the Smithsonian Institution in Washington, D.C., and the Academy of Natural Sciences of Philadelphia. I soon turned to popular writing to supplement my meager salary as a naturalist.

"I consider myself a fairly good nonfiction writer but certainly not an outstanding or prolific one. Knowledge in my field and a desire for accuracy were my fortes. I take satisfaction in seeing my name in the acknowledgements in the books of much more capable writers like Rachel Carson and Herbert Zim.

"Shall we teach our scientists to write or shall we educate our writers? Both are possible, although I prefer the former course. I have spent a large part of my career, as a reader and editor, correcting and sometimes rewriting the nature books and magazine stories written by amateur conchologists. A surprising number of publishers today produce books on science that are filled with errors created by writers not familiar with the field. Before me at the moment are two such books, each with over a hundred errors and false statements. And try to write a school book in America on the scientific subject of evolution! Religiously, it is taboo.

"There is no question that writing is mostly done by those who love to do it and those who are willing to take the time and effort. Financial reward for the average nonfiction writer is not very much. I have roughly divided the number of hours I have put into my thirty published books by the total payments in royalties and advances and have come up with the discouraging average of forty cents an hour! So it's really the enjoyment of creating and the satisfaction of completion that lures me into writing a book."

HOBBIES AND OTHER INTERESTS: Clixology, the study and taxonomy of paper clixs in the phylum Clixa; vegetable gardening; world environmental destruction; political world affairs; history of conchology.

FOR MORE INFORMATION SEE:

Register of American Malacologists, 2nd edition, American Malacologists, 1987.

COLLECTIONS

De Grummond Collection at the University of Southern Mississippi.

ADAMS, Florence 1932-

PERSONAL: Born May 18, 1932, in New York, N.Y.; daughter of Francis Joseph and Florence M. (White) O'Neill; married Donald L. Adams, August 25, 1962 (divorced, 1967); children: David G., Sam T. *Education:* Hunter College (now Hunter College of the City University of New York), B.A., 1955. *Home address:* P.O. Box 1944, Orleans, Mass. 02653.

CAREER: Computer consultant, painter, writer. Has taught computer courses at graduate level, and classes in home repair for women. Featured in "Take a Hammer in Your Hand, Sister," WBAI, New York, N.Y., 1970s. *Exhibitions:* Brewster Unitarian Church, Mass., 1988. *Member:* Authors Guild.

WRITINGS:

Mushy Eggs (juvenile), Putnam, 1973.
I Took a Hammer in My Hand: The Woman's Build-It and Fix-It Handbook, Morrow, 1973.

FLORENCE ADAMS

Catch a Sunbeam: A Book of Solar Study and Experiments (illustrated by Kiyo Komoda), Harcourt, 1978.
Make Your Own Baby Furniture: Projects for the Pregnant Woman, Evans, 1980.

PLAYS

(With Jane Greenawalt) "Susan B" (a musical), first produced in Hartsdale, N.Y., 1976.

WORK IN PROGRESS: Writing and illustrating a new children's series.

ALENOV, Lydia 1948-

PERSONAL: Born October 4, 1948, in Rochester, Minn.; daughter of Eugene John (a farmer) and Florence (a waitress and homemaker; maiden name, Wendel) Phillips; married Nikolai Alenov (a restaurateur), September 1, 1972; children: Nikolai, Nadia, Noah. *Education:* Attended Mount Mercy College, 1967-68; Minneapolis College of Art and Design, B.F.A., 1972. *Religion:* Orthodox. *Home:* 1896 Feronia Ave., St. Paul, Minn. 55104. *Office:* Russian Tea House, 1758 University Ave., St. Paul, Minn. 55104.

CAREER: Children's book illustrator. Franklin Nursing Home, Minneapolis, Minn., nurse's aide, 1969-70; Fair Oaks Nursing Home, Minneapolis, nurse's aide, 1970-71; Mount Sinai Hospital, Minneapolis, nursing assistant, 1971-75; Russian Tea House, co-owner, St. Paul, Minn., 1979—.

ILLUSTRATOR:

(With husband, Nikolai Alenov) Etolin Wittanen, *Auke Lake Tales,* Syraxis Press, 1978.

SIDELIGHTS: "I grew up on a secluded farm, surrounded by forest on three sides, with a creek flowing lazily through the pasture. I loved the quiet atmosphere. You could hear the train blowing its long lonesome warning whistle as it went through the crossing in Meridian a few miles away every evening at around six o'clock, and the sound of the milking machines going in the barn. I felt great security in the seasonal routine of farm life. I could not imagine being happy anywhere else.

"I remember waking one morning to the sound of chain saws and heavy equipment. The phone company was leveling the rows of huge oaks that canopied the long 'public' driveway that led to our farm. They were tired of fixing lines 'done in' by fallen oak branches. They had to keep herbiciding to prevent future growth. They took great care—in this regard—we never again delighted at the sight of a deer grazing along the driveway. I have never again felt such a sickening loss as I did then. But also came the grace of realizing for the first time what it means to be truly Orthodox.

"Nothing material is permanent or can be held on to. I longed to gather a treasure that moths, mold, rust, or man could not destroy. As men become more remote from God they also do battle with nature. Instead of working with it, they rely on chemical fertilizers, herbicides, etc., destroying valuable farmland and water supplies, creating acid rain which further destroys resources, creating wastes that create more wastes for which there is no safe disposal. Men forget that they are also disposable and will one day face God. But God's face can be seen in nature, and if there is only a tiny flower or the song of one bird left amid a decaying planet, the beauty of it will take flight to the heart and

LYDIA ALENOV

remind man that God will never abandon him until he comes home. In the meantime, we find great joy and comfort in the timeless, changeless tradition, the cycle of the church year. The one sure thing, the one hope worth living for in any circumstance, is the same, yesterday, today, and tomorrow."

HOBBIES AND OTHER INTERESTS: Painting, hiking.

ARMOUR, Richard (Willard) 1906-1989

OBITUARY NOTICE—See sketch in *SATA* Volume 14: Born July 15, 1906, in San Pedro, Calif.; died after suffering from Parkinson's disease, February 28, 1989, in Claremont, Calif. Educator, administrator, poet, columnist, and author. Armour was an authority on English romantic poetry and a prolific writer of humorous prose and light verse. In the mid-1940s he joined the faculties of Scripps College and Claremont Graduate School, serving both institutions as professor of English. He was also dean of the faculty at Scripps College in the early 1960s and became professor emeritus of Claremont Graduate School in 1966. Armour's first poetry was published by the *New Yorker* and the *Saturday Evening Post* in 1937; since then he contributed poetry and prose to more than two hundred periodicals. He also wrote the widely syndicated newspaper column "Armour's Armory" and more than sixty books, many enjoyed by young adults, including *Punctured Poems: Famous First and Infamous Second Lines, It All Started with Columbus, Twisted Tales from Shakespeare,* and *Through Darkest Adolescence. Going around in Academic Circles* was adapted into a musical. His books for children include *On Your Marks: A Package of Punctuation,* which was made into a film, *Have You Ever Wished You Were Something Else?,* and *Strange Monsters of the Sea.*

FOR MORE INFORMATION SEE:

Martha E. Ward and Dorothy A. Marquardt, *Authors of Books for Young People,* Scarecrow, 1971.
D. L. Kirkpatrick, *Twentieth-Century Children's Writers,* St. Martin's, 1978.
Sally Holmes Holtze, *Fifth Book of Junior Authors and Illustrators,* H. W. Wilson, 1983.
Steven H. Gale, editor, *Encyclopedia of American Humorists,* Garland, 1988.

OBITUARIES

Los Angeles Times, March 1, 1989.
New York Times, March 2, 1989 (p. B-16).
Washington Post, March 2, 1989.

BARBERIS, Juan C(arlos) 1920- (Kumpa; My)

PERSONAL: Born June 11, 1920, in Cordoba, Argentina; son of Antonio R. (an educator) and Maria Justa (a homemaker; maiden name, Negrete) Barberis; married Alcira A. Ibanez (an artist), February 20, 1947; children: Carlos Alberto, Giovanna Alcira Hershman. *Education:* Attended School of Fine Arts, Buenos Aires, Argentina, and Real Academy of Fine Arts, Madrid, Spain. *Religion:* Catholic. *Home:* 14 Willow Dr., Port Washington, N.Y. 11050.

CAREER: Free-lance artist, 1959—; American Museum of Natural History, New York, N.Y., artist and illustrator, 1963-85. *Exhibitions:* Circulo of Fine Arts, Buenos Aires, Argentina, 1945, 1950; (one-man show) Biblioteca Villaespesa, Almeria, Spain, 1949; National Exhibition of Fine Arts, Madrid Spain, 1950; Institute of Hispanic Culture, Madrid Spain, 1950; (one-man show) Biblioteca Municipal, Cadiz, Spain, 1959; National Park Service, Harpers Ferry Center, W.Va., 1979.

ILLUSTRATOR:

Thomas Fall, *Dandy's Mountain,* Dial, 1967.
Jack London, *The Call of the Wild,* adapted by Lillian Nordlicht, Raintree, 1980.

Also illustrator of *Isfendiar and the Wild Donkeys,* and *Ali,* both Atheneum. Contributor of illustrations to *Reader's Digest, Life, Reporter, Medical World News, Newsweek, Natural History, Animal Kingdom,* and *Cardiovascular Medicine.*

BASSETT, Lisa 1958-

PERSONAL: Born January 26, 1958, in Winter Park, Fla.; daughter of Samuel Taylor III and Barbara (an art teacher; maiden name, Crisler) Bassett. *Education:* Rollins College, B.A. (with honors), 1984; University of Texas at Austin, M.A., 1986, doctoral study, 1987—. *Religion:* Christian. *Home:* Austin, Tex. *Agent:* Dilys Evans, P.O. Box 400, Norfolk, Conn. 06058. *Office:* Department of English, 108 Parlin Hall, University of Texas at Austin, Austin, Tex. 78712.

CAREER: University of Texas at Austin, assistant instructor in English, 1986—. *Member:* Lewis Carroll Society of North

America, Modern Language Association of America. *Awards, honors: A Clock for Beany* was exhibited at the Bologna International Children's Book Fair, 1985, and selected one of Child Study Association of America's Children's Books of the Year, 1986; Fellowship to Oxford University from University of Texas at Austin, 1986; Scholarship to University of Birmingham (England) from the English Speaking Union of Austin, Tex., 1989.

WRITINGS:

JUVENILE

A Clock for Beany (Junior Literary Guild selection; illustrated by sister, Jeni Bassett), Dodd, 1985.
Beany and Scamp (Junior Literary Guild selection; illustrated by J. Bassett), Dodd, 1987.
Very Truly Yours, Charles L. Dodgson, Alias Lewis Carroll, Lothrop, 1987.
Beany Wakes Up for Christmas (illustrated by J. Bassett), Putnam, 1988.

WORK IN PROGRESS: Research on Shakespeare and Renaissance literature.

SIDELIGHTS: "I hope that in writing for children I can create the kind of world I always found in books. As a child I could enter the fantasy world of a book wholeheartedly, particularly the world of magical animals. My children's books are about animals, Beany Bear and Scamp Squirrel, and they are inspired by the whimsical drawings of my sister, Jeni Bassett. The friendship between Beany and Scamp is beautifully embodied in the warmth and charm of Jeni's illustrations. I write the stories with Jeni's pictures in mind.

LISA BASSETT

"My biography of Lewis Carroll, *Very Truly Yours, Charles L. Dodgson, Alias Lewis Carroll,* is also about friendship. I wanted to introduce children to the Carroll who befriended hundreds of children in his lifetime. I want my readers to meet the man as he revealed himself to the children who knew him. Biographies for juvenile readers that are written like novels never appealed to me. I always had the feeling I was reading a fictional account rather than a realistic portrayal of the biographical subject. In my book, I want to let children meet Carroll and form their opinions about the man by reading his own words (in letters to children) and the words of the children who wrote about their relationships with him.

"My interest in Carroll began long ago when I read the 'Alice' books to my sister. She had been ill for quite a while and to entertain her, I read about Alice's adventures. We laughed together, especially over Humpty Dumpty. Later as a college student, I read Carroll's letters and found the same hilarious nonsense in his epistles to children. I also found a man whom I thought children would like to know. I hope young people and adults finish my book about Carroll with a special sense of the man's love of childhood and children."

BAUGHMAN, Dorothy 1940-

PERSONAL: Surname is pronounced *Bock*-man; born July 13, 1940, in Prattville, Ala; daughter of Charles Ross (a pharmacist) and Thelma (a homemaker; maiden name, Cooper) McCartney; married James Baughman (a water company superintendent), April 22, 1960; children: James, Jr., Vicki Lynn, Toni Marie. *Education:* Attended high school in Elmore County, Ala. *Religion:* Baptist. *Home address:* P.O. Box 176, Eclectic, Ala. 36024.

CAREER: Telephone switchboard operator in Montgomery, Ala., 1959-61; Elmore County Hospital, Wetumpka, Ala., cardiogram technician, 1968-73; free-lance writer, beginning 1973; Elmore County Hospital, Ala., part time lab secretary, 1987-88; Whitehead Clinic, Tallahassee, Fla., veterinarian assistant, 1989. Emergency Medical Technician; substitute teacher and conductor of writing workshops. Member of local City Council, 1976-80; member of Methodist Church board. *Member:* Creative Writer's Club (Montgomery, Ala.). *Awards, honors:* Juvenile Pen Woman's Contest First Prize from the Alabama Pen Women and Press and Authors Club, 1975, for "Chester the Fraidy Cat"; Juvenile Pen Woman's Bicentennial Contest First Prize from the Alabama Pen Women, 1975, for "The Golden Locket"; *Piney's Summer* was selected one of Child Study Association of America's Children's Books of the Year, 1976.

WRITINGS:

Piney's Summer (juvenile; illustrated by Tom Allen), 1976.

GOTHIC ROMANCES

The Mystery of Aronov Point, Avalon, 1980.
Secret of Montoya Mission, Avalon, 1981.
Icy Terror, Avalon, 1984.
Secret Wishes, Secret Fears, Avalon, 1987.

Contributor of articles and stories to popular magazines for adults and children, including *Harper's Weekly, Woman's Cir-*

DOROTHY BAUGHMAN

cle, Home Life, Antique Trader, Children's Playmate, Red Cross Youth News, Junior Discoveries, Friend, Vine, Highlights for Children, and *Jack and Jill.*

WORK IN PROGRESS: A young adult mystery for Bantam; Civil War background novel based on great-grandparents; several short stories.

SIDELIGHTS: "I was born in the South and have been here all my life, so I am what you call the typical southern woman. My husband is a rebel by choice, I guess, since he is from Pennsylvania and has lived here for thirty-one years. I am a Peter Pan character having never grown up, and relate to children and teens better than most. I'm a nut to my children, my youngest daughter calls me a cross between Angela Lansbury and Lucille Ball, which to me is a compliment."

FOR MORE INFORMATION SEE:

Montgomery Advertiser, February 15, 1976, October 15, 1976.

BEILER, Edna 1923-

PERSONAL: Born October 24, 1923, in New Paris, Ind.; daughter of John A. (a farmer) and Magdalena (a homemaker; maiden name, Byler) Beiler. *Education:* Attended Arizona State University, 1944-45; Goshen College, graduate, 1968. *Religion:* Episcopal. *Home:* 125 North Munsie, Cumberland, Ind. 46229.

CAREER: Mennonite Publishing House, Scottdale, Pa., free-lance writer, 1950-55; Mennonite Relief and Service Committee, Elkhart, Ind., roving reporter, 1955-58; Mennonite Board of Missions and Charities, Elkhart, editorial assistant, 1959-66; Department of Public Welfare, Hancock County, Ind., social worker, 1968-76; Indiana State Department of Public Welfare, Indianapolis, institutional specialist, 1976-86. *Member:* Quilters Guild of Indianapolis.

WRITINGS:

Ten of a Kind, Herald, 1953.
Adventures with the Buttonwoods, Herald, 1960.
Bringing Jesus to Our Neighbors, Herald, 1962.
Yuishu Sahai, Herald, 1963.
Mitsy Buttonwood, Herald, 1963.
Tres Casas, Tres Famillias, Friendship, 1964.
Fly High! (study course), Herald, 1965.
White Elephant for Sale, Friendship, 1966.
Mattie Mae (illustrated by E. R. Graber), Herald, 1967.

WORK IN PROGRESS: A devotional book for adults, tentatively titled *Overflowings;* a children's book, tentatively titled *Melissa and Malinda.*

SIDELIGHTS: "I started writing for children because I loved reading as a child. And I get a lot of joy from thinking of the children who enjoy my writing. *Hans Brinker and the Silver Skates* was a favorite of mine as a child.

"I grew up in a Mennonite home and my parents had been Amish. *Mattie Mae* is about a little Amish girl."

EDNA BEILER

HOBBIES AND OTHER INTERESTS: Oil painting, piecing quilt tops, gardening, ecology.

BILIBIN, Ivan (Iakolevich) 1876-1942

PERSONAL: Born August 4, 1876, in Tarkhovka, near St. Petersburg, Russia (now U.S.S.R.); died February 7, 1942; son of Yakov Ivanovich (an assistant chief physician) and Varvara Alexandrovna (Bubnova) Bilibin; married Maria Chambers (an artist), April 28, 1902 (divorced, 1911); married Renee O'Connell (a ceramicist and stage designer), 1912 (divorced, 1917); married Alexandra Shchekatikhina-Pototskaya (an artist, draughtsman, and stage designer), February, 1923; children: (first marriage) Alexander, Ivan; (third marriage) Mstislav (stepson). *Education:* Attended School of the Society for the Advancement of the Arts, 1895-98; studied art at the studio of Anton Azbe, Munich, May-July, 1898; studied under Ilya Repin at the art school of Maria Tenisheva, 1898-1900; St. Petersburg University, certificate of completion in law study, 1900; Novorossiisk University, lawyer's diploma, 1900; studied art at the Higher Art School of the Academy of Arts, 1900-04.

CAREER: Illustrator, designer of stage sets and costumes, cartoonist, painter, and educator. Illustrator of books, beginning 1899; contributor of cartoons to the satirical magazines *Adskaia Pochta* (*Hell's Post*) and *Zhupel* (*The Bugbear*), beginning 1905; Higher School (sponsored by the Society for the Advancement of the Arts), St. Petersburg, Russia, teacher of graphic art, 1907-17; Higher Women's Polytechnical Courses, Department of Architecture, St. Petersburg, professor of watercolor painting, 1910-12; Fernand Nathan Publishing House, Paris, France, illustrator, beginning 1931; Leningrad Institute of Painting, Sculpture, and Architecture of the All-Russian Academy of Arts, Leningrad, Russia, professor of graphic art, 1936-42.

Designer of numerous stage sets and costumes for theater, ballet, and opera, including Rimsky-Korsakov's "Snow Maiden," Prague National Theatre, 1905; Moussorgsky's "Boris Godunov," Grand-Opera, Paris, 1908, and Theatre des Champs Elysses, Paris, 1931; Rimsky-Korsakov's "The Golden Cockerel," Zimin Theatre, Moscow, 1909; Igor Stravinsky's "The Firebird," Colon Theatre, Buenos Aires, 1931; and Igor Bakhterev and Alexander Pazumovsky's "Field Marshal Suvorov," Pushkin Drama Theatre, Leningrad, 1939. Member of the jury, "Art in Crimea" exhibition, Yalta, 1918; author of articles on Russian art and culture for Russian and European magazines.

EXHIBITIONS: Works included in more than fifty exhibitions in St. Petersburg, Moscow, Petrograd, Kiev, Odessa, Leningrad, Yalta, Berlin, Leipzig, Alexandria, Prague, Amsterdam, Belgrade, Vienna, Rome, Paris, Brussels, New York, and Washington, D.C., including First Exhibition of the Union of Russian Artists, Moscow, 1903-04; International Art Exhibition, Brussels, 1910; Exhibition of Theatrical Design, Petrograd, 1922; "Great Exhibition of Russian Art," Belgrade, 1930; and Exhibition of Russian Theatrical Designs from the Collection of N. Lobanov-Rostovsky and G. Riabov, New York, 1966. One-man shows in Alexandria, 1924-25; Prague, 1927; Leningrad, Moscow, Tallin, and Kiev, 1952-53; also "Bilibin's Theatrical Designs and Costumes Devoted to the Centenary of the Artist's Birth," Bakhrushin Central Theatre Museum, Moscow, 1976. Shows with wife, Alexandra Shchekatikhina-Pototskaya in Amersterdam, 1929; Exhibition Hall of the Leningrad Branch of the RSFSR Union of Artists, Leningrad, 1977; Exhibition Hall of the Association of Museums of the Leningrad Region, Leningrad, 1978-80. Work in permanent collections, including Goznak Museum, Moscow, Russian Museum, Leningrad, All-Union Pushkin Museum, Leningrad, Bakhrushin Central Theatre Museum, Moscow, Theatre Museum, Leningrad, Board of the Association of Museums of the Leningrad Region, and private collections.

Bilibin in the 1920s.

MEMBER: Artel of Russian Artists (co-organizer, 1901), Union of Russian Artists (founding member, 1903), World of Art (founding member, 1910; chairman, 1916), Commission for the Preservation of Monuments of Russian Art, Commission for the Preservation of the Artistic Treasures of the Crimea, Union of Artists of the U.S.S.R. *Awards, honors:* D.S.C. from the Leningrad Institute of Painting, Sculpture and Architecture of the All- Russian Academy of Arts, 1939; *The Tale of the Golden Cockerel* and *The Tale of Czar Saltan* were each selected one of Child Study Association of America's Children's Books of the Year, 1975; *The Tale of Czar Saltan* was included in the Children's Book Showcase of the Children's Book Council, 1976.

ILLUSTRATOR:

TRANSLATED WORKS; RUSSIAN FAIRY TALES

Skazka ob Ivane-tsareviche Zhar-ptitse i o serom volke, [St. Petersburg], 1901, translation and retelling by Irina Zheleznova published as *The Tale of Tsarevich Ivan, the Fire- Bird and Grey Wolf,* Central Books (London), 1977, published in America as *The Tale of Tsarevich Ivan, the Firebird, and the Grey Wolf,* Imported, 1979.

The Frog Princess, [St. Petersburg], 1901, Imported, 1979.

(From "Sister Fox and the Wolf" by Alexander Pushkin. Illustrated by Ivan Bilibin.)

(From *The Tale of the Fisherman and the Fish* by Alexander Pushkin. Illustrated by Ivan Bilibin.)

Peryshko finista iasna Sokola, [St. Petersburg], 1902, translation and retelling by I. Zheleznova published as *Fenist the Falcon,* Central Books, 1977, Imported, 1979.
Vasilisa prekrasnaia, [St. Petersburg], 1902, published as *Vasilisa the Beautiful,* Imported, 1974, translation and retelling by I. Zheloznova, published as *Vasilisa the Beautiful,* Central Books, 1976.
Mar'ia Morevna, [St. Petersburg], 1903, translation and retelling by I. Zheleznova published as *Marya Morevna,* Central Books, 1976, Imported, 1979.
Sestritsa Alenushka i bratets Ivanushka/Belaia utochka, [St. Petersburg], 1903, published as *Sister Alyonushka and Brother Ivanushka* [and] *The White Duck,* Imported, 1979.
A. Pushkin, *Skazka o zolotom petushke,* [St. Petersburg], 1906, translation and retelling by James Reeves published as "The Tale of the Golden Cockerel" in *The Golden Cockerel and Other Stories,* Dent, 1969, translation and retelling by Patricia Tracy Lowe published as *The Tale of the Golden Cockerel,* Crowell, 1975.
A. Pushkin, *Skazka o tsare Saltane,* [St. Petersburg], 1907, translation by Louis Zellikoff published as *The Tale of Tsar Saltan, of His Son, the Glorious and Mighty Knight Prince Guidon Saltanovich, and of the Fair Swan-Princess,* Progress (Moscow), 1968, translation by Elizabeth Millar published as *The Tale of Tsar Saltan,* adapted by Olive Jones, Methuen (London), 1974, translation and retelling by P. T. Lowe published in America as *The Tale of Czar Saltan; or, The Prince, and the Swan Princess,* Crowell, 1975.
Post Wheeler, *Russian Wonder Tales,* Century, 1912.
Nathan Haskell Dole, *White Duckling,* Crowell, 1913.
(Contributor) Frances Carpenter, *Tales of a Russian Grandmother: Genuine Stories of Old Russia,* Doubleday, Doran, 1933.
Aleksandr Nikolaevich Afanas'ev, *Russian Folk Tales,* translated by Robert Chandler, Random House, 1980.
A. Pushkin, *Tales by Alexander Pushkin* (contains *The Tale of the Golden Cockerel* and *The Tale of Tsar Saltan*), Imported, 1981.
Mikhail Lermontov, *The Lay of Tsar Ivan Vassilyevich, His Young Oprichnik and the Stouthearted Merchant Kalashnikov,* translated by I. Zheleznova, Raduga, 1984.

ILLUSTRATOR OF ADDITIONAL PUBLICATIONS IN RUSSIAN AND FRENCH

(Contributor) *Contes de l'isba* (Russian folk tales), Boivin, 1931.
(Contributor) *Contes de la couleuvre,* Boivin, 1932.
Helene Isserlis and G. Piquet, *Pierre le Grand,* Fernand Nathan, 1935.
(Contributor) *Le tapis volant, le tuyau d'ivoire et la pomme magique,* Flammarion, 1935.
Jacob Grimm and Wilhelm Grimm, *Contes des freres Grimm,* Boivin, 1935.

COLLECTIONS

Alexander Pushkin, *Tales by Alexander Pushkin* (illustrated by Ivan Bilibin), Malysh (Moscow), 1981.

SIDELIGHTS: "Besides being an artist, I also consider myself a bit of a philologist, so to speak, or student of folklore."[1]

Ivan Bilibin was born on **August 4, 1876** near St. Petersburg. "As far as I remember I have always drawn. At the end of my school days and in my early years at university I attended the drawing school of the Society for the Advancement of the Arts. While I was still a student I became a pupil of the late Jan Ciaglinski, and later his fellow teacher at that same school.

"He was an excellent teacher. He strode into the class proudly and energetically and demanded from his pupils gallant devotion towards that 'Belle Dame,' holy art."[1]

At his father's insistence, Bilibin began studying at the Law Faculty of St. Petersburg University in 1896, but within a couple of years, his interest in art gained precedence. "I spent the **summer of 1898** in Munich. I worked there in a private art studio where I first tasted the free spirit of foreign ateliers and became infected with the Stueck and Boecklin mania. Completely intoxicated by my new way of life, I returned to St. Petersburg in the autumn in a despondent mood.

"Suddenly, quite by chance, I found out that the Princess Maria Tenisheva had just such a free art studio in her home on Galernaya Street, and it was headed by no one other than Ilya Repin himself. I immediately went there and joined it . . . . Ilya Repin was a different kind of teacher than Ciaglinski—he did not effuse enthusiasm like a fire-spitting volcano. He entered the studio quietly, but all the same everyone in the studio was aware that Repin had come.

"In any branch of art a pupil will have a particular respect for his teacher if he sees that the latter is not only correct in the advice that he gives, but that he can also practise what he preaches. There are some teachers who prefer to talk and not take the pencil or the brush from the pupil, but the pupil always senses this.

"Repin was one of those rare masters who thought and talked in forms and lines as simply as we think and talk to each other in words.

"In the **spring of 1899,** when the artist Leon Bakst, a member of the Serge Diaghilev circle, saw some of my first drawings, which were to a certain extent already graphic art, he introduced me to Serge Diaghilev and his colleagues from the *World of Art* journal, which was already being published. After that I received an order for several drawings for this journal."[1]

The *World of Art* group had a particular interest in those areas of art which had been regarded less important, such as theater design and book illustration, and in consideration of these disciplines, arranged for exhibitions and the publication of their journal. "I learned a lot from the *World of Art.* Its pages acquainted me with the works of Finnish artists, with the Scandinavian Werenskiold and with the latest developments in Western art. This journal was, as it were, a 'window on Europe' for me.

"What was I equipped with in the **summer of 1899** when I started my first fairy-tales? Why, I had nothing at all. Drawings of the countryside, people, buildings, and objects, studies of the same and the book *Relics of Old Russia* by Sipovsky which I borrowed from the village library there. Thus equipped, I embarked on my long voyage. I had youth, youthful ardour, and a love for my country on my side. I knew nothing of the Russian *lubok* or icons at that time."[1]

In **1900,** Bilibin was graduated from law school. "This year marks the end of my career as a lawyer. I've got my diploma to please my father, although I've already told him that I shall never practise law."[1]

The same year, his first illustrations of Russian fairy tales were exhibited. V. Stasov, who wrote about the exhibition commented: "These are all illustrations to Russian folk tales, extremely well thought out, showing a real grasp of the Russian folk spirit and using forms that are truly national."[1]

In **1902,** Bilibin married a fellow student at the Tenisheva studio, Maria Chambers. A son followed the next year. In **1904,** the Ethnographic Department of the Russian Museum sent Bilibin to study in Northern Russia. "I have never seen such imaginative architecture as I did at Kizhi in the Olonets Province, near Petrozavodsk. Even from afar, as you sail towards this church in Lake Onega, you can distinguish something extraordinary in its architectual forms; and when the boat comes closer to it, and you see a whole pyramid of cupolas heaped up on top of one another, then you can't help feeling that you really are about to enter some kind of fairy-tale world.

"In the twilight, especially later on in the evening, the sight of these churches against the background of the long summer sunset of the North is enchanting. I wonder what kind of architect it was who built these churches!

"The main principle in old Russian wooden architecure is that the detail should never drown the whole. The overall form is of prime importance. If the structure appears a little bizarre, this is due to its general outline, as for example is the case with the church of Kizhi. The decoration is only pronounced in places, like a pretty vignette at the end of the text; it emphasizes the overall charm of the structure. Virtually every decorative element has some practical structural importance. Thanks to this, even a tent-roof church displays a classical strictness in its sense of balance between the overall outline and detail. The builder of Kizhi realized, perhaps unconsciously, that it is possible to erect a plain log wall and then to decorate it simply with a window, with a ring of slender balusters, or with a richly ornamented porch. He was well aware that it would not make a poor impression, that on the contrary an excess of unnecessary details would strike a false and unpleasant note; he possessed that harmonious sense of balance that makes itself felt in every really serious style."[1]

Because of his satiric drawings which had appeared in the journal *Zhupel,* in particular one of Czar Nicholas II, Bilibin was subjected to administrative arrest in 1906 and the journal was suppressed. The Union of Russian Artists, to which Bilibin belonged voiced its views: "Only free art is full of life, creative work alone brings pleasure, and if our country so rich in talent has not yet managed to leave its mark in the field of art, and to release the great artistic forces concealed within it, if our art has no real links with the Russian people, then we are firmly convinced that the main reason for this is the suffocating guardianship which not only kills art but also suppresses all other creative activities in Russian society.

"On the strength of this, we cannot but feel sympathy towards those representatives of Russian society who are bravely and steadfastly struggling for the liberation of Russia . . . such as Alexander Benois, Igor Grabar, Konstantin Somov, Victor Borisov-Musatov, Konstantin Pervukhin, Vasily Perepliotchikov, Ivan Bilibin, Yevgeny Lanceray, Mstislav Dobuzhinsky, Valentin Serov, Osip Braz, Pavel Shcherbov, and Konstantin Yuon."[1]

This would not be the only source of frustration for Bilibin. Like many Russian artists of the time, his attitude would cause him to spend much of his time abroad. Nonetheless, Bilibin remained faithful to classical Russian themes. Of the traditional Russian costume upon which he frequently based his designs, he wrote: "Was this dress attractive? It was splendid. There is such a thing as the beauty of movement, and there is also the beauty of serenity. The Russian national dress is a dress of serenity.

"Let us take, for example, the Russian dance. The man dances like a demon, performing every possible trick at dizzy speeds to try and disturb the majestic tranquility displayed by the focal point of the dance, namely the woman who stands almost immobile, in her beautiful serene dress, just moving her shoulders slightly.

"As far as Russian style is concerned, my own early style is by no means my favourite. I like either something timeless, not restricted to any particular epoch, like *The Golden Cockerel* [an opera based on Pushkin's story, which Bilibin designed in 1909], or something from the sixteenth or seventeenth century. Now I feel drawn to the East and would very much like to work in its spirit."[1]

In **1907,** Bilibin was appointed to teach at the Higher School of Art (sponsored by the Society for the Advancement of the Arts), where he attempted to elevate graphic design to an art form. "Our understanding of graphic art at the beginning of the twentieth century was based on a strict sense of discipline and a cult of the line. Free drawing, where the line was not cultivated, was not included in the graphic art proper.

"Nowadays our concept of the illustrated book is much broader than it was at the beginning of the twentieth century; true, if you start with a completely free technique, you may find an easier path, but the very framework of the strictly constructed book will be lost. The mature artist, who is disciplined and possesses sound experience, can allow himself deviations, but these may be dangerous for the beginner.

"Most artists don't know how to deal with styles, looking for some kind of historical authenticity in them. We are a new type of people, people of the twentieth century. For us style is only a starting point."[1]

In **1911** when Bilibin joined other distinguished artists in designing the season for the Starinny Theatre, *World of Art* member Alexander Benois said: "With such artists as Roerich, Lanceray, Bilibin, Shervashidze and Kalmakov it is possible to create something highly original, something that Russian society really needs and that will be truly beneficial to it."[1]

That same year, Bilibin separated from his wife. Among his students was artist Renee O'Connell, who was to become his second wife. She wrote of their early relationship: "The fragrance of resin from the pines and juniper, the chirping of the cicadas, the hot cliffs, the sound of the waves breaking in this spot where the water was deepest, and the complete absence of people. A north-east wind blew in the autumn, stones fell from the cliffs, the foxes barked hoarsely, and the breakers crashed noisily against the shore. In this romantic situation I became more closely acquainted with Ivan Iakolevich Bilibin. He was a cheerful person, very good company, always inclined to be optimistic; he approached people with an open heart and got on easily with them. A sociable, witty companion, he not only liked to converse with people who were intellectually his equals, but he enjoyed talking to workers and fishermen, too. He and I looked upon the Crimea as a newly discovered country. The Crimean landscape, similar to that of the Greek archipelago, and the ancient Hellenic culture dating back some two thousand years, to the times of the Scythians and of the Greek colonists, profoundly excited and attracted Bilibin.

"As far as knowledge and artistic culture are concerned Ivan Bilibin gave his pupils a great deal. He taught us to understand the creative work of such masters of drawing as Duerer, Cranach, Vallotton, and Beardsley. Bilibin thought very highly of Beardsley's precise lines. He was extremely pedantic in demanding precision from his pupils in their drawing of graphic ornaments and insisted on the firmness and beauty of the line.

(From *The Tale of Tsar Sultan* by Alexander Pushkin. Illustrated by Ivan Bilibin.)

Much time and patience was devoted to studying the various scripts of different epochs according to his own particular method. In view of the firmness of his own hand he called himself Ivan the Iron Hand.

"Bilibin particularly drew our attention to the Russian folk pictures collected by Rovinsky, and also showed us his own collection of cheap popular prints which he had brought back from his trip to his beloved Russian North. He taught us to understand and love Russian folk art."[1]

O'Connell and Bilibin were married in **1912,** and divorced in 1917, the same year in which Bilibin left his teaching job at the Higher School of Art. "In a fit of panic and fear and tempted by an opportunity of seeing exotic lands, something that an artist is always dreaming of, in February **1920** I boarded a steamship for an unknown destination with a crowd of refugees. Fate took me to Egypt.

"There are two Egypts . . . ancient, classical Egypt and Moslem Egypt. To begin with, I was captivated by the latter, since it is easier to understand and is more familiar to us. Moreover, the Moslem past is, if you like, still alive today, and life goes on much the same as ever. The Moslem part of Cairo has its own specific features; the architecture is magnificent, much of the past remains, and everywhere there are bazaars, little shops, street-traders, Bedouin beggars, Negroes, camels, donkeys arrayed in all kinds of ornaments, carpets, sweet-meats, fruit—in short, you can just sit down and draw an eastern fairy-tale.

"Ancient Egypt, incomprehensible and frightening, is speechless. While the noisy bustle of Moslem Egypt, with its different-coloured people with skins ranging from white to pitch- black, is deafening to the ears, the vestiges of that remote world of Ancient Egypt are engulfed in a majestic silence. I did not really take to either Egypt, and specialized in Byzantine art.

"I received an order for several icons for a small Greek church. I dream of painting something for the big Greek cathedral; they keep on promising me I will, but this is a country where promises are freely given but rarely kept.

"Nevertheless things do, slowly but surely, seem to be getting better, but I would only go abroad again if I was made a definite offer of work. People are beginning to get to know me in Cairo. I'm the only genuine artist in all of Egypt . . . . The standard of the rest of them is even lower than that of the Society of St. Petersburg Artists. You would think everything was splendid, just one artist for the whole country, no competition, I should be rolling in money, but in actual fact I can hardly afford to have my shoes soled. But it doesn't actually matter!

"Today when I drew my Byzantine rider I thought that it would be quite possible to create an entire theory of rhythm and harmony, and, of course, colour as well. This theory could be set out with laws well put together, like the theory of music and counterpoint.

(From *The Tale of the Fisherman and the Fish* by Alexander Pushkin. Illustrated by Ivan Bilibin.)

"Most artists base their work on feeling and intuition, and many would scorn such an established theory, believing that it would be dry as dust, but this is nonsense. Awareness only improves art.

"I cannot merely copy any kind of Byzantine mosaic composition, for there is always something in it that shocks me, but I like a lot of things about it; no matter what kind of style I have in front of me, I have to put my finger on the rhythm that I discern in this raw material, its harmony, and what I make of it will be my own, even though I work according to the canons of the style in question. Mere copying is an imbecile occupation . . . . An artist should not only be talented but clever as well."[1]

In **1923,** Bilibin took a third wife, Alexandra Pototskaya, a fellow artist. Two years later, the family moved to Paris where Bilibin became part of the thriving art movement of Russian expatriots centered there. He designed costumes and sets for theaters all over Europe; for composers such as Stravinsky, Rimsky-Korsakov, and Moussorgsky, and for stage adaptations of stories by Alexander Pushkin, but his heart remained in Russia. "For several years now I have dreamed of returning to my homeland and of working for my country in my speciality.

"It is above all morally difficult to live here in Europe, whose culture is in the grips of a crisis.

"I cannot become assimilated into another nation.

"I simply cannot take the citizenship of a country that is alien to me, as many of our colleagues have done.

"Instead of putting all my efforts into the cultural life of another country I would like to work for my own homeland."[1]

In **1936,** Bilibin returned to Leningrad and was appointed professor of graphic art at the Leningrad Institute of Painting, Sculpture, and Architecture. "Today a new period in my life begins, a period of Soviet artistic activity.

"I want to work here in the hope that my many years of experience in art will allow me to make my own contribution to the grandiose work being done in my great homeland.

"In our time, we, the World of Art artists, laid the foundations for many things. Naturally, many mistakes were made, and there were many extremes, many things were unjust and demanded revision later, but the main merit of the World of Art was that it waged a campaign against complacency, against those moments when art becomes self-satisfied and begins to acquire, so to speak, a bourgeois paunch.

"Now we have entered another age . . . when an entire people, from top to bottom, ha[ve] been roused into action. The tasks facing the artist have become more complicated and many-faceted.

(From *The Feather of Finist the Falcon*. Illustrated by Ivan Bilibin.)

(From *Vasilisa the Beautiful* by Alexander Pushkin. Illustrated by Ivan Bilibin.)

"Yesterday on the one hand we had the peaks of human artistic achievement, which were accessible to a chosen few, and on the other hand there were millions of others who were denied access to these peaks. It must now be the task of every artist, whatever his skill, to help these millions find their way to the peaks and thus to sample the delights which art can offer."[1]

Bilibin continued to teach until his death on **February 7, 1942.**

FOOTNOTE SOURCES

[1]Sergei Golynets, *Ivan Bilibin,* translated by Glenys Ann Kozlov, Abrams, 1982.

FOR MORE INFORMATION SEE:

Horn Book, December, 1975.
Bertha E. Mahony and others, compilers, *Illustrators of Children's Books: 1744-1945,* Horn Book, 1947.
Graphis 4, Graphis Press (Zurich), 1979.
Maurice Horn, editor, *The World Encyclopedia of Cartoons,* Volume 1, Gale, 1980.

BILLAM, Rosemary 1952-

PERSONAL: Born August 3, 1952, in London, England; daughter of John (a lawyer) and Mary (a teacher; maiden name, Armitage) Billam. *Education:* Attended Corona Academy of Theatre Arts, 1969-72; Norland Nursery Training College, N.N.E.B., 1982, R.S.H.N.N., 1983. *Home:* 31 Wunulla Rd., Point Piper, Sydney, New South Wales 2027, Australia. *Office:* c/o William Collins, Publishers, 8 Crafton St., London W1X 3LA, England.

CAREER: Actress and stage manager in theaters and on television, 1972-80; author. *Member:* Society of Authors, British Actors Equity.

WRITINGS:

JUVENILE

Alpaca (illustrated by Vanessa Julian-Ottie), Collins, 1982, published in the United States as *Fuzzy Rabbit,* Random House, 1984.
Alpaca in the Park (illustrated by V. Julian-Ottie), Collins, 1985, published in the United States as *Fuzzy Rabbit in the Park,* Random House, 1985.
Come on Alpaca (illustrated by V. Julian-Ottie), Collins, 1988, published in the United States as *Fuzzy Rabbit and the Little Brother Problem,* Random House, 1988.
Mr. Pando and Peter's Big Dam (illustrated by V. Julian-Ottie), Macmillan, 1989.
Alpaca Saves Christmas, Collins, 1990, published in the United States as *Fuzzy Rabbit Saves Christmas,* Random House, 1991.

PLAYS

"The Reluctant Dragon," first produced at Chichester Festival Youth Theatre, 1989.
"The Ladybird," first produced in Hammersmith at Lyric Studio, 1990.

Alpaca has been translated into four languages.

ADAPTATIONS:

"Fuzzy Rabbit" (cassette), Random House, 1985.

WORK IN PROGRESS: Children's books.

BOND, Bruce 1939-

PERSONAL: Born June 9, 1939, in Rockford, Ill.; son of Oriel E. (an artist) and Dorothy (a homemaker; maiden name, Swanson) Bond; married Margaret Weiler, April 7, 1967 (divorced, 1979); married Katherine Miller (a business manager), October 1, 1983; children: (first marriage) Elizabeth, Scott. *Education:* Attended Art Center School, Los Angeles, Calif. *Home:* 5809 Sugarbush Lane, Greendale, Wis. 53129.

CAREER: Artist and illustrator of children's books. Hulick Bros. Printing, Jamesville, Wis., art director, 1961-63; Hoffman-York Advertising, art director, 1963-67; painter and private teacher through Alaska, 1967-68; Picard-Didier Studios, Milwaukee, Wis., 1969-75; Bruce Bond's Artworks, Glendale, Wis., 1975—. *Exhibitions:* American Watercolor Society Show, 1974; Illustrators Club of New York, 1985; additional exhibitions in Illinois, Wisconsin, and Alaska. *Military service:* Illinois National Guard, 1961-62; U.S. Air Force Reserve, 1962-67. *Member:* Illustrators and Designers of Milwaukee. *Awards, honors:* Recipient of awards for artwork in Milwaukee, including Illustrators and Designers of Milwaukee, and from Art Directors Club.

ILLUSTRATOR:

Amanda's Tree, Ideals Publishing, 1979.
Gale Brennan, *Here Come the Clowns,* Ideals Publishing, 1980.
Richard L. Allington and Kathleen Krull, *Autumn,* Raintree, 1981.
Isaac Asimov, Martin Greenberg, and Charles Waugh, editors, *Thinking Machines,* Raintree, 1981.

BRUCE BOND

G. Brennan and Tom LaFleur, *Woolly the Wolf,* Ideals Publishing, 1981.

Contributor to *Astronomy*.

SIDELIGHTS: "I think a strong sense of fantasy is a valuable tool for the artist. If we can retain that sense of wonder we felt as children and apply it in tandem with our adult skills, we will be better able to communicate with our audience. A sense of humor helps as well.

"My hobbies are reading, painting, model making, and astronomy. I have written, researched, and illustrated articles for *Astronomy* magazine and am an active observer.

"Most of my illustration work is commercial rather than editorial, and I have worked for many major corporations."

BROWN, Anne Ensign 1937-

PERSONAL: Born March 9, 1937, in Phoenix, Ariz.; daughter of Ormsby Herbert (an engineer) and Josephine Marie (a homemaker; maiden name, Carmean) Ensign; married Joseph Edward Brown (a writer), April 30, 1976. *Education:* Colorado College, B.A., 1960; graduate study at Sorbonne, University of Paris, 1961-62. *Politics:* Republican. *Religion:* Episcopalian. *Home:* 376 C Avenue, Coronado, Calif. 92118.

CAREER: Scripps Clinic and Research Foundation, La Jolla, Calif., assistant director of development for Friends of Research (public relations and publications department), 1963-65, medical translator for microbiology department, 1966-67; University of California, Literature Department, San Diego, writer, translator, and coordinator on the *Machiavelli Project,* 1967-68; Oceanic Research Institute (now Pollution Abstracts, Inc.), La Jolla, writer, translator, and editor for *Oceanic Abstracts* and *Pollution Abstracts,* 1968-71; U.S. Department of Interior, Environmental Protection Agency, Washington, D.C., project director and principal writer for research grant on *Coastal Pollution for Selected Water Resources Abstracts,* 1971-73; U.S. Department of Commerce, National Oceanic and Atmospheric Administration, Washington, D.C., project director and editor for contract on *Subsurface Currents,* 1971-73; free-lance writer, illustrator, and photographer, 1973—.

WRITINGS:

(With husband, Joseph E. Brown), *Harness the Wind* (juvenile), Dodd, 1977.
Wonders of Sea Horses (juvenile; self-illustrated), Dodd, 1979.
Monarchs of the Forest: The Story of Redwoods (self-illustrated), Dodd, 1984.
(Contributor) *Lincoln-Homework Encyclopedia,* Harcourt, 1986.
(With J. E. Brown) *Frontier Forts,* Southwest Parks and Monuments Association, 1990.

ILLUSTRATOR

J. E. Brown, *Wonders of Seals and Sea Lions,* Dodd, 1975.
J. E. Brown, *The Sea's Harvest,* Dodd, 1975.

Contributor to travel section, *San Diego Tribune,* 1987-89.

WORK IN PROGRESS: Translating, retelling, and illustrating a Turkish fairy tale for children; writing and illustrating a book on American Indian legends.

ANNE ENSIGN BROWN

SIDELIGHTS: "Myths and legends from foreign lands, travel, nature, and wildlife are my major writing interests.

"I've always loved writing and as a child I was encouraged to read anything and everything. I enjoyed illustrating the unillustrated books that I read on Greek mythology, poetry, fairy tales, and nature. I really didn't plan on becoming a writer and in college was in international relations with the idea of getting into the diplomatic service in order to enjoy travel and to learn languages. However, by accident I kept falling into jobs that used what writing and illustrating skills I had and eventually decided that that's what I enjoyed most even though free-lancing is a tough way to go."

HOBBIES AND OTHER INTERESTS: Travel, sailing, wildlife, photography, reading.

BROWN, Pamela (Beatrice) 1924-1989

OBITUARY NOTICE—See sketch in *SATA* Volume 5: Born December 31, 1924, in Colchester, Essex, England; died January 26, 1989. Actress, television producer, and author. Brown became a successful children's author while still a teenager herself, using her own fascination with the theater as the basis for her 1941 novel, *The Swish of the Curtain*. Proceeds from the book enabled her to attend the Royal Academy of Dramatic Art, after which she worked as an actress during the 1940s. From 1950 to 1963 she was a television producer, first with the British Broadcasting Corporation and later with Scottish Television and Granada Television, producing children's programs such as "Zoo Times" and "Criss-Cross Quiz." Several of Brown's novels— including *Maddy Alone, Golden Pavements,* and *Blue Door Venture*— are sequels to *The Swish of the Curtain*. Her numerous other writings for children include *To Be a Ballerina and Other Stories,* the play "The Children of Camp Fortuna," and *Louisa,* a biography of Louisa May Alcott.

FOR MORE INFORMATION SEE:

Martha E. Ward and Dorothy A. Marquardt, *Authors of Books for Young People*, Scarecrow, 1964.
Brian Doyle, editor, *The Who's Who of Children's Literature*, Schocken, 1968.
Contemporary Authors, Volume 13-16R, Gale, 1975.
D. L. Kirkpatrick, *Twentieth-Century Children's Writers*, 2nd edition, St. Martin's, 1983.

OBITUARIES

Times (London), February 1, 1989.

BROWN, Richard (Eric) 1946-

PERSONAL: Born October 25, 1946, in Philadelphia, Penn.; children: one son. *Education:* Attended Philadelphia College of Art.

CAREER: Illustrator of books for children. *Awards, honors: Even the Devil Is Afraid of a Shrew* was selected one of American Institute of Graphic Arts Fifty Books of the Year, 1972, and was included in the Children's Book Showcase, 1973.

"The bigger the box, the more stuffing it holds," answered Adam. (From *Egg-Drop Day* by Harriet Ziefert. Illustrated by Richard Brown.)

WRITINGS:

JUVENILE

Valerie Stalder, reteller, *Even the Devil Is Afraid of a Shrew*, Addison-Wesley, 1972.
Franklyn M. Branley, *The Great Moon Hoax*, Ginn, 1973.
Patty Wolcott, *The Marvelous Mud Washing Machine*, Addison-Wesley, 1974.
Can We Eat Now?, Macmillan, 1974.
The Breakfast Buffalo, Macmillan, 1974.
Ashes for Sale, Harper, 1975.
Elizabeth Burrowes, *A Sleepy Story*, Golden Press, 1982.
Kathy S. Kyte, *Play It Safe: The Kids' Guide to Personal Safety and Crime Prevention*, Knopf, 1983.
K. S. Kyte, *The Kids' Complete Guide to Money*, Knopf, 1984.
Earlene R. Long, *Gone Fishing*, Houghton, 1984.
Jeffrey Moss, *People in Your Neighborhood*, Golden Books, 1984.
Brenda Nelson, *Mud for Sale*, Houghton, 1984.
Jane K. Hilleary, *Fletcher and the Great Big Dog*, Houghton, 1988.
Amy Ehrlich, *Emma's New Pony*, Random House, 1988.
Gulliver's Travels: A Kid's Guide to Southern California, Harcourt, 1988.
A Kid's Guide to New York City, Harcourt, 1988.
A Kid's Guide to Texas, Harcourt, 1989.
A Kid's Guide to National Parks, Harcourt, 1989.
One Hundred Words about Animals, Harcourt, 1989.
One Hundred Words about My House, Harcourt, 1989.
One Hundred Words about Transportation, Harcourt, 1989.
One Hundred Words about Working, Harcourt, 1989.

"SESAME STREET" SERIES

Cookie Monster's Book of Cookie Shapes, Golden Press, 1979.
Emily Perl Kingsley, *I Can Do It Myself*, Golden Press, 1980.
Deborah Kovacs, *Frazzle's Fantastic Day*, Golden Press, 1980.
Valjean McLenighan, *Special Delivery*, Golden Press, 1980.
Ellen Weiss, *The Tool Box Book*, Golden Press, 1980.
Do-It-Yourself Alphabet Book, Golden Press, 1980.
(With others) Linda Hayward, *Sesame Seasons*, Golden Press, 1981.
Good Time to Eat!, Golden Press, 1982, published as *Cookie Monster's Good Time to Eat!*, Golden Books, 1989.

Brown was not associated with other books in the series.

ALL WRITTEN BY HARRIET ZIEFERT, EXCEPT AS NOTED

The Small Potatoes Club, Dell, 1984.
The Small Potatoes and the Magic Show, Dell, 1984.
Birthday Card, Where Are You?, Penguin, 1985.
Nicky's Christmas Surprise, Penguin, 1985.
The Small Potatoes and the Sleep-Over, Dell, 1985.
Where's My Easter Egg?, Penguin, 1985.
H. Ziefert and Jon Ziefert, *The Small Potatoes and the Birthday Party*, Dell, 1986.
Where's the Halloween Treat?, Penguin, 1985.
Let's Watch Nicky, Viking, 1986.
Nicky's Noisy Night, Penguin, 1986.
Nicky's Friends, Viking, 1986.
Nicky's Picnic, Penguin, 1986.
No, No, Nicky!, Viking, 1986.
Where Is Nicky's Valentine?, Penguin, 1987.
Say Good Night!, Penguin, 1987.
Pet Day, Little, Brown, 1987.
Trip Day, Little, Brown, 1987.
Worm Day, Little, Brown, 1987.
Nicky Upstairs and Down, Viking, 1987.
Thank You, Nicky!, Penguin, 1988.
Don't Cry, Baby Sam, Penguin, 1988.

SIDELIGHTS: "From elementary school through college I enjoyed drawing and accepted it as what I would do. I enjoy it even more now. Art is a great way to reach people—a most powerful means of communicating ideas and feelings. Illustration, I feel, is the concentration of the communication idea as opposed to say, 'fine art.' In many ways this is not a discernable difference because much illustration has attained acceptance as 'fine art.' I feel that illustration will remain a very important part of our basis of communication, and for the artist, this is good."[1]

FOOTNOTE SOURCES

[1]Lee Kingman and others, compilers, *Illustrators of Children's Books: 1967-1976,* Horn Book, 1978.

BROWNE, Anthony (Edward Tudor) 1946-

PERSONAL: Born September 11, 1946, in Sheffield, England; son of Jack Holgate (a teacher) and Doris May (Sugden) Browne; married Jane Franklin (a violin teacher), July 26, 1980; children: Joseph, Ellen. *Education:* Leeds College of Art, degree in graphic design (with honors), 1967. *Home and office:* The Chalk Garden, The Length, St. Nicholas-at-Wade, Birchington, Kent CT7 OPJ, England.

CAREER: Victoria University of Manchester, Manchester, England, medical artist at Royal Infirmary, 1969-71; Gordon Fraser Greeting Cards, London, England, designer, 1971—; author and illustrator of children's books, 1975—. *Exhibitions:* "Alice's Adventures in Wonderland," Barbicon, London, England, 1988.

AWARDS, HONORS: Kate Greenaway Medal Commendation from the British Library Association, 1982, and International Board on Books for Young People Honor List, 1984, both for *Hansel and Gretel;* Kurt Maschler/"Emil" Award, 1983, Kate Greenaway Medal, 1984, selected one of *New York Times* Best Illustrated Children's Books of the Year, 1985, *Boston Globe-Horn Book* Honor Book for Illustration, and one of Child Study Association of America's Children's Books of the Year, both 1986, and Silver Pencil Award (Netherlands), 1989, all for *Gorilla;* Deutscher Jugendliteratur Preis (German Youth Literature Prize; with Annalena McAfee), and selected a Notable Children's Trade Book in the Field Social Studies from the National Council for Social Studies and the Children's Book Council, both 1985, both for *The Visitors Who Came to Stay;* Parents' Choice Award from the Parents' Choice Foundation, 1988, for *Look What I've Got;* Kurt Maschler/"Emil" Award, 1989, for *Alice's Adventures in Wonderland.*

WRITINGS:

SELF-ILLUSTRATED CHILDREN'S BOOKS

Through the Magic Mirror, Hamish Hamilton, 1976, Greenwillow, 1977.
A Walk in the Park, Hamish Hamilton, 1977.
Bear Hunt, Atheneum, 1979.
Look What I've Got, Macrae, 1979, Knopf, 1988.
(Reteller) Jacob Grimm and Wilhelm Grimm, *Hansel and Gretel,* Macrae, 1981, F. Watts, 1982.
Bear Goes to Town, Hamish Hamilton, 1982, Doubleday, 1989.
Gorilla (*Horn Book* honor list), Macrae, 1983, Knopf, 1985.
Willy the Wimp, Macrae, 1984, Knopf, 1985.
Willy the Champ, Macrae, 1985, Knopf, 1986.
Piggybook, Knopf, 1986.
(Reteller) Lewis Carroll, *Alice's Adventures in Wonderland,* Knopf, 1988.
The Little Bear Book, Hamish Hamilton, 1988, Doubleday, 1989.
A Bear-y Tale, Hamish Hamilton, 1989.
I Like Books, Knopf, 1989.
Things I Like, Knopf, 1989.
The Tunnel, Macrae, 1989, Knopf, 1990.
Changes, Macrea, 1990, Knopf, 1991.

ILLUSTRATOR

Annalena McAfee, *The Visitors Who Came to Stay,* Hamish Hamilton, 1984, Viking, 1985.
Sally Grindley, *Knock, Knock! Who's There?,* Hamish Hamilton, 1985, Knopf, 1986.
A. McAfee, *Kirsty Knows Best,* Knopf, 1987.

Also illustrator of Gwen Strauss' *Trail of Stones,* a book of poems for young adults.

ADAPTATIONS:

"Bear Hunt" (filmstrip), Weston Woods, 1982.

WORK IN PROGRESS: Illustrating Gwen Strauss' *The Night Shimmy.*

SIDELIGHTS: "I was born in Sheffield, England, September 11, 1946 where my parents ran a pub called the Brinkcliffe Oaks Hotel. I don't have a lot of childhood memories of that particular place, because we moved when I was still quite young to yet another pub called The Red Lion, in Wyke, near Bradford, a pretty rough area in the north of England. I remember my father having to physically boot people out. I was five years old the first time I saw men fighting in a field out back. 'Hold me back!' 'Lemme at him!' they were yelling as they took off their coats. There was lots of shouting and shoving, but little real violence. I remember my fear turning to amusement. I found them ridiculous.

"It always struck me as odd that my father could cope with it, for he was not a violent sort of man. He'd been in North Africa during the war, had been a boxer and a rugby player, but his ways remained gentle. He used to draw soldiers and battle scenes for my brother and me, and was good at it. Both he and my brother would draw a British and a German soldier, for instance, with all the details of uniforms and guns. I, on the other hand, would draw battle scenes with jokes thrown in—a decapitated head speaking or a picture of an invisible man. Knights on horseback and cowboys and Indians shared the same battle. Looking back I see that my pictures took on a narrative form.

"I'm told that I used to stand on a table in the tap room and tell stories to the assembled company. What a horrible thought! But apparently I had this hero called Big Dumb Tackle, who had Superman-like powers. My mother told me that in one of my stories Big Dumb Tackle went to heaven and knocked on the door of heaven and said, 'Can Jesus come out to play?' I shudder to think what the answer might have been!

"I was a kid with terrors—people coming after me, things under the bed, in the wardrobe. We had a lot of dark furniture which looked very menacing to me. I was terrified of circuses and was carried screaming from the movie of *Pinocchio* when I was two or three. Looking back, I was quite the wimp.

"Books were not a huge part of our lives. We had annuals, *The Beano Annual* or *The Dandy Annual,* that sort of thing. And fairy

Browne with children Ellen and Joseph. (Photography by Cathy Courtney.)

stories, particularly *Hansel and Gretel*. I do remember *Alice in Wonderland* which must have been read to me. Perhaps I have better recall of the Tenniel pictures than the story.

"Radio was something of a ritual. One of our favorite bedtime programs was 'Journey into Space.' My brother and I would get into bed, turn out the lights, and my father would come and listen with us."

When Browne was seven years old the family moved away from the pub scene, so that his father could pursue employment as a sales rep. "We lived in a proper house, still in Yorkshire, just a few miles from the pub. Among my father's many past jobs was that of private school teacher, and so it was decided that private school was a good place for us. My brother Michael and I were in the same class, even though he was almost two years older. I was learning Latin by the age of five. Walking home from school, we'd bang into all the kids from the Church of England school. The following year when we transferred to the same, we became immediate targets. The very first day I got into a fight and was taken to the headmaster.

"My most memorable teacher introduced me to the work of Beckett and Pinter. Encountering Beckett was a bit like discovering surrealism in painting—something at once totally unexpected and yet deeply familiar. It struck a chord, because I seemed to recognize something in it.

"My father, a frustrated painter all his life, came from a non-artistic family where it would not have been possible to consider art as a career choice. He had been a drummer, however, had had a jazz band, used to sing and do pantomime. When I announced that I wanted to go straight from high school to art college at sixteen, without sitting for my A level exams, there was no family objection. Though I did register for Graphic Arts because it had commercial possibilities.

"Three-quarters through my first year, my father died during Easter holidays when we were all home. We had gone on a family outing to a rugby match and as soon as we got home, he keeled over and died. I saw it. It was terrible. His two previous massive heart attacks should have prepared me, but I didn't take in the significance of that.

"My father and I were just starting to have arguments about music and politics. Not that things ever raged between us, but it was particularly unnerving that he died just then. The first thing I did was get my hair cut—partly for the funeral, but partly because it was one of the things we had argued about.

"My fairly traditional mother had been overprotected by her father, overprotected by her husband, and then overprotected by me. It seemed completely inappropriate for me to become rebellious towards her.

"During the first year in art school, they tried to make us forget everything we had learned. We were not permitted to draw the

And he went to a body-building club. (From *Willy the Wimp* by Anthony Browne. Illustrated by the author.)

way we had in the past. For one thing, we had to use big, black brushes. One exercise went on for three weeks and consisted of drawing matches. We had to drop a handful of matches and draw them in exactly the position they'd landed. Whatever you did, the tutor wouldn't accept. At first this was exciting and challenging, but then became hopelessly boring.

"Color was a big revelation to me. I had a teacher who made me aware of complementary colors—how a certain blue and a certain orange can be made to 'sing,' as he put it, against one another.

"I started going to galleries. At that time I was most impressed with Graham Sutherland, much more so than with Henry Moore or Barbara Hepworth. And then I came across Francis Bacon's work and was totally bowled over.

"My own work was morbid, no doubt in response to my father's death. I spent a lot of time in life-drawing classes, because I enjoyed painting women with no clothes on, and later making grotesque images based on the insides as well as the outside of the human body. I was reacting against the ambiance of the graphic design department in which I was formally enrolled. The students there wore white shoes and jackets—like real graphic designers. I made a point of looking like 'a painter,' working in oil and charcoal. There were no 'happy mediums' in my work. I went from massive oil paintings to tiny pencil drawings, nothing in between.

She found herself in a long, low hall. (From *Alice's Adventures in Wonderland* by Lewis Carroll. Illustrated by Anthony Browne.)

(From *Willy the Champ* by Anthony Browne. Illustrated by the author.)

"The first good project I did was a school project, called 'It's a Game, Only a Game,' about rugby. On one page of the spread were blokes playing rugby and on the opposite page was a long list of poetic free-associated images.

"Another project was supposed to be the first three letters of an alphabet book. I spent three weeks inside a triangle-shaped A, drawing a room with peeling wallpaper, bare floorboards, an exposed light bulb and an unmade, soiled bed and some medical instrument. The caption read 'A is for Abortion.' Terribly adolescent.

"The idea of doing children's books in those days would have been laughable. I couldn't paint a happy picture to save my life. Only one teacher was sympathetic, the others all thought I was a waste of time. When people asked my advice about going to art school, I'd say, 'The only thing I've learned is to keep my paper clean and present it neatly.'

"The problem was that I didn't belong in graphic design in the first place. I wanted to go to London and paint." Browne traveled to London to investigate other schools. Disappointed in his efforts he returned home with his mother and took up residence in the attic. "It turned out quite well, but it wasn't all roses, of course, I mean I was living on the dole.

"I spent a lot of time at the local library. One day, while looking through a book on careers for girls, I saw something called 'medical illustration.' Why it was regarded a female profession, I will never know. Anyway, I learned that there was a course taught at a hospital in London. I decided to apply. I bought some rabbit's legs from the butcher, a rat for dissection from the local biology teacher and put together a portfolio. It was the best work I'd done. I used every medium—gouache, water color, pen and ink, even some diagrams of how a heart works, etc. I got a microscope and did drawing from that. I realized that finally I'd found something I could do well. I went to the interview—with nine elderly women and one young man—and thought it went okay. But then I got a letter saying, 'Sorry.' I was devastated. It was the first time I'd ever been denied academics. A few days later I got a letter from the man who'd interviewed me, saying there was a job open as assistant medical artist in Manchester. I was hired.

"In 1969, I moved to Fallowfield for this medical illustration job. I was nervous because I had basically lied during the interview, letting them think that we did anatomy in art school. But it was actually all right. When surgeons were giving lectures on a technique they had developed, we'd make drawings while they operated, followed by more explanatory drawings for the *British Medical Journal* and similar publications. The only time I felt squeamish was when we were taken down to the mortuary to be shown something on a corpse. That was unimaginably horrible. But the job did exorcise my morbidness forever.

"Since we were paid as university lecturers, we had dining room privileges. I used to lunch with medical artist Richard Mead until he told me that there had been some comments about my hair and clothes and shoes. He obviously felt uncomfortable to be with me. I never felt that I really fit. From then on I had lunch in the student canteen. Oddly enough, I didn't make friends with any students, but with the mortician! He and I used to eat together.

"The art I did told the story of an operation in pictures. I didn't realize how narrative my work was. I also learned a lot about water color with which I had had relatively little experience. You need to learn to allow the whiteness of the paper to do its work and to control the pigment. I had to use water color in a very tight way, which is my one small regret about the job. I sometimes wish I had had a freer hand.

"My imagination was feeling very squelched and I had to move on. So I did a little teaching, and some work for a friend who had just set up an advertising agency. I did it only for the money. I was working on a collection of greeting cards on the side. Eventually I sent them to Gordon Fraser, a large card manufacturer, who thought my cards showed promise.

"Gordon Fraser became very important to me. I liked being part of the publishing world, and seeing my cards in shops was a tremendous thrill. Gordon was a gentle and highly intelligent man. He was a patron, really. He bought me my first house. Visiting me one day, he asked me how much rent I paid. 'Twenty pounds,' I said. And then he said, 'Let me buy you a house, and you pay me back at twenty pounds a month, interest free.' I never would have been able to do it alone. He did this for a couple of other artists, as well.

"I began thinking about books, because cards weren't a proper living, really. Gordon gave me the names of some publishers of children's books, including Hamish Hamilton, who immediately said, 'Why don't you have a go at a picture book?' So I came up with a story about a little elephant lost in a jungle who asks all the other animals for directions. Well, everything about this book was wrong—wrong shape, size, colors, etc. I was handed over to editor Julia Macrae who explained to me the ins and outs of dummies, and the basic thirty-two page layout. The obvious things. But they were interested in 'talent,' not slick

(From *A Bear-y Tale* by Anthony Browne. Illustrated by the author.)

appeal, so I was extremely fortunate. Another publisher would have said good-bye.

"My first book, *Through the Magic Mirror,* started with images—a picture of a door, with the phrase, 'Maybe outside there is a . . . ' (excuses for these wild drawings I wanted to do). Julia helped me craft a story out of it all. What tremendous excitement to have a book out!

"My next book was *A Walk in the Park,* which drew on a project I'd begun in art school. Two dogs go to the park with their owners and immediately mix with the other dogs, but the owners do not. They're locked into their class identities. For the book, I added children and parents. Eventually, the kids follow their dogs' example and edge nearer each other and start to mingle. Two or three years later Elaine Moss in a piece about picture books for older children, cited *A Walk in the Park* as a harbinger of a new genre.

"*Look What I've Got* is another book that started with a theme about two lads of different social backgrounds. One keeps getting lots of things and lords it over the other. He gets a new bike, rides no hands and crashes. All the way through the book he comes unstuck with all these new objects. To date, that was my best book.

"The first book I illustrated written by someone else was *Hansel and Gretel*. I did it in fifties dress, a style of my own childhood, I suppose. I felt very vulnerable with this book, because so many fine illustrators had had their crack at it. I wanted each picture to be a painting in its own right. And I wanted to illustrate what was between the lines, so to speak. Early on I adopted an image of a black triangle: the witch's hat, the shadow behind the stepmother's head, the church steeple, the mouse hole. This book earned me some of my best and some of my worst reviews. One woman complained that the social services should have intervened in this story, and wondered why anyone would wish to give such a tale to children.

(From *The Visitors Who Came to Stay* by Annalena McAfee. Illustrated by Anthony Browne.)

"*Gorilla* had its roots in a card I'd done for Gordon Fraser. It was a picture of a great big male gorilla holding a teddy bear. I think the image goes back to my father, who in some ways was like a gorilla, big and potentially aggressive during his pub days. I spent a lot of time at a zoo near Canterbury. The story, of course, hinges on the mixture of a big powerful gorilla and a small vulnerable little girl (who had metamorphosed from the original teddy bear).

"No one realized that *Gorilla* was going to be a runaway success. We all thought it was good work, felt hopeful and that was it. I must confess that it has changed my life. The Kate Greenaway Medal was a thrill, and it was published two years later in the United States.

"Then Julia had the idea that I should break away and make a big change. She suggested a number of classics, among them *Alice's Adventures in Wonderland*. 'After Tenniel,' I thought, 'who am I to even attempt.' But the story seeped into my consciousness, and Julia allowed me totally free rein (no standard thirty-two-page format, no rules). It's one of the very few books I'm pleased with, and the reviews were mostly very good. However, one said I was being 'clever-clever,' like a child who keeps saying 'look at me.' I was amused and thereafter took great delight in spotting the reviewers' mistakes. He talked about the 'Red Queen,' for instance, who isn't even in *Alice in Wonderland,* and wrote an incredibly convoluted sentence saying I did very convoluted drawings. The original illustrations have had gallery exhibits. Though I must say those pictures are best seen in a book, not on a wall.

"It's interesting to compare the reactions a book gets in different countries. In my experience, children's book reviewing is much more sophisticated in the States than in England. The French take books seriously, yet seem to retain a lightheartedness that I like. Germany can be very pedantic. I traveled to West Germany to receive an award for *The Visitors Who Came to Stay*. One woman had traveled forty miles to take issue with one of the character's wearing a bathing suit at the beach. She held that this girl would have kept her clothes on, and kept hammering at the point like there was no tomorrow. There were quite a few questions like that. Serious, combative, somewhat nit-picking. Interesting, though, definitely interesting.

"Life is now considerably calmer and more secure. I live with my wife and two children in a small village in southeast England. I usually start working at about half past nine and work until six. But sometimes in the summer school holidays I'm easily distracted, living near the sea and with the children at home. I am very much involved with my son and daughter. They're my favorite people in the world, and there's no one with whom I'd rather spend my time."[1]

FOOTNOTE SOURCES

[1]Based on an interview by Cathy Courtney for *Something about the Author*.

FOR MORE INFORMATION SEE:

Aidan Chambers, "Letter from England," *Horn Book,* December, 1981.
"Through the Magic Mirror: The Work of A. Browne," *British Book News,* autumn, 1984.
"The Object Lesson: Picture Books of A.B.," *Word and Image,* April/June, 1986.
Publishers Weekly, September 26, 1986 (p. 32ff), July 29, 1988.
Ms., March, 1987 (p. 55ff).
Books for Keeps, May, 1987 (p. 16ff).
Douglas Martin, *The Telling Line,* Macrae, 1989.

BURNS, Florence M. 1905-1988

PERSONAL: Born June 28, 1905, in Blackstock, Ontario, Canada; died September 26, 1988; daughter of John Richardson (a farmer) and Ellen (a homemaker; maiden name, Proutt) McLaughlin; married Harold B. Burns (a retired principal), September, 1972. *Education:* Attended Teacher's College, Peterborough, 1923-24; Queen's University, Kingston, B.A. 1933. *Home:* 7 Faircroft Blvd., Scarborough, Ontario, Canada M1M 2W9.

CAREER: Teacher and librarian in Toronto Public Schools; free-lance writer. *Member:* Canadian Authors Association (president of Toronto branch, 1971-72), Canadian Society of Children's Authors, Illustrators, and Performers.

WRITINGS:

First Lady of Upper Canada, Burns & McEachern, 1968.
William Berczy, Fitzhenry & Whiteside, 1977.
Jumbo: The Biggest Elephant in All the World, Scholastic-TAB, 1978.
John Beverley Robinson and the War of 1812, Irwin, 1984.

Also author of *No School till March,* 1989. Contributor of articles and stories to *Junior Red Cross Magazine, Toboggans and Turtlenecks, Antique Collector* and to the SRA Reading Lab. Contributor of two stories to *Gage's Grade 4 Anthology*.

CAPP, Al 1909-1979

PERSONAL: Born Alfred Gerald Caplin, September 28, 1909, in New Haven, Conn.; died November 5, 1979, in Cambridge, Mass.; name legally changed, 1940s; son of Otto Philip (a salesman) and Matilda (Davidson) Caplin; married Catherine Wingate Cameron, 1929 (some sources say 1932); children: Julie Ann Caplin Cairol, Catherine Jane Caplin Pierce, Colin C. *Education:* Studied at Pennsylvania Academy of the Fine Arts, Philadelphia Museum of Fine Arts, Designer's Art School, Boston Museum School of Fine Arts, Boston University, Harvard University.

CAREER: Began career as cartoonist working for Associated Press on the comic strip "Colonel Gilfeather" in 1932, *Sunday Post,* Boston, Mass., illustrator, 1933; ghost artist for several major comic strips including Ham Fisher's "Joe Palooka"; creator, developer, and author of comic strip "Li'l Abner," 1934-1977; writer and host of television's "The Al Capp Show," 1952-53; creator and author of comic strip "Abbie an' Slats"; author of comic strip "Long Sam"; author of comic strips "Private Li'l Abner, Infantry" for the *Infantry Journal,* "Small Change" for the Treasury Department, and *'Al Capp,' by Li'l Abner,* for the Red Cross, all during World War II; columnist, New York Daily News Syndicate, 1960-72; daily syndicated radio and television commentator, 1970-73. Commentator, "Today" television show; teacher of cartooning workshop course at New York University; has lectured at Harvard University. Exhibited paintings at New York Culture Center, 1975.

AL CAPP

WRITINGS:

The Life and Times of the Shmoo, Simon & Schuster, 1948.
The World of Li'l Abner, introduction by John Steinbeck and foreword by Charles Chaplin, Farrar, Straus, 1953.
Bald Iggle: The Life It Ruins May Be Your Own, Simon & Schuster, 1956.
Fearless Fosdick, Simon & Schuster, 1956.
The Return of the Shmoo, Simon & Schuster, 1959.
(With David Manning White) *From Dogpatch to Slobbovia: The (Gasp!!) World of Li'l Abner, as Seen by David Manning White, with Certain Illuminating Remarks by Al Capp,* Beacon Press, 1964.
(With George Wallace) *Great Issues: A Forum on Important Questions Facing the American Public,* Troy State University Press, 1970.
The Hardhat's Bedtime Story Book, Harper, 1971.
The Best of Li'l Abner, Holt, 1978.
(With Raeburn Van Buren) *Abbie an' Slats,* K. Pierce, 1983.
(With others) *Abbie an' Slats, Volume 2,* K. Pierce, 1984.
Li'l Abner Dailies, Volume One: 1934-1936, Kitchen Sink Press, 1988.
Li'l Abner Dailies, Volume Two, Kitchen Sink Press, 1988.
Li'l Abner Dailies, Volume Three: 1937, Kitchen Sink Press, 1988.
Li'l Abner Dailies, Volume Four, Kitchen Sink Press, 1989.
Li'l Abner Dailies, Volume Five: 1939, Kitchen Sink Press, 1989.

Contributor to *Encyclopaedia Britannica.*

ADAPTATIONS:

"Li'l Abner" (motion picture), starring Granville Owen and Martha O'Driscoll, Vogue/RKO, 1940, (Broadway musical), first produced at St. James Theater, November 15, 1956, (motion picture based on the Broadway musical and comic strip), starring Peter Palmer and Leslie Parish, Paramount, 1959, (television movie), ABC-TV, April 26, 1971, (television movie), NBC-TV, November 9, 1978.

SIDELIGHTS: Al Capp grew up in Connecticut where his father managed to make only a small income as a salesman. Having studied law at Yale, Otto Caplin was an optimistic and cheerful man, but inwardly unhappy with his life. It was his wife's strength and ingenuity that saw the family through tough times.

LI'L ABNER **By Al Capp**

LI'L ABNER **By Al Capp**

LI'L ABNER *Daisy Mae Disappears* **By Al Capp**

Earliest of the Li'l Abner strips. (From *Li'l Abner Dailies, Volume One: 1934-1936* by Al Capp. Illustrated by the author.)

Matilda Caplin talked bakers into giving her stale bread, would not deal with a grocer when he refused to hire one of her sons, worked out agreements with butchers and merchants, and dealt with unpaid landlords. There were also times, late at night, when she led her children through the neighborhood, sifting through ash cans for pieces of coal or usable items of clothing. "Her hair turned white before she was thirty-five. She was cheerful enough but she had sort of a haunted look—she never had any pretty clothes or good times.

"My father's real talent was drawing. He was a most naturally gifted comic artist. I grew up watching [him] do comic strips on brown paper bags with my mother and himself as the two principal characters. He always triumphed over her in those strips. But only in them. Never in real life.

"I inherited just a little bit of my father's gift for drawing. He was absolutely amazing—I'm not as naturally gifted as he was. I had a little bit of talent and I worked hard and now I'm a competent illustrator. But my father had a great bug-winning sense of humor and I inherited just a little bit of that."[1]

"I became a candidate for a wooden leg on August 21, 1919, when I was nine-years-old. That day my father, a vague and unworldy man, gave me 50 cents to get a haircut: 35 cents for the haircut, 5 cents for a tip, 10 cents for trolley fare. At least that was the way he figured it. I, a calculating and worldly kid, figured it a little differently. I had seen a tantalizing offer on a sign in a downtown New Haven window: 'Prof. Amoroso, Barber Academy—Haircuts 15 cents—No Tipping.' By hitching a ride on the back of an ice wagon I could step into Professor Amoroso's with 50 cents and, with luck, step out again with most of the money (and possibly some of my scalp) intact. Clutching that 50 cent piece, blinded with dreams of riches and power, I hopped off the ice cart in front of the barber academy—and directly in the path of a huge old-fashioned trolley car. I was caught under the wheels and before the car could be stopped my left leg was severed at the thigh.

"During the ride to the hospital and later while I was under anesthetic, I never once unclutched that half dollar. My mother finally took it from me.

"Losing a leg at nine is not all loss. For one thing it made me a celebrity among the other kids, to whom I had previously been merely another vague and grubby menace. True, I was not much good at baseball, wrestling or apple-orchard raiding, but then I never had been much good at them, and now I was spared the embarrassment of displaying my awkwardness. As for grownups, suddenly they noticed spiritual qualities in me as a slow-moving, one-legged boy which had been totally hidden from them when I was a hooting, howling, fast-moving two-legger. Gifts poured in from formerly unenchanted, unprofitable and unheard-of relatives. Yes, at nine, I reveled in the drama and distinction of that shocking pinned-up pants leg and those swagger crutches. With two legs I had been a nobody. With one leg I was somebody.

"Then came the day that had been hailed so glowingly by my doctor, my parents and the local wooden leg salesman—the day when I could strap on my new leg and walk around again like everyone else. It was one of the most shattering letdowns of my life. I damn well did *not* walk around like everyone else. I went through weeks of stumbling, of toppling, of aching, cursing and weeping before I mastered the gadget. And still I did not walk around like everyone else. I walked like everyone else who had a wooden leg. I swayed and I dragged.

"For a while the other kids were even more fascinated by the wooden leg than they had been by the absence of the real one, and that made a satisfyingly unique figure of me for as long as it lasted. But the novelty wore off."[2]

During his two-year convalescence, Capp began drawing and took to creating comic-strips. On the dining room table he churned out strips which his brothers and sister would sell to neighborhood kids for two or three cents.

After reading about cartoonist Bud Fisher, creator of "Mutt and Jeff," Capp decided that he too wanted to become a cartoonist. "[Fisher] was making $4,000 a week and constantly marrying French countesses. I didn't understand about the French countesses then but I sure did understand about the money."[1]

When Capp was twelve, the family moved to Brooklyn, New York. "I was thrown into a big public school, just when its principal had agreed to turn over fifty students—twenty-five brilliant children and twenty-five degenerates—to a man who was conducting an educational experiment. I think I was supposed to be one of the smart kids and that the morons were supposed to benefit by association with us, but it worked the other way around. The experiment went on for a couple of months, and it made thieves and monsters and perverts out of us nice kids. It was horrible, like a leper colony. The boy directly in back of me spent all day drooling over French postcards; the one in front of me kept picking his neighbor's pocket. We never got any textbooks or anything, and to pass the time away I used to draw a lot. Well, one day a twelve-year-old boy—a rapist, I think—sidled up to me and said, 'Jeez, you're a good drawer.' He offered me a quarter for an indelicate portrait of the teacher, and when I had no idea what he was talking about, he described in detail what he wanted. I was just a kid from the country, but soon I became an expert in pornography. My price was a quarter a drawing, and with twenty-five steady customers, I was doing fine until I got so many commissions that I started taking extra work home and my father found out about it."[3]

In general, Capp found school boring and did not do well. But he was an avid reader and a number of writers influenced him, particularly humorists. "Dickens, Benchley, Tarkington—he was a special favorite. I really didn't like most of the *New Yorker* writers, but Perelman, the way he fooled around with words, a master. I loved him because I understood everything he said! I can't forget to mention the great army of American humorists—totally unknown but named Nat and Sol—all of whom were writing for radio."[1]

He also had favorite cartoonists. "I grew up with Opper ['Happy Hooligan,' 'Alphonse and Gaston'] and Sterrett ['Polly and Her Pals']—now Sterrett! That's the guy who was the greatest. To think that a whole generation has grown up worshipping Picasso when the guy who did it far better was Sterrett. Far better than Picasso—and Herriman. I like Herriman—he has his own special place—but I love Sterrett: he belongs someplace else. He was a great man. I grew up on *Judge* and *Life* magazines and read what every other kid read. I loved the comics from the start."[4]

A book about Alfred the Great had a particularly strong impact on young Capp. The book was given to him by his aunt a few years after his accident. "Through Alfred's exploits I discovered there really isn't anything a person can't do if he convinces himself that he *can* do it. I identified like mad with Alfred. Things I thought I couldn't possibly do because of my disability I found myself doing. I supercharged myself into an arrogant, cocky young man.

Two of Capp's daily strips, circa 1935. (From *Li'l Abner Dailies, Volume One: 1934-1936* by Al Capp. Illustrated by the author.)

"Actually, it wasn't difficult identifying with Al. After looking at the illustrations repeatedly, I was positive I looked just like him. True, he had a beard (I didn't even have a stubble), blond hair (I'm a dark beauty myself) and was about twenty-five, but that, plus the fact that he wasn't even Jewish (which I was), still didn't deter me from thinking I looked just like him.

"All kidding aside, this man, this book changed my life. Alfred the Great convinced me that nothing is impossible if one has courage, spirit and, I suppose, a certain amount of foolhardiness."[5]

"I became a teen-ager with all the routine problems of teen-agers—and one special problem; namely, how to get myself treated by girls in their teens as though I did not have a special problem.

"A teen-ager wants more than anything else in life to look, act and be treated like all other teen-agers. On the first two counts I did fine. I am sure that I looked and behaved as oddly as all the other teen-agers at Central High School in Bridgeport, Conn., where I then lived. But I got different and special treatment, especially from the girls, and that made life hell for me. My rooster roughness and rowdiness was forgiven with sweet understanding, when what I wanted was the same thrilled contempt that was accorded two-legged rowdies of the same behavior.

"So I took to hanging out on street corners. Every afternoon I would leave the high school world, limp a half-dozen blocks along Main Street and prop myself against the corner of D. M. Read's store at the city's busiest intersection. I was then in a different world, and I was then a different guy. As long as I stayed in one place, the girls I stared at and whistled at treated me like any other street-corner wise guy—with the exaggerated disdain that a nicely behaved girl uses to tell a boy on a street corner who is not behaving very nicely that she would not dream of acknowledging him because she is terribly interested in him. If a girl did look back invitingly, I would look away, pleased but immobile. On a good afternoon there might be as many as a dozen look-backs and look-aways before the streets thinned out. I would go home delighted, having had a remarkably few hours of being treated ordinarily.

"[My wooden leg] and I had been through a lot together. On it I . . . learned how to live without resentment or embarrassment in a world in which I was different from everyone else. The secret, I found, was to be indifferent to that difference.

"Learning that took years, years in which, every now and then some wildly unpredictable mishap would shatter my spirit and occasionally, me. But now that I look back at those incidents, they don't seem shattering at all. They seem, instead, like the normal, predictable and hilarious adventures anyone might have who relies so heavily on a gadget. Because that's all a wooden leg is: a simply made, useful, rather good-looking gadget, no different from a sports car or a pair of suspenders—and just as apt to suddenly make a damn fool of you."[2]

At fifteen, Capp, without his parents' permission, hitchhiked through the South. In the hills of Tennessee he was exposed to a

LI'L ABNER The Strange Case of Sadig Hawkins—Part 1 **By Al Capp**

LI'L ABNER He Didn't Ask to Be Born **By Al Capp**

Two Sadie Hawkins strips from 1937. (From *Li'l Abner Dailies, Volume Three: 1937* by Al Capp. Illustrated by the author.)

region that he would later use to create a comic strip that brought him fame and fortune.

"I knew then that cartooning was not just a trick but a step beyond illustration—a kind of illustration of your own point of view. I knew you couldn't do humorous drawing until you could do straight drawing."[3] So, at nineteen, having never graduated from high school, he decided to pursue his ambition as cartoonist. Starting art school in Boston, he was forced to leave when he could no longer stall paying his tuition. In four years he repeated this process three times.

During this time Capp met and married Catherine Cameron, and together they moved to New York City in 1932. Having very little money, the Capps lived in "airless little rat holes" in Greenwich Village while Capp tried to find work. He was ekeing out a living drawing advertising strips for a few dollars when "Harry Resnick [my uncle] called the Associated Press and asked them to see me. They did, and they actually gave me a job drawing a panel called 'Col. Gilfeather.'

"I began doing this tremendous imitation of Phil May. He was a great artist, and I was copying his stuff from his prime. I was in my twenties—I didn't know anything but that I wanted to draw like him.

"When I left 'Gilfeather,' Milt Caniff took it over and probably made it a masterpiece.

"Now, after I had done 'Col. Gilfeather,' for a few months, that's when I knew—or thought I knew—something more about anatomy, plots, perspective."[4]

Having left Associated Press, Capp decided to return to Boston and resume his studies of anatomy and perspective. Needing money, he went to see the art editor of the Boston *Post*'s Sunday magazine. "I took along a portfolio full of elegant, dignified drawings. On the cover of the portfolio, I had done some offhand sketches of dames. I had always been a pretty good hip-and-thighman. Well, the editor looked at the outside of the portfolio, beamed, and, being a Bostonian, said, 'My, you have a very nice pen line.' He asked me to illustrate an article about a crooked roulette wheel at Monte Carlo. I was no fool. I did an interior view of the Casino with a terrific wind blowing up the skirts of all the dames' evening gowns. He liked it. I was invited to do a dozen or so more illustrations for the *Post*. Whatever the subject was, even if it was a bunch of people freezing to death in Alaska or trapped in the Black Hole of Calcutta, I always managed to have a strong wind blowing up the skirts of some dame."[3]

Nineteen thirty-four found the Capps back in New York where he landed a job helping Ham Fisher with his "Joe Palooka" comic strip. But Capp didn't last long, not having the temperament to be an assistant. While working for Fisher, Capp introduced a hillbilly character, Big Leviticus, into an episode of the Palooka strip.

When he left Fisher, Capp kept working on this character which soon evolved into Li'l Abner Yokum who lived with his pa and corncob-pipe-smoking ma and two pigs in a log cabin in fictitious Dogpatch, Kentucky. "He was then six feet three, and nineteen years old, and still is. Being a typical, red-blooded One Hundred Percent American boy, his main interests were eating, sleeping, not working much and avoiding marriage. Mainly what he always wanted from life was no trouble. So, mainly, that's what life has always given him. All this trouble, however, [never] made him any more careful, or less hopeful. For years his Mammy and Pappy nagged him to marry Daisy Mae Scragg. For years, Daisy Mae herself tried to catch him on Sadie Hawkins Day."[6]

"[I] brought the 'Abner' samples up to King Features and they offered me 250 bucks a week, which is the equivalent of a thousand—even more—today.

"But the big guy there—[Joseph] Connolly—said, 'Great strip, great art, yes sir. A couple of things though: That Abner's an idiot. Make him a nice kid, with some saddlestrip shoes on him. And Daisy Mae's pretty, but how about some pretty clothes? As a matter of fact, why not forget the mountain bit and move them all to New Jersey: and that Mammy, she's got to go—you need a sweet white-haired lady.'

"Well, I thought all about it and I realized that I would have had 'Polly and Her Pals!' But I would have had 250 bucks a week, wouldn't I? Well, I was pretty sick about it. I walked up to United Features—[Monte] Bourjaily was the head of it then—and they looked at it, showed it to Colin Miller and the other salesmen, were amazed by it, and wanted to take it out just as it was. They offered me fifty bucks a week—which was the lowest—and I grabbed it and forgot King Features because I was now able to do my own strip exactly as I wanted to."[4]

Catherine and Al Capp at Seabrook Beach, New Hampshire, early '30s.

"Li'l Abner" made its debut in eight newspapers on August 13, 1934. He now signed his work "Al Capp," having legally changed his name in the late '40s. "When I was in my early twenties and about to start a comic strip, I found myself in a terrible dilemma. The funny comic strip, the kind I wanted to do, was vanishing from the funny page. A frightening new thing had been discovered: namely, that you could sell more papers by worrying people than by amusing them. Comic strips which had no value except that they were comic were beginning to vanish from the funny papers. Rube Goldberg's dazed 'Mike and Ike,' Fred Opper's 'Happy Holligan,' who wore a tomato can on his head, Mil Gross's 'Count Screwloose,' who regularly escaped from the booby hatch only to return to it because things were more normal there—this beloved procession of clowns, innocents and cheerful imbeciles— slowly faded. In their place came a sobbing, screaming, shooting parade of the new 'comic'-strip characters: an orphan who talked like the Republican platform of 1920; a prize-figher who advised children that brains were better than brawn while beating the brains out of his physically inferior opponents; detectives who explored and explained every sordid and sickening byway of crime and then made it all okay by concluding that these attractively blueprinted crimes didn't really pay; and girl reporters who were daily threatened with rape and mutilation.

"Don't get me wrong. I was terrified by the emergence of this new kind of comic strip . . . only because I didn't have the special qualities they required—not because they didn't have quality. 'Dick Tracy' is a magnificently drawn, exquisitely written shocker comparable, in its own terms, with Poe. But 'suspense' strips, though enormously effective, disdain fun and fantasy. Suspense was what editors wanted when I was ready to create my own comic strip—but all I could do was fun and fantasy.

"So I tried to draw straight-faced suspense comic strips. I tried to create smart and superior heroes, and submerged them in blood-curdling tragedies, increasing in complexity, hopelessness and horror and thereby creating reader anxiety, nausea and terror—*i.e.*, suspense. But I couldn't do it. I just couldn't believe in them. The suspense strips require one-dimensional characters: good guys and bad guys, and no fooling around with anything in between. I simply couldn't believe in my one-dimensional good guys and bad guys—as I drew them. I discovered good things in the bad guys, and vice versa. So my hero [Li'l Abner] turned out to be big and strong like the suspense-strip heroes, but he also turned out to be stupid, as big, strong heroes sometimes are. His mammy, like mine, and possibly yours, turned out to be a miracle of goodness, but at the same time she was kind of bossy, quite self-righteous and sweetly ridiculous. His girl [Daisy Mae], although wildly beautiful, is vaguely sloppy and, although infinitely virtuous, pursues him like the most unprincipled seductress.

"The good people in my hero's town [Dogpatch], possibly like those in your town, often are a pain in the neck. And the bad 'uns, like some bad 'uns in real life, are often more attractive than the good 'uns. The Scragg Boys, Lem and Luke, are fiendish when they are snatching milk from whimpering babies or burning down orphan asylums to get some light to read comic books by (only to realize that they can't read, anyway); but even the most horrified reader can't help being touched by their respectfully asking their pappy's permission to commit all this manslaughter and mayhem. Monsters they certainly are, but they are dutiful children too.

Self-portrait of Capp surrounded by some of his famous characters. (Copyright © by Chicago Tribune-New York News Syndicate, Inc.)

"The society people in 'Li'l Abner' always have impressive names, but there is always something a little wrong with them too—like Henry Cabbage Cod, Daphne Degradingham, Sir Cecil Cesspool (he's deep), Peabody Fleabody and Basil Bassoon. Dumpington Van Lump seemed a harmless, hospitable kid until it developed that his favorite book was *How to Make Lampshades Out of Your Friends*. Colossal McGenius was so brilliant in giving business advice that he seemed to be justified in charging $1,000 a word for talking to worried tycoons; but it turned out that his weakness was telling long, involved jokes (at $1,000 a word) about three Bulgarians, whereupon he remembered much too late, that they were actually three *Persians,* and so he had to start the story all over again. When he finally got to the advice it was great, but by that time the tycoon had gone bankrupt.

"When I introduced a mythical country, Lower Slobbovia, I was as technical as the straightest suspense-strip creator, and gave readers a map. The map was perfectly reasonable except that the names of its parts created some distrust and disrespect for the country. The oceans were the Hotlantic and Pitziffic, and there was another body of water called the Gulf of Pincus. The capital, Ceaser Siddy, home of Good King Nogoodnik, was flanked by the twin cities of Tsk-Tsk and Tch-Tch. Its leading citizens had familiar and famous, but somehow embarrassing, names like Douglas Snowbanks Jr., Harry S. Rasputintruman and Clark Bagle. Everything in 'Li'l Abner' was my effort to be as straight as the straight strips, but colored, however, with my conviction that nothing is ever entirely straight, entirely good, entirely bad, and that everything is a little ridiculous. As in the straight suspense strips, I dutifully created the standard, popular suspense situations, but something forced me to carry them so far that terror became absurdity.

"For instance, when the Yokums make gigantic sacrifices for what they are convinced is a noble and beneficial cause, the reader knows they are swindling themselves; even victory will benefit only the enemy. When the Yokums are being heroes they are being not only heroes—they are being damned fools at the same time. When their adversaries are being villainous, they are not only vile, they are also confused and frightened.

"'Li'l Abner' had to come out that way, because that's the way things seem to me. Well, it happened to make a big hit. It was a success because it was something I hadn't thought much about as such. It was a satire. Nobody had done one quite in these terms before. I was delighted that I had. I was exhilarated by the privilege this gave me to kid hell out of everything."[7]

The strip had a decidedly liberal bent. He parodied many establishment figures and institutions of the time, as well as other comic strips. It soon became the vogue to lampoon society people in the strip. "[I strive] to create suspicion of, and disrespect for, the perfection of all established institutions. That's what I think education is. Anybody who gets out of college having had his confidence in the perfection of existing institutions affirmed has not been educated. Just suffocated.

"Some skepticism about the sacredness of all aspects of the Establishment is the priceless ingredient of education. Possibly those who read 'Li'l Abner' will be discontent with the Establishment and make it a little better. And then in another time, another Capp, hopefully a better one, but no less peevish, will come along and point out how suspect and full of flaws that *improved* Establishment is, and so on.

"My job (and the job of all humorists) is to keep reminding people that they must not be content with anything."[8]

The visual style of the strip was unique. Characters were expressive and filled the space, heavy lines were used. The Sunday editions employed bold colors and the strip's lettering undulated wildly in word balloons that exploded. The southern twang his characters spoke was catchy and they always found themselves in impossible situations which they always managed to survive. "I build fun the way an architect builds a house. I know what you place as a foundation, and how you erect the framework, and how you finish it off. It all takes thirty seconds in the reading and yet it's all put together as carefully as a new home."[1]

"I don't want to draw things right. I want to draw them so that they look vaguely like what they're supposed to."[3]

"I'd take a month of strips and throw them in the wastebasket and start over because I thought I could do better. In the beginning, for the first ten years or so, I didn't have a single day off. Not a single day off. I was just sick with anxiety about the strip."[1] Even an emergency gallbladder operation couldn't keep him away for long. "I was working two days later. In absolute agony."[1]

Capp was continuously updating the strip. "It was like living on the edge of a precipice . . . . Because Abner became the most popular comic strip in the world before I knew how to do it. And it began making an enormous amount of money and piling up an enormous list of newspapers, and I collected an endless stable of insolvent relatives—and all of this was based on an entertainment I didn't know anything about.

"It took me so long to draw anything. It took me so long to make up my mind about what I was writing. I should have served a ten-year apprenticeship, but I had no apprenticeship. I just went in and six months after I created it, I had the most popular comic strip in the world . . . . I hadn't the faintest idea— there was never a strip like this and it was out of sheer desperation that the thing was so lively and unpredictable for so many years."[1]

With the enormous success of the strip, Capp took on two assistants who worked for him for the entire forty-three year run. "When I say 'I' I mean these two guys equally with me. I'm the guy who signed the strip, and I made up our minds about what we would do but both of them had just as much effect on the strip as I: Andy Amato and Harvey Curtis.

"I only inked the faces and hands; once in a while, I inked Abner . . . . There are many sorts of things I'd do in the busy years that needed help, extra artwork.

"I'd write [the stories] in longhand at my desk, on yellow legal sheets. And I'd recite each line to the guys as I wrote and we'd knock it around. And that's how it worked for years. I would say, when we needed a new story, 'How about this?' and 'Let's try that' until we were howling with laughter—and that's how we wrote a story.

"I would know vaguely where a story was going. I had an ending, but I left myself enough choice as I went along to go anywhere with it; I would always come back to that ending. I found out through terrible, terrible agonies that you damn well better have that ending or you'll wind up wanting to kill yourself.

"I would run a story as long as I wanted. You see, from very early, the people at United wouldn't dare make suggestions . . . . They were scared to death of me."[4]

Usually his Monday-through-Saturday sequences lasted six weeks and ended on a Wednesday. "If I ended one on a Saturday, millions of my readers would have nothing to worry about over the weekend and would forget me and turn to 'Popeye.' I not only always end on a Wednesday, but sometimes in the first two of my four Wednesday panels. Then in the last two I begin a new sequence so outrageous and shocking that my readers have *got* to find out what happens next. By Saturday, they're hopelessly enslaved again."[3]

When creating the strip "the thought that is uppermost in my mind is always to make myself clear to as many people as I possible can. I think that's why I chose the comic strip as a way of working, rather than the novel, or the theater, or motion pictures. First, within fairly loose bounds, the comic strip is the freest of all mass media. There are no stockholders to dictate your next move as you have in motion pictures; you have no sponsors to give you almost unlivable restrictions as you do in television. In comics, one has so many employers that while all their voices are important enough, none of them is crucial.

"So that within bounds of almost instinctive taste, you are free to fool with any idea that interests you. The trick is to see that the idea is stated clearly enough to be understood by the greatest possible audience. I think that anyone who communicates or who makes his living by communication can measure his success in only one way, and that is by asking, with how many people does he truly communicate? To how many people does he say exactly what he wants to say?

Capp gained world recognition with his appearance on this prestigious cover. (Copyright 1950 by Time Inc. Reprinted by permission.)

(Based on the stage play, the 1959 Paramount movie "Li'l Abner" starred Stubby Kaye as Marryin' Sam.)

"My first thought is to be amusing enough, perplexing enough, so that I'll be read again the next day. I want to give enough pleasure that the reader will come back, but also I want to talk about the things that make the job fun for me to do. I do have some notions about the world and man that I want to submit to the strip's readers.

"I think that man is interested in two or three things. He is interested in death; he is exhilarated by the thought of death. That's the basis of all the adventure of 'Li'l Abner.' It is always a flirtation with death; it is always a triumph over something that we all know will eventually triumph over us. So that I think we get some escape in 'Li'l Abner' from the final certainty.

"I think people are also interested in love, every aspect of love. Most people feel themselves failures in love. In 'Li'l Abner' there is also the failure to make love fantasies come true. But the clumsy, ludicrous, pitiful failures of the folks in Dogpatch makes the rest of us, who are also failing to realize our own fantasies, feel a little less stupid and perhaps a little less incompetent.

"I think we are all interested in one other thing, which might be called 'fortune' or 'power'—all that comes as a result of winning the game of achievement against everybody else who is playing it against us. Death, love and power are the three great interests of man. They are the sources of all the stories in 'Li'l Abner,' mainly because there are no others.

"I think the whole meaning of existence, the great reward for having lived through a day, is that the day isn't as bad as it might have been. I think that's one of the satisfactions people get out of reading 'Li'l Abner,' that no matter how badly their day has gone, his went worse."[8]

During World War II many comic-strip characters joined the Armed Forces, but not "Abner." "Perhaps Li'l Abner and his friends, living through these terrible days in a peaceful, happy, free world, will do their part—by thus reminding us that this is what we are fighting for—*to have that world again.*"[3]

Despite this, in another successful strip that Capp created in 1936 and for which he wrote the text, "Abbie an' Slats" (Raeburn Van Buren drew and signed it), he had it's heroine enlist in the WACS. This was at the request of the Women's Army Corps to help in their recruiting efforts. The Army also commissioned Capp to do a strip called "Private Li'l Abner" which was used

(From the 1959 movie "Li'l Abner," starring the citizens of Dogpatch including: Appassionata Von Climax, Evil Eye Fleagle, Moonbeam McSwine, and the sisters, Available and Stupefyin' Jones.)

for training purposes and dealt with such subjects as military courtesy.

Capp also visited many Army and Navy hospitals, giving lectures and cartooning demonstrations. For the War Bond Division of the Treasury Department he did a full-page Sunday strip called "Small Change" for three years for which he received one dollar annually. This was the first time that the U.S. Government handled a comic-strip serial, and at one point it appeared in 120 newspapers.

Capp also wrote an autobiographical comic book *'Al Capp,' by Li'l Abner*. Written in the voice of Li'l Abner, the book's major focus was on the loss of Capp's leg. The Red Cross distributed 100,000 copies to disabled veterans.

By the end of the war Capp was making large sums from the continuing success of "Li'l Abner." "[In the beginning] the syndicate had control [of the script]. I could be fired at any time—they owned it. I couldn't take that after a while and said, 'I'm quitting. You can keep the strip.' I mean it.

"They got all upset, of course, and after a lot of running around they offered me a deal of a brand new contract, with new terms, and at the end of ten years, the strip would become mine. Now you see, there was an unwritten law that a successful strip had a life span of twelve years . . . . Of course after [the next] ten years I was going hotter than ever."[4]

By the 1950s the strip was running in more than 1200 newspapers world-wide. His comic characters and language and his satire were now a part of American folklore. Capp was being compared to Mark Twain and Charles Dickens and was the first cartoonist to make the cover of *Time* magazine.

To the American culture Capp added Joe Btfsplk, The Noodniks, Appassionata Van Climax, General Bullmoose, Fearless Fosdick and Kickapoo Joy Juice. Phrases such as "amoozin' but confoozin'," "natcherly," "as any fool can plainly see—I can see" and "sob!" were added to the American idiom.

In 1952, the unbelievable happened. After eighteen years of having Daisy Mae chase after Li'l Abner in hopes of ensnaring him, Capp had them tie the knot. "I had no reason for marrying Abner off to Daisy Mae. But then something happened that threatens to shackle me and my kind of comic strip. It is what I call the gradual loss of our fifth freedom. Without it, the other four freedoms aren't much fun, because the fifth is the freedom to laugh at each other.

"My kind of comic strip finds its fun wherever there is lunacy, and American life is rich in lunacy everywhere you look. I created labor-hating labor leaders, money-foolish financiers, and Senator Jack S. ('Good old Jack S.') Phogbound. When highway billboard advertising threatened to create a coast-to-coast iron curtain between the American motorist and the beautiful American countryside, I got some humorous situations out of that too. Race-hate-peddlers gave me some of my juiciest comedy characters, and I had the Yokums tell them what I know is true, that all races are God's children, equally beloved by their Father. For the first fourteen years I reveled in the freedom to laugh at America. But now America has changed. The humorist feels the change more, perhaps, than anyone. Now there are things about America we can't kid.

"I realized it first when . . . I created the Shmoo. You remember the Shmoo? It was a totally boneless and wildly affectionate little animal which, when broiled, came out steak and, when fried, tasted like chicken. It also laid neatly packaged and bottled eggs and milk, all carefully labeled 'Grade A.' It multiplied without the slightest effort. It loved to be eaten, and would drop dead, out of sheer joy, when you looked at it hungrily. Having created the animal, I let it run wild in the world of my cartoon strip. It was simply a fairy tale and all I had to say was wouldn't it be wonderful if there were such an animal and, if there were, how idiotically some people might behave. Mainly, the response to the Shmoo was delight. But there were also some disturbing letters. Some writers wanted to know what was the idea of kidding big business, by creating the Shmoo (which had *become* big business). Other writers wanted to know what was the idea of criticising labor, by creating the Shmoo, which made labor unnecessary.

"It was disturbing, but I didn't let it bother me too much. Then a year later, I created the Kigmy, an animal that loved to be kicked around, thus making it unnecessary for people to kick each other around. This time a lot more letters came. Their tone was angrier, more suspicious. They asked the craziest questions, like: Was I, in creating the Kigmy, trying to create pacifism and thus, secretly, nonresistance to Communism? Were the Kigmy kickers secretly the big bosses kicking the workers around? Were the Kigmy kickers secretly the labor unions kicking capital around? And finally, what in the hell was the idea of creating the Kigmy anyhow, because it implied some criticism of some kinds of Americans and any criticism of anything American was (now) un-American? I was astounded to find it had become unpopular to laugh at any fellow Americans. In fact, when I looked around, I realized that a new kind of humorist had taken over, the humorist who kidded nothing but himself. That was the only thing left. Hollywood had stopped making ain't-America-wonderful-and-ridiculous movies, and was making ain't-America-wonderful-but-anyone-who-says-it's-ridiculous-too-deserves-to-be-picketed movies. Radio, the most instantly obedient to pressure of all media, had sensed the atmosphere, an atmosphere in which Jack Benny is magnificent but in which Will Rogers would have suffocated.

"So that was when I decided to go back to fairy tales until the atmosphere is gone. That is the real reason why Li'l Abner married Daisy Mae. At least for the time being, I can't create any more Shmoos, any more Kigmies; and when Senator Phogbound turns up now, I have to explain carefully that, heavens-to-Betsy, goodness-no, he's not typical; nobody like THAT ever holds public office. After a decade and a half of using my characters as merely reasons to swing my searchlight on America, I began all over again to examine them, as people. Frankly, I was delighted with them. (Frankly, I'm delighted with nearly everything I do. The one in the room who laughs loudest at my own jokes or my own comic strip is me.) I became reacquainted with Li'l Abner as a human being, with Daisy Mae as an agonizingly frustrated girl. I began to wonder myself what it would be like if they were ever married. The more I thought about it, the more complicated and disastrous and, therefore, irresistible, the idea became.

"For instance, Li'l Abner has never willingly kissed any female except his mother and a pig. Well—if he got married, he'd *have* to. Even he couldn't avoid it for more than a month or so. What would happen? Would he approve of kissing? Would he say anything good about it? (And thus make it popular with millions of red-blooded young Americans whose 'ideel' he is.) Would he do it again? As a bachelor he is frankly a bum. He just sleeps, eats and goes catfishing. As a married man he would have to support his own household. How would he do it? Is there anybody stupid enough to hire someone as stupid as he is? Is there *any* profession that requires as little intelligence as he has? And how about Mammy Yokum? She has always ruled Abner with an iron fist. Would she continue to after he has his own home? And how would Daisy Mae take this? Sure, she's been sweet and docile with Mammy Yokum all these years, but that might only have been because she needed her help in trapping Abner. Now that he's her'n, will she show her true colors and tangle with Mammy for the lightweight championship of the new Yokum home? How about babies? Married people frequently have babies. Would *they* have a baby? Will he really be born on the Fourth of July? Is it possible that they'd name him Yankee Doodle Yokum? Babies have uncles. Could I freeze the blood of the entire nation by having Mammy Yokum (who can accomplish anything, even singlehanded) produce a baby of her own, five minutes after Li'l Yankee Doodle Yokum was born? Would this child be known as Oncle Yokum?

"And how about Sadie Hawkins Day? It has become a national holiday. It's my responsibility. It doesn't happen on any set day in November; it happens on the day I say it happens. I get tens of thousands of letters from colleges, communities and church groups, starting around July, asking me *what* day, so they can make plans. Well, Sadie Hawkins Day has always revolved around Li'l Abner fearing marriage to Daisy Mae. Now . . . his worst fears have come hideously true."[7]

Capp began to branch out. Capp Enterprises was established which licensed the manufacturing of Shmoos and Kigmies and many other products from Li'l Abner orangade to Daisy Mae blouses and Li'l Abner corncob pipes to skonk hats. In 1949, the film "Li'l Abner," based on his strip, was released by RKO, and in 1956 the musical "Li'l Abner," written by Norman Panama and Melvin Frank, with Capp's permission, debuted on Broadway. Three years later Paramount released it as a film.

Capp was often heard on radio as commentator and interviewer, was a frequent guest on television panel shows and began giving lectures at colleges around the country. In 1952 he had his own television show, "The Al Capp Show." It aired weekly for fifteen minutes during which Capp delivered his views on the absurdities of present-day issues in his own ascerbic humor and illustrated his monologues as he went along. Critics loved it and it lasted a year. Two years later he was the weekly commentator on NBC-TV's "Today Show."

In 1961 Capp made his debut as a columnist for the New York Daily News Syndicate. In announcing his new venture, he said, "Naturally I will deal only with those subjects on which I am an admitted authority, such as life, death, love, economics, the arts, man's inhumanity to man, metaphysics, cybernetics and atomic fusion.

"I may also deal with such trifles as how to raise children, how to survive marriage, how to tell a man's character from his necktie and how to safely insult cops who have just insulted you. I have taken up a hobby which I will pursue wearing a frown and a homburg hat."[9]

But six months later his new "hobby" was floundering. "I created a whole country in the column. Nothing happened. Gee, it was deadly. If I'd done the same thing in Abner, every editor in

(From the movie ''Li'l Abner,'' starring Granville Owen. Produced by RKO Radio Pictures, 1940.)

(From the Broadway musical ''Li'l Abner,'' starring Peter Palmer in the title role. Opened at the St. James Theatre, November 15, 1956.)

(From *Li'l Abner Dailies, Volume Three: 1937* by Al Capp. Illustrated by the author.)

the country would have been yelling for more.''[10] He continued contributing columns for many years.

With the advent of the political and social unrest of the 1960s expressed most dramatically on college campuses across the country, Capp's liberal views swung sharply to the right, and his conservative beliefs were voiced in his strip. ''I really don't think my politics changed . . . . I've always been for those who are being shamed, disgraced, ignored by other people. That group has changed. Now it's the . . . rich—well, I don't mean rich, and of course I always had Bullmoose—but the poor son-of-a-bitch who *worked,* who was being denounced by the liberals . . . . These people are keeping the country afloat. They were denounced, and it got me damn mad. So I talked about it, and I continued to talk, because one of the things I found was that when I was all for the liberal attitudes—and I believed in them—the conservatives showed me only icy- contempt. I never got a letter from them. They just hated me. When I began attacking liberals, the conservatives maintained their icy silence, but the liberals began denouncing me by the thousands of letters every week.

''I started asking myself, with these letters, 'How could a girl from Smith *know* this language?' and 'How the hell did a clergyman learn that expression?' They denounced me in the foulest terms. And I must say that it convinced me that if this is what attracted liberals, I'd better keep at it.

''When I started to knock the liberals, there came such a delu of hate mail—instantly my radio commentary show was ended; my TV show which would have started in fifty-six markets, never began; I was never again asked as a guest on the air. Critics who had recently called me the great comic historian of our time now denounced me as a bitter fascist.

''I got a lot of flack, of course, but at that time I was all right. I had all the money I needed, and thought, 'Well, gee whiz, I've simply got to do this and as long as I last with this strip I've simply got to say it.' I couldn't do anything else; I really couldn't. So I did it. One of the side effects is that I saw the strip begin to lose—but I said, the hell with it.''[4]

His popularity within social circles also began to wane. ''My neighbors are solicitous about my condition when they meet my wife in Harvard Square. 'And how is poor Al?' they ask. As if having lost my liberalism I've lost my health.''[1]

But this too did not deter him. ''Comic art not only should say something about the status quo: it must. The message is in the art that is brought to any medium. A work of art is a work of art regardless of form, size, or material. People have been brainwashed: If it's in a comic strip, in a daily newspaper, and done with pen and ink, it's supposed to be a contemptible trifle. That's self-swindling snobbishness.''[4]

A lot of Capp's anger toward the social climate at the time was directed toward college students, even targetting them in his strip

Two episodes from the first Shmoo story, 1948. (Illustration by Al Capp from *America's Great Comic-Strip Artists* by Richard Marschall.)

with such parodies as creating an organization called "S.W.I.N.E.," Students Wildly Indignant with Nearly Everything. "There's an ugliness in American life today— you see it in the way some of the kids dress, in the way some of them act. Somehow in the effort to atone for the ghetto, they've turned the whole world into a ghetto. I think this generation has made everything as ugly as the ghettos I lived in—not out of sympathy, but as a form of punishment."[1]

Despite this attitude, Capp developed a new career touring campuses with his sharp and biting speeches, sometimes hitting 240 colleges or universities in one year. He received upwards of $2,500 per appearance (an extra $1,000 for Ivy League schools which he said called for "combat pay"). A large part of that income was given to conservative organizations that fought liberal colleges, such as the Young Americans for Freedom.

But years later he reflected on that period of his life. "I kind of hated it. I felt it so bad, really so bad. But the parties on the right are so dull, and the people aren't very bright. And the left was so ludicrous. I enjoyed them. They stopped enjoying me."[11]

In 1972 Capp was forced to give up the lucrative college-lecture circuit. A married female college student accused him of attempting to seduce her after a lecture he gave at the University of Wisconsin. He was arrested, convicted of attempted adultery and fined. A year later Capp ended his three-year radio interview show. Though ABC- and NBC-TV broadcasted "Li'l Abner," and all of his books were still in print, the daily strip's popularity was slipping.

Capp turned some of his attention to painting full-size canvases from his comic strip and in 1975 held the first exhibition at the New York Cultural Center. "I hadn't painted since art school. It was fun to work in all that space, instead of small scale. Many of the paintings are at least 5-foot-4."[12]

"Whether I'm a good painter or not remains to be seen but whether you are a good painter or a bad painter, by god you can paint, that's what's nice about living in this century, you can paint, and if someone exhibits your painting then you are a painter—good, bad, or indifferent.

"I think more cartoonists should do paintings and I would like to see more artists do comic strips."[13]

In 1977, "Li'l Abner" hit its lowest point in popularity. Circulation had dropped dramatically; the public was already tired of his predictably strident politics, the stories were too short and the panels looked empty. Capp's health was failing as well. On November 13, 1977, "Li'l Abner" appeared for the last time. "The last three or four years I stopped traveling, and I knew then I was out of it. If you have any sense of humor about your strip, and I had a sense of humor about Abner, you knew that for three or four years Abner was wrong."[12]

That same year, Capp's daughter, Catherine committed suicide. Three months later, one of his granddaughters, with whom he was extremely close, was killed in an auto accident. Capp's health steadily deteriorated and in 1979 he died. "One character in 'Li'l Abner' I always figured was me: Joe Btfsplk, the little guy with the cloud always over him."[1]

FOOTNOTE SOURCES

[1]William Furlong, "Recap on Al Capp," *Saturday Evening Post,* winter, 1971.
[2]Al Capp, "My Well-Balanced Life on a Wooden Leg," *Life,* May 23, 1960.
[3]E. J. Kahn, Jr., "Profiles: Ooff!!! (Sob!!) Eep!!! (Gulp!!) Zowie!!!—II," *New Yorker,* December 6, 1947.
[4]Rick Marschall, "'Saying Something about the Status Quo': Al Capp, Master Satirist of the Comics," *Nemo: The Classic Comics Library,* April, 1986.
[5]Alan Ebert, "The Person Who Changed My Life," *Seventeen,* April, 1965.
[6]"Li'l Abner—Broadway and Dogpatch," *Life,* January 14, 1957.
[7]A. Capp, "'It's Hideously True' Creator of Li'l Abner Tells Why His Hero Is (Sob!) Wed," *Life,* March 31, 1952.
[8]David Manning White and A. Capp, *From Dogpatch to Slobbovia: The (Gasp!!) World of Li'l Abner,* Beacon Press, 1964.
[9]"Al Capp to Be a Columnist for the *Herald Tribune,*" *New York Herald Tribune,* January 8, 1961.
[10]"Li'l Al," *Newsweek,* July 17, 1961.
[11]Israel Shenker, "Al Capp, Harbinger of the Age of Irreverence, Gives Up Cartoons but Not Irascibility," *New York Times,* November 11, 1977.
[12]Eugenia Sheppard, "The Morning After," *New York Post,* April 18, 1975.
[13]Larry Rivers, "Al Capp Talks to Larry Rivers," *Interview,* June, 1975.

FOR MORE INFORMATION SEE:

Newsweek, February 26, 1940 (p. 40), July 12, 1943 (p. 70), October 28, 1946, November 24, 1947 (p. 60ff), June 14, 1954, January 16, 1961 (p. 72), April 1, 1963, April 15, 1963, July 19, 1965, June 22, 1970, October 17, 1977.
Life, June 24, 1946 (p. 58ff), December 7, 1959 (p. 94ff), April 30, 1965 (p. 97ff).
New Yorker, November 29, 1947 (p. 45ff), December 6, 1947 (p. 46ff), August 28, 1948 (p. 16ff), January 1, 1949 (p. 14ff).
Current Biography, H. W. Wilson, 1947.
Time, December 27, 1948, November 6, 1950 (p. 72ff), March 31, 1952 (p. 53), February 14, 1955 (p. 76ff), February 28, 1955 (p. 49), September 9, 1957 (p. 89), April 11, 1969, October 17, 1977 (p. 78).
New York Times, August 11, 1952, February 12, 1972.
New York Herald Tribune, August 29, 1952, January 24, 1954, August 23, 1955, November 14, 1957, December 30, 1958.
Cue, September 13, 1952.
Coronet, March, 1953 (p. 30ff).
George Mikes, *Eight Humorists,* Allan Wingate, 1954.
New York Times Magazine, December 7, 1958 (p. 27).
Cybil Dunn, "A Sharp Eye Out for Fraud," *Observer,* June 19, 1960.
Saturday Evening Post, June 1, 1963 (p. 20ff), March/April, 1973 (p. 47ff), September/October, 1973 (p. 46ff), March, 1974 (p. 48).
Esquire, December, 1963 (p. 211ff), November, 1970 (p. 161ff).
Reader's Digest, May, 1964 (p. 45ff), June, 1978 (p. 109ff).
Daily News (New York), August 27, 1967, March 3, 1970 (p. 33), March 14, 1986.
Nation's Business, September, 1967 (p. 64ff).
"Al Capp," *Cartoonist,* January, 1968.
Jack Smith, "Capp Pulls Up Fast After Shaping Snoopy," *New York Post,* October 17, 1968.
Vital Speeches of the Day, August 1, 1969 (p. 634ff), May 15, 1971 (p. 477ff).
Arthur Asa Berger, *Li'l Abner: A Sunday in American Satire,* Twayne, 1970.

Joan Baez sued Capp for his searing satire on folk singers. (Illustration by Al Capp from *Great Cartoonists and Their Art* by Art Wood.)

"Who will lead America? Us youth!" cried Senator McGrovel. (From *The Hardhat's Bedtime Story Book* by Al Capp. Illustrated by the author.)

National Review, September 22, 1970, November 23, 1979 (p. 1479).
Tom Mackin, "Capp Has Field Day," *Evening News* (Newark, N.J.), March 8, 1971.
Village Voice, July 22, 1971.
Judith O'Sullivan, *The Art of the Comic Strip,* Department of Art, University of Maryland, 1971.
W. J. Burke and Will D. Howe, *American Authors and Books: 1640 to the Present Day,* 3rd revised edition, Crown, 1972.
People Weekly, May 5, 1975, October 24, 1977 (p. 36ff).
Art News, summer, 1975 (p. 18ff).
A. Capp, "Capp, In His Own (Pow!) Words: The Comic Page Is the Last Refuge of Classic Art," *Nemo: The Classic Comics Library,* April, 1986.
Comics Journal, October, 1988 (p. 121ff), January, 1989 (p. 40ff).
Art Wood, *Great Cartoonists and Their Art,* Pelican, 1987.
R. Marschall, *America's Great Comic-Strip Artists,* Cross River Press, 1989.

OBITUARIES

Israel Shenker, "Al Capp, Creator of Li'l Abner, Is Dead at 70," *New York Times,* November 6, 1979.
Time, November 19, 1979 (p. 116).
New York Times Biographical Service, November, 1979 (p. 1497ff).

CASSEDY, Sylvia 1930-1989

OBITUARY NOTICE—See sketch in *SATA* Volume 27: Born January 29, 1930, in Brooklyn, N.Y.; died of cancer, April 6, 1989, in Manhasset, N.Y. Educator, writer. Throughout the 1970s Cassedy taught creative writing to children in Nassau County, N.Y. public schools and libraries. She also trained public school teachers in creative writing for children. Her poetry books for children include *Birds, Frogs, and Moonlight, Roomrimes,* and *Moon-Uncle, Moon Uncle: Rhymes from India.* Other juvenile titles include *M. E. and Morton, Behind the Attic Wall* and *In Your Own Words: A Beginner's Guide to Writing.* Her latest book, *Lucy Babbidge's House,* was published posthumously by Crowell.

FOR MORE INFORMATION SEE:

Dorothy A. Marquardt and Martha E. Ward, *Authors of Books for Young People,* supplement to 2nd edition, Scarecrow, 1979.
Contemporary Authors New Revision Series, Volume 22, Gale, 1988.

OBITUARIES

School Library Journal, June, 1989 (p. 28).
Horn Book, July/August, 1989 (p. 543).

CHARNAS, Suzy M(cKee) 1939-

PERSONAL: Born October 22, 1939, in New York, N.Y.; daughter of Robinson (an artist) and Maxine (an artist; maiden name, Szanton) McKee; married Stephen Charnas (a lawyer), October 4, 1968; children: (stepchildren) Charles N., Joanna. *Education:* Barnard College, B.A., 1961; New York Univer-

SUZY M. CHARNAS

sity, M.A.T., 1965. *Politics:* "Disgusted; liberal when active." *Agent:* Howard Morhaim, 175 Fifth Ave., 709, New York, N.Y. 10010. *Office:* 520 Cedar N.E., Albuquerque, N.M. 87106.

CAREER: U.S. Peace Corps, Washington, D.C., teacher of history and English at girls' high school in Ogbomosho, Nigeria, and lecturer in economic history at University of Ife, Ibadan, Nigeria, both 1961-63; junior high school teacher of ancient history and African studies in New York City, 1965-67; Flower Fifth Avenue Hospital, New York City, in curriculum development, with Division of Community Mental Health, 1967-69; writer, 1969—. Instructor, Clarion West Writers Workshop, Seattle, 1984, 1986, Clarion Writers Workshop, Michigan, 1987. Chair, Archive Project Committee, National Council of Returned Peace Corps Volunteers, 1986—. *Member:* Authors Guild, Authors League of America, Science Fiction Writers of America, Horror Writers of America, Poets and Writers. *Awards, honors:* John W. Campbell Award nominee, 1975, for *Walk to the End of the World;* Nebula Award, 1980, for "The Unicorn Tapestry"; Nebula Award nomination, 1982, for *The Vampire Tapestry.*

WRITINGS:

Walk to the End of the World (first novel in science-fiction trilogy), Ballantine, 1974.
Motherlines (second novel in science-fiction trilogy), Putnam, 1978.
(Contributor) Marleen Barr, editor, *Future Females: A Critical Anthology,* Bowling Green Popular Press, 1980.
(Contributor) George R. R. Martin, editor, *New Voices III,* Berkley Publishing, 1980.
(Contributor) Marta Randall, editor, *New Dimensions II,* Pocket Books, 1980.
The Vampire Tapestry (novel), Simon & Schuster, 1980.
The Bronze King (young adult; first novel in fantasy trilogy), Houghton, 1985.
Dorothea Dreams, Arbor House, 1986.
The Silver Glove (young adult; second novel in fantasy trilogy), Bantam, 1988.
The Golden Thread (young adult; third novel in fantasy trilogy), Bantam, 1989.

Contributor to magazines, including *Khatru, Isaac Asimov's Science Fiction Magazine,* and *Omni.*

ADAPTATIONS:

(With husband, Stephen Charnas) "Body Work" (playscript; adapted from "Unicorn Tapestry"), eight showcase performances, LaMama, New York, N.Y., February, 1987.

WORK IN PROGRESS: Stage play based on a portion of *The Vampire Tapestry;* volume three of the science-fiction trilogy; a young adult fantasy novel.

SIDELIGHTS: "I think of myself as a late bloomer, since my first book was published when I was thirty-four. This was good; I didn't leap in all at once as a youth to write the typical autobiographical first novel that so often leads to a one-book career.

"I am a devoted researcher. For *Walk to the End of the World,* I tried to learn everything there is to know about, for instance, crude plastics and the agricultural production of seaweed. For *Motherlines* I read about all sorts of nomadic stock herders, from Mongols to Lapps.

All of a sudden the sidewalk jumped under my feet. (Jacket illustration by Eric Velasquez from *The Bronze King* by Suzy M. Charnas.)

"*The Vampire Tapestry* comprises a sequential group of interrelated incidents during a period of the protagonist's life when matters have gone seriously out of control, so that he's forced to confront vital challenges to his freedom and his existence. I began with the idea of a vampire not as a figure of romance, a tarted-up Byronic hero with fangs, but as a natural creature. Frankly, he is a predator, and we are his prey. He has, of necessity, a scholarly turn of mind (there's a lot to study up on when you wake up after a fifty-year snooze that began before the turn of the century). So while he has his primitive side, ancient and ruthless, he's also a bit too intelligent for his own mental serenity—otherwise he could not cope with the computer age. I don't mean to indicate a tongue-in-cheek approach; the work is serious, but shows, I hope, some wit. Again, much of the fun of doing this book has been the opportunity for research—studying Gestalt therapy, the Santa Fe Opera and Puccini's 'Tosca,' and consulting people whose paths would not normally cross mine, such as the local zoo veterinarian.

"My interests extend to other arts (particularly music) because I am convinced that the arts feed each other. To someone like myself who has a very active inner eye, the images provided by the visual arts, stage performances of any kind, and of course those called up by words are all stimulating and rich. The arts also nourish the life of my dreams, which I feel is a distinct and powerful part of my working life.

"I've been writing scripts for the stage based on fiction of my own. Though a television option has been taken on *The Vampire*

Tapestry, I decided to create a dramatic version of this story myself for the stage. I look forward to the collaborative effort of stage-production which, unlike screen-production (at least so I understand), has a place and some respect for the writer as contributor and colleague.

"I gobble up mystery novels for fun, but reading 'serious' fiction can be a problem. Sometimes the writer's intent is too obvious, and I get bored. Often I find I can't bring myself to stomach a writer's stated or implied sexism. No matter how excellent the work, this kind of rotten place at the core invalidates all and is too insulting and distressing to put up with for the sake of whatever fragmentary insight the person may have. This does not mean that I consider myself the perfect feminist. It does mean that I try not to be either a purveyor or a victim of cultural distortions demeaning to my sex, and I have no patience with those who are proponents of those distortions.

"My advice to aspiring writers is simply what works for me: I hand over the work, at a point where it has already gelled and taken a firm shape of its own, to certain friends whose judgement I trust. After they have read it, they report back on the actual effects achieved, as opposed to what I had intended and think I have done. While I try not to bow to every wind of criticism that blows, I do value very highly the insights that come from others' perspectives. Without that, I tend to get stuck in obsessive ruts inside my own head and to communicate very little, and that faultily. A novel is not, for me, a group effort, but it invariably benefits from some outside feedback from those for whom, after all, it is intended: readers."

HOBBIES AND OTHER INTERESTS: Needlepoint, classical music.

FOR MORE INFORMATION SEE:

Times Literary Supplement, November 7, 1980.
Village Voice Literary Supplement, June, 1982.
Washington Post Book World, February 9, 1986.
Harper's, October, 1989.

COLE, Babette 1949-

PERSONAL: Born September 10, 1949, in Jersey, Channel Islands; daughter of Fred (a director) and Iris (a housewife; maiden name, Fosbray) Cole. *Education:* Canterbury College of Art, B.A. (with honors), 1974. *Home and office:* Ivy Cottage, Wingmore Lane, Wingmore, Elham, North Canterbury, Kent CT4 6LS, England.

CAREER: Author and illustrator of children's books, 1973—. *Exhibitions:* Bologna International Children's Book Fair, 1985-89; Salon International du Livre, Switzerland, 1988. *Awards, honors: Nungu and the Hippopotamus* was selected one of Child Study Association of America's Children's Books of the Year, 1980; *The Wind in the Willows Pop-up Book* was selected one of New York Public Library's Children's Books, 1983; Kate Greenaway Medal Commendation, 1986, for *Princess Smartypants;* Annabell Fargeon Award from the Library Association, 1986, for *Princess Smartypants,* and 1987, for *Prince Cinders;* Kate Greenaway Medal, 1987, for *Prince Cinders.*

WRITINGS:

JUVENILE; SELF-ILLUSTRATED

Promise Solves the Problem, Granada, 1976.
Nungu and the Elephant, Collins, 1980.
Nungu and the Hippopotamus, McGraw, 1980.
Promise and the Monster, Granada, 1981.
Don't Go Out Tonight, Hamish Hamilton, 1981, Doubleday, 1982.
Nungu and the Crocodile, McDonald, 1982.
Beware of the Vet, Hamish Hamilton, 1982.
The Trouble with Mum, Kaye & Ward, 1983, published in the United States as *The Trouble with Mom,* Putnam, 1984.
The Hairy Book, J. Cape, 1984, Random House, 1985.
The Trouble with Dad, Heineman, 1985, Putnam, 1986.
The Slimy Book, J. Cape, 1985, Random House, 1986.
Princess Smartypants, Hamish Hamilton, 1986, Putnam, 1987.
The Trouble with Gran, Putnam, 1987.
Prince Cinders, Hamish Hamilton, 1987, Putnam, 1988.
The Smelly Book, J. Cape, 1987, Simon & Schuster, 1988.
The Trouble with Grandad, Putnam, 1988.
King Changelot, Hamish Hamilton, 1988, published in the United States as *King Change-a-Lot,* Putnam, 1989.
Three Cheers for Errol!, Putnam, 1989.
The Silly Book, Random House, 1989.
Cupid, Hamish Hamilton, 1989, Putnam, 1990.
The Beastly Birthday Book, Heinemann, 1990.

ILLUSTRATOR

The Bird Whistle, Kaye & Ward, 1977.
Joan Aiken, *Mice and Mendelson,* J. Cape, 1978.
Jim Slater, *Grasshopper and the Unwise Owl,* Granada, 1979, Holt, 1980.
Norman Hunter, *Sneeze and Be Slain,* Bodley Head, 1980.
N. Hunter, *Count Bakwerdz on the Carpet and Other Incredible Stories,* Bodley Head, 1981.
J. Slater, *Grasshopper and the Poisoned River,* Granada, 1982.
Willis Hall, *The Last Vampire,* Bodley Head, 1982.
Lesley Young, *Hocus Pocus,* Hamilton, 1983.
Kenneth Grahame, *The Wind in the Willows Pop-up Book,* Holt, 1983.

Also illustrator of *The Eye of Conscience,* Follett, and Oliver Postgate's *Pingwings: A Flying Bird,* Kaye & Ward.

WORK IN PROGRESS: Hurrah for Etheleen, for Heinemann; *Ron Vandermeer and Babette Cole's Beastly Birthday Book.*

SIDELIGHTS: "I was born and grew up in Jersey in the Channel Islands. After the war, my parents wanted a fresh start and boarded a boat bound for West Africa. But my mother, who had never been outside of England, got off in the Channel Islands. There was no question of her going any further. So my father, sister, grandmother, dog, and the parrot were effectively stranded and forced to put down roots. It was before tourists and the banking community established itself there.

"I spent most of my time exploring the island with my pony. I played with animals as I wasn't encouraged to mix with other children. I don't know why that was. I had two dogs, some birds, lots of Siamese cats, and of course my pony, 'Prom,' short for Promise. I wrote two books about her. I had her flown to England, so I could have her with me while I attended art school.

My mother wasn't a particularly literary person. It was my sister, ten years older, who introduced me to books. We spent lots of time reading Lewis Carroll and Edward Lear. If I didn't like a book, I'd rewrite it and re-draw the pictures. Most of the books I

Babette Cole on her farm.

liked featured horses. I also used to write poetry, and won a prize once—a sack of pony nuts or something. All entries had to begin with, 'A rider came back from a trek . . . . ' Mine continued, 'and replied with a gasp, oh heck, to get to her yard, she found it quite hard, she was under her pony's neck!' That was my first published piece at age eight or so.

"My mother was expert at making things up. My sister always said, 'Don't take notice of your mother, she romances.' She was convinced that our neighbors had it in for seagulls, which she adored and fed on prime bacon. She concocted a whole story about how these people put barbed wire on their roof to keep the seagulls away. But there wasn't any wire at all. I'm not sure it's really fair to say she just invented this. I think she really believed it. My father worked for local builders, but was an excellent draftsman and renovated a number of our antique Japanese vases. My mother did hairdressing among other things and during the summers earned extra income working in an ice cream kiosk on the beach. I have wonderful memories of playing on the beach all day, eating free ice cream.

"I attended a convent school (although we were Protestant) where it was instilled in me to be honest and good, lest a large finger would come forth from the sky and squash me like an ant. So I was very good and always told the truth. As I got older, however, I became more devious. This is also something you learn in convent schools: how to do naughty things without getting caught. I outdid everyone else at religious subjects. We were frequently called up to tell parables. Mine were extremely elaborate and exciting, and all the students used to clap afterward. Catholicism is wonderfully theatrical—the incense, the genuflecting, and the wearing of veils in processions. In nativity plays and other major celebrations, I wasn't allowed a major role. 'How about Joseph?' I would ask, but they wouldn't hear of a Protestant playing such a part. I was blond, and all the blonds had to be angels. Although on a certain level all religions can be frightening, in particular, Purgatory. Of course, I was damned anyway for not being a Catholic. I thought about this a lot, then concluded, 'God's a jolly nice person, and I'm sure he won't damn me for eternity.'

"When I wasn't at school or playing with my horse, I would draw and make mud sculptures in the garden, complete with mud ceremonies and primeval rites in which I stewed up horrible things and danced around them. My parents would stand in the window and stare. I stuck toy animals in the privet hedge around the house. There was a whole world of creatures in those shrubs.

"For a long time I wanted to be a vet. But I got fed up with all the required science exams. I wanted lots of horses, but knew I couldn't be a professional show horse owner because that took much money. Illustration, I decided, would support my horse habit. I was turned away at an art school in Bristol. I took that first failure very hard. But they were right. I had lived an isolated existence on the island, and when they asked me what I thought of Henry Moore, I replied, 'I don't know. Does he ride?' Furthermore, my portfolio wasn't at all what they were looking for. Mine were mostly religious subjects done at the convent and sketches of Jersey farmworkers picking up seaweed on the beach.

(From *Prince Cinders* by Babette Cole. Illustrated by the author.)

"I went to work for an advertising agency, one of the darkest periods of my life. Not only did I disdain the sort of work they did, but I resented the way they acted. But I learned a lot technically, and after some time found myself running the department. It broadened me and gave me the courage to reapply to art school. I was accepted at Canterbury, but not without a good deal of drama. I hitchhiked to my interview with a friend, when the van that had stopped for us suffered a blow-out on the motorway. Needless to say, I was hours late. The man I was to see was having a gallery opening not far from Canterbury, so we went. I walked in with a great big portfolio and asked to have my interview then and there. It was a marvellous event with all the artists in attendance giving me critique. 'Well of course you can come,' they said, and off I went.

"They didn't quite know what they were getting! One of my problems in art school was that I fell in the divide between so-called fine art and graphics. I believed I was a better fine artist, but was shunted into graphics, because I was looking for illustration. There wasn't a special program for illustrators. They didn't appreciate my sculptures either. I was asked to 'make something sensuous,' so I made this lovely little black bottom that you could hold in your hand. It was made of highly polished black resin. But nobody liked it. The other students had made these enormous pieces with girders. Another time I made a lop-lop bird out of oxyacetylened scrap metal that rocked on its little rocky feet and pecked the ground. I thought it was bloody brilliant. They didn't. They only approved of very serious stuff. 'You don't take this seriously, do you?' they would ask, and I would respond, 'No. That's the point. You've missed it.'

"There was also no life drawing class—the basis of all design. So I organized one, and they didn't like it one bit. Some tutors caught a bunch of us drawing a life model and hooked us out by our ears.

"Gerald Davis taught me printmaking. This, too, was frowned on in the graphics department, leaving the press entirely to me. I made my very own children's book, which the head of one of the most important houses in England thought brilliant." This first effort was eventually published as the first 'Promise' book in 1976.

"As frustrated and unhappy as I was in art school, I got a lot out of the experience as a whole. I knew well enough that I would never again have so much time to devote to exploration, and took full advantage of the situation. I worked constantly.

(From *Three Cheers for Errol!* by Babette Cole. Illustrated by the author.)

"After I finished school, I made my living with greeting cards, illustrations for magazines, books, and projects for the BBC."

Cole was also living with a young social anthropologist, Alistair, whom she described as a "very high-minded, Marxist idealistic chap." They lived together in a manner of poverty he regarded as a "pure way of life." By now it was time for Alistair to do his fieldwork in Africa to research a people called the "Yei." "I was terrified, but promised to go, and we were very much in love.

"I spent nine months living an extremely difficult life with the Yei. Water had to be dug up and boiled before drinking, food was in shortage, and animals lay dying of starvation. People were often ill. I did a lot of drawing and writing. In fact, my three 'Nungu' stories based on myths told to me were written there. (I recently found out that these books will be appearing in African languages. So, finally the people who inspired them will get to enjoy them.)

"We traveled the countryside in a landrover and got caught in crossfire near Rhodesia, having no idea there was a war going on. Tribal border guards held us captive until they could verify Alistair's papers—awfully frightening. I was coming to terms with the fact that I could not put down roots in Africa. I felt ashamed to admit that I missed my horses and a way of life which Alistair did not approve. We had a protracted and most painful separation. We had been together for twelve years."

Cole returned to England. "The only way I could think to get back on my feet was to be totally on my own. I read an ad in *Horse and Hound* advertising cottages in Wales—'bring your own horse and dog.' So I packed everything into a trailer and headed for the mountains. I was absolutely alone and ill from the heartbreak. Then after a while I started meeting all sorts of wonderful, potty Welsh, and worked like mad. The 'Trouble With' series was born—*The Trouble with Mum* and *The Trouble with Dad* just came streaming out. Each book makes a statement. *The Trouble with Dad* is based on my father and his desire to be an artist. *The Trouble with Gran* talks about getting old."

Growing restless, again, Cole did something she thought would not have been possible. She purchased the house she and Alistair had occupied together in England to help "exorcise" her ghosts once and for all. "I needed a lot of money and was determined to work. I sat down and wrote *Princess Smartypants*, possibly my most successful book. In a sense it's my autobiography and a feminist parable on something I call 'Babettism'—going off and

(From *King Change-a-Lot* by Babette Cole. Illustrated by the author.)

doing what's best for you, damn the torpedoes.'' She refurbished the house with government grants, created a garden, and sold it three years later for a considerable profit.

Her present home, a Tudor cottage, is five hundred years old ''with tiny peg titles, Roman bricks round by the ingleknook, which is the vast fireplace once used for cooking. The windows were originally covered with skin before the use of glass. It's one of the only houses in Kent that still has its original mullioned windows. Nobody had lived here for fifteen years before I moved in. The kitchen was an earth floor. Some of the beams came from ships. Inside the ingleknook are the original hooks from which bacon was smoked. I had to adhere to the rules laid down by the Planning Commission when renovating. Everything must conform to the original style. I've done all the plastering myself—it's actually quite like making sculpture.

''I've got the land I need now for my horses and other animals. I'm involved with showing and training horses. This really is at the center of my life. The books make it possible.

''I am extremely professional about my publishing responsibilities. Once I've begun a book I work straight through until it's done. I get someone to help with the horses and isolate myself to write and draw. For *Cupid* I went to Greece and lived in a shack—no horses, no phone, no nothing. After one week of working day and night I was nearly finished. At home it would have taken three months.''

Cole's technique poses certain problems. ''My work is very hard to reproduce. The tones get muddled. So I go to the scannings and sit with the scanner telling him exactly which buttons to push and which knobs to turn. We got to a point where we relied on two printers, one German, the other Dutch. Then things changed with Hamish Hamilton. There were new people in the production department and suddenly they were sending me proofs done in Hong Kong. Some results were not good. I made such a row! Now it's written into my contract that *I* am responsible for the origination and printing of my images. Period. The end.

''I do most of my illustrations with dyes, the same things that most people use with airbrushes. I, however, paint with them. It's extremely demanding, because you cannot make a mistake. You can white out, but you can't paint over it. So you must know exactly what you intend to do before you begin.

''I have many, many copies of my books in print, not only in English but in other languages as well. Yet people keep saying,

Cole in front of Ivy Cottage, her 500-year-old house.

'You obviously write alternative children's books.' I guess it's because I tend to be a little eccentric. My books get nominated for all the prizes and are consistently named runner-up (they don't like anarchic books for prizes).

''It's interesting, you can't always predict what the reactions to your books will be. The Germans and Americans can't get enough of my books. The one truly off-the-wall response I got was to *Errol*. Errol is a rat and like all rats, is brown. He's the Errol Flynn of rats you might say, sort of swashbuckling. But he's not good at things and doesn't take himself too seriously. And in spite of the obstacles he encounters he does some very intelligent things. He may appear simple, but he can be clever. The whole point of the book is that you can't take people at face value.

''Well, the Lewisham Borough Council sent me a letter branding me a racist. Errol, like many of the West Indian children in their district, was brown. And they informed me that Errol was a West Indian name (in actual fact, it's of Scottish origin). Now quite a part of my family is West Indian, my cousins have married West Indians and live in St. Kits. I sent off a letter that blazed with my defense. I am at present working on *Hurrah for Ethelyn,* Errol's sister who is also brown and a brain surgeonette! Let them think about that!''

Cole has mixed feelings about her work. ''Sometimes I wish I could spend all my time with my horses. Just to keep my hand in, I'd do one book a year. But I keep getting ideas, and wake up in the middle of the night to jot things down and make drawings.

(From *Princess Smartypants* by Babette Cole. Illustrated by the author.)

I've got a drawer so thick with files I could do books forever. And I must admit, it's not such a bad feeling."[1]

FOOTNOTE SOURCES

[1]Based on an interview by Cathy Courtney for *Something about the Author*.

COLLIER, Steven 1942-

PERSONAL: Born June 12, 1942 in Omaha, Nebraska; son of Robert B. (a mechanic) and Mildred (a housewife; maiden name, Brunke) Collier; married Dale Anne Popkie (a secretary), March 4, 1972; children: Robert, John. *Education:* Attended Penn State, 1960-61, Art Students' League, and Famous Artist's School. *Home address:* RR3, Box 11, Calabogie, Ontario, Canada KOJ 1HO.

CAREER: Young Industries, Muncy, Pennsylvania, artist, 1966-71; free-lance artist, 1971—. *Exhibitions:* Two-man show, Williamsport, Pa., 1966. *Military service:* U.S. Army, 1961-62. *Member:* Nittany Grotto of National Speleological Society.

ILLUSTRATOR:

Joan Lyngseth (pseudonym of Joan Davies), *Martin's Starwars,* Borealis Press, 1978.

Ian P. Harris, *When Wishes Go Wrong,* General Store Publishing, 1989.

WORK IN PROGRESS: Wood carving.

SIDELIGHTS: Collier was severely injured and burned in a car accident in July, 1976. He was confined to a hospital bed for one year, and four additional months were spent in rehabilitation learning to use crutches. A nurse, discovering that he was a talented artist, asked author Joan Davies to consider Collier's illustrations for her *Martin's Starwars*.

Using artists' materials which could be manipulated in bed, Collier found pleasure in illustrating for children. "Probably it should be noted that the illustrations in *Martin's Starwars* were done in desperation when I was at least fifty pounds underweight, and the writer had been told I was near death. I had received the Last Rites of the Catholic Church they told me when I woke up. Some snafu, no doubt, or a rookie priest—I never was a Catholic.

"My wife thinks the book should be re-done from end to end. She thinks I can draw better without the pain and weakness—I could not sit up for more than an hour at a time. I had no source material whatsoever! And it shows. No one knows who helped whom the most!

"Thus far, my career in general is remarkable only for luck and durability: I should be dead or mad! There are books waiting where the unwritten ones live, and more and better illustrations.

"It seems I can't leave the art world alone. Maybe it won't leave me alone. I've worked in wood, iron, and stone. It is always there beckoning and jeering. While there is neither fame nor fortune in it, I'm more 'successful' at it than friend Van Gough was in his lifetime. My stuff has sold well enough to cover expenses. My main problem is specializing. Most of my work is commissioned and is instantly gone, so there's no 'body of work' for a show.

"Is not art the child of affluence? Is it not perverse to turn it around? Is not well-doing it's own reward? Sometimes it works!"

Collier spends his time with his wife and son on a small homestead west of Ottawa. He draws, paints, carves, and sculpts, working in a small outbuilding which he built. The family keeps goats and grows food to dry, freeze, and preserve for the winter months. "Time is desperately short here in the northern hills. The days wing by and the roof is not finished, the winter's wood needs cutting and stacking in the woodshed, spuds need digging, butchering awaits. It's tough to find time to carve, paint and draw."

STEVEN COLLIER

HOBBIES AND OTHER INTERESTS: History, theosophical ruminations, massive concrete sculptures, building with native materials, travel, movies, books, knife making, cooking.

CONEY, Michael G(reatrex) 1932-

PERSONAL: Born September 28, 1932, in Birmingham, England; son of Harold (a dentist) and Nora (a librarian; maiden name, Nettle) Coney; married Daphne Collins (a bank clerk), May 11, 1956; children: Kevin, Sally-Ann. *Education:* Educated in England. *Home:* 2082 Neptune Rd, R.R.3 Sidney, British Columbia V8L 3X9, Canada. *Agent:* (United Kingdom and foreign) Pamela Buckmaster, "Danescroft," Goose Lane, Little Hallingbury, Bishops Stortford, Herts CM22 7RG, England; (United States) Virginia Kidd, 538 East Harford St., Milford, Penn. 18337.

CAREER: Malsters Arms, Devon, England, licensee, 1962-66; Jabberwock Hotel, Antigua, manager, 1969-72; Ministry of Forests, British Columbia, management consultant, 1973-88; full-time writer, 1989—. *Member:* Science Fiction Writers of America, Institute of Chartered Accountants. *Awards, honors:* Best Science Fiction Novel of the Year from the British Science Fiction Association, 1976, for *Brontomek!; The Celestial Steam Locomotive* was selected one of *School Library Journal*'s Best Books for Young Adults, 1983.

WRITINGS:

SCIENCE FICTION NOVELS

Mirrow Image, DAW Books, 1972.
Syzygy, Ballantine, 1973.
Friends Come in Boxes, DAW Books, 1973.
The Hero of Downways, DAW Books, 1973.
Winter's Children, Gollancz, 1974.
Monitor Found in Orbit, DAW Books, 1974.
The Jaws That Bite, the Claws That Catch, DAW Books, 1975 (published in England as *The Girl with a Symphony in Her Fingers,* Elmfield Press, 1975).
Rax, DAW Books, 1975 (published in England as *Hello Summer, Goodbye,* Gollancz, 1975).
Charisma, Gollancz, 1975, Dell, 1979.
Brontomek!, Gollancz, 1976.
The Ultimate Jungle, Millington, 1979.
Neptune's Cauldron, Tower, 1981.
Cat Karina, Ace, 1982.
The Celestial Steam Locomotive, Houghton, 1983.
Gods of the Greataway, Houghton, 1984.
Fang, the Gnome, New American Library, 1988.
King of the Sceptre'd Isle, New American Library, 1989.

NONFICTION

Forest Ranger, Ahoy! The Tale of an Unusual Navy, Porthole Press, 1983.
(With Gray Campbell), *Forest Adventure: Guide to the British Columbia Forest Museum,* Porthole Press, 1985.

Coney's works have been translated into Dutch, French, German, Italian, Japanese, Spanish, Norwegian, Russian, and Serbo-Croatian. Contributor of science-fiction short stories to anthologies, and to periodicals, including *If, Worlds of Tomorrow, New Worlds Quarterly, Fantasy and Science Fiction,* and *Galaxy.*

WORK IN PROGRESS: No Place for a Sealion, a novel; *A Tomcat Called Sabrina,* a humorous/satirical fantasy novel.

MICHAEL G. CONEY

SIDELIGHTS: "'There is nothing quite so terrifying,' my mother once said to me, 'as a mad sheep.' This was probably the most influential remark made to me during my childhood. It gave me a healthy respect for the unknown, a glimpse into the strange private world of the insane, a dislike of paradoxes, a distaste for mutton, and the beginnings of cynicism. But above all it introduced me to the wonders of language. My mother's precise wording still left room for my personal ultimate fear: a nest of lobsters in my bed. A mad sheep may have been the worst, with a unique terror all its own—and for years I gave those wooly, deceptive horrors a wide berth—but lobsters were *almost* as bad.

"My mother is an extremely clever and able woman and my late father was no slouch either. It is due to their influence, genetic and otherwise, that I can do the things I do, including writing. But I have not been kind to them. As a child I saw them through perceptive and critical eyes, so I saw the worst. As an adult I wrote about them in a thinly-disguised autobiographical novel called *Rax*. This is what I wrote about my mother:

"'My mother is short and I am tall for my age, so that it is impossible for us to keep in step as we walk. She trots along beside me, legs going like pistons, and insists that she puts her arm through mine, so the pair of us reel along the street like drunks. Added to which she talks to me incessantly, looking up at me all the time and smiling fondly, and generally giving the impression that a very peculiar relationship obtains between us. I find myself praying that people think she is not my mother at all, but an old prostitute I have picked up. To emphasize this effect I try to assume a shamefaced look—which is not difficult, in the circumstances.'

"And about my father, with whom I'd had many a bitter quarrel during that period when I was challenging him for leadership of the herd:

"'Father's intelligence was waning, he was older and set in his ways, he was used to leaning on the dignity of his position; in short, he had lost the power of reasoned argument.'

"And after all that, what I write about is life, love, and beauty—with a touch of evil now and then, because nothing is quite so dull as unrelieved goodness. So I'm not above using other people's characters in my books if they fit—and in fantasy, anything fits. Blind Pew—my favourite villain—and Long John Silver both found their way into *The Celestial Steam Locomotive*. Balancing them, I wrote about the locomotive that flew through time and space.

"'Her fingers traced the brass beading around one curved splasher. The warm metal was vibrant and alive. The Locomotive is the most beautiful thing in the world. It's the distillation of everyone's idea of what a machine should look like. It's composed of a million small wishes, a million dreams of beauty.'

"Why science fiction? Well, in science fiction you can write about *anything;* flying locomotives, blind beggars, relatives—and in *Fang, the Gnome:* King Arthur, unicorns, dragons, and gnomes. Somewhere in there is a tiny line that divides science fiction from fantasy, but I try not to worry about

Now put your fists together in front of your chest, elbows out. (From *Fang, the Gnome* by Michael G. Coney. Illustrated by Tim Hildebrandt.)

it. Neither do I worry about the relevance of present-day society and its trends, concerns, issues, and woes. That will all have changed in a hundred years. But life, love, and beauty, and *Fang, the Gnome* will still be relevant.

"'I believe that when we evolved on this planet we inherited a trust. The trust was not Earth itself, with the riches that lay underground and in the oceans. Neither was the trust the stars we plundered for their wealth after we had emptied Earth. No—the trust was Life. The cells, the chromosomes, the genes. They were given to us to use wisely. And did we do this?' He paused, and the world waited. 'No, we did not. In our conceit we arbitrarily stuck our finger into the stream of history and said, "*That* is what a man is. *That* is the supreme life form, *that*, and no other." Even though the Second Species of Mankind was already beginning to evolve into something else! Even though the idiocy of what we said was right there in our mirrors! We had the vanity to consider ourselves perfect.'

"'Life is ours to use, and use it we must, because it is our only resource that is not in short supply. So let's drop this pride, this worship of a form that is changing with every generation, this nonsense about the sanctity of human life. Let's realize that we are one animal among many, and that they are all changing, and we can make a better life for everybody if we help them change.'

"I write biological science fiction. My character above has been able to resolve the conflict between the human and animal kingdoms by in effect saying that no species is sacrosanct, that all species are expendable, that it is the sum total of life that matters. I tend to agree with him, and as an animal lover I am bothered by my own sentimentality because I know my concern for endangered animals is purely selfish.

"The last moa, for instance, did not know it was the last moa. One morning it woke up with the realization that it didn't feel good. It felt old and tired, and those animals with sharp teeth seemed to be moving closer. But it had no sense of occasion. It just thought it was dying, like moas always had done. When it keeled over, rolled onto its back and stuck its scaly legs into the air, no ghostly voice whispered to it: 'This is the end of the moas. This is a moment of terrible history. This is Extinction, the big E.' No. All unknowing, it uttered a simple croak and the scavengers moved in.

"Only we humans know, and feel the regret—and don't always have the sense to realize how selfish the regret is. Perhaps I write my kind of science fiction in order to come to terms with these regrets, to invent more animals to replace the ones that have gone, to give myself and my readers some hope for the next million years."

HOBBIES AND OTHER INTERESTS: Sailing, soccer, camping, tennis.

CROFFORD, Emily 1927-

PERSONAL: Born March 3, 1927, in Lake Providence, La.; daughter of Ralph A. (a farmer) and Vera (a homemaker; maiden name, Williams) Wixson; married Robert P. Crofford (a sales manager), May 21, 1949; children: Suzanne Crofford Wick, Robert, Julia, Joyce Crofford Conway, Richard, Mary Crofford Rauchwarg, Kathleen Crofford Mirsch, Philip. *Education:* Attended Arkansas State College, 1944-45, and Pearl River Junior College, 1946. *Religion:* Roman Catholic. *Home:* 1735 Hillcrest Ave., St. Paul, Minn. 55116.

EMILY CROFFORD

CAREER: Courier News, Blytheville, Ark., reporter, and editor of women's page, 1945, 1947; *Cotton Trade Journal,* Memphis, Tenn., reporter, and assistant to editor, 1947-48; *Memphis Market News,* Memphis, editor, 1948-49; *Random Fortuitous Shots* (trade newsletter), Minneapolis, Minn., editor, 1976-79; free-lance writer, 1978—. Speaker at schools, workshops, and leader of a writer's group. *Member:* Society of Children's Book Writers. *Awards, honors:* Friends of American Writers Juvenile Book Merit Award, and National Council of English Teachers' Choice, both 1982, both for *A Matter of Pride;* Texas Blue Bonnet Award Nominee, 1983, for *Stories from the Blue Road;* Grant from Minnesota State Arts Board for a juvenile biography of Elizabeth Kenny, 1986.

WRITINGS:

A Matter of Pride (juvenile; illustrated by Jim LaMarche), Carolrhoda, 1981.
Stories from the Blue Road (juvenile; illustrated by C. A. Nobens), Carolrhoda, 1982.
Healing Warrior: A Story about Sister Elizabeth Kenny (juvenile biography; illustrated by Steve Michaels), Carolrhoda, 1989.
Frontier Surgeons: The Story about the Mayo Brothers (juvenile biography; illustrated by Karen Ritz), Carolrhoda, 1989.
Great Auk, Crestwood House, 1989.

Contributor of short stories to *Harbinger* and *Pikestaff Review. A Matter of Pride* and "Lady Merida" from *Stories from the Blue Road* were included in sixth- and seventh-grade literature textbooks published by Riverside Press, 1986.

WORK IN PROGRESS: Japanese Boy, American Boy (working title), juvenile fiction; *Sea Bear, White Giant of the Arctic,* juvenile nonfiction.

SIDELIGHTS: "Although I have spent most of my life in cities, it is the farm country where I grew up that I credit—and sometimes blame—for the part of me that must write.

"Every would-be writer reads. When I was growing up I read all the books in our tiny school library, the Mother's Oats box, and the Sears & Roebuck catalog. I also 'read' people, animals, the land, the sky. I listened to the silence and found in it marvelous dreams and knowledge from long before my birth.

"I do not wish a return to those days. This is a far better time. But the need to write, even if it is to be a story set in the present, comes when I walk again the quiet, dusty road that ran between the fields.

"In all my writing, I try to give hope. My motivations are twofold. The humor, beauty, dignity, and caring I have encountered during my life beg to be shared. At the same time, the destructive sickness I've seen—and continue to see—has to be treated and healed.

"Just as there are motivations to write, there are also motivations to cherish—or to destroy. Somehow we must nourish the creative, loving instinct of small children and discourage the emphasis on acquiring material things, an emphasis which fosters the greed that makes a shambles of those instincts.

"When I grew up in the Arkansas wetlands, there was much poverty and bigotry and physical illness. Our struggle to overcome has to a great extent been successful, but somewhere we got off track and lost the values that made it possible to overcome. We forgot that everybody on the plantation is part of one family, each member dependent on each other member. We lost the freedom of disciplining ourselves, and the dignity of believing that as individuals we are important—that how we live and what we do makes a difference.

"My advice to young people who want to write is quite simple. Listen. Watch. Feel. Daydream. Read. Then write about what you hear and see and feel and dream."

(Jacket illustration by Jim LaMarche from *A Matter of Pride* by Emily Crofford.)

HOBBIES AND OTHER INTERESTS: Walking, fishing, camping, wildlife, music, watercolor painting, travel, get-togethers with family and friends.

CURLEY, Daniel 1918-1988

OBITUARY NOTICE—See sketch in *SATA* Volume 23: Born October 4, 1918, in East Bridgewater, Mass.; died in a traffic accident, December 30, 1988, in Tallahassee, Fla. Educator, editor, and author. Curley was a novelist and short story writer who won O. Henry and Flannery O'Connor Awards as well as several arts council awards for his work. An English professor at the University of Illinois at Urbana-Champaign from 1955 until his death, he had previously taught at Syracuse University and at Plattsburgh State Teachers College (now State University of New York at Plattsburgh). Curley's writings include the novels *Mummy* and *A Stone Man, Yes,* and the children's book *Hilarion*. Among his several short story collections are *Love in the Winter* and *Living with Snakes*. Curley was a member of the editorial board of *Accent,* a literary magazine, from 1955 to 1960; he later helped to edit the book *Accent: An Anthology, 1940-1960* and became editor of the magazine in 1975 after it had been renamed *Ascent*.

FOR MORE INFORMATION SEE:

Contemporary Authors New Revision Series, Volume 18, Gale, 1986.
The Writers Directory: 1988-1990, St. James Press, 1988.

OBITUARIES

Chicago Tribune, January 2, 1989.
New York Times, January 3, 1989.
Washington Post, January 4, 1989.

DAVIDSON, Mary S. 1940-

PERSONAL: Born August 1, 1940, in Knoxville, Tenn.; daughter of William M. (a minister) and Mabelle (a teacher; maiden name, Durham) Seymour; married Tom C. Davidson (an educator), August 22, 1961; children: Dawn, Tucker, Kristen. *Education:* Emory and Henry College, B.A., 1961; Florida State University, M.S., 1967. *Religion:* Methodist. *Home:* 2029 Andrew Court, Florence, S.C. 29501. *Office:* Southside Junior High School, 200 Howe Springs Rd., Florence, S.C. 29501.

CAREER: Florida State University, Tallahassee, assistant librarian, 1967-70; Florence County Library, Florence, S.C., assistant librarian, 1972-73; Southside Junior High School, Florence, school librarian, 1973—. *Member:* South Carolina Association of School Librarians, Friends of the Florence County Library (president, 1980-82).

MARY S. DAVIDSON

WRITINGS:

A Superstar Called Sweetpea, Viking, 1980.

HOBBIES AND OTHER INTERESTS: Tennis.

DINNEEN, Betty 1929-
(Elizabeth Newark)

PERSONAL: Born August 28, 1929, in London, England; naturalized U.S. citizen, 1975; daughter of Albert Ernest and Edith Louise (Taylor) Newark; married Barry Dinneen, March 2, 1957 (divorced, 1971); children: Penelope Jane, Hugh Martin. *Education:* Educated at Tiffin Girls School. *Home:* 148 Newman St., San Francisco, Calif. 94110.

CAREER: Times Book Club, London, England, assistant librarian, 1945-47; South African Embassy, London, secretary, 1947-54; Government of Sarawak, Borneo, secretary, 1954-56; Government of Tanganyika, Department of Lands and Surveys, Dar es Salaam, Tanzania, secretary, 1956-58; Government of Kenya, Ministry of Defence, Nairobi, Kenya, secretary, 1958-59; African Medical and Research Foundation (Flying Doctor Service), Nairobi, secretary, 1963-64; Thacher, Albrecht & Ratcliff, San Francisco, Calif., legal secretary, 1970-84; Pettit & Martin, San Francisco, legal secretary, beginning 1984. *Awards, honors: The Family Howl* was named an Outstanding Science Trade Book for Children by the National Science Teachers' Association and the Children's Book Council, 1981.

WRITINGS:

JUVENILE

Lions and Karen, Dent, 1965.
A Lurk of Leopards (illustrated by Charles Robinson), Walck, 1972.
Lion Yellow (illustrated by C. Robinson), Walck, 1975.
Make Way for the Ark, McKay, 1977.
A Tale of Three Leopards (illustrated by Jennifer Emry-Perrott), Doubleday, 1980.
The Family Howl (illustrated by Stefan Bernath), Macmillan, 1981.
Striped Horses: The Story of a Zebra Family (illustrated by S. Bernath), Macmillan, 1982.

PRODUCER OF AUDIOCASSETTES

(Under name Elizabeth Newark) ''Cattails'' (contains ''The Cat That Walks by Himself'' by Rudyard Kipling, ''Puss in Boots'' by Charles Perrault, ''Two Foolish Cats'' by Yoshiko Uchida, and ''Kuching'' by Betty Dinneen), New Ark Productions, 1988.
(Under name Elizabeth Newark) ''Mousetails'' (contains ''Mouse House'' by Rumer Godden, ''Tailor of Gloucester'' by Beatrix Potter, ''Town Mouse and Country Mouse'' by Aesop, adapted by E. Newark, and ''A Christmas Wish for Crissy House'' by Betty Dinneen), New Ark Productions, 1988.

WORK IN PROGRESS: Recording ''Favorite Chapters from Jane Austen,'' on cassette for adults.

SIDELIGHTS: ''I was born in a mews in Knightsbridge, a fashionable section of London, to a working class family. Both my parents left school at thirteen. From my mother I inherit my

Her mother was dead and her brother was three hundred miles away. (From *A Tale of Three Leopards* by Betty Dinneen. Illustrated by Jennifer Emry-Perrott.)

appreciation of books and drama; from my father an instinct for gardening and a love of Beethoven. London in the thirties was a good city for a child. Hyde Park and Kensington Gardens were my playgrounds, and I wandered by myself from Chelsea to Oxford Street, from Harrods to Selfridges. I loved the Albert Memorial, and played marvellous games on its steps. I don't ever remember being lost or scared. Exhibition Road, lined with museums, was a favorite haunt. We children would run through the Science Museum, turning all the handles and pressing all the buttons, until the guards chased us out.

"Luckily we moved out of London to the suburbs (not far from Hampton Court Palace) just before World War II, and avoided the worst of the bombing, although I was evacuated to Yorkshire during the flying-bomb attacks towards the end of the war. (While I was away, a flying bomb demolished the clubhouse next door to us, and glass from my shattered bedroom window smothered my empty bed.) My education ended at sixteen, the normal English school-leaving age at that time, but my secondary school, Tiffins, was a good one (I was a scholarship kid), and I have always read widely, beginning at the age of four. My mother started me reading Dickens when I was eight. English was my favorite subject, but outside school I did not write. My hobby as a teenager was acting.

"I cannot say that I have found my lack of formal education a handicap in writing or in relating to my writer friends (most of whom have two degrees).

"I have worked most of my life as a secretary, and my jobs have taken me to four continents and five countries. My first job out of England was in Sarawak, in northern Borneo, a fascinating country where, in the rainy season, it rains all day and every day, and in the dry season, it rains at least once a day. Snakes are plentiful, and it is a haven for insects of every kind. I learned to tap a slice of bread before I toasted it, to get rid of the ants. I also learned to deal with six-inch centipedes and big black armor-plated scorpions. My short story 'Kuching' was born when I watched my tiny semi-Siamese kitten kill a four-inch scorpion.

"I was married in Dar es Salaam, Tanzania, and later moved with my husband to Nairobi, Kenya, where my two children were born, and it was there I started writing children's books. Life in Nairobi was always an adventure, and when three lions, wanderers from the National Park, were trapped on the golf course behind my house, I could not rest until I had fitted them into a story, which became *Lions and Karen*. My second book, *A Lurk of Leopards,* contains many experiences of my own—finding a leopard's footprints in the flowerbed under my window, and a dormouse's nest in my radio, having wild bees make their home in the roof, and being invaded by safari ants, after the honey bees produced.

"In all I have written ten books, seven published, and of these, nine were written while I held a full-time job. I wrote during my lunch hours, and on weekends. Evenings were for my children and I seldom tried to write then, unless I was in the last stages of revision.

"We moved to America in 1964, and in 1971 I was divorced. I have now lived happily in San Francisco for over twenty years. It is my idea of a civilized city. In 1983 I reverted to my birth name, and am now known as Elizabeth Newark. In recent years I have moved away from writing towards voice-related pastimes (and back to my early hobby of acting). I have radio experience (for about nine months I planned and read a weekly children's programme for KPFA, Berkeley), and in January, 1988, I recorded stories for two audio cassettes for children.

"Feminism has been important to me, helping me break away from the traditional (and stultifying) life patterns of the poor but respectable English; in particular it gave me the courage to buy my own house. I now own a Victorian cottage in the Bernal Heights area of San Francisco, which I have gradually renovated over the years. I also owe a considerable debt to the American belief that 'anybody can do anything' and that it's never too late to start.

"I hope to return to writing in the future, but at the present my life is fully occupied with my job as a legal secretary, and my spare time occupations of acting classes, planning new cassettes, taking care of my house and garden, meeting with my friends, reading mysteries (and Jane Austen), and talking to my cat, Zoe."

EAGLE, Ellen 1953-

PERSONAL: Born May 18, 1953, in New York, N.Y.; daughter of Arthur (a salesman) and Roslyn (a clothing designer and pattern maker; maiden name, Scheller) Eagle; married Gordon Leavitt (an account executive), August 10, 1975. *Education:* Attended State University of New York at Binghamton, 1971-73; California College of Arts and Crafts, B.F.A. (with distinction), 1975; attended Parsons School of Design, 1975, and National Academy School of Fine Arts, 1975-79; also studied with Uri Shulevitz. *Home:* 131 Hillside Ave., Glen Ridge, N.J. 07028.

CAREER: Illustrator, 1983—. *Exhibitions:* National Arts Club, New York, N.Y., 1977, 1978, 1979. *Member:* Society of Children's Book Writers, Graphic Artist's Guild. *Awards, honors:* Merit scholarships for study at National Academy School of Fine Arts, 1975-79; Certificate of Merit from the National Academy School of Fine Arts, 1976, for a drawing; Silver Medal from the National Academy School of Fine Arts, 1977, for a drawing; Award from the National Arts Club, 1978, for a drawing; Award from the Pastel Society of America, 1979, for a painting; Award from the National Academy School of Fine Arts, 1979, for a painting; *Gertie's Green Thumb* was chosen one of Child Study Association of America's Children's Books of the Year, 1983, *Someday with My Father,* 1986, and *Robin Hill,* 1987; *Star Guide* was selected an Outstanding Science Trade Book for Children by the National Science Teachers Association and the Children's Book Council, 1987; Outstanding Work of Literature from the Southern California Council of Literature for Children and Young People, 1988, for *Lila on the Landing;* Notable Children's Trade Book in the Field of Social Studies from the National Council for Social Studies and the Children's Book Council, 1988, for *The Jenny Summer.*

WRITINGS:

SELF-ILLUSTRATED

Gypsy's Cleaning Day, Morrow, 1990.

ILLUSTRATOR

Catherine Dexter, *Gertie's Green Thumb* (Junior Literary Guild selection), Macmillan, 1983.

Jean Ure, *Supermouse* (Junior Literary Guild selection), Morrow, 1984.

J. Ure, *The You Two,* Morrow, 1984.

Helen E. Buckley, *Someday with My Father* (Junior Literary Guild selection), Harper, 1985.

Mary B. Christian, *The Mysterious Case Case,* Dutton, 1986.

J. Ure, *The Most Important Thing,* Morrow, 1986.

ELLEN EAGLE

Carol Greene, *Robin Hill,* Harper, 1986.
Franklyn M. Branley, *Star Guide,* Crowell, 1987.
Sue Alexander, *Lila on the Landing,* Clarion, 1987.
C. Greene, *The Jenny Summer,* Harper, 1988.
Elizabeth Levy, *The Case of the Gobbling Squash,* Simon & Schuster, 1988.
E. Levy, *The Case of the Mind-Reading Mommies,* Simon & Schuster, 1989.
E. Levy, *The Case of the Tattletale Heart,* Simon & Schuster, 1990.

Also illustrator of numerous textbooks; newspaper editorials, including *New York Times;* stories for magazines, including "Just Bear" for *Cricket;* and book jackets.

WORK IN PROGRESS: Writing and illustrating *Gypsy Gives a Party,* for Morrow; illustrating *Tales of Tiddly* by Dolores Modrel, and three magic mystery stories by Elizabeth Levy, all for Simon & Schuster.

SIDELIGHTS: "In planning my pictures for *Someday with My Father,* as in planning all my illustrations, I was most interested in illuminating the relationship between the two characters from which the story grows.

"*Someday with My Father* is about a little girl who dreams of the fun her father has promised they will have once her leg cast comes off. By illustrating her dreams as vivid, bright, joyous, and peaceful, I hoped to communicate her unwavering faith in her father's promise and, therefore, love. Her visions are powerful: he must have kept his promises before, in this sense, her dreams are a gift from her father.

"The father has given a lot to this little girl—the hope which will become a reality, praise, and until she is well he will come into her room and read to her. This raised a problem for me: I was concerned that the little girl was too passive. I wanted her to be a more active participant in the story, to give something to her father. But what can she do, stuck at home in a cast? She can write! In between the fantasy scenes I pictured real time in which this little girl writes the story about the fun times he has promised her, about which he can now read to her. Now the dreams they share are a gift to each other.

"To underline the closeness between the two, I drew them to resemble each other. I based the father on my husband, Gordon, and drew the little girl as Gordon's sister Sharon looked at seven years old. They have the same hair color, similar haircuts, and I hope the little girl looks as though she will grow up to look like her father. They have matching sweaters. They are a team.

"When I was a little girl I had a linoleum floor in my bedroom on which were written short poems. Each poem was illustrated by a picture above: The butcher, the baker, the candlestick maker; rub-a-dub-dub, three men in a tub! I took such joy in my fellow residents—fat, round, red-cheeked, and uniformed, riding the waves across my room. These were real people to me. (Perhaps I was even careful to walk around them so as to not step on their faces.)

"The bedroom walls were mine to decorate with brush and paint. (The first picture I painted on the walls was of Miles Davis, the jazz trumpeter.) The walls of my bedroom and the floors enclosed me in a space of my own creation. It was a real live space into which I walked, peopled with characters living, moving, laughing; always there, they were loyal friends.

"Thus, I believe, was born my enthusiastic belief in character and atmosphere with which I hope to fill my illustrations today. I believe in the characters I illustrate; I am responsible for their well-being even if the character is an antagonistic one. After all, the story I am illustrating may come to an end, but if I have created full-bodied, believable characters, they will wake up the next day to face life's challenges again and again. And if they are to be victorious in the future, they must emerge from the story strong, safe, and with integrity."

FOR MORE INFORMATION SEE:

Glen Ridge Paper, April 17, 1986, July 14, 1988.
Staten Island Advance, June 6, 1986.
Essex Journal, October 30, 1986.

ENDE, Michael (Andreas Helmuth) 1929-

PERSONAL: Born November 12, 1929, in Garmisch-Partenkirchen, Bavaria, Germany (now West Germany); son of Edgar (a painter) and Luise (a physiotherapist; maiden name, Bartholomae) Ende; married Ingeborg Hoffmann (an actress), 1964 (deceased, 1985); married Mariko Sato (a translator), 1989. *Education:* Attended Waldorfschule, 1947-48 and Schauspielschule Otto Falckenberg, 1948-50. *Office:* c/o K. Thienemanns Verlag, Blumenstrasse 36, 7000 Stuttgart 1, West Germany.

CAREER: Writer. Actor in Rendsburg, Germany, 1950; film critic, 1954-62. *Member:* PEN (Germany), War Resisters International. *Awards, honors:* Literaturpreis der Stadt Berlin, 1960, for *Junge Generation;* Deutscher Jugendliteraturpreis, 1961, for

Jim Button and Luke the Engine-Driver, and 1974, for *Momo;* Hugo-Jakobi-Preis, 1967; Nakamori-Preis (Tokyo), 1976; Buxtehuder Bulle, 1979, Wilhelm-Hauff-Preis zur Forderung der Kinder- und Jugendliteratur, 1980, Premio Europeo "Provincia di Trento" (Italy), and International Janusz Korczak Prize (Poland), 1981, all for *Unendliche geschichte;* Grosser Preis der Deutschen Akademie fuer Kinder- und Jugendliteratur, Volkach, 1980; Preis der Leseratten des ZDF, 1980; Europaeischer Jugendbuchpreis, 1981; Deutscher Kinder- und Jugendschallplattenpreis, 1981; Bronzi di Riace (Kiwanis Literaturpreis), 1982; Lorenzo il Magnifico, 1982; Autor des Jahres, 1982; Silberner Griffel, 1983; Deutscher Fantasy Preis, 1987; Raffeisen Preis, 1988.

WRITINGS:

Jim Knopf und Lukas der Lokomotivfuehrer, (title means "Jim Button and Luke the Engine-Driver"; illustrated by Reinhard Michl), Thienemanns, 1960.

Jim Knopf und die Wilde 13 (title means "Jim Button and the Wild 13"; illustrated by R. Michl), Thienemanns, 1962.

Momo oder die seltsame Geschichte von den Zeit-Dieben und von dem Kind, das den Menschen die gestohlene Zeit zurueckbrachte, Thienemanns, 1973, published in England as *The Grey Gentlemen*, Burke, 1975, published in America as *Momo,* Doubleday, 1985.

Das kleine Lumpenkasperle (title means "The Little Rag Puppet"; illustrated by Roswitha Quadflieg), Urachhaus, 1975.

Lirum Larum Willi Warum (illustrated by R. Quadflieg), Urachhaus, 1978.

MICHAEL ENDE

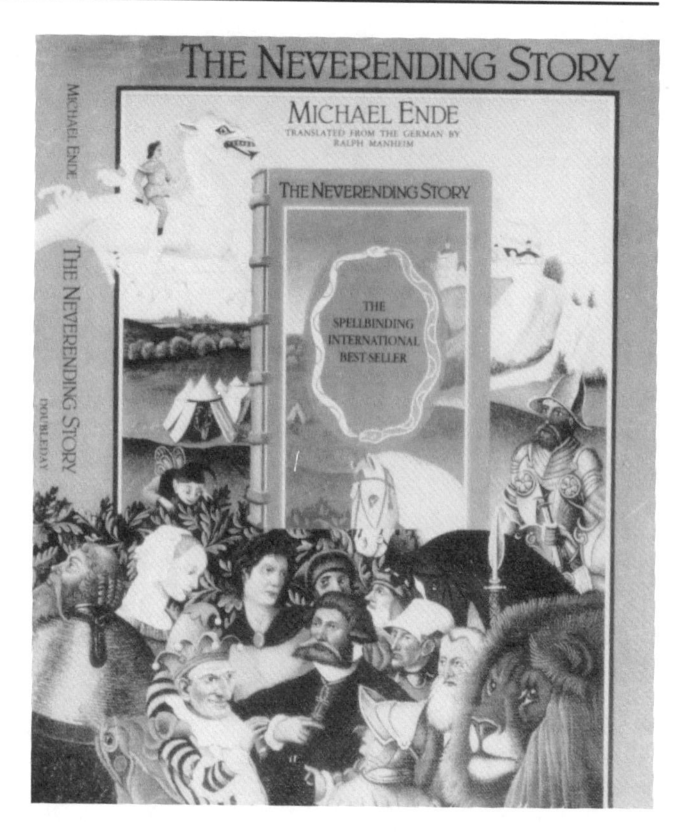

Jacket from the 1983 Doubleday edition.

Das Traumfresserchen (illustrated by Annegert Fuchshuber), Thienemanns, 1978, published as *The Dream-Eater,* translated by Gwen Marsh, Dent, 1979.

Die unendliche Geschichte (illustrated by R. Quadflieg), Thienemanns, 1979, translated by Ralph Manheim, published as *The Neverending Story,* Doubleday, 1983, large print edition, G. K. Hall, 1984.

Das Schnurpsenbuch (title means "Book of Nonsense Rhymes"; illustrated by Rolf Rettich), Thienemanns, 1979.

Der Lindwurm und der Schmetterling oder der seltsame Tausch (title means "The Dragon and the Butterfly"; illustrated by Manfred Schlueter and Wilfried Hiller), Thienemanns, 1981.

Tranquilla Trampeltreu die beharrliche Schildkroete (title means "The Persistent Turtle"; illustrated by M. Schlueter and W. Hiller), Thienemanns, 1982.

Die Schattennaehmaschine (title means "The Shadow Sewing Machine"; illustrated by Binette Schroeder), Thienemanns, 1982.

Das Gauklermaerchen (title means "A Juggler's Tale"), Weitbrecht, 1982.

(With E. Eppler and H. Taechl) *Phantasie, Kultur, Politik: Protokoll eines Gespraeches* (title means "Fantasy, Culture, Politics"), Weitbrecht, 1982.

Mein Lesebuch (anthology; title means "My Reader"), Fischer, 1983.

Der Spiegel im Spiegel: Ein Labyrinth (title means "The Mirror in the Mirror"), Weitbrecht, 1984.

Filemon Faltenreich (title means "Filemon Wrinkles"; illustrated by Christoph Hessel), Thienemanns, 1984.

Norbert Nackendick oder das nackte Nashorn (title means "Norbert Fatneck; or, The Naked Rhino"; illustrated by M. Schluter), Thienemanns, 1984.

Der Goggolori, Weitbrecht, 1984.

(With Joerg Krichbaum) *Die Archaeologie der Dunkelheit: Gesprache ueber Kunst und das Werk des Malers Edgar*

Ende (title means "Archeology of Darkness"), Weitbrecht, 1985.

Troedelmarkt der Traume: Mitternachtslieder und leise Balladen (title means "The Jumble Sale of Dreams"), Weitbrecht, 1986.

Ophelias Schattentheater, Thienemanns. 1988, translated by Anthea Bell, published as *Ophelia's Shadow Theater* (illustrated by Friedrich Hechelmann), Overlook Press, 1989.

The Wishing Punch, Theinemann, 1989.

Kunst und Politik: Ein gesprach mit Joseph Beuys (title means "Art and Politics: A Talk with Joseph Beuys"), Achberger Verlag, 1989.

PLAYS

Der Spielverderber (first performed at Schauspielhaus Frankfurt, Staedtische Buehnen, May 16, 1967), Weitbrecht, 1989.

"Die zerstreute Brillenschlange," first performed at Stadttheater Regensburg, January 11, 1981.

"Die Ballade von Norbert Nackendick oder das nackte Nashorn," first performed at Rheinisches Marionettentheater Zangerle, Duesseldorf, November 23, 1982.

RECORDINGS

"Narrenprozession," music by Hans Posegga, Emi Electrola Songbird, 1978.

"Die Fabel von Filemon Faltenreich oder Die Fussballweltmeisterschaft," music by W. Hiller, MusiCassette, 1984.

OPERA

"Die Jagd nach dem der Schlarg" (adaptation of Lewis Carroll's *Hunting of the Snark;* music by W. Hiller), first performed at Prinzregententheater, Muenchen, 1988.

ADAPTATIONS:

PLAYS

"Jim Knopf und die Wilde 13," first performed at Berliner Kammerspiele, November 20, 1971.

"Jim Knopf und Lukas der Lokomotivfuehrer," first performed at Theater fuer Kinder (Hamburg), February 12, 1970.

"Der Lindwurm und der Schmetterling oder der seltsame Tausch," first performed at Stadttheater Regensburg, January 11, 1981.

"Tranquilla Trampeltreu die beharrliche Schildkroete," first performed at Stadtmuseum (Muenchen), June 27, 1981.

"Momo," first performed at Staedtische Buehnen Muenster, October 21, 1981.

"Das Gauklermaerchen," first performed at Staedtische Buehnen Heidelberg, April 16, 1983.

"Lindwurm und Schmetterling," first performed at Katakombe Frankfurt, November 17, 1984.

"Die unendliche Geschichte," first performed at Berliner Kammerspiele, December 10, 1984.

OPERA

"Momo und die Zeitdiebe," (music by Mark Lothar), first performed at Landestheater Coburg, November 19, 1978.

"Der Goggolori" (music by W. Hiller), first performed at Munchner Gartnerplatztheater, February 3, 1985.

"Das Gauklermaerchen," [Cologne], 1988.

RECORDINGS

"Tranquilla Trampeltreu die beharrliche Schildkroete," MusiCassette, 1981.

"Die Ballade von Norbert Nackendick oder Das nackte Nashorn," music by Wilfried Hiller, MusiCassette, 1983.

"Jim Knopf und Lukas der Lokomotivfuehrer," MusicCassette, (Hamburg), 1984.

"Jim Knopf und die Wilde 13," MusiCassette, 1984.

"Momo," MusiCassette, 1984.

"Die unendliche Geschichte," MusiCassette, 1984.

MOTION PICTURES

"Die unendliche Geschichte," Neve Constantin, 1984, American version, "The Neverending Story," Neve Constantin, 1984.

"Momo," Rialto Film, Berlin, Iduna Film, Muenchen, 1986.

WORK IN PROGRESS: A collection of tales on imaginary architecture; a collection of modern legends.

SIDELIGHTS: Michael Ende is internationally recognized for creating original, multi-level fantasies that extol the power of the imagination. He is best known for his 1979 *Die unendliche Geschichte* published in America as *The Neverending Story.* With little promotion and no advertising the book held the number one spot on bestseller lists in Germany for nearly two years without a break, with 633,000 in print and another 100,000 ordered. Meanwhile K. Thienemanns, Ende's publisher which he put on the international publishing map reissued *Momo,* originally published in 1973 and since translated into 23 languages.

The rights for *The Neverending Story* have been sold for more than thirty languages. Critical reaction ranged from amazement to black rage. "You can enter the literary salon from prison, from the insane asylum, from a whorehouse—everywhere but from the children's room."[1]

In 1984 the book was adapted into a motion picture with the same name. The film (presented in two versions, German and English) enjoyed similar success. Nevertheless, "The Neverending Story" received some lukewarm reviews, the most critical of them coming directly from Ende himself. He denounced the film as "that revolting movie. The makers of the film simply did not understand the book at all. They just wanted to make money."[1] Originally Ende was not opposed to translating his work to film, and collaborated with the director on the script. "I worked as an adviser, because I wanted a beautiful movie. I trusted them. I saw the final script five days before the premiere and only as a result of a judicial verdict in Munich. I was horrified. They had changed the whole sense of the story. Fantastica reappears with no creative force from Bastian. For me this was the essence of the book."

"Neverending Story II" with a $28 million dollar budget is ready to roll as a venture between West Germany and Warner Bros. This film will deal with the principal story of the book—Bastian's adventures in Fantasia.

Born in Garmisch-Partenkirchen, Ende grew up in an artistic surrounding, the only child of surrealist artist Edgar and his physiotherapist wife, Luise. His happy childhood days were spent running about in the woods and meadows, chasing sheep, going to the circus, making sketches with his father. In 1947 he enrolled in Munich's Otto Flackenberg actors' school. "The parents of my first girlfriend paid my tuition. They wanted to get me away from her."[1]

Ende started out in life thinking that he was going to be an actor, found himself writing for the Munich cabarets in their post-World War II heyday, went on to do book reviewing for the German radio while working on his first book after an artist friend asked Ende to write the text for a children's book he was

(From the Bavarian-made fantasy film "The Neverending Story," 1984.)

illustrating. *Jim Button and Luke the Engine-Driver* was the result. "I had no idea how to write a children's book,"[1] recalled Ende, who relied on his childhood memories.

"The child that I used to be is still alive in me today, and there is no abyss of adulthood separating me from him. Basically, I feel that I am the same person now that I was then . . . a child who never loses its ability to wonder, to question, to feel excitement, who is vulnerable and exposed, who suffers, seeks comfort, senses hope . . . and who embodies our future until our dying day."[2]

When asked why he writes, Ende humorously quoted a German allegory about a millipede and a toad. The millipede was the master of dance. All the animals praised his artistry and grace. The ugly toad, very much annoyed by this, one day wrote a letter to the millipede asking him just how he used his thousand feet to dance. The letter set the millipede thinking. How did he dance? Ende said that, frankly, he felt not unlike the millipede when asked "Why do you write for children?"

"Essentially, I do not write for children at all. By this I mean that I never think of children while I am working, never consider how I should formulate my thoughts so that children will understand me, never choose or reject my subject matter as being suitable or unsuitable for children. At the very most I could say of myself that I write books which I myself would have enjoyed reading as a child. To write a fantasy is to embark on a journey to an unknown destination. It is just like starting *The Neverending Story*. It is a game, and it is at root amoral.

"It is for this child in me, and in all of us, that I tell my stories . . . . I am not guided by pedagogical or didactic principles while I work. In every person there is a child who wants to play . . . beauty can exist only in free play . . . the wondrous is always beautiful; only the wondrous is beautiful . . . and for literature for children, or for the child in each of us, I add that children are susceptible to nothing so much as genuine humor."[2]

"Nowadays the child is homogenized from his schooldays on. The fact that we kill those children by killing their creativity is fateful. I believe that especially Japan will pay a high price for this one day."[3]

Ende as a contemporary German storyteller is one of the few writers who persevered in the idea that fairy tales do neither belong to the past nor a world of sheer fiction. "Maerchen [fairy tales] are inner images. They are not, as many people believe,

Promotional ad for the 1986 movie that starred John Huston.

the description of an outer process, but rather the manifestation of an inner development in metaphorical form.

"I seek the fairy tale form of writing for the simple reason that I believe that the basis of every culture needs a myth or a story right in images . . . . This opposes the now predominant conceptual thinking, which is rigid and unequivocal. My little myths can and should be interpreted in many ways and yet they are unmistakable.

"One of the reasons why my works enjoy such a wide readership may be, that I am talking about meanings, and not only about facts."[3]

In 1970, Ende left Germany because he was fed up with having to justify his writing all the time. "At the end of the '60s the famous 'escapism debate' started. All literature that was not realistic, politically engaged, socially critical or emancipatory was considered 'flight' literature. I was called to account wherever I went."[3] He lived with his wife in a little town on the outskirts of Rome, and did not return to Germany until 1985 after the death of his wife. In 1989 he married Mariko Sato, the Japanese translator of *The Neverending Story*.

Ende's works are considered to be "positive utopia," and he states as one possible explanation for this label his faith in a "world in which the conflicts belonging to a post and not being ours any more will finally be overcome.

Nobody knew the value of an hour or a minute or even of a single second as well as they. (Jacket illustration by Fred Marcellino from *Momo* by Michael Ende.)

"We have to overcome the materialistic positivism which still haunts our conscience more than we admit . . . . And, under this aspect, fantasy is not a flight from reality. It is the capacity of forming new meanings, and bringing the old meanings in a new context. You may not realize it, but you live with a completely unmediated sense of reality.

"Giving a meaning to things, implies imagination and inner values. It is the task of literature and poetry to define these inner values and I hope to contribute as much as I can to make the culture of the 21st century worth living for."[3]

Ende doesn't think he is entirely responsible for the Ende phenomenon. "It's a disposition on the part of people. Readers are tired of realism. Ten years ago the book would not have been successful."[4] "Books float on a wave of fashion."[1]

"I believe that in order to tackle the present problems we need Maerchen like mine. By descending into the inner world of images, man may be able to realize the original values of life."[3]

FOOTNOTE SOURCES

[1]Logan Bentley "An Irate Michael Ende Blasts the 'Disgusting' Film Made from His Best-Seller *The Neverending Story,*" *People Weekly*, August 27, 1984.

[2]Michael Ende, "20th IBBY Congress in Tokyo," *Bookbird,* September 15/October 15, 1986.

[3]Ulrike Meier, "Every Culture Needs a Myth: Ende," *Japan Times,* August 26, 1986.

[4]"The Phenomenon of Michael Ende," *Publishers Weekly,* May 28, 1982.

FOR MORE INFORMATION SEE:

Washington Post Book World, October 16, 1983, March 17, 1985.

New York Times Book Review, November 6, 1983 (p. 14ff), February 17, 1985 (p. 34).

Newsweek, November 14, 1983, July 30, 1984.

Times Literary Supplement, November 25, 1983 (p. 1317).

Los Angeles Times, July 20, 1984.

Contemporary Literary Criticism, Volume 31, Gale, 1985.

Los Angeles Times Book Review, March 17, 1985.

Times (London), April 4, 1985.

FEIFFER, Jules 1929-

PERSONAL: Born January 26, 1929, in the Bronx, New York; son of David (who held a variety of jobs from dental technician to salesman) and Rhoda (a fashion designer; maiden name, Davis) Feiffer; married Judith Sheftel (a production executive with Warner Bros.), September 17, 1961 (divorced, 1983); married Jennifer Allen (a journalist), September 11, 1983; children: (first marriage) Kate; (second marriage) Halley. *Education:* Attended Art Students' League, 1946, and Pratt Institute, 1947-48, 1949-51. *Agent:* Robert Lantz, 888 Seventh Ave., New York, N.Y. 10106. *Office:* c/o Publishers-Hall Syndicate, 30 East 42nd St., New York, N.Y. 10017.

CAREER: Playwright, cartoonist, satirist. Assistant to Will Eisner (cartoonist), 1946-51; ghost-scripted "The Spirit," 1949-51; drew syndicated cartoon, "Clifford," 1949-51; held various art jobs, 1953-56, including a job making slide films, a job as writer for Terrytoons, and one designing booklets for an art firm; cartoons published in *Village Voice,* 1956—, weekly in London *Observer,* 1958-66, 1972—, and regularly in *Playboy,*

JULES FEIFFER

1959—; cartoons syndicated by Publishers-Hall Syndicate and distributed to over one hundred newspapers in the United States and abroad. Member of faculty, Yale University Drama School, New Haven, Conn., 1972-73. *Military service:* U.S. Army, Signal Corps, 1951-53; worked in a cartoon animation unit. *Member:* Authors League of America, Dramatists Guild (member of council), PEN, Writers Guild of America, East.

AWARDS, HONORS: Academy Award (Oscar) from the Academy of Motion Picture Arts and Sciences for Best Short-Subject Cartoon, 1961, for "Munro"; Special George Polk Memorial Award, 1961; named most promising playwright of 1966-67 season by New York Drama Critics, London Theatre Critics Award for Best Foreign Play of the Year, 1967, and Outer Critics Circle Award, and Obie Award from the *Village Voice,* both 1969, all for "Little Murders"; Outer Critics Circle Award, 1970, for "The White House Murder Case"; Pulitzer Prize, 1986, for editorial cartooning.

WRITINGS:

CARTOONS, UNLESS OTHERWISE NOTED

Sick, Sick, Sick: A Guide to Non-Confident Living, McGraw, 1958, published with introduction by Kenneth Tynan, Collins, 1959.
Passionella and Other Stories, McGraw, 1959.
The Explainers, McGraw, 1960.
Boy, Girl, Boy, Girl, Random House, 1961.
Feiffer's Album, Random House, 1963.
Hold Me!, Random House, 1963.
Harry, the Rat with Women (novel), McGraw, 1963.
(Compiler and annotator) *The Great Comic Book Heroes,* Dial, 1965.
The Unexpurgated Memoirs of Bernard Mergendeiler, Random House, 1965.
The Penguin Feiffer, Penguin (London), 1966.
Feiffer on Civil Rights, Anti-Defamation League, 1966.
Feiffer's Marriage Manual, Random House, 1967.
Pictures at a Prosecution: Drawings and Text from the Chicago Conspiracy Trial, Grove, 1971.
Feiffer on Nixon: The Cartoon Presidency, Random House, 1974.
Ackroyd, Simon & Schuster, 1977.
Tantrum: A Novel-in-Cartoons, Knopf, 1979.
Feiffery: Jules Feiffer's America from Eisenhower to Reagan, Knopf, 1982.
Marriage Is an Invasion of Privacy and Other Dangerous Views, Andrews, McMeel, 1984.
Feiffer's Children, Andrews & McMeel, 1986.
Ronald Reagan in Movie America: A Jules Feiffer Production, Andrews & McMeel, 1988.
Feiffer: The Collected Works, Volume 1, Fantagraphics Books, 1989.

PLAYS

"The Explainers" (satirical review), first produced in Chicago at Playwrights Cabaret Theater, May 9, 1961.
Crawling Arnold (one-act; first produced in Spoleto, Italy at Gian-Carlo Menotti's Festival of Two Worlds, June 27, 1961), Dramatists Play Service, 1963.
"The World of Jules Feiffer," first produced in New Jersey at Hunterdon Hills Playhouse, 1962.
Little Murders (two-act comedy; first produced on Broadway at Broadhurst Theatre, April 25, 1967 [closed after seven performances]; first American play produced by Royal Shakespeare Company in London at Aldwych Theatre, 1967; revived Off-Broadway at Circle in the Square, January 5, 1969), Random House, 1968.
"The Unexpurgated Memoirs of Bernard Mergendeiler," first produced in Los Angeles, Calif. at Mark Taper Forum, October, 1967, produced with other plays under title "Collision Course" Off-Broadway at Cafe au Go Go, May 8, 1968, published in *Collision Course,* edited by Edward Parone, Random House, 1968.
Feiffer's People: Sketches and Observations (first produced in Edinburgh, Scotland at International Festival of Music and Drama, August, 1968; produced in Los Angeles, Calif., 1971), Dramatists Play Service, 1969.
"God Bless," first produced in New Haven, Conn. by Yale School of Drama, October 10, 1968; produced by Royal Shakespeare Co. at Aldwych Theatre, 1968.
"Dick and Jane: A One-Act Play," first produced in New York at Eden Theatre as part of "Oh! Calcutta!," revised by Kenneth Tynan, June 17, 1969, published in *Oh! Calcutta!,* edited by K. Tynan, Grove, 1969.
The White House Murder Case: A Play in Two Acts [*and*] *Dick and Jane: A One-Act Play* ("The White House Murder Case" first produced in New York City at Circle in the Square, February 19, 1970), Grove, 1970.
(With others) "The Watergate Classics," first produced in New Haven, Conn. at Yale Repertory Theatre, November 16, 1973.
Knock-Knock (first produced in New York City at Circle in the Square, 1974), Hill & Wang, 1976.
Hold Me! (first produced in New York City at American Place Theatre, January 13, 1977), Dramatists Play Service, 1977.
"Grown-Ups" (first produced in New York City at Lyceum Theater, December 7, 1981), Samuel French, 1982.
"A Think Piece," first produced in Chicago at Circle Repertory Theatre, June 26, 1982.

The "Clifford" comic strip of July 23, 1950. (From *Feiffer: The Collected Works,* Volume 1 by Jules Feiffer. Illustrated by the author.)

(Strip from *Ronald Reagan in Movie America: A Jules Feiffer Production* by Jules Feiffer. Illustrated by the author.)

Elliot Loves (first produced in Chicago, 1988), Grove, 1989.
"Feiffer's America," first produced in Evanston, Ill. at Northlight Theater, April 13, 1988.
"Carnal Knowledge," first produced in Houston, Tex. at Stages Repertory Theater, April 23, 1988.

SCREENPLAYS

"Little Murders," Twentieth Century-Fox, 1971.
(With Israel Horovitz) *VD Blues,* PBS-TV, 1972, Avon, 1974.
"Popeye," Paramount Pictures, 1980.
(Adapter) "Puss in Boots," CBS/Fox Video, 1984.
"I Want to Go Home," Marvin Karmitz Productions, 1989.

ILLUSTRATOR

Robert Mines, *My Mind Went All to Pieces,* Dial, 1959.
Norton Juster, *The Phantom Tollbooth,* Random House, 1961.

Contributor of sketches to productions of DMZ Cabaret, New York; writer for "Steve Allen Show," 1964; author of episode "Kidnapped" for "Happy Endings" series for ABC-TV, August 10, 1975; contributor to periodicals, including *Ramparts.* Feiffer's books have been translated into German, Swedish, Italian, Dutch, French, and Japanese.

ADAPTATIONS:

"Munro" (animated cartoon; based on a Feiffer story), Rembrandt Films, 1961.
"Crawling Arnold," WEAV-TV, 1963.

(From the movie ''Popeye,'' starring Shelley Duvall and Robin Williams. With screenplay by Jules Feiffer, it was released by Paramount Pictures in 1980.)

''The Apple Tree'' (musical by Jerry Bock and Sheldon Harnick; consists of three playlets, one based on Feiffer's ''Passionella''), first produced at Schubert Theater, October 18, 1966.

Harry, the Rat with Women (play), first produced at Institute of Arts, Detroit, Mich., 1966.

Carnal Knowledge (released by Arco Embassy, 1971), Farrar, Straus, 1971.

''Academy Award Winners: Animated Short Films'' (includes Feiffer's ''Munro''), Vestron Video, 1985.

''Grown-Ups'' PBS-TV, May 9, 1986, (video), Warner Home Video, 1987.

WORK IN PROGRESS: An Off-Broadway musical based on *Harry, the Rat with Women,* starring Sylvester Stallone, with music by Alan Mencken and book by Howard Ashman; script of ''Terry and the Pirates,'' for Cinecorp; drama commissioned by the Philadelphia Festival of New Plays; cartoons.

SIDELIGHTS: Born in the Bronx, New York on **January 26, 1929,** Feiffer was the product of an unhappy marriage. ''[My mother] was not meant to be married; there wasn't a moment of married life that wasn't cruel to her. She was a bohemian, but she lived in a time when independent women had to be much stronger and tougher of spirit . . . in order to go it alone. She would have been most happy with a career and friendships and no sex life and no children . . . . [She] would have ended up in her 80s as a fairly delightful person with many, many friends, living an upper-middle class life . . . instead of being in poverty for most of her mature years and embittered and alienated from her children who were furious with her, because they felt unloved.''[1]

''[My father was] a defeated man by the time I knew him. Maybe it was that, as an immigrant, he never made an adjustment to his country. Or maybe being surrounded by wheelers and dealers, he just never had the absence of ethics to be a successful businessman. He was a sweet man, my father. He lived by avoiding living.''[2]

Feiffer discovered very early on that he did not blend well with other children, often isolating himself in his home in order to draw. ''In a way, I've used my childhood . . . as a sort of lab tryout . . . . As a kid I just wasn't there most of the time. I was hiding. The things I wanted to do had nothing to do with what was going on around me. My clock didn't tick with anybody else's time.

''I have always been a dreadful competitor—a sore loser and a guilty winner. One of my great desires to grow up was that, as I understood it, adults did not have to take gym.''[3]

''Growing up in the Bronx, as I did, during the Depression . . . I was almost always aware of this sense of victimization. First economic and then, in the forties, political, at the beginning of the witch hunts, which started long before Joe McCarthy. You felt this very strongly if your parents came, as mine did, from

Robin Williams and director Robert Altman's grandson, Wesley Ivan Hurt, as they appeared in the movie, "Popeye."

Eastern Europe, and the memory of the pogrom was still very strong in the family. There was always this undefined anxiety about political danger, and a certain uneasiness about making any sort of dissent. As a kid I felt—silenced. I didn't get beat up a lot, because I was too much of a working coward, but I was miserable."[4]

"I had a very strong sense of where the power was. It wasn't with the kids, it was with the grown-ups, and I discovered it was almost impossible for a child's evaluation of a situation to be accepted over the contradictory evaluation of a grown-up.

"I didn't seem to have a facility for anything except drawing. But even my drawings didn't look like everybody else's drawings."[5]

Comic books, World War II, the Depression, and Feiffer, all got started "at roughly the same time. I was eight. *Detective Comics* was on the stands, Hitler was in Spain, and the middle class (by whose employment record we gauge depressions) was, after short gains, again out of work.

"Eight was a bad age for me. Only a year earlier I had won a Gold Medal in the John Wanamaker Art Contest for a crayon drawing on oak tag paper of Tom Mix jailing an outlaw. So at seven I was a winner—and didn't know how to handle it. Not that triumph isn't at any age hard to handle, but the younger you are the more of a shock it is to learn that it simply doesn't change anything. Grownups still wielded all the power, still could not be talked back to, still were always right however many times they contradicted themselves. By eight I had become a politician of the grownup, indexing his mysterious ways and hiding underground my lust for getting even until I was old enough, big enough, and important enough to make a bid for it. That bid was to come by way of a career—(I knew I'd never grow big enough to beat up everybody; my hope was to, somehow, get to own everything and fire everybody). The career I chose, the only one that seemed to fit the skills I was then sure of—a mild reading ability mixed with a mild drawing ability—was comics.

"Instead of being little and consequently ridiculed for staying in the house all day and drawing pictures, one was big, and consequently canonized for staying in the house all day and drawing pictures. Instead of having no friends because one stayed in the house all day and drew pictures, one grew up and had millions of friends because one stayed in the house all day and drew pictures. Instead of being small and skinny with no muscles and no power because one stayed in the house all day and drew pictures, one grew up to be less small, less skinny, still perhaps with no muscles, but with lots of power: a friend of Presidents and board chairmen; an intimate of movie stars and ball players—all because one stayed in the house all day and drew pictures.

"I swiped diligently from the swipers, drew sixty-four pages in two days, sometimes one day, stapled the product together, and

(From *Feiffer's Children* by Jules Feiffer. Illustrated by the author.)

took it out on the street where kids my age sat behind orange crates selling and trading comic books. Mine went for less because they weren't real.

"My interest in comics began on the most sophisticated of levels, the daily newspaper strip, and thereafter proceeded downhill. My father used to come home after work, when there was work, with two papers: the *New York Times* (a total loss) and the *World-Telegram*."[6]

"I had to steal newspapers, the *Daily News* and the Hearst press, from other neighbor's garbage cans or befriend kids who I didn't particularly like in order to get their papers. To see 'Terry and the Pirates,' we'd have to get the *Daily News,* which my family wouldn't allow in the house.

"I came from a New Deal Democratic family and they considered Captain Patterson, who ran the *News,* and Hearst to be anti-Semites and racist and all of those other things. And they weren't far off the mark."[1]

The secret to acceptance in the Feiffer home was to remain unobtrusively successful. "Both my parents were concerned about me without having the faintest understanding or interest in my interests. And the only advice I got from them was bad advice because it was always conservative and cautious. My mother was very ambitious for me, but being an immigrant with memories of Polish pogroms, she was never far from feeling that if you offended the gentiles, they would throw you out of the country."[2]

"It was obviously not the dream of most Jewish immigrants . . . to have their only son grow up to become a cartoonist."[7]

"When I was a kid in high school, which were four very mixed-up, unhappy years, I still hadn't learned what to listen to or where I was going, obviously. And we'd always have to go into the auditorium and listen to some successful, famous graduate tell us about the wonderful times he had in high school. I was absolutely cut off from this. I didn't understand how this guy could ever be a former student or care. You know, he looked like the enemy—he had a moustache. And my boyhood dream was always to someday become successful and famous and come back to my school and look around and tell them the way it really was."[8]

"My idea of going to school was to mark time until I got into the comic-strip business. But I was never rebellious as a kid. It never occurred to me that I could be. I saw who had the guns. I assumed I was outnumbered from the start, so I went underground for the first twenty years of my life. I observed, registered things, but commented as little as possible."[9]

At the age of fifteen, Feiffer attended the Art Students' League. "My mother dragged me. I was a very shy kid, and very nervous, truly nervous about putting this talent that I fantasized a lot about on the line . . . . [So] when she . . . took me by the hand and took me to the Art Students' League, I remember screaming bloody murder, I didn't want to go. But she thought I should study anatomy, and it was wonderful."[1]

Shy a few credits for college, Feiffer found he would have to attend summer school. "I hated high school . . . . I liked people in it, and I liked some teachers in it, but the whole notion of going back was anathema to me. So, I forgot about college, which is probably the best accident that ever happened to me [and] went to Pratt for one year. But Pratt at that time was very much under the influence of the Bauhaus school, and had a lot of transplanted Europeans, and its mode of thinking was towards abstract art about which I knew nothing and cared nothing . . . . Certainly those teachers weren't going to make it more sympathetic to me, because they were overblown with their own self-importance, and belonged to that school of thought which was not unpopular in those years—that the more you demean the students, the more they learned. Well, the more I was demeaned, the more I disappeared, and so I vanished altogether from the day school, switched over to the evening school, where I ran into a wonderful teacher, wonderful perhaps because he actually worked in the field. He was an advertising art director for Grey Advertising named Lenny Kusokov. He was very sympathetic, and I learned a lot from him in a period of three years or so."[1]

1946. Became an assistant to Will Eisner, one of his childhood idols. "He said I was worth absolutely nothing, but if I wanted to hang out there, and erase pages or do gofer work, that was fine, which I did a few weeks, and then he came upon bad times. I forget what was going on at the time, but he let virtually everyone go . . . . He kept me around for $10 a week, just to fill in, to do blacks and rule borders and things like that . . . . Then I got promoted to $20 a week and did more of the same. But the main reason he kept me on was because I was the only real fan he had.

"At some point, we got into one of our arguments—and we got into a lot of them—about his stories. I said that his post-'46 stories weren't really up to his '39, '40, '42 stories. He had heard enough of this, and he said, if you think you can do better, write me a story. So I did. He liked it, and from that point on I was writing a lot of them . . . . We worked well together, and when we didn't, he would win.

"I was writing 'The Spirit' and laying it out. I thought that was worth $30 a week. He informed me that it really wasn't. So I threatened to quit. And to keep me on, he said he'd give me the back page of 'The Spirit' section, which then had a nice strip, but rather predictable and tired by then, called 'Jonesy' by a wonderful old cartoonist named Bernard Dribble. Stibble or Dribble. But I was a cut-throat competitor, so the hell with him, and I got the 'Clifford' page."[1]

1951. Feiffer was drafted into the Army during the Korean War against his will—"not having the courage to be a conscientious objector."[7]

"It was the first time I was truly away from home for a long period of time, and thrown into a world that was antagonistic to everything I believed in, on every conceivable level. In a war that I was out of sympathy with, and in an army that I despised. [An army that] displayed every rule of illogic and contempt for the individual and mindless exercise of power. [That] became my material."[1]

"I had never appreciated the luxury in being able to hate—the clear freedom in facing pure evil—and the Army was it . . . . I was totally on my own in what you might consider a serious man's world, and discovered that reason, or even simple basic idiot logic, had very little to do with day-to-day existence."[3]

"After two years of discovering hate, I turned into a satirist."[10]

During that first year in the Army, Feiffer began the story of the five-year-old boy, "Munro." "I did a couple of dummies [and] couldn't get it tight, I couldn't finish it. It was the first work of this kind that I had ever toyed with, and I didn't understand exactly what I was doing . . . what I was going after . . . . It went along fine up until the last third and then I seemed to blow it . . . . [By] the time I finished it [in 1953,] I was ready to get out of the Army . . . . [Finally it] became clear that the answer was in a sense dictated right from the first ten pages."[1]

Animators had a hard time dealing with Feiffer's anti-military stance. "This was at a time when McCarthyism was officially over, but the resultant suppression and fear were still very much hallmarks of society. In fact, the blacklist in the entertainment industry didn't end until some years later, so the entertainment industry wasn't likely to take to anything with a message such as this."[1]

Publishers had a hard time reconciling the innocence of the form with the bleakness of the satire. "They also didn't know how to market it. They explained to me over and over that unfortunately I was not William Steig (who was famous) or James Thurber (who was famous) or Saul Steinberg or Robert Osborne (who were famous), therefore nobody would buy since nobody had heard of me, even though they thought the work was very good. I understood instantly the necessity of becoming famous in order to sell my work."[11]

October, 1956. Feiffer began drawing a weekly comic strip for the *Village Voice*. "My approach to the *Voice* was totally cynical. I had been turned down over and over and over again by book publishers . . . [who all] thought I was terrific . . . . 'It's wonderful stuff, but there's no market for it.' . . . [It] was a Catch-22 situation. I had no name, so who was going to buy this work that looked like children's drawings, but was very adult material? . . . I had to figure out a way of becoming Steig, Steinberg or Thurber in order to get what I wanted into print. I thought of all sorts of things. I could kill somebody . . . . I could commit suicide . . . . Suicide was not then established as a form of self-promotion, as it later became with several poets.

"But short of suicide or murder, I didn't know what to do until the *Voice* came along . . . . [The] very people who were rejecting me read that paper, because it was hip, it was inside. It was very modestly circulated, but to all the right people. I was smart enough to know, even at the age of twenty-seven, which I was then, that if I could get the stuff they're turning down in print . . . they will change their minds, which is what happened."[1]

"We cut a stiff deal. They would publish anything I wrote and drew as long as I didn't ask to be paid . . . . [But] it worked just as I had fantasized . . . . An editor said, 'Oh boy, this guy is good, he's in the *Voice,*' and accepted the same stuff his company had turned down when I had come to their offices as an unpublished cartoonist."[11]

"All my advisers advised me to never do anything for free—get paid for everything, they said. Before I started doing the cartoons in the *Voice* I got paid for everything; I was doing more and more work and earning less—probably because I was doing things I hated to do—things I got no enjoyment from. I was quickly turning into a hack. I'd wanted to become a cartoonist since I was a child. I loved to draw, I loved to invent fantasies, and I loved to combine words with pictures. But after being a professional for several years the word 'love' went out the window. I was doing it because I *had* to, because it was the only way I could make a living, the way most people do their jobs—because they know of no way to get out.

"Becoming an amateur again—going to the *Village Voice* and saying 'I just want to get in print somehow'—re-created the element of love in the work, and revived the pleasure of being an *amateur,* of doing something for the hell of it. It was easily the most valuable lesson I've learned in my career.

"So—be warned of the good advice of others. Be warned when they tell you that your attitude is immature . . . . All *good* advice is necessarily *safe* advice, and though it will undoubtedly follow a sane pattern, it will very likely lead one into total sterility: one of the crushing problems of our time."[12]

Now that Feiffer had the job, he was struggling for style. In dealing with reproduction, he would stiffen up. He couldn't handle a brush well; he couldn't handle a pen. He could handle a pencil but you can't reproduce in pencil. Finally he stumbled on a technique of using wooden dowels that gave him a dry line approximating pencil. He'd draw those in poster and black ink, diluted. "That gave me a line that I liked for a while. But it took forever . . . . In those years I was very influenced by William Steig and Osborn, and the closer I could get my work to look like them, the happier I would be. I must have been doing the weekly strip for . . . six months to maybe a year, before I hit on the drawing style I liked."[1]

1956. While continuing with the *Voice,* he took a monetary job at Terrytoons. "I met people I really liked, and whose talents I respected . . . . There was a man I never heard of named Ernie Pintoff doing a cartoon called 'Flea Bits' which I think is still a brilliant piece of work. There was a man I never heard of named Bob Blechman, who was going up on the same train I was, working on an animated version of 'The Juggler of Our Lady.' There was a lot of talent around. So, for the first time, I felt that I was among constituents, that there were peers around. They put me . . . to coming up with the morning animated series that would replace 'Tom Terrific' when that ran out, so it would run four or five minutes a day. So I designed a series called 'Easy Winners' about a bunch of kids living in a neighborhood like the Bronx. Something that would have been vaguely autobiographical . . . a kind of spin-off of 'Clifford.' . . . They all loved it . . . . Then some muckety-muck from CBS was coming who had to O.K. it . . . . He came in a three-piece suit, very expensive looking, and very well coiffed, and I knew I was dead.

"The storyboards are pinned up by push-pins on the wall, and it looks like a comic strip . . . . My idea of a comic strip is you read a comic strip. That's not the way it works in animation. The people who come in to O.K. it . . . expect to be performed for. And you get these fifty- or sixty-year old animators who quack like ducks and jump up and down and flap their wings [acting] out the drawings. So you have a middle-aged animator, or a story layout man flapping his wing, and then being his own laugh-track, so as to encourage the clod who's looking on to think this is amusing, because how would he know? He wouldn't know from the drawings and he wouldn't know from the performance. But from his laugh and from the laughs of the claque in attendance.

"I didn't quack once, and I was kind of mumbling. I could see my support system . . . all around me, grinning, beaming, [but] by the time I had finished the last drawing, I was standing alone and they were all surrounding this guy from CBS.

"And he said, well, it's a little too *New Yorker*-ish . . . . The worst curse word in the world. And then he said, what I mean is—and this is a direct quote I will never forget—'It's a little closer to Dostoevsky than it is to *Peter Pan*.' . . . That afternoon they cancelled the series.

"The next day I went in and quit, and I got a $50 a week raise to stay on. By that time I knew that my days there were numbered, but I needed the money, and I would take it until something else came along. What came along was Mr. Hefner offering me 500 bucks a month to do a cartoon for *Playboy*."[1]

1961. "Munro," made into an animated cartoon, won an Academy Award. "The Explainers," a musical revue based on his cartoons, was directed by Paul Sills and produced by Chicago's Playwrights of the Second City. "I was quite dissatisfied with

Feiffer, as he appeared in the March 5, 1989 issue of the *Daily News Magazine* (N.Y.). (Photograph by Joyce Ravid.)

seeing the cartoons acted out. They were much too one-dimensional. At the same time I became interested in seeing if I could write for the stage, and do a full-length play, rather than these little vignettes.

"Transferring the cartoons to live action, whether on stage or on film, presents very difficult problems."[13]

On **September 17, 1961,** Feiffer married Judy Sheftel. A few years later his daughter, Kate, was born. "I didn't want a kid, I'd never liked kids. Then they showed me Kate at the hospital. Wow! Five seconds and I was won for life."[14]

"It wasn't funny when my baby threw a spoon on the floor the first time. But when I put it back on the table, when I watched her examine it, when she threw it on the floor again, when I picked it up again, I began to see that it was funny.

"We were embroiled in a comedy routine. It was a team. I was the straight man. The baby was the clown. There were an infinite variety of pauses and expressions, but it was all part of the same gag. If it wasn't such a gag, you'd want to kill the baby."[5]

Begun originally as a novel, Feiffer's first full-length play, "Little Murders," was produced on Broadway in 1967. "[I] realized that whatever the fate of the play, I was stuck as a playwright. I felt as at home with a play as with the cartoon."[15]

"Once you fall in love with the form, you can't fall out of love with it, whatever the travail. Also, it's fun. The production

But poor Munro was very tired. So he went to the sergeant and he said:

(From *Feiffer's Children* by Jules Feiffer. Illustrated by the author.)

process, the collaboration in the rehearsal process—I take lots of pleasure in that.''[16]

1971. Separated from his wife.

1980. Feiffer's film, ''Popeye'' was released. ''My love of 'Popeye' really started late. In some bookstore or other, I ran into the Bill Blackbeard collection of 1936 Popeyes that Woody Gelman put out. And it was a revelation to me, because I had not remembered 'Popeye' as being that witty . . . . But more importantly, it created a kind of universe, and had a philosophy that seemed to be apt for our time . . . a social-Darwinian world . . . . There was something Kafkaesque in that world, and there was something Beckett-like . . . . [His] use of time—certain sequences could stretch on for days and days, where virtually nothing happened, [yet] it was so full of events.

''Then I got a call from Robert Evans maybe a year or so later, saying he was doing a movie of 'Popeye,' and was I interested in doing the screenplay . . . . I said, it depends, if you want to do Max Fleischer's 'Popeye' I am not your man. If you want to do Segar's 'Popeye' no one else can write it but me. He said, 'I want to do any ''Popeye`` you want to do.' So that's how it started . . . . There was great enthusiasm for the project from the beginning. Dustin Hoffman was originally supposed to play Popeye . . . . He read the first fifty pages of the script, loved it.

Cover from the published edition of *Little Murders* by Jules Feiffer.

''Evans loved the first draft. Dustin hated it. At one point it became a question of him or me. Evans stayed with the script, which he supported completely. Dustin pulled out. You don't get many cases of a Hollywood producer losing his financing in order to stay with a script . . . . A year or so later Robin [Williams] became a hit in 'Mork and Mindy' and Evans suggested him for the part, and that's how the film got off the ground again. Otherwise it would have been still on the shelf.''[1]

1981. Feiffer's autobiographical play, ''Grown- Ups,'' opened at the Lyceum Theatre to rave reviews. It is the story of Jake, a young *New York Times* reporter, whose parents place more importance on his success than on his work. ''My mother had died in February of 1973. I knew that I could handle that because I'd spent eighty-five years in psychotherapy talking about my mother and working out all of our problems. Except that the day that she was buried, I couldn't go to the funeral because I had a fever of 104 and no voice. Something had gone wrong. Since I couldn't get a refund on my psychotherapy, I decided that this needed looking into in some other way. I had started another novel, but I'd stopped working on it and didn't really want to work on anything. I had simply quit everything. The best thing about a contract is that, whatever personal breakdown you may be having, you have to stop it in order to earn your living. So I did the work I was supposed to do, and then went back to my breakdown.

''I decided after a couple of months that this was kind of silly, and I'd better find out what's going on here and learn a little about who I am and was in regard to this woman and her life and history with me. So maybe I'd better write a family play. There was a problem: I am cursed with instant boredom and immediately move into nap-time when I touch on anything directly autobiographical. When I start telling people about something that's really happened, I lose interest instantly because I know the ending. I see no point in telling it. So I had to create characters who were related to me and my family but weren't simply photographs or paste-ups of those people.

''The parents in 'Grown-Ups' I made as close to my parents as I could. In the first draft of the play, I had a hard time recreating their voices. When I finished it, I realized that I hadn't written the Feiffers but Portnoy's parents. They were the conventional Jewish parents of modern-day novels and plays. They weren't my parents. So I went through my files and was fortunate enough to discover letters that my parents had written to me from the Forties through the Fifties. In going over those letters, I rediscovered their voices. I remembered again how they talked, how they sounded, and I started jotting down notes. Then I rewrote the play with the real parents.

''After I revised the script, I put it all on tape to hear what it sounded like. It was chilling. I shuddered with the realization that I had raised Dave and Rhoda Feiffer from the dead. It was scary and wonderful and moving, but the one thing it wasn't was a play. It was just an act of memory. So I had to go back like a playwright and do the difficult job of cutting all the stuff that was nice writing as I wrote it but turned out not to be so nice when it was all put together. So I did that and then decided, for personal reasons, that it was simply too potent a piece of work to put on the stage at that particular time. My first child was seven or eight years old then, and I really didn't like the idea of her seeing this on stage until she was older. So I waited seven years.''[11]

''How would my parents have reacted if they saw it? I think they would have been mortally offended and would have prayed desperately for its success.''[2]

"Now, young man, what can you do to entertain us?" (From *The Phantom Tollbooth* by Norton Juster. Illustrated by Jules Feiffer.)

In **1983** Feiffer divorced his wife and married Jennifer Allen. On **November 20, 1984,** his daughter, Halley, was born.

April 17, 1986. Received the Pulitzer Prize for editorial cartooning. "I've only wanted what all nice Jewish boys want .... To be honest, collect paychecks and get a few prizes, and actually I've done pretty well.

"The Pulitzer certainly helps me to go on, because often you feel you're having no effect, and that nothing will change .... Now, at least, I have won a prize. So I can continue to feel this way, and still get on with it."[17]

"As wonderful as winning the award was the response from friends and strangers. It reaffirmed the reason I've been doing the cartoons all these years ... and gave me a sense of rejuvenation. One assumes there's an audience out there, but it's not always evident."[18]

Throughout his career as a playwright and screenwriter, Feiffer has remained dedicated to his weekly strip. The dream is "to get to the very core of people ... to reduce the story of mankind to eight panels."[8]

The differences between playwrighting and cartooning have presented more pleasures than problems for Feiffer. "The use of the language is very different, and what it has to say .... I love that .... If I do cartoons about men and women, it's usually about what's not working and how it falls apart. And it has to be succinct, it has to be pithy, it has to make a point, and it better be fun. And it's got to be in six panels. In theater, I have much more range, and it doesn't have to be funny. It can be anything I damn please.

"Normally, the assumption is that when you move out of cartooning into a second profession which is taken more seriously, then you'll forget the cartooning. I found it was just the reverse. Because the more I got into theater the more important retaining the cartoon became.

"There is something that's exciting to me about going from one form to another."[1]

Throughout his career as a playwright, Feiffer has been accused of writing characters that are less deeply developed, more like cartoon characters. "The irony of all this is that during all the years when I was doing only the cartoons, what was being said and written about me was that I wasn't really a cartoonist—that these were little plays or little short stories. So in my cartoons, I'm a writer, and in my stage work, I'm a cartoonist."[19]

With a career that has touched many mediums, Feiffer allows each piece of work to lead him into a new direction. "I can only understand my career when the latest piece of work is finished. Then I can connect it to the last thing I did. There's a kind of trail that I'm following, and I don't know what the hell it is."[19]

FOOTNOTE SOURCES

[1]Gary Groth, "Memories of a Pro Bono Cartoonist," *Comics Journal,* August, 1988.
[2]Michiko Kakutani, "In Writing 'Grown-Ups,' Jules Feiffer Found He Really Liked His Parents," *New York Times,* December 15, 1981.
[3]Julius Novick, "Jules Feiffer and the Almost-in-Group," *Harper's,* September, 1961.
[4]Tom Burke, "Feiffer: If at First You ... ," *Boston Globe,* January 26, 1969.
[5]Marian Christy, "Conversations," *St. Louis Post-Dispatch,* November 3, 1985.
[6]Jules Feiffer, compiler, *The Great Comic Book Heroes,* Dial, 1965.
[7]Mimi Leahey, "Jules Feiffer Writing a Serious Play," *Other Stages,* June 17, 1982.
[8]Eve Auchincloss and Nancy Lynch, "An Interview with Jules Feiffer," *Mademoiselle,* January, 1961.
[9]Robin Brantley, "'Knock Knock' 'Who's There?' 'Feiffer,'" *New York Times Magazine,* May 16, 1976.
[10]Rex Reed, "Breaking All the Rules—and Winning," *Sunday News,* February 15, 1976.
[11]Christopher Durang, "Jules Feiffer, Cartoonist—Playwright," *Dramatists Guild Quarterly,* winter, 1987.

(From *Ronald Reagan in Movie America: A Jules Feiffer Production* by Jules Feiffer. Illustrated by the author.)

[12]Roy Newquist, "Jules Feiffer," *Counterpoint,* Rand McNally, 1964.

[13]Jordan R. Young, "The Screenplay According to Jules Feiffer," *Millimeter,* April, 1981.

[14]"The Prolific Pen of Jules Feiffer," *Life,* September 17, 1965.

[15]Samuel G. Freedman, "Jules Feiffer's West Side Story," *New York Times,* May 3, 1987.

[16]Helen Dudar, "Jules Feiffer on the Tyranny of Trivia," *New York Times,* June 20, 1982.

[17]Clarke Taylor, "Feiffer Surviving on Anxiety," *Los Angeles Times,* May 8, 1986.

[18]David Astor, "An Unexpected Pulitzer for Jules Feiffer," *Editor and Publisher,* May 31, 1986.

[19]John Engstrom, "Has Feiffer Switched Pens?," *Horizon,* November, 1981.

FOR MORE INFORMATION SEE:

Mademoiselle, January, 1958 (p. 70).
Village Voice, May 14, 1958, April 13, 1967 (p. 5), May 4, 1967, October 25, 1976.
Mayfair, September, 1958.
Time, February 9, 1959 (p. 36), May 26, 1961, June 28, 1963.
New Republic, June 6, 1960 (p. 17ff).
Realist, February, 1961.
Cue, March 18, 1961 (p. 11).
New York Post, March 29, 1961 (p. 46), January 13, 1976, February 19, 1976, May 21, 1987.
Horizon, November, 1961.
Commentary, November, 1961, December, 1964 (p. 52ff).
Newsweek, November 13, 1961 (p. 93), May 8, 1967.

(Strip from *Feiffer's Children* by Jules Feiffer. Illustrated by the author.)

Harper's, June, 1962 (p. 74ff), February, 1968 (p. 48).
Current Biography, H. W. Wilson, 1962.
Holiday, June, 1963 (p. 66ff).
Saturday Evening Post, October 3, 1964 (p. 38ff).
Look, January 11, 1966 (p. 60).
New York Times, February 26, 1967 (p. 15), April 23, 1967, April 27, 1967, October 12, 1968, November 28, 1972, February 10, 1976 (p. 42), July 24, 1981 (p. C-2).
Ramparts, May, 1968 (p. 36), August, 1969 (p. 23ff).
Lydia Joel, "Happy Holidays to You and Jules Feiffer," *Dance*, December, 1968.
Plays and Players, January, 1969 (p. 35ff).
"Jules Feiffer," broadcast on Artists in America series, PBS-TV, 1971.
Graphis, Volume 28, number 159, 1972/73 (p. 76ff).
Carolyn Riley, editor, *Contemporary Literary Criticism*, Volume II, Gale, 1974.
"The Dancer Tripping the Light Fantastic Is Really the Cartoonist on a Fantastic Trip: Jules Feiffer," *People Weekly*, November 1, 1976.
Nation, July 1, 1978 (p. 19), December 30, 1978 (p. 734ff), July 11-18, 1981 (p. 39).
David Badder and Bob Baker, "Jules Feiffer," *Film Dope*, September, 1978.
Dictionary of Literary Biography, Volume 7, Gale, 1981.
Los Angeles Times, January 18, 1981, November 7, 1982 (part V, p. 1), March 20, 1983.
Focus on Film 37, March, 1981 (p. 10).
Frank D. Gilroy, "Broadway Playwrighting: An Impossible Dream?," *Dramatists Guild Quarterly*, spring, 1981.
James Vinson, editor, *Contemporary Dramatists*, 3rd edition, St. Martin's, 1982.
Progressive, January, 1983 (p. 28).
Wilson Library Bulletin, November, 1985 (p. 50).
James Harney, "New York's Prize City," *Daily News*, April 18, 1986.
Esquire, July, 1986 (p. 60).
Video, May, 1987 (p. 15).
Jerry Tallmer, "Feiffer's Fun and Prophecy," *New York Post*, May 21, 1987.
Variety, May 11, 1988 (p. 137).
Daily News Magazine, March 5, 1989 (p. 11ff).

FREEMAN, Nancy 1932-

PERSONAL: Born December 4, 1932, in Toronto, Ontario, Canada; daughter of W. B. (an electrical engineer) and Alma (a nurse; maiden name, Henderson) Buchanan; married Norman S. Freeman (a civil engineer), May 19, 1956; children: Heather (Mrs. R. W. Jennings), Lee (Mrs. J. P. Regimbal), John. *Education:* Toronto Teacher's College, Teaching Certificate, 1952; correspondence courses, Institute of Children's Literature, 1977, 1979; attended St. Lawrence College, 1988-89. *Politics:* "Freedom of Choice." *Religion:* Anglican. *Home and office:* Freehaven Farm, R.R.2, Milford, Ontario, Canada K0K 2P0.

CAREER: Etobicoke Schools, Toronto, Ontario, Canada, teacher, 1952-57; writer, 1982—. Has also worked as a volunteer, peer counsellor, community choir director, and Golden Retriever breeder. *Awards, honors: Ginny and the General* was a Children's Book Centre Choice, 1984-85.

WRITINGS:

Ginny and the General (illustrated by Ineke Standish), Borealis, 1983.

NANCY FREEMAN

Sandy (illustrated by I. Standish), Borealis, 1984.

SIDELIGHTS: "It had never occurred to me to write for publication until I was in my forties. At that time an experience with a disturbed golden retriever gave me something important to say to young people—a message of self-worth as seen through the heart of a fine dog. This circumstance presented me with a requirement to learn the writer's craft. Two correspondence courses through the Institute of Children's Literature in Redding Ridge, Connecticut followed.

"My dog story, *Ginny and the General*, was published in 1983 by a small Canadian publishing house, Borealis Press of Ottawa. I knew nothing about illustration at that time, and though I respected what the illustrator had done with my story, it was obvious that she did not see the same dog that I saw. Hence rumblings within me about wanting to be able to illustrate my own work began.

"My second book, *Sandy*, does not have a dog in it. It was chosen, however, by the Ontario 4-H leaders to be recommended reading for 4-H groups throughout the country because it depicts Ontario rural life so well. The country approach therein contained is fresh and unsophisticated. Fresh, because my general husband had recently retired from the military and we were new country dwellers. Unsophisticated, because there is no place in the book for the terrific traumas of many of today's teenagers, merely the ever present concerns of family relationships and growing up with traditional values. I felt that I said what I had to say well enough in both books.

"Now I am learning to draw and paint. I have three grandchildren. What I may have to say, in a more up-beat style, I suspect, should prove interesting to me, at least, to you, at most.

"I consider that young people (and old) should be taught and shown sensitivity. Therein lies my strength and I shall do what I can where I can."

HOBBIES AND OTHER INTERESTS: Music (choir, piano, and organ), spinning, weaving, dying, felting, leatherwork, painting, gardening, nature walks, travel, reading, people.

GANZ, Yaffa 1938-

PERSONAL: Born March 26, 1938, in Chicago, Ill.; daughter of George and Dorothy Siegel; married Abraham Ganz, (a teacher of Bible and Talmud), 1958; children: four sons, one daughter. *Education:* University of Chicago, B.A., 1962. *Home:* Jerusalem, Israel. *Office:* Feldheim Publishers, P.O. Box 6525, Jerusalem, Israel.

CAREER: Writer, 1979—; Feldheim Publishers, Jerusalem, Israel, editor of Young Readers Division, 1978-88.

WRITINGS:

JUVENILE

Our Jerusalem, Behrman, 1979.
Savta Simcha and the Incredible Shabbos Bag, Feldheim, 1980.
Yedidya and the Esrog Tree, Feldheim, 1980.
Savta Simcha and the Seven Splendid Gifts (illustrated by Bina Gewirtz), Feldheim, 1980.
The Riddle Rhyme Book, Feldheim, 1981.

YAFFA GANZ

The Adventures of Jeremy Levi, Feldheim, 1981.
Who Knows One? A Book of Jewish Numbers (illustrated by Harvey Klineman), Feldheim, 1981.
Follow the Moon: A Journey through the Jewish Year (illustrated by H. Klineman), Feldheim, 1984.
Savta Simcha and the Cinnamon Tree (illustrated by Bina Gewirtz), Feldheim, 1984.
The Story of Mimmy and Simmy (illustrated by H. Klineman), Feldheim, 1985.
The Gift That Grew, Feldheim, 1986.
Shuki's Upside-Down Dream (illustrated by B. Gewirtz), Feldheim, 1986.
The Terrible-Wonderful Day, Feldheim, 1987.
The Jewish Factfinder: A Bookful of Important Jewish Facts and Handy Information, Feldheim, 1988.
From Head to Toe: A Book about You, Feldheim, 1988.
Alef to Tav, Artscroll-Mesorah, 1988.
Tali's Slippers, Tova's Shoes, Artscroll-Mesorah, 1989.
The Little Old Lady Who Couldn't Fall Asleep, Artscroll-Mesorah, 1989.
The Wonderful World We Live In, Artscroll-Mesorah, 1989.
Where Are You Hashem?, Artscroll-Mesorah, 1989.
Hello Heddy Levi, Feldheim, 1989.
Teasers, Twisters, Stumpers, Feldheim, 1989.
Sharing a Sunshine Umbrella, Feldheim, 1989.

Ganz's books have been translated into Hebrew, German, and French. Contributor of over 200 stories and articles on Israel and Jewish topics to magazines and newspapers in the United States, Canada, England, South Africa, and Israel.

WORK IN PROGRESS: An anthology of humorous articles on the Jewish scene for adults.

SIDELIGHTS: "Having learned in Jewish all-day schools through grammar and high school, I was 'incubated' in a warm, happy, secure, Jewish environment until I was seventeen. These years were spent absorbing Jewish knowledge and values which I simply took for granted.

"My mother had always prodded me to put my writing skills to some use, but somehow, that never seemed like a *real* thing to do, especially when I was always so busy with school, working, counseling in a youth group and in summer camps. It was only many years later, after receiving my degree and raising my own children, that I began to think about sharing my wonderful world with other Jewish children.

"When my youngest went off to school, I wrote my first novel, found a publisher, and together with the publisher, I found—or one might say: founded!—a job as the first juvenile editor of a large Jewish publishing firm. In my spare time, I wrote about any and everything—from a Jewish perspective: funny books, serious stories, factual presentations—and I still can't believe how far and wide the books have gone. (Of course my *own* Hebrew speaking kids considered reading English a chore when they were young, and they rarely read anything I wrote! Fortunately, my grandchildren will be able to read at least some of the books in Hebrew translation.)

"I think that one of the reasons for the books' popularity is that many Jewish children's books on the market are either for religiously observant children who are very strong in their Jewish identity, or for children whose Jewish focus is vague or marginal. I try to hit the middle of the spectrum. I present serious, authentic Jewish material, but in a light, contemporary, often humorous manner which any Jewish kid can relate to, identify with, and enjoy. Or at least, I hope so.

"Away with you! Shoo!! Off you go!" (From *Savta Simcha and the Seven Splendid Gifts* by Yaffa Ganz. Illustrated by Bina Gewirtz.)

"To sum it all up, I'd say that the story of the Jew and his Torah is the unending story of Man, the Divine, and the wondrous world we live in. Bringing even a tiny bit of this vast wealth, wisdom, and beauty to light—this is my task, my pleasure, my delight. And I work very hard getting it all down on paper!"

GOFFE, Toni 1936-

PERSONAL: Surname is pronounced "goff"; born October 5, 1936, in Southampton, England; son of Cecil Charles (a manager) and Hannah (a homemaker; maiden name, Miller) Goffe; married Jill Rosemary Chatfield (a teacher), August 6, 1960; children: Tim, Tobin. *Education:* Southampton College of Art, National Diploma in Art and Design, 1956. *Home and office:* The Manse, Ackender Rd., Alton, Hampshire GU34 1JS, England. *Agent:* Linda Rogers Associates, P.O. Box 330, 1 Bloomsbury House, 9 Guildford St., London WC1N 1PX, England; Carol Bancroft, 185 Goodhill Rd., Weston, Conn. 06883.

CAREER: Free-lance artist, 1956—; band musician, London, England, 1956-63; judo instructor, London and Hampshire, England, 1963—; author, 1972—; Pendulum Gallery, Selborne, Hampshire, art gallery director, 1972-79; John Stobart Gallery, Boston, Mass., art gallery director, 1982-85. *Exhibitions:* Lion and Lamb Gallery, Farnham, England, 1986, 1987; John Stobart Gallery (one-man show), Boston, Mass., 1987; Garden Gallery (one-man show), London, 1987; Godalming Gallery, Surrey, 1987; has also exhibited throughout Europe, Germany, and the eastern United States. *Military service:* Served seven months in Royal Army Ordinance Corps National Service.

WRITINGS:

SELF-ILLUSTRATED

Monkey Tricks, Key Facts, 1969.
Sleepy Toy Soldier, Key Facts, 1969.
Sue and Peter's Holiday Diary, Key Facts, 1969.
The XYZ of Sport, Transworld, 1977.
Judo Games, Corgi-Carousel, 1977, second edition, Pendulum Gallery Press, 1986.
The XYZ of Musical Instruments, Transworld, 1978.
The XYZ of Dogs, Transworld, 1979.
The XYZ of Horses, Transworld, 1981.
Toby's Animal Rescue Service, Hamish Hamilton, 1981.
Love Wars, Exley, 1984.
Judo for Juniors, Pendulum Gallery Press, 1986.
"Is There Sex after 40?" (cartoons), Pendulum Gallery Press, 1987.
Joe Giant's Missing Boot, Walker, 1990.
The Dog with the Awful Laugh, Walker, 1990.
The Fish That Made a Difference, Collins, 1990.
Jessie's Mum Is Ill, Collins, 1990.

TONI GOFFE

ILLUSTRATOR

Ian Niall, *Trout from the Hills,* Heinemann, 1961.
The Twins at the Fair, Purnel, 1967.
The Twins in London, Purnel, 1968.
The Twins in France, Purnel, 1969.
Richard Musman, *Robert en Vacances,* Nelson, 1969.
Robert en France, Edward Arnold, 1969.
Jocelyn Phillips, *Sir Prancelot and the Dragon,* Purnel, 1972.
J. Phillips, *Sir Prancelot and the Magic Machine,* Purnel, 1973.
Jennifer Vaughan, *Noah and the Flood,* Macdonald, 1973.
J. Vaughan, *Ali Baba,* Macdonald, 1973.
J. Phillips, *The Sir Prancelot Annual,* Purnel, 1974.
Diana Finley, *A Book of Sounds: A, B, C,* Macdonald, 1974, Raintree, 1979.
J. Vaughan, *Onia and the Animals,* Macdonald, 1974.
J. Vaughan, *The Pied Piper of Hamelin,* Macdonald, 1974.
J. Vaughan, *King Midas's Ears,* Macdonald, 1974.
The Little Red Hen, Macdonald, 1975.
D. Finley and S. Connell, *A Book of Sounds: ee, oo, ai,* Macdonald, 1975, Raintree, 1979.
D. Finley, *A Book of Sounds: sl, ch, pr,* Macdonald, 1975, Raintree, 1979.
Anne Toppina, *Formidable,* Edward Arnold, 1975.
Stephanie Connell, *A Book of Sounds: Blends and Ends,* Macdonald, 1976, Raintree, 1979.
Brian Read, *Wonder Why Book of Building a House,* Transworld, 1977.
Tony Allan, *Pharaohs and Pyramids,* Usborne, 1977.
R. E. Boyce, *The Gay Way,* (series of 7 books), Macmillan, 1977.
Kipper the Kitten, MacDonald, 1977.
B. Read, *Building a House,* Transworld, 1977, Silver- Burdett, 1987.
B. Read, *How Your House Works,* Transworld, 1977.
R. E. Boyce, *The Red Book,* Macmillan, 1978.
Peter Emmens, *Looking into English, Book 1,* Longmans, 1978.
P. Emmens, *Looking into English, Book 2,* Longmans, 1978.
Sing a Song, Book 1, Nelson, 1978.
Clare Gault and Frank Gault, *How to Be a Good Soccer Player,* Scholastic, 1978.
The Moose Is Loose, Scholastic, 1979.
This Is France, Transworld, 1981.
This Is the U.S.A., Transworld, 1981.
Jeremy Strong, *Lightning Lucy,* Blackie, 1982.
Looking into English, Collins, 1983.
J. Strong, *Money Doesn't Grow on Trees,* Blackie, 1984.
Witches of Halloween, Hodder & Stoughton, 1984.
Word Games: Books One and Two, Hodder & Stoughton, 1984.
Michael Bond and Karen Bond, *Paddington's Wheel Book,* D. C. Thomson, 1984, Macmillan, 1986.
J. Strong, *The Woff,* Blackie, 1985.
Two Times Teddy, David Booth, 1985.
M. Bond, *Paddington Bear,* Century/Hutchinson, 1986.
M. Bond and K. Bond, *Paddington at the Airport: An Activity Board Book,* Macmillan, 1986.
M. Bond and K. Bond, *Paddington Mails a Letter,* Macmillan, 1986.
M. Bond and K. Bond, *Paddington's Clock Book,* Macmillan, 1986.
Headway English IV, Collins Educational, 1986.
The Silver Skating Books, D. C. Thomson, 1986.
A Toy Shop Tale, D. C. Thomson, 1986.
The Tall Story of Wilbur Smith, Blackie, 1986.
Catherine Storr, *Find the Specs,* Belitha Press, 1986, Silver Burdett, 1987.
Gran Builds a House, Belitha Press, 1986.
C. Storr, *A Safe Move,* Belitha Press, 1986, published in the United States as *A Fast Move,* Silver-Burdett, 1987.
C. Storr, *Grandpa's Birthday,* Belitha Press, 1986, Silver-Burdett, 1987.
Sarah Hayes, *Clap Your Hands: Finger Rhymes,* Walker Books, 1986, Lothrop, 1988.
S. Hayes, *Stamp Your Feet: Action Rhymes,* Walker Books, 1986, Lothrop, 1988.
All Year Round: Summer, Macdonald, 1986.
All Year Round: Spring, Macdonald, 1986.
The School with the Troll, Hodder & Stoughton, 1986.
Beginning to Count, Octopus Books, 1986.
Duff Up at the Disco, Ward Lock Educational, 1986.
Skyways-Ghost-Hunters, Collins Educational, 1986.
Beginning to Count Workbook, Octopus Books, 1986.
Lightning Lucy Storms, A. & C. Black, 1986.
Ahead, A. & C. Black, 1986.
Penelope Lively, *Debbie and the Little Devil,* Heinemann, 1987.
Going Places, Oyster Books, 1987.
Word Work Book, Collins Educational, 1987.
Batty Adventures, BBC Enterprises, 1987.
The Same and Not the Same, Ginn, 1987.
How Do We Know?, Collins Educational, 1987.
Family Gathering, Dent, 1987.
The Little Lighthouse Keeper, Viking Kestrel, 1987.
The Little Military Horse, Ginn, 1987.
Connection Anthologies, Ginn, 1987.
Questron: A Day at the Zoo, PSS, 1987.
Martin Waddell, *Class Three and the Beanstalk,* Blackie, 1987.
The Digger, Macdonald, 1987.
My Friends Book, Geepap Oy, 1987.
Word Patterns, Collins Educational, 1987.
Playons Colouring: Aesop's Fables, Price, Stern, 1987.
Teach Your Child to Swim, Usborne, 1987.
What Can I Taste, Hodder & Stoughton, 1987.
What Can I Touch, Hodder & Stoughton, 1987.
What Can I See, Hodder & Stoughton, 1987.
What Can I Hear, Hodder & Stoughton, 1987.

(From *Stamp Your Feet: Action Rhymes* by Sarah Hayes. Illustrated by Toni Goffe.)

(From *Joe Giant's Missing Boot* by Toni Goffe. Illustrated by the author.)

Cat in the Custard, Hodder & Stoughton, 1987.
Leo Gale, *"Why Me?,"* Pendulum Gallery Press, 1987.
Felicity Henderson, *My Little Box of Prayers* (four books), Lion, 1988.
Ann Jungman, *The Day Teddy Didn't Clean Up,* Baron, 1989.
A. Jungman, *The Day Teddy Got Very Worried,* Baron, 1989.
A. Jungman, *The Day Teddy Made New Friends,* Baron, 1989.
A. Jungman, *The Day Teddy Wanted Grandpa to Notice Him,* Baron, 1989.
Constance A. Keremes, *I Wanted to Go to the Circus,* Harbinger, 1989.
Jim Aylesworth, *Mother Halverson's New Cat,* Macmillan, 1989.
Will Watkins, *Sid Seal, Houseman,* F. Watts, 1989.
Norma Jean Sawicki, *The Little Red House,* Lothrop, 1989.
Ian Whybrow, *The Sniff Stories,* Bodley Head, 1989.
Our Peculiar Neighbour, Dent, 1990.
Little Boy Soup, Ladybird, 1990.
Gertie's Gang, Viking Kestrel, 1990.
Sniff Bounces Back, Bodley Head, 1990.
My Little Christmas Box, Lion, 1990.
Adelaide's Naughty Granny, Heinemann, 1990.
Max and the Quiz Kids, Piccadilly, 1990.

Also illustrator of A. Toppina's, *Die Familie Neuman,* Macmillan; John Pudney's, *Living in a One- Sided House,* 1976; *Robert in Spain,* Edward Arnold; John Noakes', *The Flight of the Magic Clog,* and *Noakes at Large,* both Hamish Hamilton; *Stories for the Very Young;* and of series "Let's Read Together," Belitha Press, 1986, and "Owl," Hodder & Stoughton, 1987.

WORK IN PROGRESS: More books in the "Toby" series; "Mother Gooseville" series, based in a town full of nursery rhyme characters; writing and illustrating *Staying This Night at Granny's.*

SIDELIGHTS: "I was born in Southampton in 1936 on October 5th. My father worked on the Southampton docks, where he later expected me to work and was very surprised when I wouldn't." An only child, Goffe left to his own devices created imaginary friends. "I may have invented an older brother at some point."

The river which flowed near his childhood home provided many hours of amusement. "We made boats and played games defending little islands on the river. With the boats we made there was a great need to learn how to swim very quickly."

But most of all, Goffe remembers "drawing all the time. I used to copy photographs and Disney characters and book illustrations with varying successes." Neither of his parents was artistically oriented and did not view his talents as something to be nurtured.

Goffe's school years began during the war and unlike other children in England he was not evacuated. "I went to infant school in Ludlow, a three-mile walk. It was a bit hairy during air raids to have a three-mile run home because there were no shelters at the school. I will never forget the day I went home with a friend of mine who had taken a completely different route. My mother, who would always meet me, missed me. When I arrived home, I couldn't get into the house and she was left wandering around searching for me.

"Our house was bombed while we were in the shelter. It didn't actually land on the house, but the blast brought down many a ceiling. I was fascinated by the spectacle, thinking about how I

(From *Clap Your Hands: Finger Rhymes* by Sarah Hayes. Illustrated by Toni Goffe.)

must get up on the roof to have a look around.'' The family lived among the rubble of the fallen ceiling until it was rebuilt.

''The war was terrifically exciting. We would watch the dogfights between the Spitfires and the Messerschmidts. We weren't frightened at all; it was good fun, especially going into the shelter at night and camp down with my mother and father and sometimes neighbors and other children.''

Goffe would rush home from school to listen to the ''Children's Hour'' on the radio. ''It was absolutely riveting—the plays, the stories, the competitions, the characters, the readings from *Wind in the Willow*, and *Winnie the Pooh*. Norman Shelley was the best 'Pooh' I've ever heard.''

School was often disrupted by the war and a variety of childhood diseases—whooping cough, mumps, and diptheria—causing him to fail the ''eleven plus'' examination which would promote him to the next level in his education. He had another try at it the following year and passed to attend Merryoaks, an all boys school. From there he went to Bittern Park. He was thirteen years old by this time and hoped to pursue a career in art. ''My father wouldn't let me go to an art school. He held fast to the idea that a general education would serve me better, and the argument made sense at the time. 'You can do art later if you really want,' was his reasoning.

''He bought me a whole set of tools and wanted me to become an engineer or an electrician and work on the docks much as he had always done. He used to get jobs for me down there. It was terrible.

''When I left school, I left a bit early. I was getting expelled and didn't know what to do next. Perhaps I could go to the school that concentrated on art, I thought. But I realized that I was too old to do that. So the next alternative was art college.

''I went with a bundle of drawings which were pretty awful at that stage—watercolors and gouache of bowls of flowers and a piano. There were jazz drawings because I was getting interested in music. I showed them my drawings and they said, 'Yes. Start next September.'

''At the time I had no idea you could earn a living with art. I just knew that that was the direction I wanted to go. I wasn't encouraged by my parents. As a matter of fact, I was discouraged by my father.''

Art school was a terrific experience for Goffe from a social point of view. The teaching, however, was ''bloody awful. We were left on our own too much. Art schools did not prepare the student for earning a living. They didn't even guide us.''

It was during this time that his interest in music and jazz, in particular, flourished. Many of his friends and associates were musicians and he began playing in bands. ''I had no idea what I was doing. No idea at all. I don't think I have a very good ear, but I could hear what key the whole thing was in.

''I had to have a bass. For some reason it was the perfect instrument for me. My mother found one in the paper that was being advertised for twenty-five pounds. My father went crazy. I already had a piano and an organ. He was always trying to get rid of them because they were too big for our small bungalow.''

After four years of college, Goffe received his diploma in art and design in 1956. ''I couldn't draw very well after college. They didn't put much emphasis on drawing. The next big problem for me was the National Service.''

Sent to Blackdown, he began his stint in the army. ''I enjoyed it for the first three weeks—meeting all those very strange guys from all over the country was an education. Once the excitement of the first three weeks wears thin, they stick you into some job. Mine was teaching people how to drive. I made films for the learner drivers and did all the drawings of how to drive. I built a room in the corner of greatcoats (a room in which greatcoats were stored for the summer) and called it my studio.

''I was also sending cartoons to *Jazz Journal*. I did ten headings for them for which I was paid sixteen pounds. At first I thought they were paying sixteen pounds for each heading—my first brush with commercialism. It was exciting to have my first work published.

''I also drew for *Soldier* magazine. When I sold a cartoon to them, the acceptance came in an official-looking War Office envelope with forms in triplicate which was rushed down to me. I would never tell anyone what they were for. They thought I was working for MI5 and was well treated because of that.''

Goffe soon realized, however, that it was going to be a long two years of sitting in army camps. After seven months he received a medical discharge. ''I'd injured my back at judo and I couldn't stand for long periods of time. Trying to tell someone in the army that your back hurts is like talking to a brick wall.''

After his discharge, he immediately headed for London, where the action was, and landed a job in advertising, earning six pounds a week. ''I could hardly afford a room. I didn't know anything about feeding myself. My mother's suggestion was to go to restaurants. She had no idea how little money I was earning. I got into a terrible state of health and suffered malnutrition.''

The job with the agency lasted six months at which point he was sacked. It seemed a friend had introduced him to lunchtime drinking. ''We used to get going on these 'stingos' at lunch and come back to cause absolute havoc. I'm surprised we lasted as long as we did.

''I started joining bands then and became a musician. That was my primary source of income for the next ten years. But all this time I was drawing during the day and trying to sell my work. I was sending out fifty cartoons a week to all the magazines. I'd start at the top—*Punch*—and when they came back, would send them to the next one. It was a complicated list and went all the way down to *She*, which paid the worst. I was lucky to sell two or three a week.''

Goffe described this time in his life as a ''Ten Year Party.'' ''As I became better known I played with better bands and played more regularly with such bands as Bruce Turner, Al Fairweather, and Sandy Brown. I once played for Grace Cole's All Girls' Orchestra. I spelled my name Toni [while doing a leaderhead once, he discovered that the 'y' was missing and substituted the 'i'], which is the feminine version of Tony. I toured with All Girls' Orchestra and was asked if I'd dress in drag. I didn't, but I had a lot of fun.''

Goffe had met his wife at art school in Southampton, but did not marry her until the end of the ''Ten Year Party.'' Their first son, Tim, was born in 1960. It was time to earn a living in earnest and Goffe found himself wrestling with the decision ''shall I be a musician or shall I be an artist?'' The artist won.

''We bought a house down in Hampshire because it was near both sets of parents and near London as well. I did two pages a

Goffe in his studio, 1989. (Photograph by Cathy Courtney.)

week for a magazine called *Finding Out* and had regular money coming in.

"We moved to Hedley and our second son Tobin was born. I was hanging around the house a great deal of the time and saw a lot of my children. I told them stories. Tobin became very interested in animals and we made up this story about him caring for animals in danger." *Toby's Animal Rescue Service* was the result.

"This book was yet another downfall. It was the first book I wrote in a series of six which I had planned for Hamish Hamilton. It took years of plodding. I put three solid years of work into the job and did a lot of free work for publicity." Eventually, after much effort, the book was published. "But the publishers failed to publicize my book and it went down the tube."

With a new agent, Goffe was commissioned to illustrate more children's books. "Some of the stories you read are abysmal. You're putting all the skills you've developed over the years into these stories to try to make them good, and they are good because of your drawings. If the stories are awful, it reflects on you as well as the author. So I decided that I should write my own stuff." An admirable ambition for one who suffers with dyslexia. "I put the first letter of the next word on the end of the last word and things like that. The writing can be quite difficult to read after a while."

In 1980 he embarked on trip to the United States to visit an artist friend. The two started a gallery in Boston, selling the works of other artists as well as a few pieces of their own.

"In the final analysis I find England more conducive to work than America. The landscape means a lot to me. One of the main reasons I came back was because I missed the English countryside. It's quieter here with fewer distractions. America makes you want to be on the move, which is great in its proper time and place in your life. But as I get older I have less energy, and I don't want it dissipated."

When he returned to England, he went back to his agent who advised him to "just do some drawings and see what happens." "I was drawing in a completely different style—less cartoony and more thoughtful. I was still very interested in humor as a way of communicating and use it in my writing rather than my drawings. It seems to work better. It's a new depth."

The new depth is demonstrated in some his recent publications. One is a combination of stories called *Stories for the Very Young*, another, *I Wanted to Go to the Circus* for which Goffe did the illustrations only, is about a little boy who wanted to go to the circus but was taken to the ballet instead. And although he thought it was awful at the beginning, he was very excited about the ballet at the end. *Mother Halverson's New Cat,* written by Jim Aylesworth, is a story about a farmer's wife whose cat has just died and she wants another to take its place. The farmer had four cats in the barn and ûsed his ingenuity to pick the best one. The story examines the process of how he goes about picking the cat.

Getting together with the author of the book for which he is executing illustrations is more of a hindrance than help, claims Goffe. He reads the story and depends on his first visual impressions. "What happens if you read it over and over again, you may be drawing as you get ideas and as you go into it more and more the whole idea may change."

The number of drawings for a book is usually determined by the publishers, depending on whether they elect full color, black and white, or half and half. "Usually it's left up to me to decide what to illustrate. Roughs are sent in and OK'd by the author. Then drawn to finish."

Goffe maintains a nine-to-five working schedule—thinking in the morning, drawing in the afternoon. His visual memory is acute. If it fails him, however, he researches by "going to take a look."

Although he tries not to put real people into his painting, "I'm heavily influenced by people around me. My family appears. Jill is always the mother figure. In *Toby's Animal Rescue Service,* Tobin was the principal character, Tim his uncle, and I the villain. A lot of my musician friends were in my 'gang.'"

When working on his own books the ideas come first. "I don't know the process exactly. For instance, the ideas for the series that I'm working on now came to me while I was in America and it's been bubbling for a year. I've been writing it in my head ever since. Traveling is very stimulating because I'm relaxed and that opens me up to seeing things.

"I find that I have to do text and drawings together. I rough out thumb nail sketches of the action on each double page, and try to resolve it so it makes for a good ending and the whole thing flows and works. I write and draw as I go, always thinking visually of how it should look. You've got to be careful that you're not describing what is happening in the picture.

"I'm reading more children's books than I did before to get a better feeling of what they're like. I use terrible cliches and the word 'just' too often. There are always editors around, however. But you have to watch them so that they don't change the whole book around and lose your style of writing."

Goffe is presently busier than ever with his books. "I've got about ten books in my head at the moment and haven't been able to write them—all children's books." His interest in music is never far behind. "I'm on the local jazz scene and play locally. Jazz is very practical and realistic, very down to earth. When you're playing in a band, people tend to ignore you, giving the players an excellent vantage point for observing people more intimately."

Goffe also enjoys judo and scuba diving. "I am a third degree black belt at judo and have instructed at the Budokawi in London. After moving to Hampshire I started my own judo club. I enjoy sub aqua (scuba) diving and am a second class diver. My favorite dives are the Red Sea and Bermuda."[1]

FOOTNOTE SOURCES

[1]Based on an interview by Cathy Courtney for *Something about the Author*.

GREENBERG, Jan 1942-

PERSONAL: Born December 29, 1942, in St. Louis, Mo.; daughter of Alexander (a manufacturer) and Lillian (an advertising executive; maiden name, Rubenstein) Schonwald; married Ronald Greenberg (an art dealer), August 31, 1963; children: Lynne, Jeanne, Jacqueline. *Education:* Washington University, B.A., 1964, Webster University, M.A.T., 1971. *Home and office:* 3 Brentmoor Park, St. Louis, Mo. 63105.

CAREER: St. Louis Public Schools, St. Louis, Mo., teacher, 1969-72; Forest Park Community College, St. Louis, instructor of English composition, 1973-75; Webster University, St. Louis, director and instructor of aesthetic education, masters degree program, 1974-79, instructor, 1989—; *St. Louis Post-Dispatch,* St. Louis, book reviewer, 1975-80; CEMREL (National Education Laboratory), St. Louis, researcher, 1976-78; free-lance writer, 1978—. Has presented speeches and workshops in aesthetic education and on writing books for young readers. Missouri Arts Council, literature committee, 1984—; Big River Association, board of directors, 1985; member of Daniel Webster Society Board, Webster University. *Member:* PEN, Society of Children's Book Writers. *Awards, honors: No Dragons to Slay* was selected one of American Library Association's Best Books for Young Adults, 1984; Webster University Distinguished Alumni Award, 1986.

WRITINGS:

NOVELS FOR YOUNG READERS

A Season in-Between, Farrar, Straus, 1979.
The Iceberg and Its Shadow, Farrar, Straus, 1980.
The Pig-Out Blues, Farrar, Straus, 1982.
No Dragons to Slay, Farrar, Straus, 1983.
Bye, Bye Miss American Pie, Farrar, Straus, 1985.
Exercises of the Heart, Farrar, Straus, 1986.
Just the Two of Us, Farrar, Straus, 1988.

WORK IN PROGRESS: Let's Look: Introduction to Contemporary American Painting.

JAN GREENBERG

SIDELIGHTS: Jan Greenberg was born in St. Louis, Missouri in 1942 and grew up loving to read. "My parents' library was filled with an assortment of books ranging from Plato's *Dialogues* to *Gone with the Wind*. It was there in that cozy room with a fireplace that I developed my eclectic tastes in literature."

When Greenberg was ten, she began writing a journal. Even now she finds it helpful to jot down some of her thoughts during the day. "All the characters in my books represent some part of my own personality, and they often surprise me by behaving in ways I never suspected. I learn about myself through writing.

"In the early seventies my husband and I began collecting contemporary American art. Soon our rambling house was filled with bright canvases, the yard with large steel sculpture." Later, the Greenbergs opened an art gallery which has now become a center for young American artists and musicians. "The energy and excitement engendered by my contact with other artists inspired me to write and develop my own creative skills.

"I am a storyteller. I write books with a beginning, a middle, and an end. I agree with Virginia Woolf that the 'proper stuff of fiction' does not exist. 'Everything is the proper stuff of fiction.' In my case, that content was revealed in the voice of a teenager during a difficult time of her life. That voice was my own. When I write, I see the streets of my childhood—the long treelined sidewalk on Buckingham Drive. I hear the voices of my mother and aunt calling me and my cousins in for dinner. I smell the wisteria growing near our white picket fence. I use autobiographical material, but that doesn't mean that I'm attempting to recreate a situation exactly as it happened. The advantage to writing fiction is that you can exaggerate, embellish, and expand on a real experience. For example, when I was a young girl growing up in St. Louis, I had a terrible crush on the boy next door. He never paid a bit of attention to me. But in my first novel, *A Season in-Between,* guess who ends up with the boy next door? In terms of truth telling, the only thing I'm willing to grant is that I'm attempting to present an honest expression of a human emotion. We all have a primal urge to be remembered, not to let our lives pass unmarked. I write when I'm haunted by a plot that I must write out of an inner necessity.

"My work has been stimulated by the ever-present concerns I have as a mother and a participant observer in a strong family life. My books deal with domestic issues: illness or death in a family, sibling rivalry, or problems with friends or parents. I'm not drawn to the more sensational aspects of teenage life—sex, drugs, abuse, etc.—mainly because they're out of the range of my experience. I'm writing about ordinary boys and girls who are experiencing ordinary, day to day problems growing up in a complex society. I am writing to cheer them on, to say, 'Yes, sometimes it's hard. But keep trying. Keep up the good work!'

"Most of my stories take place in the Midwest. But unlike Mark Twain's *Huckleberry Finn*, which relies on the Missouri landscape, my books could take place in suburbia almost anywhere in America. Whenever a student raises his hand at one of my talks and says, 'Mrs Greenberg why don't you write science fiction?,' I console myself that my favorite authors, Jane Austen, Emily Dickinson, and Virginia Woolf, also wrote domestic novels. So I'm in good company. The only difference between these three writers and me, aside from obvious stylistic considerations, is that they didn't have three daughters to raise. That prompts me to tell you that I'm not writing about tidy, perfect children who behave like the Brady Bunch. I fall more into the Dennis the Menace category. Many people have asked me what kind of a miserable childhood did I have to invent such weird and cranky characters. The truth is that my childhood wasn't unusually miserable at all. Yes, I had eye allergies and boy troubles. I was too tall, I thought my parents too strict, my teachers unfair, but then these complaints and a host of new ones cropped up in regular cycles with my own daughters as well. Perhaps this is why I started writing about teenagers in the first place.

"The fact is that trauma is the business of adolescence, and along with these traumas, large or small, come negative feelings. And yet, always the eternal optimist, I'd rather have my characters walk out of a snowstorm than into one at the end of a novel.

"Sometimes, however, I get trouble from my daughters, who tell me I'm stealing their material. That's what happens, I tell them, when you have a mother who's a writer. So the stories continue, and until those teenage voices cease bubbling in the back of my head like a pot ready to boil over, I will continue writing for young people."

For Jan Greenberg writing is a process of discovery. Her novels focus on the development of characters who face problems. "After my first novel, *A Season in-Between*—which is the story of a thirteen-year-old girl who, in the throes of a difficult adolescence, must face the illness and death of her father—some people told me how courageous I was to admit weakness and negative feelings in print. But writing is an act of sharing. A book is never a total figment of the imagination. It begins as a stomach ache, a slight quiver of discomfort. It's like falling in or out of love. If the feeling is strong enough, a book may evolve. Or maybe not. But when something happens and a year later I'm holding a new novel in my hand, I want to jump up and down, throw confetti, and stop everyone on the street and say, 'Look what I've done.'"

HOBBIES AND OTHER INTERESTS: Skiing, jogging, drawing, playing with bulldog, Jasper.

GREENFIELD, Eloise 1929-

PERSONAL: Born May 17, 1929, in Parmele, N.C.; daughter of Weston W. (a truck driver) and Lessie (a clerk-typist and writer; maiden name, Jones) Little; married Robert J. Greenfield (a procurement specialist), April 29, 1950 (separated); children: Steven, Monica. *Education:* Attended Miner Teachers College (now University of the District of Columbia), 1947-49. *Agent:* Marie Brown, Marie Brown Associates, 412 West 154th St., New York, N.Y. 10032. *Office:* Honey Productions, Inc., P.O. Box 29077, Washington, D.C. 20017.

CAREER: U.S. Patent Office, Washington, D.C., clerk-typist, 1949-56, supervisory patent assistant, 1956-60; worked as a secretary, case-control technician, and an administrative assistant in Washington, D.C., 1964-68. District of Columbia Commission on the Arts and Humanities, writer-in-residence, 1973, 1985-87. Participant in numerous school and library programs and workshops for children and adults. *Member:* District of Columbia Black Writers' Workshop (co-director of adult fiction, 1971-73, director of children's literature, 1973-74), African American Writers Guild, Authors Guild.

AWARDS, HONORS: Carter G. Woodson Book Award from the National Council for Social Studies, 1974, for *Rosa Parks;* Irma Simonton Black Award from Bank Street College of Education, 1974, for *She Come Bringing Me That Little Baby Girl; Sister* was selected one of *New York Times* Outstanding Books of the Year, 1974; *She Come Bringing Me That Little Baby Girl,* and *Sister* were each selected one of Child Study Association of

ELOISE GREENFIELD

America's Children's Books of the Year, 1974, *Me and Neesie,* 1975, *First Pink Light,* 1976, *Honey, I Love and Other Poems,* 1978, and *I Can Do It by Myself,* 1979.

Paul Robeson was selected a Notable Children's Trade Book in the Field of Social Studies by the National Council for Social Studies and the Children's Book Council, 1975, *Childtimes,* 1980, and *Alesia,* 1982; Citation from the Council on Interracial Books for Children, 1975, Citation from the District of Columbia Association of School Librarians, 1977, National Black Child Development Institute Award, 1981, and Mills College Award, 1983, all for body of work; Jane Addams Children's Book Award from the Jane Addams Peace Association and the Women's International League for Peace and Freedom, and Coretta Scott King Award Honor Book from the American Library Association, both 1976, both for *Paul Robeson;* Coretta Scott King Award, 1978, for *Africa Dream;* Classroom Choice Book Citation from the International Reading Association and the Children's Book Council, 1978, for *Honey, I Love and Other Poems.*

Boston Globe-Horn Book Award Nonfiction Honor Book, and Carter G. Woodson Book Award for Outstanding Merit, both 1980, and one of New York Public Library's Books for the Teen Age, 1980, 1981, all for *Childtimes;* Washington, D.C. Mayor's Art Award in Literature, 1983; *Grandpa's Face* was selected one of *School Library Journal*'s Best Books, 1988; Parents' Choice Silver Seal Award from the Parents' Choice Foundation, 1988, for *Under the Sunday Tree;* Coretta Scott King Award Honor Book, 1990, for *Nathaniel Talking.*

WRITINGS:

Sister (novel; illustrated by Moneta Barnett), Crowell, 1974.

Honey, I Love and Other Poems (ALA Notable Book; "Reading Rainbow" selection; illustrated by Diane Dillon and Leo Dillon), Crowell, 1978.

Talk about a Family (novel; Junior Literary Guild selection; illustrated by James Calvin), Lippincott, 1978.

Nathaniel Talking (poems; illustrated by Jan S. Gilchrist), Writers and Readers, 1989.

PICTURE BOOKS

Bubbles (illustrated by Eric Marlow), Drum & Spear, 1972, published as *Good News* (illustrated by Pat Cummings), Coward, 1977.

She Come Bringing Me That Little Baby Girl (ALA Notable Book; *Horn Book* honor list; illustrated by John Steptoe), Lippincott, 1974.

Me and Neesie (ALA Notable Book; illustrated by M. Barnett), Crowell, 1975.

First Pink Light (illustrated by M. Barnett), Crowell, 1976.

Africa Dream (illustrated by Carole Byard), John Day, 1977.

(With mother, Lessie Jones Little) *I Can Do It by Myself* (illustrated by C. Byard), Crowell, 1978.

Darlene (illustrated by George Ford), Methuen, 1980.

Grandmama's Joy (illustrated by C. Byard), Collins, 1980.

Daydreamers (ALA Notable Book; "Reading Rainbow" selection; illustrated by Tom Feelings), Dial, 1981.

Grandpa's Face (ALA Notable Book; illustrated by Floyd Cooper), Philomel, 1988.

Under the Sunday Tree (ALA Notable Book; illustrated by Amos Ferguson), Harper, 1988.

BIOGRAPHIES

Rosa Parks (ALA Notable Book; illustrated by E. Marlow), Crowell, 1973.

Paul Robeson (illustrated by G. Ford), Crowell, 1975.

Mary McLeod Bethune (illustrated by Jerry Pinkney), Crowell, 1977.

(With L. J. Little) *Childtimes: A Three-Generation Memoir* (autobiography; illustrated by J. Pinkney), Crowell, 1979.

(With Alesia Revis) *Alesia* (illustrated by G. Ford, and with photographs by Sandra Turner Bond), Philomel, 1981.

CONTRIBUTOR TO ANTHOLOGIES

Alma Murray and Robert Thomas, editors, *The Journey: Scholastic Black Literature,* Scholastic Book Services, 1970.

Karen S. Kleiman and Mel Cebulash, editors, *Double Action Short Stories,* Scholastic Book Services, 1973.

Joseph Claro and Katherine Robinson, *Love,* Scholastic Book Services, 1975.

William K. Durr, John Pescosolido and Willie Mae Poetter, *Encore* (textbook), Houghton, 1978.

Louise Matteoni and others, *Daystreaming,* Economy, 1978.

L. Matteoni and others, *Forerunners,* Economy, 1978.

Zena Sutherland, *Burning Bright,* Open Court, 1979.

Child Study Children's Book Committee at Bank Street College of Education, *Friends Are Like That,* Crowell, 1979.

Betsy Feist, Kate Wilson, and Louise E. May, editors, *Language Activity Kit: Teachers' Edition,* Harcourt, 1979.

Carol Steben, *Building Reading Skills,* McDougal, Littell, 1980.

Gloria Paulik Sampson, *New Routes to English: Book 5,* Collier, 1980.

G. P. Sampson, *New Routes to English: Advanced Skills One,* Collier, 1980.

Jumping Up, Lippincott, 1981.

William K. Durr and others, *Emblems,* Houghton, 1981.

Dorothy Strickland, *Listen, Children,* Bantam, 1982.

Bonus Book, Gateways, Level K, Houghton, 1983.

Joanna Cole, *New Treasury of Children's Poetry,* Doubleday, 1984.

Z. Sutherland and Myra Cohn Livingston, *Scott, Foresman Anthology of Children's Literature,* Scott, Foresman, 1984.

Contributor to *World Book Encyclopedia;* author of 1979 bookmark poem for Children's Book Council. Also contributor to periodicals, including *Black World, Cricket, Ebony, Jr.!,*

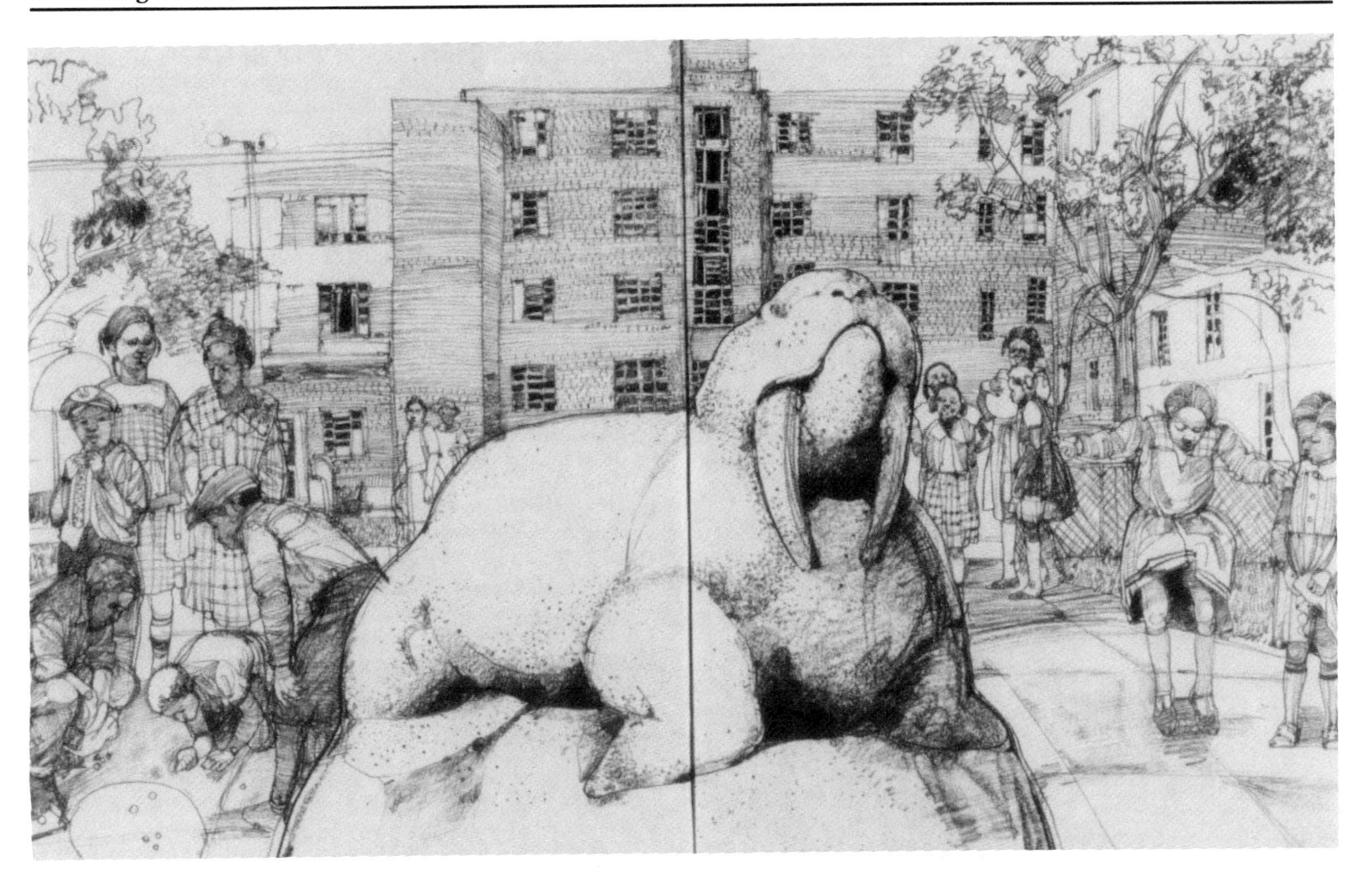

There were so many games to play and things to do. (From *Childtimes: A Three-Generation Memoir* by Eloise Greenfield and Lessie Jones Little. Illustrated by Jerry Pinkney. Photographs from the authors' family albums.)

Horn Book, Negro Digest, Interracial Books for Children Bulletin, Ms., Negro History Bulletin, Scholastic Scope, and *Washington Post.*

ADAPTATIONS:

"Honey, I Love" (record; cassette), Honey Productions, 1982.

WORK IN PROGRESS: A novel for children aged eight to eleven.

SIDELIGHTS: Eloise Greenfield was born on **May 17, 1929,** in Parmele, North Carolina. "Mama wasn't expecting me until the end of the month, but I fooled her—I was ready to see the world on the seventeenth of May. Daddy was downtown playing checkers in front of Mr. Slim Gordon's store, and Mama wanted to wait until he came home, but his mother told her, 'That young'un ain't going to wait for nobody! I'm going to get Mrs. Mayo now!'

"I was born at six o'clock that evening. My great-aunt Mary was there to welcome me, and both of my grandmothers, Williamann Little and Pattie Ridley Jones. My brother Wilbur was there, too, but he didn't think my arrival was anything to get excited about.

"When Daddy came home, I was all of half an hour old, and did I give him a surprise!

"In the spring of 1926, Daddy had graduated from high school, Parmele Training School. He had been offered a scholarship by Knoxville College in Tennessee, but he hadn't taken it. He and Mama had gotten married that fall, and now they had Wilbur and me to take care of. Mama had been teaching school since her graduation from Higgs, but she had decided to stop.

"When I was three months old, Daddy left home to make a way for us. He went North, as thousands of black people had done, during slavery and since. They went North looking for safety, for justice, for freedom, for work, looking for a good life. Often one member of a family would go ahead of the others to make a way—to find a job and a place to live. And that's what my father did.

"Nineteen twenty-nine was a bad time for Daddy to go away, but a worse time for him not to go. The Great Depression was about to begin, had already begun for many people. All over the United States, thousands of people were already jobless and homeless.

"In Parmele, there were few permanent jobs. Some seasons of the year, Daddy could get farm work, harvesting potatoes and working in the tobacco fields. Every year, from August to around Thanksgiving, he worked ten hours a day for twenty-five cents an hour at a tobacco warehouse in a nearby town, packing tobacco in huge barrels and loading them on the train for shipping. And he and his father were house movers. Whenever somebody wanted a house moved from one place to another, Daddy and Pa would jack it up and attach it to a windlass, the machine that the horse would turn to move the house. But it was only once in a while that they were called on to do that.

"So, one morning in **August, 1929,** Mama went with Daddy to the train station and tried to hold back her tears as the Atlantic Coast Line train pulled out, taking him toward Washington, D.C. Then she went home, sat in the porch swing, and cried.

"In Washington, friends helped Daddy find a room for himself and his family to live in, and took him job hunting. He found a job as a dishwasher in a restaurant, and in a few weeks, he had saved enough money for our train fare.

"Mama brought Wilbur and me to our new home on a Saturday night. Two days later, Daddy was out of a job. The restaurant manager had tricked him. He hadn't told Daddy that he was being hired just until the regular dishwasher came back from vacation.

"Daddy's next job lasted only two months. Then, finally, he found one at a Peoples Drug Store, making deliveries on a bicycle and cleaning the store. So we were in Washington to stay. Daddy worked at the drugstore for several years, and whenever they put a new display in the window, he would bring home the material from the old one, and Mama would dye it and make dresses and slips for herself and for me.

"I'm three years old, sitting on the floor with Mama. Cutting out a picture for my scrapbook, a picture of a loaf of bread. Cutting it out and pasting it in my book with the flour- and-water paste I had helped to make.

Nobody had ever told her that being picked for a leaf to rest on was good luck. She just knew it. (From *Talk about a Family* by Eloise Greenfield. Illustrated by James Calvin.)

"As far as I know, that was the day my life began.

"My school life began two years later. Mama walked my cousin Vilma and me down P Street, through the open doors of John F. Cook School, and into Mrs. Staley's kindergarten class. Vilma and I were both scared. I was scared quiet; she was scared loud. I sat squeezed up in my chair, and Vilma screamed.

"When I was in the fifth grade, I was famous for a whole day, and all because of a play. The teacher had given me a big part, and I didn't want it. I liked to be in plays where I could be part of a group, like being one of the talking trees, or dancing, or singing in the glee club. But having to talk by myself—*uh uh!*

"I used to slide down in my chair and stare at my desk while the teacher was giving out the parts, so she wouldn't pay any attention to me, but this time it didn't work. She called on me anyway. I told her I didn't want to do it, but she said I had to. I guess she thought it would be good for me.

"On the day of the play, I didn't make any mistakes. I remembered all of my lines. Only—nobody in the audience heard me. I couldn't make my voice come out loud.

"For the rest of the day, I was famous. Children passing by my classroom door, children on the playground at lunchtime, kept pointing at me saying, 'That's that girl! That's the one who didn't talk loud enough!'

"I felt so bad, I wanted to go home. But one good thing came out of it all. The teacher was so angry, so upset, she told me that as long as I was in that school, I'd never have another chance to ruin one of her plays. And that was such good news, I could stand being famous for a day."[1]

When Greenfield was nine years old, her family moved into a new housing project at 21st Street and Benning Road, in Northeast Washington. It was one of the nation's first public housing projects. "I fell in love with Langston Terrace the very first time I saw it. Our family had been living in two rooms of a three-story house when Mama and Daddy saw the newspaper article telling of the plans to build it. It was going to be a low-rent housing project in northeast Washington, and it would be named in honor of John Mercer Langston, the famous black lawyer, educator, and congressman.

"So many people needed housing and wanted to live there, many more than there would be room for. They were all filling out applications, hoping to be one of the 274 families chosen. My parents filled out one, too.

"I didn't want to move. I knew our house was crowded— there were eleven of us, six adults and five children [and sister, Vedie, born in 1939]—but I didn't want to leave my friends, and I didn't want to go to a strange place and be the new person in a neighborhood and a school where most of the other children already knew each other. I was eight years old, and I had been to three schools. We had moved five times since we'd been in Washington, each time trying to get more space and a better place to live. But rent was high so we'd always lived in a house with relatives and friends, and shared the rent.

"Finally, one evening, a woman came to the house with our good news, and Mama and Daddy went over and picked out the house they wanted. We moved on my ninth birthday. Wilbur, Gerald, and I went to school that morning from one house, and when Daddy came to pick us up, he took us home to another one. All the furniture had been moved while we were in school.

(From *Africa Dream* by Eloise Greenfield. Illustrated by Carole Byard.)

"Langston Terrace was a lovely birthday present. It was built on a hill, a group of tan brick houses and apartments with a playground as its center. The red mud surrounding the concrete walks had not yet been covered with black soil and grass seed, and the holes that would soon be homes for young trees were filled with rainwater. But it still looked beautiful to me.

"We had a whole house all to ourselves. Upstairs and downstairs. Two bedrooms, and the living room would be my bedroom at night. Best of all, I wasn't the only new person. Everybody was new to this new little community, and by the time school opened in the fall, we had gotten used to each other and had made friends with other children in the neighborhood, too.

"I guess most of the parents thought of the new place as an in-between place. They were glad to be there, but their dream was to save enough money to pay for a house that would be their own. Saving was hard, though, and slow, because each time somebody in a family got a raise on the job, it had to be reported to the manager of the project so that the rent could be raised, too. Most people stayed years longer than they had planned to, but they didn't let that stop them from enjoying life.

"They formed a resident council to look into any neighborhood problems that might come up. They started a choral group and presented music and poetry programs on Sunday evenings in the social room or on the playground. On weekends, they played horseshoes and softball and other games. They had a reading club that met once a week at the Langston branch of the public library, after it opened in the basement of one of the apartment buildings.

"The library was very close to my house. I could leave by my back door and be there in two minutes.

"There were so many games to play and things to do. We played hide-and-seek at the lamppost, paddle tennis and shuffleboard, dodge ball and jacks. We danced in fireplug showers, jumped rope to rhymes, played 'Bouncy, Bouncy, Bally,' swinging one leg over a bouncing ball, played baseball on a nearby field, had parties in the social room and bus trips to the beach. In the playroom, we played Ping-Pong and pool, learned to sew and embroider and crochet.

"For us, Langston Terrace wasn't an in-between place. It was a growing-up place, a good growing-up place. Neighbors who cared, family and friends, and a lot of fun. Life was good. Not perfect, but good. We knew about problems, heard about them, saw them, lived through some hard ones ourselves, but our community wrapped itself around us, put itself between us and the hard knocks, to cushion the blows."[1]

One of the persistent problems was racism. "Almost every summer, the police would drag nearby Kingman Lake—we called it a river—and bring up the body of a boy who had drowned. He would be a black boy, most likely from some part of northeast Washington. He would be a boy for whom fireplug showers were not enough. And because he wanted to swim, he would have died in the filthy water of Kingman Lake.

"The boy could have gone to a pool and been watched over by lifeguards. Of course, he couldn't have gone to Rosedale pool, right down the street, or to most of the pools in my city— they were for white children only. But if he had the streetcar fare, or if he felt like walking thirty or more blocks each way, he could have stood in a line three blocks long at one of the few black pools and hoped that enough children would get tired of the water and leave, so that he could take his turn before closing time.

"But he hadn't wanted to do that. So he swam in the lake, and he died.

"On the streetcars, we could sit anywhere, but we couldn't sit down at the drugstore soda fountains. We could shop downtown, but we might have to stand at the counter while the saleswoman waited on all the whites first, even if they had come in last, or we might not get waited on at all. The schools were segregated. The white newspapers carried only bits of news about black people, none of it good. The newspaper ads for all the best jobs said, 'White Only.' And if a 'For Rent' sign in front of a house didn't say 'Colored,' black people could forget it.

"There were a lot of things we couldn't do and places we couldn't go. Washington was a city for white people. But inside that city, there was another city. It didn't have a name and it wasn't all in one area, but it was where black people lived.

She was my best friend. (From *Me and Neesie* by Eloise Greenfield. Illustrated by Moneta Barnett.)

The pedal on our school piano squeaks. (From *Honey, I Love and Other Poems* by Eloise Greenfield. Illustrated by Diane and Leo Dillon.)

"As with all places, there were both good and bad things about our city within a city. We had all the problems that the other Washington had, plus the problems caused by racism. Some people tried to drink their problems away. Some took their anger at racism out on each other. But most did what they could to help their friends and neighbors and relatives, and many got together to work for black freedom. There was always, in my Washington, a sense of people trying to make things better."[1]

Meanwhile, Greenfield lived the life of a typical teenager, studying the piano and singing in a group called the Langston Harmonettes. "[Music] has always been part of our lives. It's so much a part of me that if you could somehow subtract it from who I am, I would be a stranger to myself. I wouldn't know how to act. Spirituals, gospel, blues, rhythm-and-blues, jazz. Black music.

"At church, the choir would sing the gospel, or take a white hymn and bend it black. And the male quartet at Grandma's church would stomp and shout in harmony, looking hard at something in the air, straining the veins in their necks, until people here and there in the room got the Holy Ghost and did their shout-dances, even Grandma, a prim shouter, jumping up and down in one spot.

"We sang spirituals in the glee club at school, and danced to black music on records, and I don't think we could have fallen in love if Billie Holiday hadn't sung 'Lover Man' in that sad, lonely way.

"I don't know how many hours, all together, I spent at the Howard Theater where the great musicians came to play. I could never see a show just once, I'd have to stay there and see it at least one more time. We called it 'bucking the show.' My cousin Vilma and I bucked the show three times one Saturday, went to the one o'clock afternoon show and didn't get home until ten that night. Mama was waiting at the bus stop, worried to death, when we got off the bus. We just couldn't leave that music."[1]

On visits to her grandparents, Greenfield was reminded of what it meant to be Black in the South. "It was an eight-hour trip to Norfolk, Virginia, where we always went first. Grandma Pattie Ridley Jones and Grandpa had moved there by that time, and we'd spend about a week with them, then go on to Parmele for another week.

"One thing that we saw on the road frightened me. Chain gangs. We saw them often, the lines of black men in their black-and-white-striped jail suits, chained by their ankles and watched over, as they repaired the roads, by white men with guns.

"I wasn't afraid of the men, and I didn't think about maybe getting shot. But for a reason I didn't understand, I was afraid of the whole thing. Those bent-over striped backs, the sharp points of the picks the men swung, the sound of the picks hitting the concrete, the sight of men with long guns, pacing. It scared me.

"Something happened to me one day in Norfolk that I won't ever forget. I was about twelve, and I was taking my first bus ride alone there. I can't remember where I was going, maybe to visit one of my cousins, but I remember what happened. The bus was crowded, so I got on and paid and stood next to the people who had gotten on in front of me, the way I would have done at home. But a drunk man sitting on the long side seat near the driver got very angry. He said, 'You better get on back in the back where you belong!' I had forgotten that in Norfolk black people couldn't sit or stand in the front of the bus.

"The people close by heard the man say it and they looked embarrassed, but they didn't say anything, so I squeezed through the crowd to get to the back, and then I just stared out the window. I hated that drunk man and I hated those people for looking embarrassed. I felt as if everybody knew what had happened and I didn't know what look to put on my face. I was so glad when I got to my stop and I could get off the bus.

"That was a terrible thing that happened, but it didn't ruin Norfolk for me. With so many relatives living there, every time we went, it was like a family reunion."[1]

The advent of World War II began to change life in America. "In the beginning, I thought war was exciting. At twelve, I hadn't been paying much attention to all the news on the radio and in the movie newsreels about the fighting in Europe, Africa, and Asia. Then, all of a sudden, the United States was at war with Japan. President Franklin D. Roosevelt came on the radio to say so. Mama and Daddy had known war before, and they were worried, but I wasn't.

"The war changed our lives in a lot of ways. At school, they changed the way we saluted the flag so that it wouldn't look even slightly like the Nazi salute to Hitler, Germany's dictator. We sold savings stamps for ten cents apiece, or bought them and pasted them in little books, lending money to the government to help buy guns and ships and bullets. We learned new patriotic songs that we sang at all the assemblies. One song was written especially for black children to sing. We sang, 'We Are Americans, Too.'

She saw a little black stone with sparkly silver specks in it, and she picked it up. (From *Grandmama's Joy* by Eloise Greenfield. Illustrated by Carole Byard.)

"And then, one night a woman received a telegram and screamed, screamed into the night and into my fading excitement. Her husband had been killed in the war.

"War became real for me that night. I knew, then, what my parents had known all along.

"In the **spring of 1945,** Bobby Greenfield was drafted into World War II. The night before he left, a bunch of us gathered around the stone horse in Langston and talked and joked with him about nothing important. It was our way of saying that we would miss him.

"Bobby had moved into our neighborhood, right down the block from Langston, when I was thirteen. His friends told me he liked me. My friends told him I liked him. But the years passed, and we never told each other. The night before he left for the army, he promised to write.

"The whole time Bobby was away, we wrote long, friendly letters to each other. Nobody reading them would have guessed that five years later we would be married."[1]

At seventeen, Greenfield graduated from high school. The next year her mother had another baby, sister Vera.

1947-1949. Greenfield attended Miner Teacher's College (now University of the District of Columbia) but dropped out after two years and took a job as a clerk-typist at the U.S. Patent Office.

April 29, 1950. Greenfield married Robert Greenfield, who worked as a procurement specialist. They subsequently had two children, Steven and Monica.

1956-1960. Greenfield was promoted to a supervisory patent assistant, continuing to work for the U.S. Patent Office, and working on her writing. "Writing was the farthest thing from my mind when I was growing up. I loved words, but I loved to read them, not write them. I loved their sounds and rhythms, and even some of their aberrations, such as homonyms and silent letters, though the pluralizing of 'leaf' annoyed me. I could think of no good reason for getting rid of that f.

"I wish I could remember just what it was that made me sit down one day and write my very first rhyme. But I can't. I remember only that I was a young wife and mother working full-time as a clerk-typist, and that for some reason I began to write. First, rhymes that I hoped were humorous, then songs. There was a television program called 'Songs for Sale' that invited the viewing audience to send in original songs, the best of which would be played on the air, and I submitted one of mine. I waited anxiously for a favorable reply, but instead the song was returned with the information that the show was going off the air. I've always had the unpleasant suspicion that after looking at my song, the musical director had flung it across the room, lifted his arms and his eyes heavenward, and quit, followed by the rest of the staff.

"My next attempts were short stories. I wrote three, and they were promptly rejected. It was obvious that I had no talent, so I gave up writing forever.

"Forever lasted five or six years, during which time I learned what writing was—that it was not the result of talent alone, but of talent combined with skills that had to be developed. So I set about practicing them."[2]

Greenfield did not give up. Instead, she kept writing and finally, in 1963, she published her first poem "To a Violin" in the *Hartford Times*. Then she joined the D.C. Black Writers Workshop, and later became a co-director of adult fiction. "I felt the need not only for the exchange of ideas and criticisms but also to learn where the opportunities were."[3]

"When I joined the D.C. Black Writers Workshop, I met Sharon (Bell Mathis) and she was so deeply involved in children's literature and talked so passionately about the need for good black books that it was contagious. Once I realized the full extent of the problems, it became urgent for me to try, along with others, to build a large collection of books for children. It has been inspiring to me to be a part of this struggle."[4]

1972. Greenfield's first book, *Bubbles,* was published. It was later reissued as *Good News.*

1973. In addition to being director of the children's literature division of the D.C. Black Writers Workshop, Greenfield became a writer-in-residence for the D.C. Commission on the Arts and Humanities. She began working on a series of biographies about famous Black Americans: Rosa Parks, Paul Robeson, and Mary McLeod Bethune. Her goal was "to make children aware of the people who have contributed to the struggle for black liberation."[4]

"I enjoyed doing them. The research is always interesting. There's so much information that I hadn't known before. And also I feel good about presenting those subjects; I selected them because I felt they were people children needed to meet. But I really prefer work that is totally my own creative effort. As far as

Doretha started to worry about tomorrow. (Jacket illustration by Moneta Barnett from *Sister* by Eloise Greenfield.)

getting satisfaction from the writing process is concerned, that's more satisfying to me."[5]

Throughout the seventies, Greenfield wrote one or two books a year. In 1976 she published her fourth picture book for children, *First Pink Light*. "One Christmas, when my nephew, Darren, was five or six years old, he received a camera as a gift, but no flash attachment. He'd gotten up at 3:00 a.m., as so many children do on Christmas, and he wanted to use his camera immediately. My sister explained that he needed daylight and suggested that he go back to bed and sleep until morning. But he said, 'No,' that he'd sit up and wait for daylight, and that's what he did. Then he went outdoors and took pictures of the trees. As soon as my sister told me about it, I said, 'There must be a story there.'"[4]

1978. Greenfield explains how another book began. "*Talk about a Family* began life as just a shadowy character and a single, disconnected sentence. They came from nowhere that I can trace. I could just see this little girl riding her bike down the sidewalk on a sunny, fall day, and a leaf landing on her shoulder as she passed under a tree. 'It had to mean good luck,' was the sentence that came, isolated. The rest I would have to work out. Who was this little girl, and why did she need good luck? She became Genny, facing the painful experience that so many children are facing today—the breaking up and rearranging of the family unit. Children are so powerless in this kind of situation, and so confused about their own feelings. I wanted to say something that might help them get through the worst of it without severe and permanent trauma."[6]

In the same year, Greenfield also published a book of poems, titled *Honey, I Love*. "I wrote the title poem as a picture book and sent that to my editor. She thought that it didn't work as a picture book but that she would like it as a poem, and she suggested that I write some other poetry to go with it to form a collection. That left me with a decision to make, because I still feel that it works as a picture book. When you submit your work, you have to have confidence in your own opinion too. It means that you listen to editors and consider their opinions because they are expert opinions based on knowledge and experience in the field, but then yours is too. I had to decide whether to submit it elsewhere as a picture book. But the idea of writing poetry was intriguing to me, so then I did write the rest of the poems in one period of a few months. The other interesting thing is that I had written a picture book called *Africa Dream,* and I decided I might as well include that in this collection of poetry, because I had not submitted it as yet to my editor. So I included that as a poem, and my editor said, 'Well, I think this works as a picture book.' I ended up with two books anyway!"[5]

Childtimes was a collaborative effort between Greenfield and her mother. "With *Childtimes,* I was sitting at my desk one night, just daydreaming, and I was thinking about my grandmother and some material that she had written before her death. I realized that my mother's writing had filled in this space between my grandmother's writing and mine, and that there should be something that we could do for children. I didn't know what right away, but I thought it through and came up with the idea, then suggested it to my mother. She liked it, and that's how that book came about.

"We enjoyed doing that book very much, and it was special for me. Of course, my mother had told me some things about her childhood, but there were so many details that I hadn't known as a child and learned because we were doing the book. Also, because the material my grandmother had written was not really sufficient for the book, we interviewed her sisters. Two of them were living at the time: one is still living—she's ninety-seven. That rounded out my grandmother's section of the book. All of the family were so cooperative. Sometimes there'd be a little hole in the information, and we'd have to call somebody. Everyone was very excited about it, and furnishing snapshots and things like that. It was really a family project."[5]

1980-1981. Greenfield wrote two books about handicapped children, *Darlene* and *Alesia*. "Actually there's not a connection between the two, although you would think so. I visit schools fairly often, here in Washington. I enjoyed that visit, and the children and some of the teachers suggested that I write a book about a disabled child. The children said, 'Why don't you write a book about a child in a wheelchair?' and I said I would try to do that. It was a few years later that the idea for *Darlene* came to me.

"Alesia was a neighbor of mine. At the time of her accident, when she was nine, she was living a few doors down from me. It was a real tragedy for the neighborhood. We shared in that problem and in that tragedy and in just watching Alesia develop over the years. She did attend Sharpe Health School and I dedicated *Darlene* to her, but when she was in the eleventh grade, she decided that she wanted to attend a regular school. I happened to be talking to her mother and she mentioned to me that Alesia was attending Woodson High School, and that's when I got the idea that maybe Alesia and I could tell her story. I didn't know the details of it. I had seen her over the years and knew that she was improving and developing, but I didn't know, for example, how she decided that she was going to walk, that it was her idea, that she was the one who pushed for a lot of things. And I didn't know about the great amount of courage she had. I just felt that she would have an interesting story to tell, but her courage was a bonus, and it gave a focus to the book that I hadn't anticipated."[5]

Her own children are often involved with her writing. "They often read my manuscripts before they are submitted and I value their opinions. Usually at least one of them will read the manuscript before I send it out. They are very supportive, but honest. They will tell me if they think something doesn't work; and I ask their opinions if I run into problems or if I'm not sure about something. I call them my in-house editors."[4]

"And I've consulted them on specific points of passages to get their opinion. They are well into adulthood now, but they are still helpful, because of their sense of words—and I guess because they were more recently children than I."[5]

"Writing is now, along with my relationship with my family, an important and enriching part of my life. I make it the major pursuit of most of my days. Writing and rewriting. Trying always to write a book that children will want to live with, live *in,* for as long as it takes them to read it: hoping that some part of the book will stay inside them for the rest of their lives. Reading can generate a special kind of excitement that I call word-madness, and it is this that I try to create. The attempt itself is exciting. Moving words around on paper. Accepting gratefully the miracle of words that come without effort. Struggling to find those that don't.

"And then, there's that added dimension—a cause. There's a desperate need for more Black literature for children, for a large body of literature in which Black children can see themselves and their lives and history reflected. I want to do my share in building it."[2]

Greenfield confesses to daydreaming a lot. "I believe everyone spends time daydreaming. With writing, sometimes an idea will come, or a word will come, or a title, or an opening sentence, or

He picked her up and carried her into the front room. (From *Good News* by Eloise Greenfield. Illustrated by Pat Cummings.)

an image, and then it may be months or years later before it really develops into a story. I think it's all working in the subconscious or somewhere in your daydreaming during the period that it's developing.

"At a certain point, the words begin to build. My head gets so full—I'll put it like that—that there's danger that I will forget the words. Then I know it's time to start putting them down. There's a signal; I can't describe it, but I just know the feeling when it's time to start writing. Things have built to a point where it's time to start putting it on paper.

"When I'm on my schedule I work every day. There are times when other things become rather overwhelming—my mail, especially—and I have to move from my regular schedule and just try to catch up for a while. But my normal schedule is to write in the morning after breakfast until lunchtime. And then after lunch I will either continue to write or do some other things, depending on what needs to be done. Sometimes, if the story is moving well, I'll just continue to write regardless. Also, sometimes I'll take a nap in the evening and begin writing late at night. That's an especially quiet time, so things seem to work better then."[5]

"Writing is my work. It is work that is in harmony with me; it sustains me. I want, through my work, to help sustain children.

"My attempts and those of other writers to offer sustenance will necessarily be largely ineffectual. Not only do we as human beings have limitations—so also does the written word. It cannot be eaten or worn; it cannot cure disease; it cannot dissipate pollution, defang a racist, cause a spoonful of heroin to disintegrate. But, at the right time, in the right circumstances, falling on the right mind, a word may take effect.

"Through the written word I want to give children a love for the arts that will provoke creative thought and activity. All children are creative. They create music, art, poetry, dances, daydreams and nightmares, fads, myths, and—as I'm sure you know—mischief. A strong love for the arts can enhance and direct their creativity as well as provide satisfying moments throughout their lives.

"I want to encourage children to develop positive attitudes toward themselves and their abilities, to love themselves. When they are infants, other people have the complete responsibility for their health and safety; but when they are older, they must say, 'I am the only human being who is always with me, and I must care enough, must love myself enough, to make the decisions that are best for me.' As for abilities—self-confidence is half the battle. Children must be able to face their mistakes and weaknesses without losing sight of their strengths.

"I want to present to children alternative methods for coping with the negative aspects of their lives and to inspire them to seek new ways of solving problems. One of these alternative methods—so beautifully expressed in the words of Lucille Clifton, 'Oh children think about the good times'—I used in *Sister*. Sister, who is Doretha, discovers that she can use her good times as stepping stones, as bridges, to get over the hard times—the death of her father, the alienation of her older sister, her struggles with schoolwork. My hope is that children in trouble will not view themselves as blades of wheat caught in countervailing winds but will seek solutions, even partial or temporary solutions, to their problems.

"I want to give children an appreciation for the contributions of their elders, contributions that may not be news but that make daily survival possible. At one time, not so very long ago, it would not have been necessary to make a conscious effort to acquaint children with their elders. But with the decline of the extended family and the magnification of the youth culture, it has become necessary. Children who are unaware of the practical guidance, moral support, and wisdom that older people have given and are willing to give are deprived of valuable assistance in growing up.

"I want to give children a true knowledge of Black heritage, including both the African and the American experiences. The distortions of Black history have been manifold and ceaseless. A true history must be the concern of every Black writer. It is necessary for Black children to have a true knowledge of their past and present, in order that they may develop an informed sense of direction for their future.

"I want to write stories that will allow children to fall in love with genuine Black heroes and heroines who have proved themselves to be outstanding in ability and in dedication to the cause of Black freedom. Rosa Parks, Paul Robeson, Harriet Tubman, Nat Turner, Sojourner Truth, Marcus Garvey, Malcolm X, Dr. Martin Luther King, Nina Simone, and so many others deserve our love and our respect. And this love and respect must be given for the right reasons. Jackie Robinson was a great athlete long before the major leagues decided they needed him. The fact that he was selected for entry into the major leagues does not enhance his worth nor does it diminish the worth of all the great ones who were never allowed to enter.

"Accompanying all of my other wants for children is the desire to share the feeling that I have for words .... While reading Keorapetse Kgositsile's book, *The Present Is a Dangerous Place to Live*, I came across the words, 'Home is where the music is'—plain words, quiet words, understated. But the excitement they created was too much for me to contain. I had to repeat them softly. I wanted to stand up and shout them, but I was afraid the neighbors would think that I had suddenly gone mad. And they would have been right—I had gone mad, word-mad. Because, if you love home and you love music and you love words, the miracle is that the poet chose *those* words and put them together in *that* order, and it is something to shout about. I felt like the Southern Black preachers who, in reciting from the Scriptures, would suddenly be surprised by an old, familiar phrase and would repeat it over and over to savor and to celebrate this miracle of words.

"I want to be one of those who can choose and order words that children will want to celebrate. I want to make them shout and laugh and blink back tears and care about themselves. They are our future. They are beautiful. They are for loving."[7]

FOOTNOTE SOURCES

[1]Eloise Greenfield and Lessie Jones Little, *Childtimes: A Three-Generation Memoir*, Crowell, 1979.
[2]Anne Commire, editor, *Something about the Author*, Volume 19, Gale, 1980.
[3]Jacqueline Trescott, "Children's Books and Heroes," *Washington Post*, October 29, 1976.
[4]Rosalie Black Kiah, "Profile: Eloise Greenfield," *Language Arts*, September, 1980.
[5]*Contemporary Authors New Revision Series*, Volume 19, Gale, 1987.
[6]*Junior Literary Guild*, March, 1978.
[7]E. Greenfield, "Something to Shout About," *Horn Book*, December, 1975.

FOR MORE INFORMATION SEE:

Washington Post Book World, December 18, 1973 (p. C4), May 1, 1977, January 13, 1980 (p. 10), May 10, 1981, October 27, 1982 (p. DC1).
Ann Allen Shockley and Sue P. Chandler, *Living Black American Authors: A Biographical Dictionary*, Bowker, 1973.
New York Times Book Review, May 5, 1974 (p. 16), November 3, 1974 (p. 48).
Interracial Books for Children Bulletin, Volume VI, number 1, 1975 (p. 4), Volume XI, number 5, 1980 (p. 14ff), Volume XI, number 8, 1980.
Social Education, January, 1975 (p. 60).
Negro History Bulletin, April-May, 1975, September-October, 1978.
Theressa Gunnels Rush and others, *Black American Writers Past and Present: A Biographical and Bibliographical Dictionary*, Scarecrow, 1975.
Encore, December 6, 1976.
Horn Book, April, 1977, June, 1983 (p. 243).
School Library Journal, December, 1979 (p. 85), January, 1985 (p. 60).
Top of the News, winter, 1980.
Africa Woman, March-April, 1980.
Freedomways, Volume XXI, number 1, 1981, Volume XXII, number 2, 1982.
Washington Post, December 15, 1981 (p. C5).
Children's Literature Review, Volume IV, Gale, 1982.

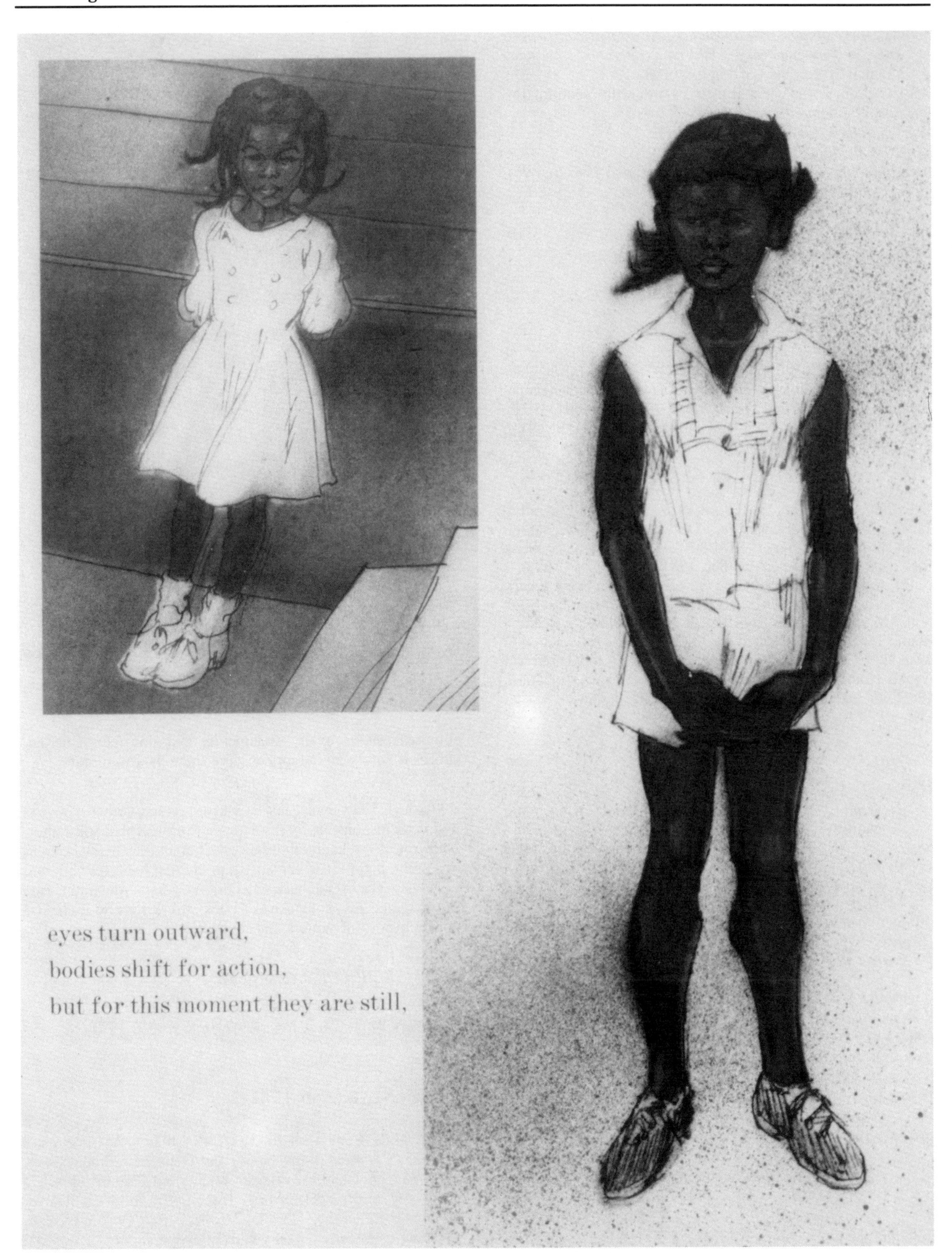

(From *Daydreamers* by Eloise Greenfield. Illustrated by Tom Feelings.)

Rudine Sims, *Shadow and Substance: Afro-American Experience in Contemporary Children's Literature,* National Council of Teachers of English, 1982.
Pearl C. Lomax, "Poems Bursting Forth with Youthful Energy," *Atlanta Journal,* May 23, 1982.
Metropolitan Washington, August, 1982.
HCA Companion, first quarter, 1984.
Journal of Youth Services in Libraries, summer, 1988 (p. 396).
Wilson Library Bulletin, April, 1989 (p. 92).

COLLECTIONS

Kerlan Collection at the University of Minnesota.

HARVEY, Brett 1936-

PERSONAL: Born April 28, 1936, in New York, N.Y.; daughter of Robert (a stockbroker) and Marjorie (a writer; maiden name, Abbott) Harvey; married Louis Vuolo, 1960 (divorced, 1971); children: Robert, Katherine. *Education:* Attended Northwestern University, 1956-59. *Home:* 305 8th Ave., Brooklyn N.Y. 11215.

CAREER: WBAI-FM, New York, N.Y., drama and literature director, 1971-74; *Feminist Press,* Old Westbury, N.Y., publicity and promotion director, 1974-80; free-lance journalist, book critic, and children's book author, 1981—. *Member:* Author's Guild, National Writer's Union (co-chair of New York local). *Awards, honors:* Drexel Citation from Drexel University, Book of the Month Selection from Philadelphia Children's Reading Round Table, 1986, selected one of Child Study Association of America's Children's Books of the Year, 1987, Golden Sower Award Nomination from the Nebraska Library Association, 1988, and included on the William Allen White Award Master List, 1988-89, all for *My Prairie Year.*

WRITINGS:

My Prairie Year: Based on the Diary of Elenore Plaisted (juvenile; ALA Notable Book; illustrated by Deborah Kogan Ray), Holiday House, 1986.
Immigrant Girl: Becky of Eldridge Street (juvenile; illustrated by D. Kogan Ray), Holiday House, 1987.
Cassie's Journey: Going West in the 1860s (juvenile; illustrated by D. Kogan Ray), Holiday House, 1988.
(Editor) *Various Gifts: Brooklyn Fiction,* Fund for Borough of Brooklyn, 1988.
My Prairie Christmas, Holiday House, 1990.

Contributor of articles to periodicals, including *Mother Jones, Village Voice, New York Times Book Review, Psychology Today,* and *Mademoiselle.*

WORK IN PROGRESS: A book about American women in the 1950s, for Harper & Row.

SIDELIGHTS: "An incorrigible activist, the moment I became a freelancer in 1981 I realized that isolation and low pay were my deadly enemies, and joined the then-fledgling National Writer's Union (NWU) to remedy both. I now juggle my writing with union organizing—sometimes one takes precedence, sometimes the other. I'm co-chief-steward of the NWU's campaign to get a contract for *Village Voice* freelancers, and serve as co-chair of the New York local. Also, I've become keenly aware of the importance of the NWU's 'fair pay and fair treatment' campaign for book authors. Our initial goals include timely payments,

BRETT HARVEY

comprehensible royalty statements, and non-returnable advances—surely all authors deserve these as a minimum!

"Although I never met her, it was my grandmother who was indirectly responsible for my career as a children's book author. She wrote down her reminiscences of her journey to the Dakotas as a child, and I made her story into my first book for children. Curiously, she herself became a children's book illustrator. And her daughter, my mother, was a cookbook writer. So we have a family history of writers and illustrators."

FOR MORE INFORMATION SEE:

New York Times Book Review, September 13, 1987.

HIRSCH, Karen 1941-

PERSONAL: Born April 16, 1941, in Ashland, Wis.; daughter of Oscar Clarence (a mechanic) and Demrise (a homemaker; maiden name, Gaudreau) Hagstrom; married Timothy Hirsch (a university professor), April 16, 1966; children: David, Stephanie. *Education:* Northland College, B.A., 1963; Wisconsin State University—Eau Claire (now University of Wisconsin—Eau Claire), M.A., 1969. *Politics:* Democrat. *Religion:* Unitarian-Universalist. *Home:* 1744 Coolidge Court, Eau Claire, Wis. 54701. *Office:* Eau Claire Board of Education, 1222 Mappa St., Eau Claire, Wis. 54701.

CAREER: Wausau Public Schools, Wausau, Wis., teacher, 1963-67; Wisconsin State University—Eau Claire (now University of Wisconsin—Eau Claire), teacher at campus school, 1969-71; Eau Claire Academy, Eau Claire, teacher, summers, 1971-73; University of Wisconsin—Eau Claire, part-time teacher of remedial reading, 1973-76; Leysin American School, Leysin, Switzerland, high school English teacher, 1977-78; Eau Claire Board of Education, Eau Claire, elementary school teacher, 1976-77, 1978-81, resource teacher for high achieving students, 1981—. Active in civic and religious groups. *Member:* Association for the Gifted, League of Women Voters, Wisconsin Council of Teachers of English, Wisconsin Council of Writers. *Awards, honors: Becky* was selected one of Child Study Association of America's Children's Books of the Year, 1981; Woodward Park School Annual Book Award Honorable Mention, 1982, for *My Sister.*

WRITINGS:

JUVENILE PICTURE BOOKS

My Sister (illustrated by Nancy Inderieden), Carolrhoda, 1977.
Becky (illustrated by Jo Esco), Carolrhoda, 1981.
Mr. Schnizzel's Wonderful Invention, Davenport, 1984.

Contributor to periodicals, including *Jack and Jill, Wisconsin English Journal,* and *Good Apple.*

WORK IN PROGRESS: A juvenile novel, *Only One Year;* a novel for nine- to twelve-year-olds.

SIDELIGHTS: "I was born and raised in a small Wisconsin town on the south shore of Lake Superior. My home, a small white

KAREN HIRSCH

She put the string around her hands and started flipping it every which way. (From *Becky* by Karen Hirsch. Illustrated by Jo Esco.)

frame house, surrounded by fields, woods, apple orchards, and a few other houses, was across the street from the lake. I was literally raised on the shore of Gitchiegumie! The youngest of three girls, I seemed to have a great deal of freedom to explore the fields, woods, and lake. My friends and I searched for driftwood and pig iron along the shore, built rafts of washed-up boards and spikes swiped from my father's workbench. We built forts, had secret clubs, stole apples, visited the gypsies, and shared countless nickel popsicles from Lokken's Market.

"When I was very young I began visiting the tidy brick building on our brick main street, downtown. This place—this heaven for me—was the Vaughn Public Library. The children's area was at the back of the library and was guarded by a sweet but iron-protective tiny lady. We were *quiet* in that library! But she was kind, too, and helped me find books. One of my earliest book-memories was a series of biographies, all bound in orange covers. Each title consisted of the name of a person and then a descriptive phrase: *Ben Franklin: Boy Inventor; Amelia Earhart: Girl Pilot.* I read them and dreamed of greatness.

"I read the Laura Ingalls Wilder books, the Beverly Cleary books, the 'Betsy' books, adventures, mysteries, and funny books. For birthdays I received a Nancy Drew mystery, a special treat since they weren't available in my library. My interest in reading sparked my interest in writing and I wrote stories and poems beginning in third grade.

"My first published book, *My Sister*, grew out of a childhood experience. Across the street from me lived a child who was mentally retarded. We included this girl in our games, but never at the same level as the other neighbor kids, and sometimes we got her to do embarrassing or silly things for us, and when she naively agreed, we laughed. That experience made me think about writing a book to help children see a retarded child as a *person,* with needs, goals, and worth.

"*Becky* is about a handicapped child also—a hearing impaired child. This was much harder for me to write because I didn't know anyone with a hearing loss. After trying several drafts, I visited a family who had a little girl living with them during the week so she could attend school. I met the girl, a profoundly hearing impaired, but charming and delightful child, and I knew that I had my story.

"Writing for me is a part-time hobby. I teach school full time, working with gifted and talented elementary school children. My own two children are in college now and we enjoy travelling to visit them at Harvard and Swarthmore. Of course they come home, too, and we spend hot summer days in the clear water of Long Lake, where we have a cottage. My husband is a university English professor, and an author too. He is writing a book which shows college students how to write a research paper. He and I love to travel. During the summer of 1986 my husband and I and our children went to Poland to teach in a UNESCO English language camp for Polish teenagers. In the summer of 1988 my husband and I went to northern Italy to teach in another English language camp for Italian teachers. In 1989 we taught at a UNESCO English language camp in Debrecen, Hungary.

"I have unpublished books and stories in my desk, some of which are good, but which haven't yet been accepted. I have other ideas for books, but I've put writing on a back burner of my mind where the ideas simmer and I hope will boil over soon and force me to write again!"

HOBBIES AND OTHER INTERESTS: Cross-country skiing, downhill skiing, hiking, reading, swimming.

HOLLAND, Marion 1908-1989

OBITUARY NOTICE—See sketch in *SATA* Volume 6: Born July 7 (one source states July 17), 1908, in Washington, D.C.; died of cancer, April 5, 1989, in Washington, D.C. Illustrator and author. After illustrating articles for a children's magazine, Holland wrote and illustrated her own books for young people, including *Billy Had a System, A Tree for Teddy, A Big Ball of String,* and *Casey Jones Rides Vanity.* Her book *Billy's Clubhouse* won the Boys' Club of America Junior Book Award. She was an avid correspondent with the *Washington Post,* chiding editors for bad grammar and discussing community affairs with columnist William Raspberry, who wrote of her as his "friend in Chevy Chase."

FOR MORE INFORMATION SEE:

Who's Who in American Women 1961, Marquis, 1960.
Martha E. Ward and Dorothy A. Marquardt, *Authors of Books for Young People,* Scarecrow, 1971.
Contemporary Authors, Volumes 61-64, Gale, 1976.

OBITUARIES

Washington Post, April 8, 1989.

HUGHEY, Roberta 1942-

PERSONAL: Surname rhymes with "phooey"; born May 28, 1942, in Washington, D.C., daughter of (stepfather) Malvern Frye (a banker) and Patricia (a social worker; maiden name, Proctor) Morse; married Philip Jan Hughey (a health administrator), March 22, 1967; children: Stephanie, Patrick, Elizabeth. *Education:* Miami University, Ohio, B.A., 1963; Ohio State University, M.A., 1970; University of Florida, Ed.D., 1976; attended George Washington University and Austin Peay State College.

CAREER: Teacher in Washington, D.C. Public Schools, 1964-68; Teacher Corps, University of Florida, Gainesville, Fla., editor, 1977-80; free-lance editor, 1980—. *Member:* Society for Children's Book Writers, Assembly on Literature for Adolescents. *Awards, honors:* Delacorte Press Prize for Outstanding First Young Adult Novel Honorable Mention, 1983, for *The Question Box;* Individual Artist Fellowship Award in Literature from the Florida Arts Council, 1987-88.

WRITINGS:

The Question Box, Delacorte, 1984.

Contributor of short stories to *Highlights for Children.*

WORK IN PROGRESS: Working titles, *Margaret and Sam,* and *Ride the Glass-Bottomed Boat.*

SIDELIGHTS: "Ever since I've wanted to be anything, I've wanted to be a writer. It was a shock to me when I recently became aware not only that everyone else had not cherished the same dream, even secretly, but that most people didn't worship writers the way I did and that most of them, upon learning I had written a book, were no more impressed than if they had learned I could bake a mean batch of brownies—possibly less, since you can't eat a book. I have also over the last several years met and gotten to know a number of writers and found out that everyone was right and I was wrong. Most writers, at least those I have met, have about the same number of positive qualities and character defects as any other segment of the population. We can be just as jealous, petty, or selfish, just as enthusiastic, funny, or loving as your average fire fighter or computer programmer. Still, I have always loved books and reading and no one but a writer can give me those.

ROBERTA HUGHEY

Genevra had on one of her regular school outfits. Tight Jordaches, . . . high-heeled boots. (Jacket illustration by Mark Gerber from *The Question Box* by Roberta Hughey.)

"My first memory of books comes from Los Angeles, across the country from Florida, where I now live, and across time, forty-two years ago, when I was three and lived with my grandparents. At night they would be sure to pile enough books by my bed to keep me occupied in the morning until they were ready to get up, and I can see those books strewn around me on the bed, *Angus and the Cats, Make Way for Ducklings*. Every week my grandmother and I walked to the public library, for me the beginning of a love affair with libraries and bookstores that I am still faithful to today. My kids try to distract me whenever we pass a bookstore, unwilling to wait while my 'just a few minutes' stretch into thirty, forty-five. I don't believe I've ever left a bookstore emptyhanded. For many years my dearest dream was to walk into a bookstore or a library and see on the shelf a book with my name on it. And I always pictured a novel, which was what I loved to read, not something as ordinary and unmagical as a biography or a travel book or something on glaciers.

"A third grade teacher, Miss Langston at Holton-Arms School in Washington, D.C., is the first person I remember telling me I had a knack for writing. My English teachers at Bethesda-Chevy Chase (Maryland) High School encouraged me further, and though I wanted to major in journalism in college, I was a coward, very afraid of not measuring up, and signed up for elementary education instead. That turned out for me to be the other extreme, far too unchallenging, and I compromised on English. Even there, I failed to sign up for the second semester of a short story writing course because I didn't get all A's the first semester. I chose to coddle my fragile ego and low self-esteem, which I have since learned are as common among writers as in the rest of the population, and as deadly to growth.

"When I graduated from college with general honors and honors in English but with not one math course under my belt (at least I knew one of my weaknesses), I went to work in Washington, D.C., as an editorial assistant, later as assistant editor (more pay) on the magazine of a national college fraternity. I spent a year in Europe looking for myself. I got married, earned a masters degree, adopted a child, moved to Florida, adopted another child, gave birth to a third child, and worked toward a doctorate in curriculum and instruction—it was back to the classroom for me, I thought. By the time I finished the degree, I never wanted to see a classroom again. Instead, I edited newsletters for several years, taught workshops for teachers, and, finally, began to edit books.

"In about 1981, almost twenty years after that short story writing course, I signed up for a community education course called 'Writing and Selling Short Stories and Articles,' and within months had sold a story to *Highlights for Children*. Within the next few years I wrote a mystery for young adults and published several other stories. I helped found the Gainesville Writers' Workshop, which still flourishes as a home for beginning writers and their work. Finally, in July, 1983, I got a phone call from an editor at Delacorte Press in New York saying I was runner-up in their contest for first young adult novels and they would like to publish my book. I managed to sound so calm during the call that the editor asked me if I was interested. Too bad she couldn't see me leaping around my living room, shrieking, after we hung up. The book came out in October, 1984, the paperback in January, 1986. Since then, I've finished another mystery (the first one, which I now consider a practice run, is in my drawer after fifteen publishers said no thanks) and begun a third.

"This spring I was back in the high school classroom with the Writers in the Schools project in the Florida town where I live, teaching creative writing. I told each of the four classes I taught that I assumed at least one person in that room would become a better writer than I am, and I meant it. Wonderful writers are out there, if only they don't let their fear get in the way.

"Today I can go into a bookstore or a library and find my book on the shelf. In the bookstore, I always turn a copy front cover out, the better to attract browsers."

KRESH, Paul 1919-

PERSONAL: Born December 3, 1919, in New York, N.Y.; son of Samuel and Jean (Finesilver) Kresh. *Education:* Attended Columbia University, 1936-38; City College (now City College of the City University of New York), B.A., 1940. *Politics:* Independent liberal. *Religion:* Jewish. *Home:* 1 David Lane, Yonkers, N.Y. 10701. *Office:* Paul Kresh Communications, Inc., Suite 1114, 32 Union Square E., New York, N.Y. 10003.

CAREER: Radio Station WNYC, New York City, scriptwriter, 1939-41; National Jewish Welfare Board, New York City, staff publicity writer, 1941-46; Nathan C. Belth Associates, New York City, account executive, 1946-48; American ORT (Organization for Rehabilitation through Training) Federation, New York City, publicity director, 1948-49; United Jewish Appeal, New York City, assistant national public relations director and motion picture coordinator, 1949-59, creative director of Jewish Philanthropies Campaign, 1974-81; Union of American Hebrew Congregations, New York City, public relations director and editor of *American Judaism,* 1959-67; Spoken Arts, Inc., New Rochelle, N.Y., vice-president, 1967-70; Caedmon Records, New York City, recording director and projects editor, 1970-71; United Jewish Appeal of Greater New York, New York City, public relations director, 1971-74; Paul Kresh Communications, Inc., New York City, communications consultant, 1981—; Artists and Repertoire in North America, Listen for Pleasure Ltd., Toronto, director, 1985-87; Richard Cohen Associates, senior associate publicist, 1988-90; originator, host, and producer of "The Story Department" (daily radio program), WQXR-AM, 1989—.

Member of White House Record Library Commissions, 1981—; panelist, "First Hearing," WQXR Radio, 1984—; producer and recording director for Listening Library of "George Orwell: A Portrait in Sound," 1988, and "Short Stories of Katherine Mansfield," "High Spirits by Robertson Davies," and "Virginia Woolf: A Portrait in Sound," all 1989. *Member:* National Academy of Recording Arts and Sciences, National Academy of Television Arts and Sciences, Authors League, Authors Guild of America, American Society of Journalists and Authors, PEN American Center, Writers Guild of America, American Jewish Public Relations Society.

AWARDS, HONORS: Radio Award from Ohio State University, 1940 and 1941, for "Adventures in Music," and 1965, for "Adventures in Judaism"; Golden Eagle Award for Filmscript from the Committee on International Non-Theatrical Events, 1965, for "The Day the Doors Closed"; Faith and Freedom Award in Broadcasting from the Religious Heritage Foundation, 1968, for contributions to religious broadcasting; Award from the Council of Jewish Federations, 1972, for Best Organizational Newspaper; Silver Award from the International Television and Film Festival of New York, 1972, for film "The Jewish Year in Review"; Bronze Medal from the International Television and Film Festival, 1974, for "Broken Sabbath"; Chris Award from the Columbus Film Festival, 1974, for "May It Be," and 1980, for "On the Brink of Peace"; Ohio State Award, 1975, for "Jewish World" radio series; Silver Medal for Commitment from the International Film Festival, 1976; Fellow, MacDowell Colony, Virginia Center for Creative Arts; Emmy Award from the National Association of Television Arts and Sciences, 1980, for "Movin' into the Eighties"; Armstrong Award from Dupont-Columbia University, 1982, for "The World of Jewish Music."

PAUL KRESH

WRITINGS:

(With Stephen M. Young) *Tales out of Congress,* Lippincott, 1964.

(Editor) *An American Judaism Reader,* Abelard, 1965.

The Power of the Unknown Citizen, Lippincott, 1969.

Isaac Bashevis Singer: The Magician of West 86th Street, Dial, 1979.

Isaac Bashevis Singer: The Story of a Storyteller (illustrated by Penrod Scofield), Lodestar, 1984.

An American Rhapsody: The Story of George Gershwin, Lodestar, 1988.

Author of twenty film scripts for United Jewish Appeal, of television scripts, "Trail in Heaven," "The Stranger in the Empty Chair," and "Movin' into the Eighties," and of filmscript, "The Day the Doors Closed"; author of opera libretto, "The Marble Faun." Author and director of Columbia Broadcasting System series "Adventures in Judaism," 1965, and of WQXR series "The Jewish World," 1974, and "Jewish Lives," 1977. Also author of "The World of Jewish Music."

Monthly columnist, *Words Only,* and *American Record Guide,* 1959-63; contributing editor and critic, *Hi Fi-Stereo Review,* 1963-80, and *High Fidelity,* 1984-89; book reviewer, *Saturday Review,* 1967—; editor of "The Spoken Arts Treasury of 100 Modern American Poets Reading Their Poems," 1969; record reviewer, *New York Times,* 1974—; spoken word critic, *Musical Heritage Review,* 1980—; *Musical America,* 1984-88, *Ovation,* 1988-89, and *Classical Music,* 1989—; contributing editor, *Jewish Week,* 1990—.

SIDELIGHTS: "I have worn any number of hats during my long career of trying to make a living—author, publicist, scriptwriter, radio and documentary film director, record critic, record producer—but the thing that has always mattered most to me has been writing.

"My father died when I was twelve and my mother and I went to live with her rather large family in a crowded apartment in the neighborhood of the upper reaches of Manhattan known as Washington Heights. Closest to me was my aunt, who also lived there and who happened to work as a secretary on the *Saturday Review.* She had read me the 'Winnie-the-Pooh' books as they came out starting when I was six, and it was she who inspired me to want to write.

"I started pursuing this demanding craft when still a child. In high school, I, of course, was one of the editors of our newspaper—it being George Washington High School it was called the 'Cherry Tree'—and I later edited our yearbook the *Lantern.* During the year or so I attended the 'progressive' college called

Isaac would explore Warsaw itself, the great city beyond the ghetto. (From *Isaac Bashevis Singer: The Story of a Storyteller* by Paul Kresh. Illustrated by Penrod Scofield.)

New College at Columbia University I also worked on the newspaper there. Soon afterwards I started my extensive collection of rejection slips. I wrote poems, several novels, stories, and an opera libretto, and got them all back. I was forty-four when I published my first book, and that was a ghostwriting job for a senator. Since then I have published four more along with countless reviews and articles and scripts of every kind.

"What I'd really like to be able to do is stay home and write fiction, but the old problem of having to earn a living is still with me, and I have to keep my dog in dog food. My last two books—a biography of Isaac Bashevis Singer and one of George Gershwin—have both been part of Lodestar/Dutton's 'Jewish Biography' series for young adults. I never thought I would be able to write for youngsters but these turned out to be thoroughly congenial assignments. Anyhow, I think a writer should be able to write *anything* from a television commercial to a chant royal—and that is what I tell my students when I teach creative writing."

Kresh, who has been involved in the field of spoken word recordings which has grown tremendously in the past two decades, is now the originator, host, and producer of "The Story Department," on WQXR-AM in New York. "One of the things I convinced Spoken Arts of was that you could get a great star to do the right vehicle. If Julie Harris really wanted to do something, she would do it for the same price as some far less famous personality. And so it turns out.

"Yet there are many fine readings by unknown readers. And some of the best ones I've used have been done by obscure actors that nobody remembers, but they were awfully good at reading aloud. But for the most part and for the glamour of it—after all, you can't ignore that—if I have somebody like Sir Laurence Olivier reading something and I get the rights to it, I'll use it. And you can be pretty sure it's going to be wonderful."[1]

According to Kresh, a primary task of a recording director is "to get on the phone and try to persuade the right person to do the right job. You try to get—as I did . . . for Listening Library—Irene Worth to do Virginia Woolf or Rosemary Harris to do Katherine Mansfield or Eli Wallach and Anne Jackson to do Bernard Malamud. Or whoever matches up in your imagination as the person to record this book. And you go after the person, and finally you settle for the best you can get.

"Then you have to get the script prepared. Some books you record complete, others abridged. There are people who are extremely skilled at reducing a 500-page book to a 100-page script. So you get that ready. And then you sit in the recording studio with the actor who has received the script and has had a chance to rehearse it.

"I lean . . . toward dramatic readings. I like it when the actor does the characters, does the accents. When I recorded *Huckleberry Finn* with Dick Cavett, everybody said, what do you mean Dick Cavett, why Dick Cavett? But it turned out that Dick Cavett knew every single one of the 150 dialects that Mark Twain used in his book. So we said, well, let's ask him. He was delighted. When you hear him read *Huckleberry Finn*—he does a three-hour condensation of the novel—you never hear Dick Cavett at all. You hear all the Mark Twain characters. And how he kept track of them God only knows, but he did.

"The director's job is to get the best possible performance out of an actor, just as he would in a stage production. To discuss all the ways which a character can be projected through sound alone. To eliminate phrases in the story that are not necessary because you're hearing the character speak. To think about pacing and changes of pace and volume and building to a climax.

"I remember recording Edgar Allan Poe with Hurd Hatfield. We did *The Mask of the Red Death* which is a story that takes only twenty minutes to hear, but we spent hours on it because we wanted it to build to such a spine-chilling climax that the person who heard it would never forget it."[1]

Many recordings of "The Story Department" are of the author reading his or her own works. "In most cases the interest in listening to the author is that he will probably read the story the way he heard it in his head. There's some interest in that even if it isn't a great performance. Usually the author tends to understate and for that reason I tend to favor dramatic readings.

"But some authors are just natural-born performers. People like James Joyce and Dylan Thomas. Dickens himself who made a living by reading his stories in public—not that there are any recordings of him. And James Baldwin, who was the son of a preacher, reads *Another Country* with such eloquence. People like Truman Capote, who had that nasal, funny little drawl, who sounded so ridiculous—and he did a recording for RCA of chapters from *In Cold Blood* and it's enthralling. You forget all about that voice because he was a spellbinding storyteller.''[1]

Why storytelling on the radio? ''We think of our audience as the educated listener who's home or driving at the time, but who doesn't want to watch soap operas—who wants something where his or her intelligence won't be insulted.

''Music has become kind of commonplace. It's everywhere. It's coming out of your ears at the supermarket, in the elevator. So this idea of listening to stories, people are discovering it.

''People like to go a little beyond themselves. And we all feel that we missed a lot. We all feel that we avoided the classics in school. We have a sort of secret curiosity to find out what *Moll Flanders* was really about. So if you're not going to have time to read it, it's nice to be able to hear it.''[1]

FOOTNOTE SOURCES

[1]''Spellbinding Storytellers Spin Their Tales on WQXR-AM,'' *Talk Radio Guide,* February, 1990.

FOR MORE INFORMATION SEE:

New York Times, June 29, 1979.
New York Times Book Review, October 28, 1979.
Washington Post Book World, November 11, 1979.
''Westchester Bookcase,'' *New York Times* (Westchester edition), July 3, 1988.

LALICKI, Barbara

PERSONAL: Born in Middletown, Conn.; married Tom Lalicki. *Education:* State University of New York at Stony Brook, B.A. *Address:* c/o Lothrop, Lee & Shepard Books, 105 Madison Ave., New York, N.Y. 10016.

CAREER: Has worked as an editorial assistant at Coward, McCann, at Four Winds Press, Bristol, Fla., and as senior editor at Lothrop, Lee & Shepard Books, New York, N.Y. *Awards, honors: If There Were Dreams to Sell* was selected one of *New York Times* Best Illustrated Children's Books of the Year, and one of the National Council of Teachers of English Choices, both 1984.

WRITINGS:

(Compiler) *If There Were Dreams to Sell* (juvenile; illustrated by Margot Tomes), Lothrop, 1984.

SIDELIGHTS: ''I want children to enjoy big words and not to be afraid of those they don't understand. The poems and Margot Tomes's pictures in *If There Were Dreams to Sell* invite children to look and to listen to sounds. They can imagine meanings from context. These imaginings will always play a part in the connotative associations they bring to the words.''

FOR MORE INFORMATION SEE:

COLLECTIONS

Kerlan Collection at the University of Minnesota.

LAPP, Eleanor J. 1936-

PERSONAL: Born January 7, 1936, in Wausau, Wis.; daughter of Gustav (a mechanic) and Bertha (a teacher; maiden name, Luetschwager) Schram; married Richard Lapp (a logger), June 11, 1955; children: Rick. *Education:* University of Wisconsin, Stevens Point, B.S., 1967. *Home:* 2355 South Shore Rd., Land O'Lakes, Wis. 54540.

CAREER: Elementary school teacher, 1955—. Resort owner and operator, 1955-76. *Member:* Society of Children's Book Writers, Council for Wisconsin Writers, Wisconsin Regional Writers Association. *Awards, honors:* Council for Wisconsin Writers Picture Book Award, 1977, for *Duane, the Collector,* and 1983, for *The Blueberry Bears.*

WRITINGS:

Hey, Elephant! (picture book; Junior Literary Guild selection; illustrated by John Paul Richards), Steck-Vaughn, 1970.
Duane, the Collector (picture book; illustrated by Christine Westerberg), Addison-Wesley, 1976.
The Mice Came in Early This Year (picture book; illustrated by David Cunningham), A. Whitman, 1976.
In the Morning Mist (picture book; illustrated by D. Cunningham), A. Whitman, 1978.
The Blueberry Bears (picture book; illustrated by Margot Apple), A. Whitman, 1983.
Orphaned Pup (juvenile novel), Scholastic, 1988.

Contributor to children's magazines.

ADAPTATIONS:

''The Mice Came in Early This Year'' (filmstrip), Instructional/Communications Technology, 1977.

WORK IN PROGRESS: Picture books and a juvenile novel.

SIDELIGHTS: Eleanor J. Lapp has lived most of her life in Wisconsin. There were few children in her small town and they played mostly boys' games—she learned the rudiments of hunting, fishing, skiing, and skating and has continued these activities into her adult life.

Today Lapp lives in the resort and lake region of northern Wisconsin. ''My husband, Dick, and I built a log home back in the woods on a small lake that is part of our large acreage. We watch deer, bear, fox, eagles, ducks, and many other forest animals. We also have two horses and three dogs that enjoy life here with us.

''I always wanted to be a teacher and I do that in my small village of Phelps. I have taught first or second or third grades; sometimes I have taught two grades at the same time. I have always taught in the same school and now I have children of children that I had before.

''Reading is one of my favorite pastimes and I think that brought me to writing books. For several years I wrote picture book stories and magazine stories for very young children.

''The stories I write come from my own experiences. *Hey, Elephant!* was my first book and my son, Rick, was the model for James in that story. *Duane, the Collector* came from a little boy named Duane that was in my school and had unusual collecting habits.

There were bears in the closet and bears under the stove. (From *The Blueberry Bears* by Eleanor Lapp. Illustrated by Margot Apple.)

"I took a class from Uri Shulevitz and learned how to use very simple experiences for picture books. My love of the outdoors and the change of seasons became *The Mice Came in Early This Year*. The mists of August mornings became *In the Morning Mist*.

"One year I picked so many blueberries (I dearly love to pick) that my family wondered what I was going to do with all of them. We also had a family of young bears in our area that climbed the trees in our yard many nights. I put those things together and wrote *The Blueberry Bears*. My favorite recipe for blueberry muffins is in that book.

"*Orphaned Pup* is my first novel for juveniles. I began that story in April when the weather in northern Wisconsin usually hasn't made up its mind whether there will be spring or more snow. I got up at five o'clock in the morning and wrote for an hour before school. The idea for the story came from an incident in my adult life where I heard the repeated crying of a dog out in the woods. I investigated and found a single, lonesome puppy. I have enjoyed the letters that I have received from children all over the country about Op, the orphaned pup.

"I usually do my writing during the summer vacations and the school vacations. I write the first draft of a story in longhand. I work on the second and third and sometimes fourth drafts of the story on my typewriter or word processor. I read the picture books aloud to hear the rhythm that I like to have there. I love to work out the details of the longer novel.

"One of the children in a school I visited pointed out that there is always an animal or two in my stories and I am sure that is because I like animals. My latest story has a cat in it.

"I am currently working on more picture book stories and another novel for juveniles, still teaching children, and enjoying life in the northwoods."

HOBBIES AND OTHER INTERESTS: "I have a vegetable garden and an herb garden. I am fascinated by antiques. I enjoy riding my mountain bike and going on bike tours in other parts of the country. In the winter I like to cross country ski on the trails in and through the woods in our area."

LEDER, Jane M(ersky) 1945-

PERSONAL: Surname is pronounced "leader"; born July 25, 1945, in Detroit, Mich.; daughter of Morris (a manufacturer) and Helen Shirley (a housewife and teacher; maiden name, Saulson) Mersky; married Marc Kahan, July 8, 1968 (divorced, 1976); married Alan J. Leder (a director of visual and media arts), September 6, 1981; children: Joshua. *Education:* University of Michigan, B.A., 1967; Roosevelt University, M.A., 1973.

Home and office: 3531 North Bosworth, Chicago, Ill. 60657. *Agent:* Berenice Hoffman, 215 West 75th St., New York, N.Y. 10023.

CAREER: Junior high school English teacher in Marblehead, Mass., 1967-68; high school English teacher in Royal Oak, Mich., 1968-70, and in Chicago, Ill., 1970-72; Singer Society for Visual Education, Chicago, writer and producer, 1977-80; WLS-TV, Chicago, researcher and field producer, 1980-81; free-lance writer, 1981—. Independent documentary filmmaker, films include "Mama Florence and Papa Cock." *Member:* International Association of Business Communicators, National Organization for Women, Independent Writers of Chicago, National Writers Guild. *Awards, honors:* Gold Award from the International Film and Television Festival of New York, 1983, for "Orwell's 1984: The Prophecy and the Reality"; *Dead Serious: A Book for Teenagers about Teenage Suicide* was chosen one of American Library Association's Best Books for Young Adults, 1988; Blue Ribbon from the American Film Festival, 1988, for film "Dead Serious."

WRITINGS:

JUVENILE

Champ Cars, Crestwood, 1983.
Cassettes and Records, Crestwood, 1983.
Video Games, Crestwood, 1983.
Martina Navratilova, Crestwood, 1985.
Marcus Allen, Crestwood, 1985.

(From the 1987 movie "Dead Serious." Copyright © by MTI Film & Video.)

Walter Payton, Crestwood, 1985.
Moses Malone, Crestwood, 1985.
Wayne Gretzky, Crestwood, 1985.
Stunt Dogs, Crestwood, 1985.
Exotic Cars, Crestwood, 1987.
Amelia Earhart, Greenhaven, 1989.
Powers of the Mind, Capstone, 1989.

YOUNG ADULT

(With K. Lee Zorn) *How to Use Apple Writer* (illustrated by Dale Janzen), Flip Track, 1983.
Dead Serious: A Book for Teenagers about Teenage Suicide, Atheneum, 1987.

Author of audio-visual scripts, including "Understanding Your Sexuality," "Orwell's 1984: The Prophecy and the Reality," and "When Your Parents Drink Too Much." Contributor to magazines and newspapers, including *McCall's, Woman's Day, Glamour, Seventeen, Chicago Reader,* and *Chicago Sun-Times.*

ADAPTATIONS:

"Dead Serious" (film; videocassette), MTI Film & Video, 1987.

WORK IN PROGRESS: How Brothers and Sisters Shape Our Lives, for St. Martin's.

SIDELIGHTS: "As a result of my brother's suicide and the publication of *Dead Serious: A Book for Teenagers about Teenage Suicide,* I became more and more interested in the relationship between brothers and sisters. How do we shape each other's personalities? Do our relationships change as we grow older? Do we draw closer together under stress? Why have professionals put the sibling relationship on the back burner or assumed that rivalry is the major component?"

HOBBIES AND OTHER INTERESTS: Modern jazz dancing, travel (Galapagos Islands, most of Europe and Scandinavia), speaking on teenage suicide and AIDS, Pro-choice Alliance.

LEROE, Ellen W(hitney) 1949-

PERSONAL: Born April 26, 1949, in Newark, N.J.; daughter of Bernard William (a mechanical engineer) and Iris (an educational secretary; maiden name, Brienza) Leroe. *Education:* Elmira College, B.A., 1971; University of Leicester, Certificate, 1970. *Home and office:* 2211 Stockton St., Apt. 409, San Francisco, Calif. 94133. *Agent:* Baltzell and Chleboun Literary Agents, 366 Collingwood St., San Francisco, Calif. 94114.

CAREER: Hahne's (retail store), Newark, N.J., fashion buyer, 1971-74; free-lance writer and illustrator, 1974-76; International Engineering Co., San Francisco, Calif., editorial assistant, 1976-77; San Francisco Junior Chamber of Commerce, San Francisco, administrative manager, 1977-79; full-time free-lance writer, 1979—. *Member:* Media Alliance, Society of Children's Book Writers. *Awards, honors:* New Jersey Institute of Technology Authors Award, 1983, for *Confessions of a Teenage TV Addict;* San Francisco Fair Poetry Competition First Prize, 1985.

WRITINGS:

Single Bed Blues (adult poems), Tandem Press, 1982.

ELLEN W. LEROE

Confessions of a Teenage TV Addict (young adult), Lodestar, 1983.
Enter Laughing (young adult romance novel), Silhouette, 1983.
Give and Take (young adult romance novel), Silhouette, 1984.
The Plot against the Pom-Pom Queen (juvenile), Lodestar, 1985.
Robot Romance (young adult science-fiction novel), Harper, 1985.
Have a Heart, Cupid Delaney (young adult fantasy), Lodestar, 1985.
Robot Raiders (young adult science fiction), Harper, 1985.
Personal Business (juvenile; novelization of ABC-TV "Afterschool Special"), Bantam, 1986.
The Peanut Butter Poltergeist (juvenile mystery), Lodestar, 1987.
Meet Your Match, Cupid Delaney (young adult fantasy), Lodestar, 1989.
H.O.W.L. High (juvenile mystery), Simon & Schuster, 1989.

Contributor of articles and poems to periodicals, including *Cosmopolitan, Travel, National Business Woman, California Living, Good Housekeeping, Ladies' Home Journal, Frequent Flyer, Total Fitness,* and *WomensWeek.*

WORK IN PROGRESS: A children's picture book, *The Day Danny Stopped Digging Dinosaurs;* an adult comedy/thriller, tentatively titled *Come Back, Bogey.*

SIDELIGHTS: "After getting off the roller coaster of my own adolescence in the late 1960s—shaken and somewhat thankful—I've decided that the ride was fun after all and definitely worth writing about. Through rereading my old high school diaries and happily befriending a family of four teenagers I have become a Born Again Teen. I enjoy reading about young adults, writing about them, and, most importantly, talking and listening to them.

"Because I put so much of myself and my own experiences into my novels I tend to focus on main characters confronting, and eventually successfully altering, their insecure and vulnerable self-images. I start with a crisis—a girl who's hopelessly addicted to soap operas (*Confessions of a Teenage TV Addict*), a boy who bucks authority in a computer high school (*Robot Romance*), a teen whose use of sarcasm is shutting out friends and dates (*Enter Laughing*)—and then I mix in complications such as well-meaning but misguided friends, strict parents, and tension with the opposite sex. But the true growth and action come with the main character's discovery that the answers have been hidden within himself the whole time.

"Humor plays a strong part in all my writing, as it does in my own life. I strive to make my dialogue as realistic and as natural as possible. Basically I write about the subjects that interest me most. Those seem to be the subjects that also interest teens: becoming popular without selling yourself short; realizing that other things in life are more important then popularity; and learning to cope with such problems as being overweight, possessing a hyperactive funnybone, having a less than loving and supportive brother or sister, or parents who are too demanding. I try to impart a personal message with my books, but not a heavy-handed moralistic one. I respect young adults; they are bright and intelligent enough to ask the right questions. I don't write to preach but to entertain. And, hopefully, in the entertaining I can give my readers a new perspective about their problems, which will enable them to form their own conclusions.

"Taking the plunge into full-time writing was the most difficult thing I ever chose to do. Now, seven years and twelve published books later, it is still the most difficult thing I choose to do, but it is also the most rewarding, the most personally satisfying, and the most liberating. The nine-to-five job syndrome is one I consciously set out to avoid. Though I often become discouraged

"Will you kindly stop doing that?" the red-haired boy snapped. (Jacket illustration by Eric Jon Nones from *Have a Heart, Cupid Delaney* by Ellen Leroe.)

when checks are late or when publishers reject my material, an inner voice still urges me to keep going. As Henry Ford so succinctly put it, 'You can't build a reputation on what you are GOING to do.'''

HOBBIES AND OTHER INTERESTS: Reading (particularly British murder mysteries and biographies of movie stars), exercising, working as an extra on the local San Francisco television shows shot on location.

LESSAC, Frane 1954-

PERSONAL: Given name is pronounced ''Fra-*nay;*'' born June 18, 1954, in Jersey City, N.J.; daughter of Arthur J. (a philosopher) and Estelle (a travel agency owner; maiden name, Siegel) Lessac; married Mark Greenwood (a musician), April 19, 1986; children: Luke. *Education:* Attended New School for Social Research, 1973, University of Southern California, 1974, and University of California—Los Angeles, 1975-76. *Address:* c/o Bon Venture Studios, 49B British Grove, London W4 2NL, England.

CAREER: Filmmaker, artist, and illustrator, 1983—. *Exhibitions:* Fowler Mills Gallery, Los Angeles, Calif., 1980, 1982; Courtyard Gallery, Montserrat, 1981; Exhibition de Intercaribe de Peinture, Guadeloupe, 1981; Gallerie Aintoinette, Paris, France, 1981; Centre des Arts et de la Culture, Guadeloupe, 1982; Bankside Gallery, London, England, 1983, 1984; Libertys Gallery, London, 1983; Sugar Mill, Montserrat, 1984, 1986; Barbican Center, London, 1984; Brixton Art Gallery, London, 1984; Chelsea Manor Street Gallery, London, 1984; Rona Gallery, London, 1984; Craft and Folk Art Museum, Los Angeles, 1985; Metropolitan Museum of Art, New York, N.Y., 1985; Riverside Studios, London, 1985; Commonwealth Institute, London, 1986; Yellow Poui Art Gallery, Grenada, 1987; Vanessa Devereux Gallery, London, 1987. Work in also included in many private collections worldwide. *Awards, honors:* Children's Book of the Year from the Island of St. Martin, 1984, for *The Little Island.*

WRITINGS:

JUVENILE, EXCEPT AS INDICATED; ALL SELF-ILLUSTRATED

My Little Island (''Reading Rainbow'' selection), Lippincott, 1984 (published as *The Little Island,* Macmillan Caribbean, 1984).
(With Jan Jackson) *The Dragon of Redonda,* Macmillan Caribbean, 1986.
Caribbean Canvas (adult), Macmillan Caribbean, 1987, Harper, 1989.
(With husband, Mark Greenwood) *Caribbean Alphabet,* Macmillan Caribbean, 1989.

ILLUSTRATOR

Charlotte Pomerantz, *The Chalk Doll,* Harper, 1988.
Aleph Kamal, *The Bird Who Was an Elephant,* Cambridge University Press, 1989, Harper, 1990.
Barbara Ker Wilson, *The Turtle and the Island,* Harper, 1990.

Also illustrator of *The Magic Boomerang* by Mark Greenwood.

WORK IN PROGRESS: Illustrating *Nine O'Clock Lullabye* by Marilyn Singer; a picture story book set in Australia.

SIDELIGHTS: ''My aim is to produce multi-cultural, non-sexist books for children, to break down racial barriers and educate at the same time. I also want children to be aware of our precious environment.

''When I was at school, the art teachers considered me unteachable. Because my lines were never straight and my paintings didn't have dimension, the art teachers told me that they were wrong. My school wasn't progressive enough to recognize my work as a legitimate art form. Sometimes I even climbed in through the classroom window after school to change my grade in the professors' book.

''At the age of eighteen, I headed for film school in California. My aim was to make films about 'primitive' tribes before they were swamped by Western culture. Initially I borrowed camera equipment and, given film, took off on the road in the American Southwest, documenting a rodeo team, a long distance trucker, and even the birth of a baby.

''Then in 1978, I moved from California to the small Caribbean island of Montserrat, and, stunned by its visual beauty I concentrated on painting the old style West Indian architecture and its peoples. The locals would say to me, 'You live in de cement house, no worry de hurricanes,' and my feelings were torn as the houses were torn down. I wish there was a house museum. The beautiful images of Montserrat were the inspiration for my book of paintings, *The Little Island.*

''Montserrat is also the home of one of the world's finest recording studios, Air Studios, which attracts an extraordinary number of international musicians and producers. These people became patrons of my paintings, and my work is now in private collections worldwide.

''In 1987, I published *Caribbean Canvas,* a collection of works, painted on my recent travels to Barbados, Grenada, Antigua, Palm Island, and St. Kitts. This is aimed at a more extensive audience and also includes poetry by Caribbean writers.

''*The Dragon of Redonda* is a fairy tale endorsed by the 'real' King of Redonda. *The Bird Who Was an Elephant* is my favorite book. How could a bird have been an elephant? Children will understand this, of course. But grown-ups, who always need explanations, may need to know that in India it is believed that we have many lives and that when we die, we can become another human being—or an animal. So this is the story of the bird.''

FOR MORE INFORMATION SEE:

New York Times Book Review, January 12, 1986, June 18, 1989.

LEWIS, Jean 1924-

PERSONAL: Born June 2, 1924, in Shanghai, China; daughter of David (a businessman) and Nettie Craig (a music teacher and missionary; maiden name Lambuth) Lewis. *Education:* Tutored at home. *Politics:* Republican. *Religion:* Protestant. *Home:* 601 East 20th St., Apt. 13H, New York, N.Y. 10010.

CAREER: Actress and singer in radio, television, and theater, mainly in New York City, 1940-53; American Theatre Wing's Hospital Committee, New York City, program director, 1947-51; Rehabilitation through Photography, Inc., New York City, executive director, 1953—; writer of children's books,

1962—. Writer of sales promotion and continuity for women's television shows.

WRITINGS:

JUVENILE

Pebbles Flintstone, Artists & Writers Press, 1963.
Bamm-Bamm and Pebbles Flintstone, Artists & Writers Press, 1963.
Touche Turtle and the Fire Dog, Whitman, 1963.
The Flintstones at the Circus, Whitman, 1963.
Boo Boo Bear and the V.I.V., Whitman, 1965.
The Flintstone's Picnic Panic, Whitman, 1965.
(Contributor) *Golden Prize and Other Stories about Horses,* Whitman, 1965, revised edition, 1972.
The Flintstones Meet the Gruesomes, Golden Press, 1965.
Hoppity Hooper Versus Skippity Snooper, Whitman, 1966.
Alvin and the Chipmunks and the Deep Sea Blues, Whitman, 1966.
The Road Runner and the Bird Watchers, Whitman, 1968.
Frankenstein, Jr. and the Devilish Double, Whitman, 1968.
Tom and Jerry Scairdy Cat, Whitman, 1969.
Tom and Jerry under the Big Top, Whitman, 1969.
Gumby and Pokey to the Rescue, Western, 1969.
H. R. Pufnstuf, Western, 1970.
Jane and the Mandarin's Secret, Hawthorn, 1970.
Dr. Leo's Pet Patients (illustrated by Don Madden), American Heritage Press, 1971.
Wacky Witch and the Royal Birthday, Western, 1971.
Hot Dog, Grosset, 1971.
Kathi and Hash San and the Case of Measles, Rand McNally, 1972.
Wacky Witch and the Mystery of the King's Gold, Western, 1973.
Lassie and the Busy Morning, Western, 1973.
Nancy and Sluggo and the Big Surprise, Western, 1974.
Scooby Doo and the Pirate Treasure, Western, 1974.
Bullwinkle's Casserole, Western, 1975.
The Sleeping Tree Mystery, Rand McNally, 1975.
Hong Kong Phooey and the Fortune Cookie Caper, Rand McNally, 1975.
Scooby Doo and the Haunted Dog House, Rand McNally, 1975.
Scooby Doo and the Mystery Monster, Rand McNally, 1975.
Bugs Bunny: Too Many Carrots, Western, 1976.
Mickey Mouse and the Pet Show, Western, 1976.
Santa's Runaway Elf, Rand McNally, 1977.
Mumbley to the Rescue, Rand McNally, 1977.
Benji, the Detective, Western, 1978.
Donald Duck in It's Play Time, Western, 1980.
Around the Year with Pooh, Western, 1980.
Little Golden Book of Dogs, Golden Books, 1982.
Shags Finds a Kitten, Grosset, 1983.
The Teddy Bear Clan from Evergreen Woods, Grosset, 1984.
Planetanimals Mission Zapton (illustrated by John Costanza), Grosset, 1985.
Rainbow Brite: Starlight Saves the Day, Golden Books, 1985.
Rainbow Brite: Twink's Magic Carpet Ride, Golden Books, 1985.
Tom and Jerry's Big Move, Golden Books, 1985.
Bugs Bunny Rides Again, Golden Books, 1986.
Little Golden Book of Holidays, Golden Books, 1986.
The Dragon and the Tiger (fifth grade reader), Macmillan, 1986.
Lady LovelyLocks: Silkypup's Butterfly Adventure, Golden Books, 1987.
Tweety and Sylvester: A Visit to the Vet, Golden Books, 1987.
Tabitha Tabby's Fantastic Flavor, Golden Books, 1988.
Raggedy Dog to the Rescue, Macmillan, 1988.
The Big Book of Dogs, Grosset, 1988.

ADAPTER

Swiss Family Robinson, Artists & Writers Press, 1961.
The Tortoise and the Hare, Whitman, 1963.
The Jungle Book, Golden Press, 1967.
Old Yeller, Golden Press, 1968.
The Absent-Minded Professor, Golden Press, 1968.
Chitty-Chitty-Bang-Bang, Golden Press, 1968.

Contributor to periodicals, including *Professional Photographer* and *Human Services.*

WORK IN PROGRESS: The Temple Summer, young adult fiction set in China during the Boxer Rebellion of 1900; *I Remember Amah,* memoirs of her childhood in China; retelling of Bible stories for Checkerboard Press' "Read-Along" series.

SIDELIGHTS: Lewis, who is the executive director of Rehabilitation through Photography in New York City, writes in her spare time. Author of more than fifty books she comments, "Writing, I think, is fun. I hope I can always do it and that somebody will always want to read it."

HOBBIES AND OTHER INTERESTS: Animals, particularly cats.

FOR MORE INFORMATION SEE:

Town & Village (New York), February 9, 1984 (p. 12), November 17, 1988 (p. 13).

LINES, Kathleen Mary 1902-1988

OBITUARY NOTICE: Born September 24, 1902, in Edmonton, Alberta, Canada; died December 24, 1988, in Winchester, Hampshire, England. Librarian, editor, and author. Lines was primarily known for establishing high standards in children's literature through her guidebooks that have helped parents select books for their children. A librarian for the Toronto Public Library and later a consultant to Oxford University Press's children's book department, Lines was commissioned by the National Book League in 1946 to write *Four to Fourteen,* a book that quickly became a vital resource tool for English librarians because of its annotated listing of more than twelve hundred children's books. She also edited *The One Hundred Best Books for Children,* commissioned in the mid-1950s by the London *Sunday Times; The House of the Nightmare and Other Eerie Tales,* a Junior Literary Guild selection in 1968; and *Stories for Christmas,* and *The Faber Story Book,* both published in the 1980s. She compiled many anthologies, including a collection of nursery rhymes entitled *Lavender's Blue,* which received a Carnegie Special Commendation in 1954, was an International Board on Books for Young People honour list selection in 1956, and received the Lewis Carroll Shelf Award in 1960.

FOR MORE INFORMATION SEE:

Martha E. Ward and Dorothy A. Marquardt, *Authors of Books for Young People,* supplement to the 2nd edition, Scarecrow, 1979.

OBITUARIES

Times (London), December 29, 1988.

MARIE, Geraldine 1949-
(Marie Christie)

PERSONAL: Born September 9, 1949, in Kew Gardens, N.Y.; daughter of Salvatore A. (a video engineer) and Louise A. (a secretary; maiden name, Ingargiola) Lettieri; children: Elizabeth. *Education:* Queens College of the City University of New York, B.A., 1971; C. W. Post College, Long Island University, M.S., 1976. *Address:* 515 East 72nd St., New York, N.Y. 10021.

CAREER: St. Patrick's School, Bay Shore, N.Y., elementary school teacher, 1971-81; free-lance writer, 1981—. *Member:* Society of Children's Book Writers, International Reading Association. *Awards, honors:* Children's Choice from the International Reading Association and the Children's Book Council, 1982, for *The Magic Box.*

WRITINGS:

JUVENILE

(Adapter) Arthur Conan Doyle, *The Hound of the Baskervilles,* A/V Concepts Corp., 1980.
Reading Comprehension Series of Games, Comprehension Games, 1980.
The Magic Box (illustrated by Michele Chessare), Dutton, 1981.
Reading Skills Games, Learning Well, 1981, fourth edition, 1982.

CASSETTE SERIES

"The Golden Touch," Gamco Industries, 1979.
"Alice and the Mad Tea Party," Gamco Industries, 1979.
"Thumbellina," Gamco Industries, 1979.
"Rumpelstiltskin," Gamco Industries, 1979.
"Pinocchio," Gamco Industries, 1979.
"Beauty and the Beast," Gamco Industries, 1979.

Also author of educational stories for Troll, 1981. Contributor of stories for children to magazines.

WORK IN PROGRESS: A supplementary reading series for preschool and kindergarten; *The Devil's Necklace,* a young adult gothic novel; *Love's Full Fury,* a contemporary adult novel, under pseudonym Marie Christie.

SIDELIGHTS: "I began writing as a hobby in 1976. Originally, I had hoped to publish a children's literature guide for parents. When it did not sell, I thought that if I published something else, editors might then be more receptive to the idea of the guide. I started writing stories for educational publishers. Although the literature guide has still not sold, the educational stories, cassettes, adaptations, and even games for all grade levels have been successful continually.

"I am still very interested in educational writing. However, the publication of *The Magic Box* and its being voted a Children's Choice of 1982 has intensified my interest in writing trade books for children.

"About my writing: I keep as busy and active as possible in the field. I love writing and consider it not only my job but my hobby. I enjoy being versatile by writing for all ages, preschool through adult.

GERALDINE MARIE

"Most recently, I have become involved in writing contemporary adult romances. I am a romantic at heart, and find I fit in with the genre, naturally and easily.

"I am picky with my writing. No matter what I write, I try to keep my standards high. As for my characters, I feel there is a little bit of me in all my main characters and a little bit of the people I know in the others.

"In my opinion, the most pressing issue in our society is our educational system, both informally in our families and neighborhoods and formally in our schools. The education of each individual (and consequently of our society as a whole) is the basis of our society. The importance of this issue is too often neglected or ignored because of its too obvious impact. The formation of each individual for good or bad—his thoughts, words, attitudes, values, and actions—can be traced back to the education provided and the example set in families, neighborhoods, and schools. If our families, neighborhoods, and schools fail, how can the individuals who make up our society succeed?"

HOBBIES AND OTHER INTERESTS: Reading, classical music, museums, the arts, the countryside, cooking.

McDANIEL, Becky B(ring) 1953-

PERSONAL: Born September 16, 1953, in Ashland, Ohio; daughter of Walter Dale (a painter) and Ethel (a homemaker; maiden name, Ernst) Bring; married Larry Craig McDaniel (a power plant administrative manager), October 18, 1972; children: Jennifer Ann, Kristopher Craig, Katie Eileen. *Education:* Attended Santa Fe Community College, 1983—, and University of Florida, 1984. *Politics:* Republican. *Religion:* Presbyterian. *Home:* 3931 N. 40th Court, Gainesville, Fla. 32606. *Office:* 3800 N.W. 6th St., Gainesville, Fla. 32609.

CAREER: Free-lance writer of children's books, poetry, and puzzles. *Member:* Phi Theta Kappa.

WRITINGS:

JUVENILE

Katie Did It (illustrated by Lois Axeman), Childrens Press, 1983.

Katie Couldn't (illustrated by L. Axeman), Childrens Press, 1985.

Katie Can (illustrated by L. Axeman), Childrens Press, 1987.

Also author of "Animals from the Bible Puzzle," High Adventure, 1983-84. Contributor to periodicals, including *Creative Years, Trail Signs, Poet's Corner, Whisky Island, Alura, Lady's Circle, Writer's Opportunities,* and *High Adventure.*

WORK IN PROGRESS: Several children's books, *Katie Shouldn't, Katie Forgot, Wednesday Kris Eats Macaroni and Cheese;* articles for magazines; poetry for children.

SIDELIGHTS: "I was born in Ashland, Ohio on September 16, 1953, and lived on a small farm until I was eleven years old. I still believe that the love I have for nature and animals (mostly cats) all began in the apple orchards and small town atmosphere of my early childhood. Living in the country, I learned to use my imagination during time alone and with friends as we spent countless hours inventing new games, camping out, sledding, and scaring the daylights out of each other at Halloween in a neighbor's old, red barn!

BECKY B. McDANIEL

"At the same time that I was turning into a teenager, I also turned into a city dweller as my parents sold the small farmhouse and moved into the city. Although I was sure I would never be so happy or have so many friends again, I learned that happiness is generally where we find it—not necessarily where we expect it! I quickly made many new friends—including one whose father owned an old semi-trailer that seemed to be just right for parties, dances, or creating an imaginary world that belonged only to us.

"Our new house was located near Brookside Park where I spent many hours swimming, playing baseball, and hanging out with friends in the summer before turning to ice skating and sledding in the winter. My favorite season was usually the season I was then enjoying—but the season I remember the most was the sun-filled summer.

"It was during these early years of my life that I first began the attempt to share my thoughts and feelings with the world by writing them on paper. My first target turned out to be my very own mother as I wrote countless poems to her to express my sincere love. She kept some of these poems and, as I read them today, they still say the things I feel; however, the form and format is much the same as those displayed by many of the students that I speak to on my frequent talks to elementary and middle school classes.

"About the time of my fourteenth birthday, our family made the large transition of moving from our small Ohio town to the larger university town of Gainesville, Florida. Perhaps it was because of the loneliness of moving away from all the friends or perhaps it was just from my natural love of writing, I began to keep a journal. Virtually everything and everyone I met, liked, disliked, loved, hated, wanted, and believed was systematically logged in this book that anyone else would simply have named, 'The Best and Worst Times of Becky Sue Bring!'

"After high school I attended Santa Fe Community College for several semesters, taking the required courses at that time. English was a required course, but one I truly loved.

"Not unlike countless other people everywhere, my life began to take some unexpected twists and turns that prevented me from attending college as I had always dreamed of. At the age of twenty-seven, I once again enrolled in Santa Fe Community College in Gainesville. This proved to be the turning point in my writing career.

"Although others had told me that I had the talent to write, I never really believed it. It was not until I took a writing class from an instructor named Barbara Kirkpatrick that I really found that not only could I write but I also seemed to possess the ability to entertain others with my writings. Barbara encouraged me to write, write often, and send things off to various publishers. Through her supervision and genuine caring, I ventured forth into the unknown world of publishers. The first manuscript I sent off was, *Katie Did It.*

"I received my manuscript back along with a rejection letter. I sent *Katie Did It* off again and received a letter saying it had been accepted for publication by Childrens Press. It was a dream come true for me and at times even now its hard for me to believe I have three books published that children all over the United States are reading. I enjoy writing children's books most of all, and beginning readers give me the most pleasure. My poetry consists of serious work and some poems for children. Here again I am drawn to works for children. I derive the most pleasure from these and hope that the children that read them do too.

(From *Katie Did It* by Becky Bring McDaniel. Illustrated by Lois Axeman.)

"*Katie Did It* is a story that has a lot to do with my own childhood. I was the youngest of three children, just as Katie is the youngest of my three children. By watching and listening to my children, I found some of the things happening with them were the same things that had happened to me. I was blamed for virtually everything in our household. If the mayonnaise was not put away, I was blamed. If one of my brother's model cars was moved a fraction of an inch, I was blamed. It was never my other brother that touched those cars, it had to be Becky. Like I really wanted to touch his stupid, old cars anyway!

"*Katie Couldn't* was, again, my childhood revisited by Katie. My brothers constantly reminded me of all the things I couldn't do. I would try to keep up with them, but usually without success. And then, once in a while something would come along to make me realize I was happiest being the youngest, because there truly were some things only the youngest of the family could do!

"*Katie Can* was a story that came out of a situation like many situations for the youngest, where he/she tries and tries to show others she can do things just like them. However, it usually never works out when someone is watching; it works out when no one else is around. Well, Katie tried things but never succeeded when Jenny and Kris watched. Finally, she succeeded when no one was around, so she thought, and to her delight, Jenny and Kris did see her accomplish something. This is another story that happens to the youngest in the family, just as it did to me. By watching my three children, a lot of my childhood memories have come back to visit me again. They have been very welcome memories!"

HOBBIES AND OTHER INTERESTS: Sharing my work with area schools, family outings and vacations, decorating, gardening, raquetball, swimming and the beach.

MEAKER, Marijane 1927-
(Ann Aldrich, M. E. Kerr, M. J. Meaker, Vin Packer)

PERSONAL: Born May 27, 1927, in Auburn, N.Y.; daughter of Ellis R. (a mayonnaise manufacturer) and Ida T. Meaker. *Education:* Attended Vermont Junior College, and New School for Social Research; University of Missouri, B.A., 1949. *Home:* 12 Deep Six Dr., East Hampton, N.Y. 11937. *Agent:* Julia Fallowfield, McIntosh & Otis, Inc., 475 Fifth Ave., New York, N.Y. 10017.

CAREER: Worked at several jobs, including assistant file clerk for E. P. Dutton (publisher), 1949-50; free-lance writer, 1949—. *Member:* Ashawagh Hall Writers' Workshop (founder), PEN, Authors League of America, Society of Children's Book Writers.

AWARDS, HONORS: Dinky Hocker Shoots Smack! was selected one of *School Library Journal*'s Best Books of the Year, 1972, *The Son of Someone Famous,* 1974, *I'll Love You When You're More Like Me,* 1977, *Little Little,* 1981, *What I Really Think of You,* 1982, and *Night Kites,* 1987; *Dinky Hocker Shoots Smack!* was selected one of American Library Association's Best Books for Young Adults, 1972, *Is That You, Miss Blue?,* 1975, *Me, Me, Me, Me, Me: Not a Novel,* 1983, *I Stay Near You,* 1985, and *Night Kites,* 1986; *If I Love You, Am I Trapped Forever?* was selected one of *New York Times* Outstanding Books of the Year, 1973, *Is That You, Miss Blue?,* 1975, and *Gentlehands,* 1978; *Book World*'s Children's Spring Book Festival Honor Book, and one of Child Study Association of America's Children's Books of the Year, both 1973, both for *If I Love You, Am I Trapped Forever?; Media and Methods* Maxi Award, 1974, for *Dinky Hocker Shoots Smack!;* Christopher Award, 1979, and one of New York Public Library's Books for the Teen Age, 1980, and 1981, both for *Gentlehands;* Golden Kite Award for Fiction from the Society of Children's Book Writers, 1981, and one of New York Public Library's Books for the Teen Age, 1982, both for *Little Little.*

WRITINGS:

YOUNG ADULT FICTION; UNDER PSEUDONYM M. E. KERR

Dinky Hocker Shoots Smack! (ALA Notable Book), Harper, 1972.
If I Love You, Am I Trapped Forever?, Harper, 1973.
The Son of Someone Famous, Harper, 1974.
Is That You, Miss Blue? (ALA Notable Book), Harper, 1975.
Love Is a Missing Person, Harper, 1975.
I'll Love You When You're More Like Me, Harper, 1977.
Gentlehands, Harper, 1978.
Little Little, Harper, 1981.
What I Really Think of You, Harper, 1982.
Him She Loves?, Harper, 1984.
I Stay Near You, Harper, 1985.
Night Kites, Harper, 1986.
Fell, Harper, 1987.
Fell Back, Harper, 1989.

YOUNG ADULT NONFICTION; UNDER PSEUDONYM M. E. KERR

Me, Me, Me, Me, Me: Not a Novel (autobiography), Harper, 1983.

CONTRIBUTOR; YOUNG ADULT

Sixteen: Short Stories by Outstanding Writers for Young Adults, edited by Donald R. Gallo, Delacorte, 1984.

ADULT FICTION

(Under name, M. J. Meaker) *Hometown,* Doubleday, 1967.
Game of Survival, New American Library, 1968.
(Under name Marijane Meaker) *Shockproof Sydney Skate,* Little, Brown, 1972.

ADULT NONFICTION; UNDER NAME M. J. MEAKER

Sudden Endings, Doubleday, 1964, paperback edition under pseudonym Vin Packer, Fawcett, 1964.

NONFICTION; UNDER PSEUDONYM ANN ALDRICH

We Walk Alone, Gold Medal Books, 1955.
We Too Must Love, Gold Medal Books, 1958.
Carol in a Thousand Cities, Gold Medal Books, 1960.
We Two Won't Last, Gold Medal Books, 1963.
Take a Lesbian to Lunch, MacFadden-Bartell, 1972.

ADULT FICTION; UNDER PSEUDONYM VIN PACKER

Spring Fire, Gold Medal Books, 1952.
Dark Intruder, Gold Medal Books, 1952.
Look Back to Love, Gold Medal Books, 1953.
Come Destroy Me, Gold Medal Books, 1954.
Whisper His Sin, Gold Medal Books, 1954.
The Thrill Kids, Gold Medal Books, 1955.
Dark Don't Catch Me, Gold Medal Books, 1956.
The Young and Violent, Gold Medal Books, 1956.
Three-Day Terror, Gold Medal Books, 1957.
The Evil Friendship, Gold Medal Books, 1958.
5:45 to Suburbia, Gold Medal Books, 1958.
The Twisted Ones, Gold Medal Books, 1959.
The Damnation of Adam Blessing, Gold Medal Books, 1961.
The Girl on the Best Seller List, Gold Medal Books, 1961.
Something in the Shadows, Gold Medal Books, 1961.
Intimate Victims, Gold Medal Books, 1962.
Alone at Night, Gold Medal Books, 1963.
The Hare in March, New American Library, 1967.
Don't Rely on Gemini, Delacorte Press, 1969.

Teacher's guides are available for *Dinky Hocker Shoots Smack!, If I Love You, Am I Trapped Forever?, Is That You, Miss Blue?* and *Love Is a Missing Person.*

ADAPTATIONS:

"Dinky Hocker" (television film; based on *Dinky Hocker Shoots Smack!*), starring Wendie Jo Sperber, Learning Corporation of America, 1978.
"If I Love You, Am I Trapped Forever?" (listening cassette), Random House, 1979.

WORK IN PROGRESS: An adult book set in Oak Ridge, Tenn. in 1942.

SIDELIGHTS: Marijane Meaker was born on **May 27, 1927** in Auburn, New York, the only daughter of Ellis and Ida Meaker. Her father owned Ivanhoe Foods, whose chief product was mayonnaise, and she often joked of the family monopoly, because her grandfather owned many of the local grocery stores. "I grew up always wanting to be a writer. My father was a mayonnaise manufacturer, with a strange habit, for a mayonnaise manufacturer, of reading everything from the Harvard Classics, to all of Dickens, Emerson, Poe, Thoreau, Kipling, and John O'Hara, Sinclair Lewis, John Steinbeck, all the Book-of-the-Month Club selections, plus magazines like *Time, Life,*

MARIJANE MEAKER

Look, and *Fortune,* and all the New York City newspapers, along with the local Auburn, New York *Citizen Advertiser*."[1]

Meaker's father was not the only one to encourage her interest in reading and writing. "So did English teachers . . . and librarians who had to pull me out of the stacks at closing time. And there were my favorite writers like Thomas Wolfe, Sherwood Anderson, the Brontes, and our hometown hero, Samuel Hopkins Adams. (I'd pedal past his big house on Owasco Lake, just to see where a real writer lived!) But in my heart, I know who was responsible for this ambition of mine to become a writer: it was my lifelong abettor . . . my . . . mother.

"One of the most vivid memories of my childhood is of my mother making a phone call. First, she'd tell me to go out and play. I'd pretend to do that, letting the back door slam, hiding right around the corner of the living room, in the hall. She'd have her pack of Kools and the ashtray on the desk, as she gave the number of one of her girlfriends to the operator . . . . My Mother would begin nearly every conversation the same way: 'Wait till you hear this!'

"Even today, when I'm finished with a book and sifting through ideas for a new one, I ask myself: Is the idea a 'wait till you hear this?'"[1]

On Saturday nights in summer mother and daughter would drive downtown together and park in different spots, observing their neighbors and collecting gossip. "Then home . . . and a lesson from my mother on the importance of fiction. Fiction, I learned early on, spins off grandly from fact. Our trip downtown would be related over the phone, beginning, 'Wait till you hear this! Carl Otter sent poor little Polly off to see "Brother Rat" so he could have a night on the town, that dear little woman with her face down to her shoes, standing in line by herself while he treats Ellie Budd to old-fashioneds down at Boysen's.'

"Long before the character in one of Salinger's short stories ever peeked into someone else's bathroom cabinet to inspect its contents, I'd learned from my mother that that was the first thing you did once the bathroom door was closed in other people's homes.

"'What are you looking for?' I'd ask.

"She'd say, 'Shhhh! Run the water!'

"I learned that the first thing you look for is prescription medicine, then all the ointments and liquids that tell you what ailments are being treated in the house you're visiting.

"My mother taught me all a writer'd need to know about socio/economic/ethnic differences, too.

"She taught me to cut out all the labels from my coats and jackets, anything I might remove in Second Presbyterian Church on a Sunday morning, so that no one knew that we often bought out-of-town.

"I'm not explaining my philosophy of life to you," Dinky answered. (Jacket illustration by Jay J. Smith from *Dinky Hocker Shoots Smack!* by M. E. Kerr.)

"My mother'd come from a poor immigrant German family twenty-six miles from Auburn, where she'd been raised in a convent. She'd taken a step up in her marriage, a fact she was always defensive about in Auburn, always proud of in her hometown, Syracuse; and the labels she'd cut out were sewn back in for visits there.

"She took an unusual interest in the boys who came to call on me when I was in my early teens. She warned me that if I married a Catholic, there'd be one baby right after the other; that if I married an Italian I wouldn't be allowed to wash the salad bowl, they just wiped it dry; and that any boy whose father was bald, would be bald himself one day."[1]

At age ten, Meaker and her friends were in love with the movie star, Ronald Reagan. She wrote him a letter pretending to be a little crippled girl in the hope of getting his autograph. He wrote back:

"Dear Marijane, Thank you for your letter. Remember that a handicap can be a challenge. Always stay as cheerful as you are now. Yours truly, Ronald Reagan"[2]

Her parents found the letter and she was forced to admit she had lied tc the actor. "After my father read the letter, and got the truth out of me concerning my correspondence with Ronald Reagan, he told me what I was to do.

"What I was to do was to sit down immediately and write Ronald Reagan, telling him I had lied. I was to add that I thanked God for my good health. I was to return both the letter and the photograph.

"No Saturday in my entire life had ever been so dark.

"My father stood over me while I wrote the letter in tears, convinced that Ronald Reagan would hate me all his life for my deception. I watched through blurred eyes while my father took my letter, Ronald Reagan's letter, and the signed photograph, put them into a manila envelope, addressed it, sealed it, and put it in his briefcase to take to the post office."[2]

1939-1940. Her younger brother, "Butchie," was born and Meaker's life changed. "Twelve was the age I was when my baby brother was born, and my older brother went off to military school.

"Thirteen was the year I became a hundred.

"Three things contributed to my rapid aging: the new baby in the house, the dramatic change in my older brother's personality, and my forced enrollment in Laura Bryan's ballroom dancing classes.

"No new budget was going to make up for the fact that both my parents were suddenly swooning daily over Butchie, my baby brother.

"No new budget was going to make me feel better about the sight of my older brother coming through the door on vacation from military school, a Riverside Military Academy cadet, caped and epauletted and sabered.

"I was suddenly the nothing, sandwiched between two stars.

"Locked in my room, I wrote stories about murder and suicide, tried on clothes, daydreamed about boys, and listened to records like 'Blues in the Night' and 'Let's Get Away from It All.'

"I was in a slump, and my mother's answer to this was to enroll me in Laura Bryan's school, this time for ballroom dancing. I had already suffered through toe and tap dancing, with Laura Bryan wincing while I performed grotesque tour jetes and did the buck-and-wing to any rhythm but the one the pianist was playing. Dancing was not one of my gifts."[2]

1943. Another answer to Meaker's "slump" was to send her to boarding school at Stuart Hall in Staunton, Virginia. She resented the move and soon got into trouble at the Episcopal, all-girls' school.

1944. Meaker's family bought a summer cottage on Owasco Lake, at Burtis Point, a point of land farthest away from town. Meaker was isolated from her friends. "The summer of 1944 I became Eric Ranthram McKay.

"I think one reason for this was all the sailors pouring into our small town. There were some soldiers and marines around, too, but we knew them. They were hometown boys, coming and going from war. The sailors were another matter. On leave from nearby Sampson Naval Base, they came to us fresh from boot camp, lonely and looking for fun.

"'The kind of fun a sailor is looking for might fill a few empty hours for him, but you could pay for it the rest of your life,' my father said."[2]

Meaker, naturally, wanted to be where the sailors were, instead of babysitting for her kid brother. "There, at the beginning of the

(From the television film "Dinky Hocker," based on *Dinky Hocker Shoots Smack!*, starring Wendie Jo Sperber. Courtesy of Learning Corporation of America.)

summer, I was marooned. My father drove into work every morning at seven, and returned at six every evening. Gas rationing made it hard for anyone to get to and from Burtis Point. There were no buses. Hitchhikers didn't fare well on the empty roads at night, which discouraged local boyfriends from visiting. 'Life' was going on back in town, at the movies, at the Teen Canteen and the USO, at the kids' hangouts like Murray's.

"By day I swam and sailed and looked after my kid brother, listening to my girl friends' accounts of what was happening, for hours on the telephone. By night I wrote, using my first pseudonym: Eric Ranthram McKay.

"The pseudonym was chosen because my father's initials were E. R. M. After I wrote a story, I mailed it off to a magazine with a letter written on my father's stationery, engraved with his initials and our home address.

"I don't know why I chose Eric, Ranthram, or McKay—I guess I just felt the name had a good ring to it.

"All of Eric Ranthram McKay's stories were sad, romantic ones about the war. I subscribed to a magazine called *Writer's Digest*, which listed the needs of publications like *Good Housekeeping*, *Ladies' Home Journal*, and *Redbook*. I mailed off my stories in manila envelopes with a stamped, addressed envelope enclosed, and they came back like boomerangs, with printed rejection slips attached.

"Sometimes these rejection slips had a 'sorry' penciled across them, or a 'try again.'

"These I cherished, and saved, and used to buoy my spirits as I began new stories, and kept the old ones circulating.

"At the same time Eric Ranthram McKay was writing stories, Marijane Meaker was writing servicemen—a soldier named Bob McKeon from my hometown, and a sailor named Eddie Herbold. Herbold was considered an okay sailor, since my family knew him. These 'romances,' by mail, were in full swing that summer."[2]

1945. On her return to Stuart Hall, she continued to be rebellious to school authorities, and in February of her senior year she was suspended for throwing darts at photographs of faculty members. From February to March she worked at American Locomotive, a local defense plant, as a file clerk. Her mother's manipulations allowed her to be reinstated in time for graduation. "I think

I am now unofficially engaged. (Jacket illustration by Fred Marcellino from *I'll Love You When You're More Like Me* by M. E. Kerr.)

(Jacket illustration by Leslie Bauman from *Is That You, Miss Blue?* by M. E. Kerr.)

my years at Stuart Hall were a provocative experience for both Stuart Hall and me. I was the class reprobate, assigned a single room the size of a large closet on Middle Music Hall to keep me out of trouble. Nevertheless, I was very familiar with Mrs. Hodges' office, where I would go after finding in my mailbox, many a morning, a note exclaiming, 'See me at once! APH.' . . . In my senior year I was expelled, and only my mother's intervention with a bishop had that changed to a suspension, so I could return to graduate with my class . . . . I had, while I was there, and well after, a great infatuation with Stuart Hall, a lover's quarrel with its rules and certain stern faculty members, and now I read it's changed and not so strict, and wonder would I love it so well these days? I don't know, but there was something stimulating and amusing, and very like life, as I came to know it, in its regulated, intense, dutiful and peculiar ambiance. I went there during World War II, and I remember so well getting there on overcrowded trains jammed with boys just a few years older than I, on their way to war. Many of us had brothers away at war. It was a difficult time . . . and I remember Mrs. Hodges calling an assembly to announce Roosevelt's death, and dear Miss Dean, the science teacher, correcting her former opinion that atoms could not be split.

"In the school yearbook, *Inlook,* **1945,** I am distinctively out of place, since it was put together during my expulsion. At the very end of the seniors' photographs comes Kathryn Walters, my roommate; then Wellford, Worthy and Yates . . . then Marijane Meaker, on record forever, the out-of-line black sheep."[2]

After graduation, Meaker went to Vermont Junior College where she edited the school newspaper, which published her first story. "I was too overwhelmed by the idea there were boys on campus (local ones, about a dozen, who were day students) and too amazed that I could wear jeans to class, and to the dining room, and that I could carry a pack of cigarettes in my shirt pocket, though I could smoke them only in the 'smoker.'

"I felt like someone who'd been let out of prison. I was finally going to school again with Yankees who talked like me, knew what deep snow was, and owned skis, skates, and toboggans. (Winters you could take skiing for gym, go off on skis before breakfast with the class, and come in to a feast of pancakes with real Vermont maple syrup poured over them.)

"I was too busy clearing out an old storage room the dean allowed me to convert into a press room.

"Before the autumn leaves had stopped falling, my first article appeared in the first issue of the school paper.

"It was called 'The Air and I,' and it was about my flying lessons, which I'd talked my father into giving me that past summer. (My father'd bought a small plane for my older brother and him to enjoy, and I suppose I was in another phase of 'brother envy.')

"I hated flying, managed to solo, then never went up again."[2]

1946. Transferred to the University of Missouri. She had to join a sorority because housing was so scarce due to the war. Her father refused to send her trunks until he was sure she had joined up, and therefore had a place to live. "At the University of Missouri, where I went despite my father's warning that if I did go there, I'd end up marrying someone from Missouri, I

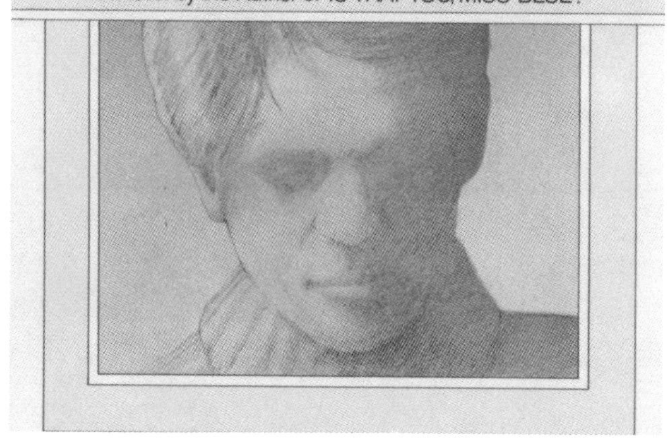

I wonder what that summer would have been like if I'd never met Skye Pennington. (Jacket illustration by Fred Marcellino from *Gentlehands* by M. E. Kerr.)

switched my major from Journalism to English . . . partly because I failed Economics, which one had to pass to get into J-School, and partly because I realized I didn't want anything to do with writing fact. I wanted to make up my own facts. I wanted to do creative writing.

"It was the end of World War II, and Columbia, Missouri, was a real college town, filled with kids right off the farm, or coming from little towns like Bolivar and Poplar Bluff, plus an abundance of young men straight out of the service. Girls who'd never been any farther than St. Louis or Kansas City were matched on blind dates with fellows who'd fought in Okinawa, or already seen London and Paris, as sorority/fraternity life commenced. My very first week there I went with some classmates to a popular hangout called the Shack, and learned the game of Chug-a-Lug, which was a beer drinking contest, in which you drained your full glass in one breather, while everyone sang 'Here's to Marijane, she's true blue, she's a drinker through and through!'"[1]

But Meaker hated the sorority teas and their process of elimination. "The sorority system, to my mind, is still one of the cruelest introductions to college life that I can imagine, and I'm not particularly proud of my participation in sorority life, even though I made my closest friends in the Alpha Delta Pi sorority.

"I tried to think what it was sororities were saying to their members, and it seemed to me they were all saying not to be individuals, but to be as much like the group as possible."[2]

Being as much like the group as possible was not Meaker's strong suit. "Although it was very much a party campus in those postwar years, it was still the end of the 1940s, and there were rules: a time to be in at night, no men above the first floor in a sorority house, no alcoholic beverages . . . and in our sorority, Alpha Delta Pi, dating men who were not in fraternities was frowned on. They were called 'independents'; they were unwelcome (though tolerated) at major sorority functions.

"I found someone to date (and fall in love with) who gave my father far more to worry about than the boy from St. Louis or Kansas City whom he'd envisioned. George was from Hungary originally, a Jew who'd barely managed to escape the Nazis in his teens by being smuggled into Venezuela.

"By the time he arrived on the Missouri campus, he was an ardent Communist.

"Under his spell, I joined the Communist party, and voted for Henry Wallace for President of the United States, the only one in Cayuga County, New York, to do so.

"I stayed on for summer sessions, too, because of George, and although he'd politicized me, he hadn't cured me of my wish to be a writer.

"I wrote story after story, sending them off to New York-based magazines, accumulating so many rejection slips that I attended a sorority masquerade party as a rejection slip, wearing a black slip with rejections from all the magazines pinned to it."[1]

Meaker also volunteered at the local mental hospital, where she dated the hospital psychiatrist. She and George discussed marriage, but eventually he left the country without her, spurred on by an F.B.I. investigation of his Communist sympathies. Meaker implies that her mother may have instigated the investigation.

1949. After receiving her B.A. from the University of Missouri, Meaker moved to New York City with several of her sorority sisters. "In those days, New York City was still a place where you could take a subway at night and not fear getting mugged. You could also find a two-bedroom apartment for $150 a month, if you wanted to live in Washington Heights, where the four of us found ours.

"My roommates all got good jobs in advertising/publishing, because they knew shorthand. In those days, a good job, for a female, was a job as a secretary, at about fifty dollars a week.

"I had never been able to master shorthand, though I had studied it at my father's insistence . . . . My first job was at Dutton Publishing Company, as something like an assistant to the file clerk, at thirty-two dollars a week.

"My job had no real title. I worked in the art department, in the bull pen, carrying my lunch every day in a paper sack, after a long subway ride with two station changes; it took me an hour to get down to lower New York from Washington Heights in hose, heels, hat, and gloves.

"I wasn't worth the thirty-two dollars Dutton paid me to file letters and answer phones and carry things from one floor to another. My own work came first with me. I was always sitting there scratching out short stories and poems. I think the only time I looked up was when an author came into the area to discuss the artwork on his/her cover. I was in awe of all the authors. I remember one young, tough fellow who never liked his covers,

On the night of the Senior Prom, I was stood up. (Jacket illustration by Andrew Rhodes from *Fell* by M. E. Kerr.)

who always gave the art director a hard time. He was Mickey Spillane, not too well known yet.''[1]

Meaker's work continued to be rejected, but she kept on with it. ''I couldn't get an agent, so I began sending out manuscripts under my roommates' names. I wanted a variety of names, and I wanted to be sure the manuscripts were safely returned to our mailbox.

''I wrote anything and everything in an effort to get published. I wrote confession stories, articles, 'slick' stories for the women's magazines, poetry and fillers.

''One manuscript was returned from *Your Life* magazine with a hopeful letter, telling me that with a little revision, they might publish it. It was one of the ones sent out under a roommate's name.

''She hit the roof when she saw the title: 'Masturbation Is Normal.'

''After that, none of my roommates wanted their names on my work.''[2]

Meaker lost her job at this point. ''In a year's time, I went from Dutton to Compton Advertising Company, to a medical house publishing the *Review of Gastroenterology* and the *Proctology Review,* to Fawcett Publications, fired almost as soon as I was hired.

''Meanwhile, I'd found a way to get an agent: I'd become my own agent, print up stationery with my name on it and 'Literary Agent,' and send out stories under pseudonyms.

''My pseudonyms were my clients.

''On lunch breaks from Fawcett Publications, I visited editors and talked about Laura Winston (who wrote slicks for women's magazines), Mamie Stone (who wrote confessions), Edgar Stone, her 'husband' (who wrote detective stories), and Winslow Albert (who wrote articles) . . . . They were all me.

''Finally, Fawcett fired me, tired of my two- and three-hour lunch breaks.''[2]

1951. Meaker made an arrangement with her roommates to cook for them in exchange for food money, and she worked full time on her writing. Finally, at the age of twenty-three, she sold her first story. ''On April 20, 1951, a letter came in the mail from the *Ladies' Home Journal,* to Marijane Meaker, Literary Agent, saying they were going to buy Laura Winston's story.

''I raced to the phone to call my roommates. I was so excited that I believed they were paying seventy-five dollars for the story. No one, in any office in New York City, was at their desks. General Douglas MacArthur was being welcomed in New York City with an enormous ticker-tape parade!

''When my roommates finally came home and read the acceptance letter themselves, one said, 'It isn't seventy-five dollars they're paying you. It's seven hundred and fifty dollars!'

''That night I took everyone out to dinner to Ruby Foo's for egg rolls, duckling chop suey, beef with snow-pea pods, et cetera, et cetera. I'd earned enough to keep on writing for another six months . . . . I was on my way!

''In **September, 1951,** when my story was published, I opened to the table of contents and cried out, 'Look, there's my name with John P. Marquand's and Dorothy Thompson's!' 'There's Laura Winston's name,' a roommate said, 'and there's your picture, with Laura Winston's name under it!' On pages 46 and 47, there was a large illustration depicting three characters from my story.

The *Journal* Presents
LAURA WINSTON
And
Her First Published Story
DEVOTEDLY, PATRICK HENRY CASEBOLT''[2]

1952. After this success, she never worked at a full-time job again. Her first novel, *Spring Fire,* was published by Gold Medal Books, a series by Fawcett Publications. ''*Spring Fire* was an instant paperback success, selling 1,463,917 copies in 1952, more than *The Damned* by John D. MacDonald or *My Cousin Rachel* by Daphne du Maurier, both published that same year in the U.S.

''Long out of print now, *Spring Fire* enabled me to become a full-time free-lance novelist, enjoy a trip to Europe, and get my first apartment, sans roommates, on East Ninety-fourth Street, off Fifth Avenue, where I would live for eight years.''[1]

Meaker began to write mysteries and thrillers under the pen names Vin Packer and Ann Aldrich. ''I was writing some paperback originals. In those days it seemed like a phenomenal amount of money that you could get for them; hardcover, of course, didn't pay as much unless you were a best-seller. Then I heard that if you wrote mysteries and suspense you would be reviewed in the *New York Times* in the mystery and suspense column, whereas, you were never reviewed if you wrote just a paperback original. So I immediately started writing mystery and suspense for that reason, and that was how I got into it. And I did get reviews; I did get noticed."[3]

1950-1964. Meaker wrote twenty novels under her two pen names. She explained how she choose the name Vin Packer. "Years and years later, I discovered I wasn't the only one who felt a female wouldn't be taken seriously. When I first began writing suspense stories for Fawcett Publications, my editor suggested that I take a male pseudonym. 'You tell a fast, tough story,' he said, 'and you'll lose your credibility with a name like Marijane Meaker.' I chose the pen name Vin Packer, after talking about the problem over dinner with one friend whose first name was Vin and another whose last name was Packer."[2]

A good friend, Louise Fitzhugh, encouraged her to write for young adults. "Louise was an artist turned writer, who had done a very successful book called *Harriet the Spy*. It was published by Harper & Row as a 'young adult' book. I had never heard of such a category.

We sat on the sand ... watching this diamond-shaped thing blink out over the ocean. (Jacket illustration by Andrew Rhodes from *Night Kites* by M. E. Kerr.)

"'You'd be a good young adult writer,' Louise would tell me, 'since you're always writing about kids.'

"'But not from their viewpoint,' I'd answer, and I'd dismiss her suggestions that I should try to write for this field."[1]

Meanwhile, Meaker was studying psychology, sociology, anthropology and child psychology at the New School for Social Research.

1964. Meaker wrote a hardcover nonfiction book on suicide called *Sudden Endings* under the name M. J. Meaker. In her "Author's Note" she wrote: "When I was a child, there was a grand eight-sided white stone house at the end of our block, with a glass-roofed cupola on top, and a tall iron fence built all the way around the sumptuous grounds. It was an abandoned house, boarded up, the lawn a field of weeds. 'The Octagon' was always a source of eerie fascination to the children; we called it 'The Octopus,' and we went there to play despite our parents' warnings to stay away. What drew us to this house was not its eight sides, nor its cupola, nor even the fact it was empty; when we sat huddled under the large front porch in our secret clubhouse, we spoke of the mysterious Mr. Slater, who had owned 'The Octopus.' The mystery revolved around the fact that Mr. Slater hanged himself in an upstairs bedroom of the house.

"We had heard that Mr. Slater was very rich, that he had married a much younger woman, and that she had run off with another man. We made up many stories to supplement what we knew about Mr. Slater. We acted out versions of his life and even fought over who would be the one to commit suicide in our strange little plays.

"Our town was near Rochester, New York. One day our parents were all whispering over the suicide of George Eastman, the founder of Eastman Kodak. Every family had a Kodak; we children used to muse over the idea that the man who had made our cameras had done what Mr. Slater had done . . . . Our town was a prison city; one of the stories about the prison, which we all knew, was that the state executioner, who had sent 141 men to death in the electric chair, had shot himself.

"We used the word 'suicide' frequently; it sounded even more ominous than murder. It was a far more taboo subject, we sensed that. There was never anything about it on the radio, nor in the magazines; we sensed there was something shameful about the subject."[4]

Hometown, published in 1967, was not successful. "It was described by *Publishers Weekly* as 'a long, boring novel, all the more surprising because it comes from the facile pen of Vin Packer.' I was beginning to believe that my real name was a jinx, though ultimately I went on to publish a successful novel called *Shockproof Sydney Skate* as a Marijane Meaker. It became a Literary Guild alternate, and a selection of the Book Find Club, and the paperback money was exceptional, enough eventually to buy me the house I live in today, in East Hampton, New York.

"Again, my friend Louise Fitzhugh was nudging me about writing a novel for young adults. Again, she reminded me that my protagonist, Sydney Skate, was a teenager. Louise, by that time was interested in writing mystery and suspense. She thought that maybe if we traded typewriters, a young adult book would emerge for me, and my typewriter would produce for her a crime story. We laughed about it. I took a look at some of these young adult novels and decided I could never write one . . . *until* I picked up one called *The Pigman* by Paul Zindel."[1]

(From *If I Love You, Am I Trapped Forever?* by M. E. Kerr. Jacket illustration by Peter Clemens.)

1968. Meaker volunteered as a teacher one day a week as part of an experiment with writers in the schools. "I'd been assigned to some classes at Central Commercial High School, in New York City, on Forty-second Street. These kids worked half a day and went to school half a day. They were wild, unruly, wonderful kids who didn't give a fig for reading, but who responded to writing assignments with great vigor and originality.

"The star of one of my classes was a very fat black girl nicknamed 'Tiny.' She wrote really grotesque stories, about things like a woman going swimming and accidentally swallowing strange eggs in the water, and giving birth to red snakes.

"I always 'published' Tiny's stories in the little mimeographed magazine we ran off for the kids. One day her mother appeared, complaining that Tiny's stories were hideous and that I was encouraging her to write 'weird.' While we discussed this, I learned that Tiny's mother was an ardent do-gooder who worked with her small church helping drug addicts. Tiny would come home from school to an empty apartment, fix herself something to eat, watch TV, and wait for her mom to come home from her churchwork. Then they'd eat dinner, her mom would go back to her good works, and Tiny would eat and watch TV . . . . In other words, while Tiny's mom was putting out the fire in the house across the street, her own house was on fire.

"That was the birth of my first book for young adults. Tiny translated into 'Dinky,' and since I knew that this story could be told about any family, black or white, rich or poor, I decided to stick close to home. I'd just moved to Brooklyn Heights, which abounded with lawyers because the courts were right nearby. I set my story there, and made Dinky's mother a middle-class lawyer's wife who was involved in rehabilitating dope addicts.

"The result was *Dinky Hocker Shoots Smack!*

"Since I love pseudonyms, I decided to call myself M. E. Kerr, a play on my last name, Meaker."[1]

"The paperback sale was enormous. It was optioned for the movies (many times) and ultimately made into an afternoon special. It is still going strong today.

"I decided to take a second look at this new, to me, young adult category. I was in my forties, by then, and not very interested any longer in murder and crime. The passion I had brought to that interest was waning, as I became more mellow, more liable to see the light in the dark, or the light *and* the dark. As I looked back on my life, things seemed funnier to me than they used to. *I* seemed funnier to me than I used to, and so did a lot of what I'd 'suffered.'

"Miraculously, as I sat down to make notes for possible future stories, things that happened to me long ago came back clear as a bell, and ringing, and making me smile and shake my head as I realized I had stories in me about *me*—no longer disguised as a homicidal maniac, or a twisted criminal bent on a scam, but as the small-town kid I'd been, so typically American and middle class and yes, vulnerable, but not as tragic and complicated as I used to imagine.

"So I had a new identity for myself in middle age: M. E. Kerr.

"I also moved to a new place, East Hampton, on Long Island, New York, which would eventually become Seaview, New York, in many of my novels. My old hometown, Auburn, would appear from time to time as Cayuta, New York."[1]

Love Is a Missing Person came from an idea she got while attending a high school football game. "At halftime I'd watched a pretty blond girl run up to the pom-pom cheerleaders, greeting them as though she hadn't seen them in a long time. She was carrying something in her arms, in a blanket. Behind her, a tall black guy was waiting for her, not joining in the reunion.

"When this blond girl unfolded the blanket, there was a tiny black baby gurgling up at everyone.

"I was standing beside my dentist's wife, and I said something about supposing that was inevitable in a community where there were blacks and whites going to school together: intermarriage.

"She said, 'Ah, but that's not the real story. The real story is the anger black girls here have because white girls date "their men."' She said many of the black boys were sports heroes, and the white girls went out with them, but white boys didn't in turn date black girls.

"This incident, on an ordinary autumn afternoon, was the background for a book called *Love Is a Missing Person.* It was the story of a girl whose sister fell in love with a black boy, and ran off with him at the end of the novel. Not a lot of local teachers and parents were thrilled about this Kerr, but it has elicited many letters from kids familiar with the problem of interracial dating."[1]

A second book was about life in a boarding school, *Is That You, Miss Blue?* Meanwhile, *Dinky Hocker Shoots Smack!* was banned in Randolph, New York, from the district high school library.

1978. Meaker published *Gentlehands*. She explains some of its inspiration. "I've never married nor had children, and I've lately thought this has been a great asset. If I'd had children, I'm sure I would have been tempted to keep them tied to something in an upstairs room, so no harm would come to them. I think the youngster in me remains vivid because I've never raised any children to compete with her, or compare with her, and I have not had to pace the floor nights worrying where they are or with whom, and what has happened to the family car.

"Again, these experiences come to me through osmosis. When I first moved to East Hampton, a sweet seventeen-year-old kid next door to me was going through his first love affair with a very rich girl who spent summers in our community. His family disapproved of this girl; his dad was a policeman, and Kippy was brought up strictly. He was working as a soda jerk the summer he met this rather sophisticated young lady. He had a new bicycle; she had a new Porsche.

"Kippy would come over to my house, agonizing about what to wear, what fork to pick up on the table when he was invited to her house for lunch. She had a butler. She lived by the ocean. She was a year older than Kippy. She'd gone to high school in European boarding schools. That same summer, I was reading a book by Howard Blum called *Wanted! The Search for Nazis in America*. That book, and what Kippy was going through, became all mixed together, until finally I sat down to write a novel called *Gentlehands*."[1]

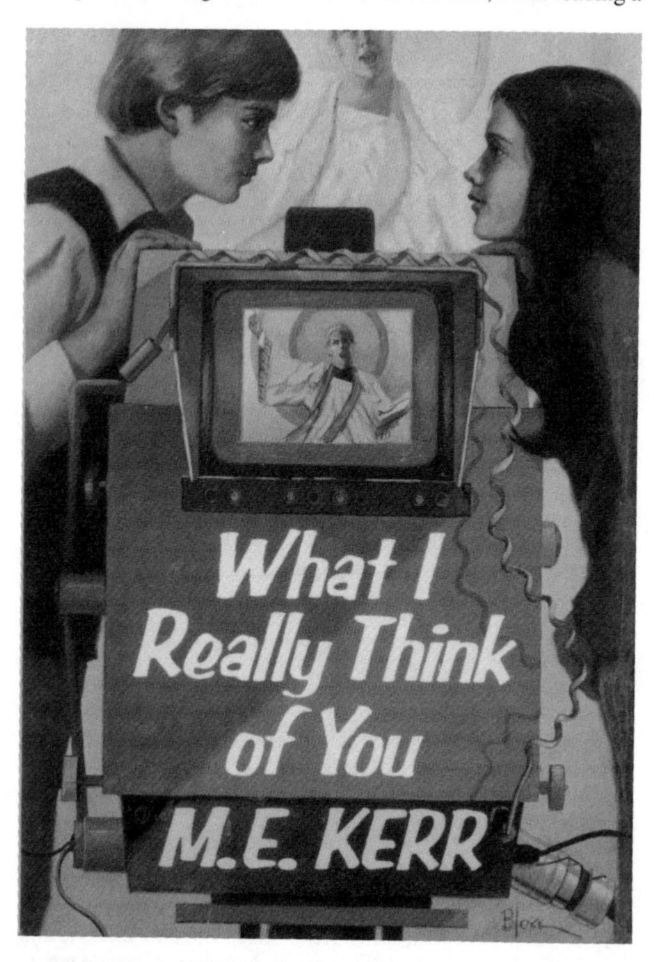

I start my story with the day I first saw Jesse Pegler. (From *What I Really Think of You* by M. E. Kerr.)

In **1981** *Little Little* was published—a book about teen-age dwarfs. Meaker says it was her most difficult to write but her favorite. "I don't know why it was so difficult, except I couldn't seem to get much humor into it, and what was there often seemed too dark . . . . Another thing was that I was afraid to tell *anyone* I was writing a book for young adults about dwarfs. I was afraid of the reaction, and of being discouraged by it. So I kept it to myself as I started the story over and over again, worked on it up to about fifty pages, then abandoned it. It seemed unworkable after several years of trying.

"One day I decided to write an essay about it for the Long Island section of the *New York Times*. It would be about the one story I wanted to write but couldn't. In the middle of this essay, I stopped, and started the book again, and this time finished it."[1]

Meaker's inspiration for the story comes from a hometown experience. " . . . The golden boy of our town went to Harvard and came back with a wife. They were everybody's idea of the marvelous young couple. And then they had a child who was a midget. This always held me fascinated: watching them cope, watching them change from an almost Scott and Zelda Fitzgerald-type of carefree couple with everything in the world, watching them having to fight for this little girl and find her friends. They joined the Little People of America, and then we had what I described in *Little Little*, an invasion by the little people. They would come every summer, which caused all sorts of problems because the town was trying to sell itself as a town for industry. We already had a prison and a Japanese steel plant, so people who were looking the town over would ride with midgets, prisoners, and Japanese businessmen! They would not think our town was a very typical small American town; they would reject it as a place for industry. Anyway, that story held me; I never forgot it."[3]

1982. Meaker's next work was *What I Really Think of You*, a book about "P.K.'s" or preacher's kids. " . . . My interest in preachers' kids probably started when I roomed with Kay Walters, the first P.K. I ever really knew."[2]

1983. Meaker published her teenage autobiography, *Me, Me, Me, Me, Me: Not a Novel*.

She has few interests that aren't related to writing. "I read like a fat person eats. I read everything from magazines like *Time, Rolling Stone, Interview, New York Magazine, Redbook, Fortune, Business Week, Vanity Fair, Woman's Day,* and *Ms.* to the best-sellers—Anne Tyler (a particular favorite), Raymond Carver, Elmore Leonard, Eudora Welty, Robert Cormier, Alice Munro, Bobbie Ann Mason, Alice Walker, Joyce Carol Oates, Barbara Pym—on and on and on. And I reread wonderful Carson McCullers. I love poetry, too—Yeats and Auden and Kastner and Rilke and Wakoski and Leo Connellan."[1]

FOOTNOTE SOURCES

[1]"M. E. Kerr," *Something about the Author Autobiography Series*, Gale, 1986.
[2]M. E. Kerr, *Me, Me, Me, Me, Me: Not a Novel*, Harper, 1983.
[3]"Marijane Meaker," *Contemporary Authors*, Volume 107, Gale, 1983.
[4]M. J. Meaker, *Sudden Endings*, Doubleday, 1964.

FOR MORE INFORMATION SEE:

Horn Book, February, 1973 (p. 56), August, 1975 (p. 365), June, 1977 (p. 288), September-October, 1986.
Times Literary Supplement, November 23, 1973, September 19, 1975, December 1, 1978.
Washington Post Book World, May 19, 1974, July 11, 1982.
English Journal, December, 1975, February, 1986 (p. 26).
School Library Journal, January, 1977 (p. 40), September, 1986 (p. 46), November, 1986 (p. 30).
Jerry Tallmer, "An Old Question for Young Adults," *New York Post,* July 8, 1978.
Lion and the Unicorn, fall, 1978 (p. 37).
Doris de Montreville and Elizabeth D. Crawford, *Fourth Book of Junior Authors and Illustrators,* H. W. Wilson, 1978.
D. L. Kirkpatrick, editor, *Twentieth-Century Children's Writers,* St. Martin's, 1978, 2nd edition, 1983.
Kenneth L. Donelson and Alleen Pace Nilsen, *Literature for Today's Young Adults,* Scott, Foresman, 1980, 2nd edition, 1985.
Contemporary Literary Criticism, Volume 12, Gale, 1980.
Washington Post Book World, May 10, 1981 (p. 15).
David Rees, *Painted Desert, Green Shade: Essays on Contemporary Writers of Fiction for Children and Young Adults,* Horn Book, 1984.
Voice of Youth Advocates, February, 1985 (p. 307).
Alleen Pace Nilsen, *Presenting M. E. Kerr,* Twayne, 1986.
New York Times Book Review, April 13, 1986.
Publishers Weekly, June 26, 1987.

COLLECTIONS

Kerlan Collection at the University of Minnesota.

MERCER, Charles (Edward) 1917-1988

OBITUARY NOTICE—See sketch in *SATA* Volume 16: Born July 12, 1917, in Stouffville, Ontario, Canada; died December 28, 1988, in Edison, N.J. Journalist, editor, and author. Mercer spent thirteen years as an editor at the New York City publishing firm of G. P. Putnam's Sons, retiring in 1979 as a vice-president and senior editor in charge of young adult books. He was also the author of seventeen novels, including *Rachel Cade,* a 1956 work about an American missionary in Africa. The book, which sold more than three million copies and was translated into fourteen languages, was made into a feature film called "The Sins of Rachel Cade." Other Mercer novels include *The Drummond Tradition, Enough Good Men,* and *The Reckoning.* His juvenile titles include *Let's Go to Africa, Let's Go to Europe, Monsters in the Earth: The Story of Earthquakes,* several juvenile biographies, *Gerald Ford, Roberto Clemente,* and *Jimmy Carter,* and *Miracle at Midway,* which was a Junior Literary Guild selection in 1977. Mercer began his career as a reporter for the *Washington Post* and was a feature writer and television columnist for the Associated Press for many years. He served in Army Intelligence during World War II and also served in the Korean War.

FOR MORE INFORMATION SEE:

Contemporary Authors New Revision Series, Volume 2, Gale, 1981.
Who's Who in America, 45th edition, Marquis, 1988.

OBITUARIES

New York Times, December 30, 1988 (p. A-18).
Chicago Tribune, January 1, 1989.

MEYNELL, Laurence Walter 1899-1989 (Valerie Baxter, Robert Eton, Geoffrey Ludlow, A. Stephen Tring)

OBITUARY NOTICE: Born August 9, 1899, in Wolverhampton, Staffordshire, England; died April 14, 1989. Educator, estate agent, editor, and writer. The author of social commentary, children's books, and biographies, Meynell is best remembered for his numerous contributions to the thriller genre. He worked briefly as a schoolmaster and estate agent and traveled extensively throughout Europe before completing his first book, *Mockbeggar,* in 1924. Writing as many as three books each year, he composed nearly 150 works in a writing career that spanned six decades. Most of his juvenile titles were written under the pseudonym A. Stephen Tring, including *The Cave by the Sea, Barry's Exciting Year, Frankie and the Green Umbrella, Peter's Busy Day, Penny Triumphant* and *The Old Gang.* He also wrote career novels for boys under his own name and for girls under the name Valerie Baxter. Meynell served as literary editor of *Time and Tide* in the late 1950s.

FOR MORE INFORMATION SEE:

D. L. Kirkpatrick, *Twentieth-Century Children's Writers,* St. Martin's, 1978, 2nd edition, 1983.
Contemporary Authors New Revision Series, Volume 15, Gale, 1985.
Who's Who, 141st edition, St. Martin's, 1989.

OBITUARIES

Times (London), April 18, 1989.

MILLAR, Margaret (Ellis Sturm) 1915-

PERSONAL: Surname is pronounced Miller; born February 5, 1915, in Kitchener, Ontario, Canada; daughter of Henry William (a businessman) and Lavinia (Ferrier) Sturm; married Kenneth Millar (a mystery writer), June 2, 1938 (died July 11, 1983); children: Linda Jane Pagnusat (deceased). *Education:* Attended University of Toronto, 1933-37. *Politics:* Democrat. *Religion:* Protestant. *Home:* 4420 Via Esperanza, Santa Barbara, Calif. 93110. *Agent:* Harold Ober Associates, Inc., 40 East 49th St., New York, N.Y. 10017.

CAREER: Warner Bros., Inc., Hollywood, Calif., screenwriter, 1945-46; mystery writer. *Member:* Writers Guild of America West, Mystery Writers of America (president, 1957-58), National Audubon Society, Sierra Club. *Awards, honors:* Edgar Allan Poe Award for Best Novel from the Mystery Writers of America, 1956, for *Beast in View,* and 1983, for *Banshee; Los Angeles Times* Woman of the Year, 1965; Edgar Allan Poe Grand Master Award, 1982.

WRITINGS:

MYSTERY NOVELS

The Invisible Worm, Doubleday, 1941.
The Weak-Eyed Bat, Doubleday, 1942.
The Devil Loves Me, Doubleday, 1942.
Wall of Eyes, Random House, 1943.
Fire Will Freeze, Random House, 1944.
The Iron Gates, Random House, 1945 (published in England as *Taste of Fears,* R. Hale, 1950).
Do Evil in Return, Random House, 1950.
Vanish in an Instant, Random House, 1952.

(Cover illustration by Roger Roth from *Rose's Last Summer* by Margaret Millar.)

Rose's Last Summer, Random House, 1952, published as *The Lively Corpse,* Dell, 1956.
Beast in View, Random House, 1955.
An Air That Kills, Random House, 1957 (published in England as *The Soft Talkers,* Gollancz, 1957).
The Listening Walls, Random House, 1959.
A Stranger in My Grave, Random House, 1961.
How Like an Angel, Random House, 1961, large print edition, Thorndike, 1989.
The Fiend, Random House, 1964.
Beyond This Point Are Monsters, Random House, 1970.
Ask for Me Tomorrow, Random House, 1976.
The Murder of Miranda, Random House, 1979.
Mermaid, Morrow, 1982.
Banshee, Morrow, 1983.

NOVELS

Experiment in Springtime, Random House, 1947.
It's All in the Family, Random House, 1948.
The Cannibal Heart, Random House, 1949.
Wives and Lovers, Random House, 1954.
Spider Webs, Morrow, 1986.

NONFICTION

The Birds and Beasts Were There, Random House, 1968.

CONTRIBUTOR

Ellery Queen's Awards: Ninth Series, Little, Brown, 1954.
Every Crime in the Book, Putnam, 1975.

SIDELIGHTS: Margaret Millar's late husband, Kenneth, was a mystery writer under pseudonym Ross Macdonald. The couple met in Kitchener, Ontario, where they were both members of the high school debating team and married after college. Shortly after the birth of their daughter, Millar was confined to bed for six months with a heart ailment. It was during this time that she began to read mystery novels and, eventually, to write her own. Her success in the field led her husband to try his hand at it. "By going on ahead and breaking trail," Kenneth Millar recounted in his introduction to *Kenneth Millar/Ross Macdonald: A Checklist,* "she helped to make it possible for me to become a novelist, as perhaps her life with me had helped to make it possible for her."

Millar attributes her interest in mysteries to reading detective magazines as a girl. Her two older brothers bought the magazines and Millar furtively read them. "They used to hide them under the mattress, and I'd fish them out . . . . They tell you always to write about what you know. What I knew was murder."

Millar works on her novels in the afternoon, sitting in the old maple chair in which she has composed all her books.

FOR MORE INFORMATION SEE:

Margaret Millar, *The Iron Gates,* Random House, 1945.
Kirkus, February 1, 1945, September 1, 1960.
Weekly Book Review, April 1, 1945.
New York Times, April 1, 1945, June 1, 1952, June 26, 1955, January 6, 1982, May 26, 1983.
New Republic, April 2, 1945, November 27, 1976.
New Yorker, April 7, 1945, November 15, 1976, January 18, 1982.
New York Herald Tribune Book Review, November 16, 1952, June 19, 1955, November 6, 1960.
Library Journal, June 1, 1955, July, 1962.
San Francisco Chronicle, July 17, 1955.
New York Times Book Review, September 6, 1970, May 12, 1974, August 29, 1979, February 14, 1982, February 19, 1984.
Saturday Review, October 31, 1970.
Matthew J. Bruccoli, compiler, *Kenneth Millar/Ross Macdonald: A Checklist,* Gale, 1971.
Times Literary Supplement, May 14, 1971, February 22, 1980.
Ms. August, 1979.
Observer, February 3, 1980, April 18, 1982, August 28, 1983.
Los Angeles Times, February 11, 1982, September 12, 1983.
Los Angeles Times Book Review, June 12, 1983.
Times (London), August 18, 1983.
Santa Barbara, July/August, 1984.
Village Voice, July 3, 1984.
Globe & Mail (Toronto), May 21, 1988.

MILLER, Deborah Uchill 1944-

PERSONAL: Born May 17, 1944, in Denver, Colo.; daughter of Sam Harry (a furniture store owner) and Ida (a teacher and author; maiden name, Libert) Uchill; married Clifford Bruce Miller (a rabbi), May 30, 1966; children: Arielle Zimrah, Adinah Sharone. *Education:* Barnard College, B.A., 1966; Jewish Theological Seminary, M.A., 1986. *Religion:* Jewish.

Home: Bayonne, N.J. *Agent:* Karen Ostrove, 249 Keats Ave., Elizabeth, N.J. 07208. *Office:* Solomon Schechter Day School, 511 Ryders Lane, East Brunswick, N.J. 08816.

CAREER: Solomon Schecter Day School, Cranford, N.J., teacher, 1977-81; Beth El/Beth o'r Religious School, Cranford, principal, 1981-82; Adath Jeshurun Jewish Congregation, Minneapolis, Minn., education director, 1982-84; Solomon Schechter Day School, East Brunswick, N.J., director, 1984—. *Member:* Association for Supervision and Curriculum Development, Coalition for Advancement of Jewish Education, Jewish Educators' Assembly, International Reading Association.

WRITINGS:

JUVENILE

Only Nine Chairs: A Tall Tale for Passover (illustrated by Karen Ostrove), Kar-Ben, 1982.

Poppy Seeds, Too: A Twisted Tale for Shabbat (illustrated by K. Ostrove), Kar-Ben, 1982.

My Siddur (illustrated by Jana Paiss), Behrman, 1984.

(With K. Ostrove) *The Modi' in Motel: An Idol Tale for Hanukah* (illustrated by K. Ostrove) Kar-Ben, 1986.

CONTRIBUTOR

Stephen Garfinkle, editor, *Slow Down and Live,* United Synagogue of America, 1981.

Deborah Miller, dressed as a sixteenth-century Jewish woman of Portugal.

WORK IN PROGRESS: With Karen Ostrove, a book about keeping Kosher (Jewish dietary laws).

SIDELIGHTS: "Originally I wanted to be a journalist. I majored in government at Barnard College, so that I would have a wide view of the world. But I gave up this career goal long ago. I fell into Jewish education and my writing for children grew naturally out of the experience.

"Writing for children is hard, but enjoyable. Sometimes, my co-author and I start talking in rhyme, and can't stop. It can go on for days. When we were writing *The Modi' in Motel,* we had a four-day laugh. We have written books that are too silly to show to any publisher. Writing with and for each other is cheap entertainment. We have books to which we keep returning, hoping to improve them enough to submit for publication.

"A major influence on my writing is Dr. Seuss. I like the way he goes for absurdity, but keeps strictly to the rules of rhyme, rhythm, and meter. He also finds ways of introducing—very subtly—important values.

"I'm not sure all of our books are for young people. Grown-ups like them, too, and sometimes get the jokes better. But you can't expect grown-ups to buy picture books for themselves.

"Jewish children's books need a lighthearted spirit, some fun—without sacrificing Jewish values and loyalty. I love to write books that make kids laugh, and am pleased to see the recent flowering of Jewish children's literature which is not pedantic or preachy.

"Karen and I enjoy visiting schools and centers, talking with kids about writing, illustrating, and publishing. The kids know all about writers' challenges and problems—especially writers' block."

HOBBIES AND OTHER INTERESTS: Israeli dancing, public speaking, Jewish history, Civil War, everything about children and education.

MINES, Jeanette (Marie) 1948-
(Jeanette Mines Ryan)

PERSONAL: Born September 9, 1948, in Chamberlain, S.D.; daughter of Leo F. (a farmer) and Ann (a homemaker; maiden name, Leiferman) Mines; married John J. Ryan, August 14, 1971 (divorced June 12, 1985); children: Marie T. *Education:* College of St. Teresa, B.A., 1970; University of Illinois at Chicago Circle, M.Ed., 1978. *Home:* 800 South Wesley, Oak Park, Ill. 60304.

CAREER: Harmony Hill High School, Watertown, S.D., dean of girls, 1970-71; St. Bridget School, Chicago, Ill., language arts teacher, 1971-77; Proviso High School, Hillside, Ill., English and reading teacher, 1977-83; University of Illinois at Chicago Circle, Chicago, lecturer in composition, 1984-87; Loyola University of Chicago, Chicago, adjunct faculty in English and education, 1987-89; Lewis University, Romeoville, Ill., assistant professor in education, 1990—. *Member:* Independent Writers of Chicago, Children's Reading Round Table of Chicago.

WRITINGS:

(Under name Jeanette Mines Ryan) *Reckless: A Teenage Love Story* (young adult novel), Avon, 1983 (later editions published under name Jeanette Mines).
Another Chance (young adult novel), Avon, 1985.
Misjudged (young adult novel), Scholastic, 1986.
Risking It (young adult novel), Avon, 1988.

Contributor of more than forty articles and stories to periodicals, including *Writing!, Chicago Tribune, ALAN Review,* and *Catholic Life.*

WORK IN PROGRESS: Don't Remind Me, a young adult novel about "a girl growing up on a farm in the Midwest and her struggle to come to terms with herself and life"; *Maura's Story,* a young adult novel.

SIDELIGHTS: "While growing up on a farm in South Dakota, I spent lots of time reading. I loved a story that transported me to places I'd never seen and introduced me to people I'd never met. The love of a good story stayed with me, and I often shared books with my students. They, too, enjoyed a good story, especially a story about people their own age, who encountered many of the same problems, frustrations, joys, and challenges they experienced themselves. Because I couldn't always find the kind of story I wanted for my students, I decided to write stories for young people myself.

JEANETTE MINES

"It has been my experience that young people will read willingly if they are able to identify with the characters and their experiences. Although the lives of the characters I create often differ from those of my readers, in telling their story I hope the commonality of life we all share is revealed.

"My readers often ask me where the ideas for my stories come from. They want to know if my characters are real people. I sometimes get ideas from the people I know and from events that happen to people I know, but none of the characters in my stories are based on real people. My characters come to life as I write. Often what my characters say and what they do surprises even me, but I listen to them because each character is unique and has something special to say and be.

"Readers sometimes tell me they know someone just like the characters in my stories or they feel exactly like the characters I write about. Growing up in a world of rapidly changing technology, shifting populations, global concerns, and everchanging expectations is extremely stressful. If even for a short while readers can identify with another person through the medium of the written word, perhaps the aloneness so prevalent among teenagers can disappear long enough for them to know there is a connection among us all."

FOR MORE INFORMATION SEE:

Wednesday Journal (Oak Park, Ill.), June 29, 1983 (p. 11), August 21, 1985 (p. 18).
"Teacher Relieves a Novel Shortage," *Pioneer Press* (Melrose Park, Ill.), July 13, 1983.
West Cook County Press (Elmhurst, Ill.), July 2, 1985 (p. 1).

MOORE, Tara 1950-

PERSONAL: Born March 4, 1950, in Baltimore, Md.; daughter of Egbert Holmes (in real estate) and Helen Louise (an editor; maiden name, Stephenson) Hawkins; divorced. *Education:* Attended University of New Mexico. *Home:* Route 1, Box 147K, Queenstown, Md. 21658.

CAREER: Artist (painter), 1970—; film director and producer; president of Elephant's Child Productions, Inc., 1983—; president of Cygnus Films, Inc. Producer of documentary "Chesapeake: Great Shellfish Bay." *Member:* Society of Animal Artists. *Awards, honors:* State of Maryland Governor's Citation for film premier and support of conservation, 1988, for "Tusks."

WRITINGS:

JUVENILE; SELF-ILLUSTRATED

A Pack of Labs, Garrard, 1982.
Elephants, Garrard, 1982.
Polar Bears, Garrard, 1982.

ILLUSTRATOR

(Contributor) Richard Wolters, *Labrador Retrievers: The History and the People,* Peterson, 1981.

FILMS; EXECUTIVE PRODUCER AND DIRECTOR

"Tusks," Elephant's Child Productions, 1990.

WORK IN PROGRESS: "Katmandu," a screenplay dealing with a modern-day relationship of an American woman and her

TARA MOORE

brother, who lives in Nepal; writing and directing film "Burning Passion," dealing with destruction of rain forests in Brazil, to be produced by Cygnus Films.

SIDELIGHTS: "The motivation behind my writings is a desire to reach and educate people through my means of entertainment. Grabbing people's attention visually with film or paintings helps to tell the story; therefore, more of the public can be reached. Writing sets up the paintings and film.

"Wildlife conservation is my main subject. I have traveled around the world, including the Arctic, Africa, Nepal, and South America, studying natural habitats with animal scientists and other guides.

"'Tusks' is based on experiences that I have had in the past, but extremely exaggerated, turning the story into total fiction—the story of an artist involved with a poacher, a game warden, and the elephants. It is an adventure story with an animal conservation message. 'Katmandu' is also based on my experiences when traveling to Nepal searching for tigers to paint and finding my brother whom I hadn't seen for seven years. Again, it is an adventure story, totally fiction, with a positive message.

"My books were written and illustrated about my own personal experiences, hoping to educate and entertain young people. My film projects are geared for adults because of the importance to generate awareness *now*."

HOBBIES AND OTHER INTERESTS: White-water rafting, ultra-light flying.

FOR MORE INFORMATION SEE:

Ray Champman, *Who's Who in Waterfowl Art,* Ambassador Graphics, 1983.
Wildlife Art News, March/April, 1987.
Sun, January 15, 1989.

MORNINGSTAR, Mildred 1912-

PERSONAL: Born June 18, 1912, in Chicago, Ill.; daughter of Harry Alvin (in public relations) and Margaret May (a teacher; maiden name, White) Whaley; married Ralph Morningstar, June 2, 1937 (divorced January 2, 1974); children: Marjorie, Marilyn Morningstar Gelsomino. *Education:* Attended University of Tulsa, 1930-32, and Denver Bible Institute, 1933-37; Wheaton College, B.A., 1954. *Religion:* Protestant. *Home and office:* 9620 West 25th Place, Lakewood, Colo. 80215.

CAREER: Chicago Child Evangelism Fellowship, Chicago, Ill., assistant to director, 1940-41; free-lance writer and editor, 1943—; public schoolteacher in Mount Prospect, Ill., 1955-56, and Glen Ellyn, Ill., 1957-58; Conservative Baptist Foreign Mission Society, Wheaton, Ill., writer, 1960-67; Baptist Publications, Lakewood, Colo., editor, 1974-75; Accent Books, Lakewood, writer and editor, 1976-78.

WRITINGS:

JUVENILE

Christian Nursery Rhymes, Zondervan, 1947.
Sing a Song for Jesus, Zondervan, 1948.
Billy Listens, Van Kampen, 1952.
The Amazon Comes Alive, Singtime Publishing, 1954.
Japan Comes Alive, Singtime Publishing, 1954.

MILDRED MORNINGSTAR

Africa Comes Alive, Singtime Publishing, 1954.
The Bible Says, Moody, 1960.
Rosa of the Philippines, David C. Cook, 1964.
Carlos of Brazil, David C. Cook, 1964.
Danger at the Sheep Ranch, Moody, 1983.

OTHER

Reaching Children, Moody, 1944.
Training to Go, Conservative Baptist Foreign Mission Society, 1962.
To All the World, Conservative Baptist Foreign Mission Society, 1963.
Holidays around the World, Conservative Baptist Foreign Mission Society, 1964.
Missions in a Revolutionary Age, Conservative Baptist Foreign Mission Society, 1965.
Missionary Moments for Girls, Conservative Baptist Foreign Mission Society, 1965, 3rd edition, 1967.
(Contributor) J. Allan Petersen and Evelyn R. Petersen, editors, *For Women Only,* Tyndale, 1974.
The Truth about Tomorrow, Baptist Publications, 1975.
Parables Made Plain, Baptist Publications, 1975.
God Tests a Nation and Its Leaders, Baptist Publications, 1975.
The Drama of Redemption, Baptist Publications, 1975.
The Book of Beginnings, Baptist Publications, 1975.
The Man Who Wouldn't Say Uncle, Baptist Publications, 1976.
Family Talk, Baptist Publications, 1976.

Editor of church school curriculum materials for Baptist Publications, 1974-76. Author of monthly column for women in *Good News Broadcaster,* 1970-74. Contributor to magazines, including *Baby Talk, His, Success* (now *Christian Education*), *My Counselor, Hi-Time, Young Ambassador,* and *Today's Child.*

WORK IN PROGRESS: Two books "dealing with the emotions and problems the hurting person encounters and the steps he will need to take in order to enjoy a happy life, one about facing difficult problems and the other about recovering self-esteem."

SIDELIGHTS: "The lives of great Christians fascinate me to the extent that I have begun research on an industrialist, a businessman, an early explorer in western North America, a befriender of neglected children, and an early American patriot.

"I write to meet a need. Seeing needs in the lives of those I contact motivates me to endeavor to help them solve their problems. Thus it began many years ago when scarcely any books told how to impart Christian values to children.

"By combining the public school training in elementary education received at the University of Tulsa with Biblical knowledge from a four-year course at the Denver Bible Institute, I worked out my own philosophy and methods. Considerable experience in children's classes solidified my thoughts and enabled me to work out practical ways to achieve my goals.

"At this point, my employment in Chicago led to training teachers in the field of Christian education. I taught a number of classes for teachers in various sections of the metropolitan area. After I received many requests to repeat the same sessions with other groups, letters began to arrive from all across the country, asking me to further explain my concepts and methods. When I committed this information and inspiration to paper, my writing career had begun.

"Writing to meet a need opened new vistas to me. After my marriage was blessed with two children, a path opened into the delightful field of children's books. That guided me later into the area of family problems—rugged, but rewarding as well. It finally brought me into the fascinating position of writing and editing for publishing companies.

"While in an Alaskan library researching the life and accomplishments of an explorer, I was taken to a separate room in the library where original, very old documents were kept. A librarian locked the door and stayed with me, watching me the whole time. She forbade me to use a pen, even in making my own notes, but did permit a pencil. She was undoubtedly protecting these books and documents from theft and defacement.

"Only two patrons were using the library, both of us occupied in research. The other was James Michener! Quite an experience!

"I did not take that trip for research alone, but always endeavor to take advantage of opportunities to collect materials that may be useful in the future.

"Clipping magazines and newspapers in areas of my interests helps too. I also make notes when observing incidents useful for illustrating points in future articles. My files bulge with helpful materials.

"Once when an article was coming due, I stopped at the library after work to search for insights and illustrations. A couple of hours work yielded absolutely nothing, but at home I found in my files everything I needed.

"Often when drifting off to sleep, an idea for a current writing project will occur to me. I snap on the lamp above my bookcase headboard, pull out a pen, and record the idea.

"Sometimes when I'm almost asleep, dialogue for a particularly difficult part of a story will run through my mind. In the past if very sleepy I was tempted to think I would remember it in the morning. Now I know if I don't act it will be gone forever. Eagerly I capture that dialogue.

"On occasion, I will puzzle over the outline for an article, perhaps at different sessions, to no avail. Then to solve the problem, I will go over my notes thoroughly the evening before my next writing session. When I start to work the next morning, I realize my subconscious mind has provided me with an excellent outline. This patient assistant doesn't even turn in a bill!

"While research gives added depth to an article or book, it does not supply the whole answer. The reader wants to hear the ring of truth, to be able to say 'This writer has been where I am. She understands what I am experiencing.' To produce this reaction in the adult reader, I found that I need to experience the problem myself or to have close association with those involved in it. Confidential relationships with members of support groups which deal with problems in which I am interested provide valuable insights. When these elements co-exist, the feedback I receive from my readers shows me I am on the right track. My readers find help, and I find great satisfaction in writing to meet their needs."

HOBBIES AND OTHER INTERESTS: Reading, travel "when I collect beautiful sights to store in my memory bank."

MORRIS, Judy K. 1936-

PERSONAL: Born August 2, 1936, in Orange, N.J.; children: two. *Education:* Swarthmore College, B.A., 1958. *Residence:* Washington, D.C.

I was trying to think how I got into this. (Cover illustration by Derek James from *The Crazies and Sam* by Judy K. Morris.)

CAREER: Writer, 1959—. *Member:* Authors Guild, Washington Independent Writers. *Awards, honors:* Superintendent's Award from the Washington, D.C. Public Schools, 1985; Artist-in-Education Grant from the District of Columbia Commission on Arts and Humanities, 1986.

WRITINGS:

The Crazies and Sam (juvenile novel), Viking, 1983.
The Kid Who Ran for Principal (juvenile novel), Lippincott, 1989.

WORK IN PROGRESS: Several children's novels.

SIDELIGHTS: "I have worked as a volunteer, teaching writing to children in a public elementary school near my home for ten years, and I have worked with elementary schoolteachers on the teaching of writing. All this has been a stimulating break from the word processor. I've learned a lot about writing and about what is on children's minds.

"Although I write children's novels, I write for myself. The stories are on serious subjects but have a great deal of humor, which usually grows from the juxtaposition of carefully drawn, varied characters. This amuses me and makes me think, and I hope it will do the same for others.

"*The Crazies and Sam* was written because someone mentioned a young boy getting into a stranger's car. I wondered if I could make that situation believable—a responsible, able child doing such a dangerous thing. I located the story near the part of Washington, D.C., where I live, a downtown area where there are many street people, people so like and so different from ourselves, fascinating to children, and to all of us.

"*The Kid Who Ran for Principal* benefited from my work in many different schools, and from a long history of working in political campaigns. Like Bonnie, I was a good little girl, and like her, I had to learn that it can be 'good' and necessary to speak out and to fight hard, when the cause is right."

NANOGAK, Agnes 1925-

PERSONAL: Born November 12, 1925; daughter of Billy Natkusiak Banksland (a guide) and Topsy (Alingnak) Steffanson; married Wallace J. Goose, October 3, 1943 (deceased, 1985); children: Billy, Roy, Shirley, Molly, Beatrice, Aldena, Douglas, J. Wallace. *Religion:* Pentecostal.

CAREER: Free-lance artist, carver, and painter of prints, 1964—; has also worked as a land claims field worker, Holman, North West Territory, Canada, 1976-80. Elders Committee Councellor, Holman. Has held exhibitions in Waterloo, Ontario, Canada, Nova Scotia, Ontario, and Edmonton, Alberta, Canada. *Awards, honors: Tales from the Igloo* was selected a Notable Canadian Children's Book; Doctor of Humane Letters, Mount Saint Vincent University, Halifax, 1985.

ILLUSTRATOR:

Tales from the Igloo, Hurtig, 1972, St. Martin's Press, 1977.
More Tales from the Igloo, Hurtig, 1985.

SIDELIGHTS: "I was born in 1925 in Baily Island which is beside Taktoyaktuk. At age eight my family went to Banksland by boat. My father had encouraged me to draw animals, people, and scenes from the land. In 1964 Father Henry Tardy had encouraged me to draw for the co-op and I have been drawing since then. I greatly enjoy drawing old Inuit myths, legends, and children's stories."

NICHOLLS, Judith (Ann) 1941-

PERSONAL: Born December 12, 1941, in Westwoodside, Lincolnshire, England; daughter of Ernest Leonard (an education officer) and Joyce (a hairdresser; maiden name, Kelsey) Sharman; married John Richard Nicholls (a university lecturer), September 9, 1961; children: Dominique, Guy, Tracey. *Education:* College of Sarum St. Michael, Certificate in Education, 1976; Bath College of Higher Education, B.Ed. (with first class honors), 1984. *Home and office:* Church View, Churchyard, Westbury, Wiltshire BA13 3DA, England.

CAREER: Modern Woman (national magazine), London, England, secretary and assistant 1960-61; Calne and Westbury Comprehensive Schools, Wiltshire, England, English teacher, 1976-79; Holt Primary School, Wiltshire, teacher, 1979-85; writer, 1985—. Writer in schools giving readings and workshops for children, parents, and teachers. *Member:* Schools' Poetry Association.

WRITINGS:

JUVENILE

Magic Mirror and Other Poems for Children, Faber, 1985.
Midnight Forest and Other Poems, Faber, 1987.
(Compiler) *Wordspells* (illustrated by Alan Baker), Faber, 1988.
Popcorn Pie (poems; contains six small books and a giant book with cassette; illustrated by Tessa Richardson-Jones), Mary Glasgow Publications, 1988, Modern Curriculum, 1989.
(Compiler) *What on Earth . . . ?* (poems), Faber, 1989.
(Compiler) *Higgledy-Humbug* (poems; illustrated by T. Richardson-Jones), Mary Glasgow Publications, 1990.

RADIO

"Pictures in Your Mind" (two programs), 1987 and 1988.

TELEVISION

"Seeing and Doing" (for schools), Channel 4 (England), 1989.

CONTRIBUTOR TO ANTHOLOGIES

John Foster, editor, *A Fifth Poetry Book,* Oxford University Press, 1985.
J. Foster, editor, *Spaceways,* Oxford University Press, 1986.
Robert Fisher, compiler, *Witchwords,* Faber, 1987.
Raymond Wilson, compiler, *Out and About,* Viking Kestrel, 1987.
David Orme and James Sale, compilers, *The Poetry Show 1,* Macmillan, 1987.
J. Foster, editor, *School's Out,* Oxford University Press, 1988.
J. Foster, *Another First/Second/Third/Fourth/Fifth Poetry Book,* Oxford University Press, 1989.

Poems broadcast regularly on BBC Radio for Schools. Contributor of articles and reviews to education journals, including *Junior Education, Child Education, Junior Bookshelf,* and *Books for Your Children.*

WORK IN PROGRESS: Poems for several juvenile anthologies; a collection of own poems illustrated by Shirley Felts, for Faber; radio recordings; another schools television program for British Broadcasting Corp.'s "Zig-Zag."

JUDITH NICHOLLS

(From *Wordspells* by Judith Nicholls. Illustrated by Alan Baker.)

SIDELIGHTS: "The first four years of my life were spent in a small farming community where most of the cottages and farms on the main street seemed to be filled with relatives. After the war we moved to the rather bleak east coast of Lincolnshire where I spent my schooldays and where my parents still live.

"After sixth form I did everything 'the wrong way round!' I moved to London, went to a smart secretarial college for a year (a great cultural shock at the time!), worked on a national woman's magazine, then married. (I'd met my husband at school when I was twelve.) We had three children, lived in several different places, including a year in Portugal, then came to Wiltshire. I took a teacher-training course as a mature student, taught for eight years (completing a degree in three of them), then began to think more seriously about writing. My children are now grown up, my husband continues to lecture at Bath University, I work full-time as a writer and a writer in schools.

"My earliest remembered poem was written when I was seven and was, in retrospect, much better than some of the awful stuff I wrote as a teenager—great thoughts on Life in the Grand Abstract school!

"I'm really interested in where poems came from, and how they get from wherever that is to the finished version on paper. Mine seem to come from all kinds of different sources which I can pinpoint in *retrospect* for several poems but, maddeningly, it's never a process that's a guaranteed 'recipe' for the next poem! Sometimes a childhood memory is involved, sometimes a recent incident or experience, a person, a few words that intrigue me, a particular form I want to try. I'm happier once I have *something* on paper. The poems then usually go through several pages of drafts over a few days, during which time various words or lines or even punctuation nag at me until they're removed, added to, reworded, transferred—and finally I'm reasonably satisfied.

"When I run workshops or give talks I always show the drafts that preceded one of my poems. Children in particular often assume that what appears in a book is what was first written down—they are intrigued to see the mess which preceded! I also like to get them to discover, at however simple a level, a little of what is *special* about a poem, and the way it differs from prose—as well as what *fun* it can be to play with words!

"It's impossible to name just one favourite or influential poet. I love e. e. cummings, Dylan Thomas, Sylvia Plath, Emily Dickinson, Norman Nicholson, Arthur Waley's translations from old Chinese poems, the poetry of the King James' Old Testament . . . and many others! I didn't set out initially to write for children, though I really enjoy children's books. Even when I'm working on a poem specifically for a class or for a children's anthology I rarely think consciously of writing 'for children.' Maybe it's just that people who write for children have at least a little corner of themselves which has never quite left childhood behind. I'm not quite sure how I shall write when I grow up!

"Children often ask me how many poems I've written. I have no idea as I never seem to have time to count them, but I *think* probably between two and three hundred."

HOBBIES AND OTHER INTERESTS: Family, walking, swimming, art lessons, cooking (mainly vegetarian food).

NOVELLI, Luca 1947-

PERSONAL: Born October 7, 1947, in Milan, Italy; son of Aurelio (an ex-sailor) and Ines (a tailoress; maiden name, Perucconi Carlaccini) Novelli; married Caterina Raia (in public relations), February 14, 1980. *Education:* University of Milan, doctor's degree in science, 1972; attended Faculty of Agriculture, Milan, 1972-73. *Politics:* Liberal. *Religion:* Catholic. *Home:* Via Breno 7, Milan, Italy 20 139. *Agent:* QUIPOS, Via Ariberto 24, Milan, Italy 20 100. *Office:* Piazza Grandi 3, Milan, Italy 20 129.

CAREER: Scientific consultant; cartoonist. Manager of advertising office, 1974-80; free-lance cartoonist, 1975—; author of educational and popular science books, 1978—. Television consultant for "RAI 2," 1986 and "RAI 1," 1988. *Military service:* Aeronautical Army, 1972-73. *Member:* Italian Journalists. *Awards, honors:* Piero Paolo Vergelio Prize for Young People's European Literature Special Mention, 1987, for the French edition of *The History of Chemistry in Comic Strip Form*.

WRITINGS:

SELF-ILLUSTRATED

Voyage to the Center of the Cell, Ottaviano, 1978.

Il mio primo libro sui computer, Mondadori, 1983, translation by Laura Parma-Viegel published as *My First Book about Computers,* Microsoft, 1986.

Il mio primo libro di BASIC, Mondadori, 1984, translation by L. Parma-Viegel published as *My First Book about BASIC,* Microsoft, 1986.

Il mio primo dizionario dei computer, Mondadori, 1985, translation by L. Parma-Viegel published as *My First Computer Dictionary,* Microsoft, 1986.

I fantastici mondi di LOGO (title means "The Fantastic World of LOGO"), Mondadori, 1986.

The Thinking Machines, Mondadori, 1987.

The Cell Planet, Mondadori, 1987.

Little History of Medicine, GM Editions, 1988.

ALL ILLUSTRATED BY CINZIA GHIGLIANO

Storia della chimica a fumetti (title means "The History of Chemistry in Comic Strip Form"), Milano Libri Editore, 1984.

La storia naturale (title means "The Natural History"), Rizzoli Editore, 1988.

WITH OTHERS

The Ball-Frame-Book, Coccinella, 1989.

The Balance-Book, Coccinella, 1990.

COMICS AND STRIPS

Gli Edenisti (title means "The Eden People"), Editrice Dardo, 1975.

E adesso dottore? (title means "And Now, Doc?"), Bompiani, 1979.

Il laureato (title means "The Graduate"), Mondadori, 1980.

L'orto diabolico (title means "The Devil's Garden"), EDTM, 1982.

Il laureato senza timberland (title means "The Graduate without Timberland"), Glenat Italia, 1986.

Il laureato diventa yuppie (title means "The Graduate Is Becoming a Yuppie"), Glenat Italia, 1987.

Il laureato cambia look (title means "The Graduate Changes His Look"), Glenat Italia, 1988.

Il laureato fo cavviera (title means "The Graduate in a Career"), Glenat Italia, 1989.

Also author of *Ecology Comics,* and of cartoon strips "Il messaggero," Rome, 1975-80, and "Il giorno," Milan, 1975—. Cartoons have appeared in *Il Mondo* and *Epoca*.

WORK IN PROGRESS: The Big Book of Communications.

SIDELIGHTS: "When I was a little boy, the Walt Disney character I liked best was Gyro Loosegear. I wanted to be like him when I grew up—a bit of an inventor and a bit of a scientist. I was not among the better students in school, but was quite adept at narrating stories by combining drawings and phrases as in the comic strips. In fact, I was an avid reader of comic strips.

"I liked the sciences very much but found textbooks to be both difficult and unappealing. It was much simpler to watch science programs on television, which in Italy at that time were limited to two channels in black and white.

"By ten I began to shop around second-hand comic book stands and discovered fantasy science and science fiction. Thanks to Isaac Asimov and other American authors, I became familiar with such terminology as 'cybernetics,''ecology,' and 'genetic engineering.'

LUCA NOVELLI

"In December of 1968, while attending college, I brought some satirical drawings to the office of a weekly publication to see if I could stir their interest. I did and that was the beginning of my adventure in the world of print and publishing.

"For a number of years I contributed to newspapers and magazines, publishing small books which contained a collection of strips and characters I had created. It was not until 1978, however, that I began to realize that my background in science and my ability to translate difficult scientific principles into simple language were well-suited for children's books.

"My first books on scientific subjects were *Voyage to the Center of the Cell* and *Ecology Comics,* both of which dealt with topics that were familiar to me from college courses. When the opportunity arose to write *My First Book about Computers,* I found that I had no prior knowledge about the subject. I studied for several months until I became knowledgeable, and even purchased a computer which I now use in my writing. The resulting work was translated into eleven languages.

"Besides working on my books, I also write the texts for a series of illustrations by my friend Cinzia Ghigliano. These are the types of books I would have been elated to find on book shelves when I was thirteen.

"I find pleasure in the hope that among my youthful readers there may be a great and truly important scientist.

(From *My First Book about Computers* by Luca Novelli, translated by Laura Parma-Veigel. Illustrated by the author.)

"I have a house which is built on the rocks above the sea. I spend most of my time here working and growing citrus fruit and rare orchids."

OBLIGADO, Lilian (Isabel) 1931-

PERSONAL: Born April 12, 1931, in Buenos Aires, Argentina; daughter of George Rafael (a senior editor and author) and Elizabeth (Kuhn) Obligado; married Pedro Simonetti (a doctor and rancher), April 29, 1960 (died, October 29, 1960); married Szabolcs de Vajay (an international civil servant), August 20, 1967; children: (second marriage) Cristina Elisabeth, Sigmund George. *Education:* Studied painting in Argentina with Vincent Puig and others. *Religion:* Catholic. *Home:* 429 South Lexington Ave., White Plains, N.Y.; Avenue Victor Hugo, Paris France; 1 place de l'Ancien-Port, CH-1800 Vevey, Switzerland. *Office:* 23 avenue des Baumes, CH-1418 la Tour de Peilz, Vaud, Switzerland.

LILIAN OBLIGADO

CAREER: Illustrator and artist. Western Printing & Lithograph Co., New York, N.Y., free-lance illustrator, 1958-89; Houghton Mifflin, Boston, Mass., illustrator of "McKee Reader" series, 1964-65. *Awards, honors: New York Herald Tribune*'s Children's Spring Book Festival Award Honor Book, 1963, for *A Dog Called Scholar; Black-Eyed Susan* was selected one of Child Study Association of America's Children's Books of the Year, 1968, *I, Roger Ellis—Know-It-All,* 1969, *Magdalena* and *The Day Luis Was Lost,* 1971, *Frere Jacques,* 1973, and *Pickles and Jake* and *A Child's Book of Animals,* 1975.

WRITINGS:

SELF-ILLUSTRATED

Little Wolf and the Upstairs Bear, Viking, 1979.
Faint Frogs Feeling Feverish and Other Terrifically Tantalizing Tongue Twisters, Viking, 1983.
If I Had a Dog, Golden Press, 1984.
Guess the Animal, Golden Press, 1990.

ILLUSTRATOR

Elspeth Bragdon, *One to Make Ready,* Viking, 1959.
Barbara Shook Hazen, *Animals and Their Babies,* Golden Press, 1959.
Carl Memling, *Little Cottontail,* Golden Press, 1960.
Carol Kendall, *The Big Splash,* Viking, 1960.
Anne Heathers, *Four Puppies,* Golden Press, 1960.
George Obligado, *Gaucho Boy,* Viking, 1961.
Vivian Laubach Thompson, *Sad Day, Glad Day,* Holiday House, 1962.
(With others) Bryna Untermeyer and Louis Untermeyer, editors and selectors, *Beloved Tales,* Golden Press, 1962.

She accepted them, but responded to none of them. (From *Lassie Come-Home* by Eric Knight. Illustrated by Lilian Obligado.)

(With others) B. Untermeyer and L. Untermeyer, editors and selectors, *Fun and Fancy,* Golden Press, 1962.
L. Untermeyer, *The Kitten Who Barked,* Golden Press, 1962.
Herbert Best, *Desmond the Dog Detective: The Cast of the Lone Stranger,* Viking, 1962.
Patricia M. Scarry, *The Wait-for-Me Kitten,* Golden Press, 1962.
Margaret Wise Brown, *The Golden Egg,* Golden Press, 1962.
Elizabeth Coatsworth, *Jock's Island,* Viking, 1963.
Anne H. White, *A Dog Called Scholar,* Viking, 1963.
Charlotte Zolotow, *The White Marble,* Abelard, 1963.
Helen Kay, *House of Many Colors,* Abelard, 1963.
Irmengarde Eberle, *Raccoon's Young Ones,* Abelard, 1963.
Jean Bothwell, *Mystery Gatepost,* Dial, 1964.
Eric Knight, *Lassie Come-Home,* Doubleday, 1964.
E. Bragdon, *There Is a Tide,* Viking, 1964.
Margaret Adair, *Far Voice Calling,* Doubleday, 1964.
H. Best, *Desmond and the Peppermint Ghost,* Viking, 1965.
Alberta Eiseman, *Candido: A Story,* Macmillan, 1965.
(With Garth Williams) M. W. Brown, *The Whispering Rabbit and Other Stories,* Golden Press, 1965.
Kay Boyle, *Pinky, the Cat Who Liked to Sleep,* Crowell-Collier, 1966.
Jacqueline Jackson, *The Taste of Spruce Gum,* Little, Brown, 1966.
Catharine Marsden, *The Secret Elephants,* Dutton, 1966.
Stuart Brent, *Mr. Toast and the Woolly Mammoth,* Viking, 1966.
Doris Gates, *The Elderberry Bush,* Viking, 1967.
Morton Friend, *Lop Ear and Little Gray,* L. W. Singer, 1968.
Evelyn Trent Bachmann, *Black-Eyed Susan,* Viking, 1968.
Polly Berrien Berends, *Who's That in the Mirror?,* Random House, 1968.
K. Boyle, *Pinky in Persia,* Crowell-Collier, 1968.
Victoria Cabassa, *Trixie and the Tiger,* Abelard, 1968.
Albert G. Miller, *A Friend for Shadow,* L. W. Singer, 1969.
Ann Grafton, *I, Roger Ellis—Know-It-All,* Funk & Wagnalls, 1969.
Aileen Olsen, *Masie and the Persian Pink Petunias,* Abelard, 1970.
Ruth G. Gilroy and Frank D. Gilroy, *Little Ego,* Simon & Schuster, 1970.
Elizabeth B. Keeton, *Esmeralda,* Little, Brown, 1970.
Edna Barth, *The Day Luis Was Lost,* Little, Brown, 1971.
Louisa Rossiter Shotwell, *Magdalena,* Viking, 1971.
E. B. Keeton, *Friday Nights and Robert,* Little, Brown, 1972.
Amalie Sharfman, *Papa's Secret Chocolate Dessert,* Lothrop, 1972.
Joan Bacon, *Pussycat Tiger,* Golden Press, 1972, reissued, 1977.
Mary J. Fulton, *My Friend,* Golden Press, 1973.
B. S. Hazen, *Frere Jacques,* Lippincott, 1973.
The Three Little Kittens, Random House, 1974.
Kathleen N. Daly, *A Child's Book of Animals,* Doubleday, 1975.
Janet Chenery, *Pickles and Jake,* Viking, 1975.

Scholar raised his head and looked at him. (From *A Dog Called Scholar* by Anne H. White. Illustrated by Lilian Obligado.)

C. Zolotow, *The Little Black Puppy,* Golden Press, 1975.
K. N. Daly, *A Child's Book of Insects,* Doubleday, 1975.
Campbell, *Peter's Angel, a Story about Monsters,* Four Winds, 1976.
The Country Mouse and the City Mouse, Random House, 1977.
Grimm Brothers, *The Wolf and the Seven Kids,* Random House, 1978.
Hans Christian Andersen, *The Ugly Duckling,* translated from the French by Ann Spencer, Knopf, 1979.
Nursey Rhymes, Golden Press, 1980.
Goldilocks and the Three Bears, Golden Press, 1980.
K. N. Daly, *A Child's Book of Snakes, Lizards, and Other Reptiles,* Doubleday, 1980.
Little Red Hen, Golden Press, 1981.
Marjorie Weinman Sharmat, *The Best Valentine in the World,* Holiday House, 1982.
Ellen Rudin, reteller, *The Three Billy Goats Gruff,* Golden Press, 1982.
Over in the Meadow: An Adaptation of the Old Nursery Counting Rhyme, Golden Press, 1983.
Mary Beth Markham, *Willie Found a Wallet,* Golden Press, 1984.
M. W. Sharmat, *One Terrific Thanksgiving,* Holiday House, 1985.
K. N. Daly, *The Four Little Kittens Storybook,* Golden Press, 1986.
Marie Tenaille, *Looking for a Friend,* translated from the French by Didi Charney, Macmillan, 1988.

Also illustrator of Josephine Wright's *Wise Dog,* published by Dutton.

ADAPTATIONS:

"The Three Little Kittens" (cassette; filmstrip with cassette), Random House, 1986.

"This is the loneliest food I've ever seen." (From *One Terrific Thanksgiving* by Marjorie Weinman Sharmat. Illustrated by Lilian Obligado.)

(From *Faint Frogs Feeling Feverish and Other Terrifically Tantalizing Tongue Twisters* by Lilian Obligado. Illustrated by the author.)

WORK IN PROGRESS: A Christmas story.

SIDELIGHTS: Lilian Obligado was born on April 12, 1931 in Buenos Aires, Argentina. "My father's ancestors settled in Buenos Aires about 250 years ago; they came from Andalusia, Spain on one side, from Berne, Switzerland on the other. My grandfather, Rafael Obligado, was one of the major classic poets of Argentina. After reading Walter Scott novels most of his youth he decided to build a castle on the hills overlooking the Parana River, and he did. It is now standing there, improved by every generation who has lived there since. It is a very odd sight in the middle of the pampas."[1]

"The very first years of my life, until the age of four, were spent there. This was the most wonderful setting, on one side miles of pastures with grazing cattle and horses, and behind the house down the hill flowed the great Parana River carrying islands of blue and yellow water flowers on which were lodged miriads of small animal life, including snakes, water fowl, and iguanas. One could hear the call of different birds and watch white egrets, herons, and sometimes a flamingo sail by. Wild honeysuckle and jasmine vines grew on the walls of the castle. I still smell their perfume in my memory. I came into contact with nature almost immediately, as I was out in the garden in my crib most of the day. Sometime later, as do most ranchers in Buenos Aires, we would live part-time in the city and part-time in the country.

"My first memories of having loved to draw and invent stories to go with these drawings are from the age of six. I used to love to draw hospital scenes, full of activities, nurses, doctors, and sick children, but since I did not know how to draw well, all these bodies were round and then I drew their clothes which you could see through over the bodies. Very 'a la mode' these days! To this day I have a horror of hospitals and never go near one unless absolutely necessary, so I can't imagine why these subjects fascinated me then.

"Subsequently my parents divorced and I went to live in Europe with my mother who was Swiss. We traveled around a lot then, and one day she took me back to Argentina to see my father. She returned to Europe where she then lived. I didn't see her again for many years, the Second World War cut us off completely. So I grew up with my father and grandmother in Argentina. When my father remarried an English-Argentine lady, we went to live in Washington, D.C.

"From there we crossed the desert (I had souvenirs of endless Saguaro cactuses and Yellowstone and the Grand Canyon all in one bundle) and reached Santa Monica, California where we stayed for several happy years. I loved my school days, my friends, my dog Trixie, and my special treat—trips to the Warner Bros. film studio and the Walt Disney studio where I was shown how 'Bambi' and 'Fantasia' were being made, including a pencil preview sketch outline of the film. I met Walt Disney, Shirley Temple, Constance Bennett, Errol Flynn, and others. I was then ten years old and stage struck like all the other kids in Hollywood. I believe the visit to the Walt Disney studio did a lot towards my becoming a children's book illustrator.

"When Pearl Harbor happened, we returned to Argentina as my grandmother was very ill. She died shortly after. I loved her dearly. From then on my life consisted of English boarding schools, and living at home on and off, but every glorious summer would be spent part-time by the seashore, and the rest on the ranch. Life on the ranch was wonderful, as we were surrounded by five other 'estancias' (ranches) filled with all kinds of aunts and uncles and cousins of all ages. Families in Argentina at that time and in that class had ample time for leisure and many servants, so we children benefited from much friendly attention coming our way. Grown-ups listened to us, told us stories, and taught us. I used to mingle with the farmers' children—we rode horses together, swam, and went to round up the cattle for miles. We were surrounded by dogs, cats, chickens, and geese. In the eucalyptus trees around us there were hundreds of green parrots streaking in and out of their nests. Other times we would go out on the river in our boats. Life on the river was a bit like being Huckleberry Finn in our minds. During those years I spent a great amount of time sitting on fences, in haystacks, on horseback, or in the chicken coop or the dairy barn with my pencil and drawing pad in hand.

"For most of my life I have sketched what was around me—people and animals mostly. I used to love to write and draw long, involved stories which I would send to my grandmother. Like everything one wants to perfect, one must practice all the time. If I don't get the opportunity to pick up a pencil for more than three days, my finger goes numb, and it will take a day or two before I get the feel of it again. It's rather like playing an instrument, you should practice all the time.

"Later I studied seriously with a wonderful teacher, Vincent Puig. He taught me a lot, he believed in me, and was very generous in letting me work along side him after classes when he did his own painting for commissioned portraits."

"Illustrating books has always appealed to me and I tried a bit of it in Buenos Aires, but when I returned to the United States in 1958, my real career as a children's book illustrator started. I began getting commissions immediately.

"I am best at free sketching, and with dinobase—it being so transparent and having a thick grain—one can just trace off from the original sketch without losing much of the light quick touch."[1]

"After my second marriage, I followed my husband's international career shared between Paris (where his institution is based) and Geneva (where he represents it). My favourite working place is at la Tour de Peilz, facing the Lake of Geneva. Off and on I stay in Paris, looking for renewed inspiration from the great classic masters.

"Besides art I oversee a small farm in Argentina whenever I go there. I love to swim in Lake Geneva and go for hikes in the mountains, always carrying my sketch pad. Switzerland is a beautiful country.

"In the summer of 1989 I was in Washington for the book fair, and I was impressed by the output in children's books and what a big industry it has become. I hope that writers, illustrators, editors, publishers, and the media don't lose the ability to really understand children, and think the way children think because, as we grow into adulthood, we seem to lose the sense of wonder and excitement and appreciation of the world which surrounds us.

"I believe it's important to remain a bit child-like as an artist if you want to reach children. Show them what's beautiful and positive in life rather than depress them with violence and the sordid details of living. They will have time enough to learn all that. That is why most of my characters are smiling or have a gleam in their eyes!"

FOOTNOTE SOURCES

[1]Lee Kingman and others, *Illustrators of Children's Books: 1957-1966,* Horn Book, 1968. Amended by L. Obligado.

There were people with all kinds of cats. (From *Pickles and Jake* by Janet Chenery. Illustrated by Lilian Obligado.)

FOR MORE INFORMATION SEE:

Lee Kingman and others, *Illustrators of Children's Books: 1967-1978,* Horn Book, 1978.

COLLECTIONS

Kerlan Collection at the University of Minnesota.

OSBORN, Lois D(orothy) 1915-

PERSONAL: Born October 22, 1915, in Cleveland, Ohio; daughter of Ralph Page (a manufacturer) and Bonita (a homemaker; maiden name, Clifford) Judd; married Robert Osborn, February 2, 1939 (deceased); children: Kathleen Osborn Burdick, Linette Osborn Stenberg, Clifford, Lawrence. *Education:* Western Reserve University (now Case Western Reserve University), B.S., 1937; Concordia College, River Forest, Ill., M.A., 1976. *Agent:* Jane Jordan Browne, Multimedia Product Development, Inc., 410 South Michigan Ave., Chicago, Ill. 60605.

CAREER: Elementary school teacher in Garfield Heights, Ohio, 1937-39, and Elmhurst, Ill., 1955-79; writer, 1979—. *Member:* Society of Children's Bookwriters, Off Campus Writers Workshop, Children's Reading Round Table.

WRITINGS:

JUVENILE

My Brother Is Afraid of Just about Everything (illustrated by Jennie Williams), A. Whitman, 1982.
My Dad Is Really Something (illustrated by Rodney Pate), A. Whitman, 1983.

WORK IN PROGRESS: A young adult novel set in the early part of the twentieth century.

SIDELIGHTS: "Several years ago I faced retirement from the teaching profession, work that I loved. I had been recently widowed. What was I going to do with the rest of my life?

LOIS D. OSBORN

"The local college (Elmhurst) offered a course entitled 'Writing for Publication.' It was an idea that appealed to me. I enrolled, and my life began to change.

"'You're either a dabbler or a writer,' our instructor told the class. The former was a dreamer, the latter a worker. His contempt for dabblers was obvious. I vowed to become a writer.

"My first success was an article published in a teacher's magazine, *Instructor*. It described a method I had devised to help fourth graders learn math facts, and have a little fun doing it.

"Later I answered a newspaper ad from Science Research Associates who needed writers for their reading laboratory kit. I sold them an article and a story.

"I was no dabbler. I had become a writer! But I knew I had much to learn, and even today I'm still in the process of mastering the craft. 'How-to' books help, but better yet are the weekly sessions of the Off Campus Writers Workshop in Winnetka, Illinois, where editors and authors lecture and critique members' work. Out of this organization came a whole new circle of friends, some of whom are very close.

"In retrospect I realize that all during my life I was being prepared for a career that I had, at the time, no thought of following. In grade school it was discovered that I had considerable dramatic talent. (Could that be why my family had nicknamed me Sarah Bernhardt?) I enjoyed appearing in plays from then on and through my college years. An actor must become the character portrayed, assume the personality, the thought processes, feel the emotions, show the body language, and this is what a writer experiences when creating characters on paper.

"In junior high school my English teacher used her free period to conduct a poetry writing class for those who were interested. I wrote daily for three years. I learned the importance of selecting just the right word, and of being concise. I got a feel for the rhythm and flow of words. My teacher submitted one of my poems to a magazine called the *Bystander* and it was printed. Fifty-four years later, I dedicated my first picture book to her memory.

"At college I was fortunate to study under May Hill Arbuthnot, a leading authority on children's literature. From her I learned the criteria a story should meet, and developed a love and appreciation for children's books.

"I taught for a year and a half, but when I was married, I was forced to resign. In those days only unmarried women were allowed to teach, the reason being that once a woman had a husband to support her, she should give up her position to one who had not. Woman's Lib had yet to be heard from.

"Soon I was bored being a housewife. 'Either I get a dog, or we start a family,' was the ultimatum I delivered to my husband. He chose the latter. We had four children, and I devoted the next seventeen years to them. Being a parent is not essential to success in writing for children, but it helps.

"Finally I returned to teaching, and taught for twenty-four years. My creative energies went into devising learning games and other educational materials. I wrote plays for my class to perform, and put together a rhyming dictionary for them. Unhappy with a reading program that ignored phonics, I augmented it with a phonics program of my own which included writing a series of preprimers.

"Little did I know then that as I used *Something about the Author* in preparing literature lessons, I would one day appear in it myself.

"My ambition now is to become a novelist for young adults. I've written three. The first two did not sell, so I consider them 'practice books.' I do have hopes for the third and fourth which are at present being considered, but not as yet sold.

"I visit schools to read my books and talk about being a writer. I don't hesitate to describe the pain of rejections and the need to persevere despite them. I also emphasize that the joy one experiences in any creative process can be an end unto itself."

HOBBIES AND OTHER INTERESTS: Playing the piano, bowling, bridge, travel, reading.

PALTROWITZ, Donna (Milman) 1950-

PERSONAL: Surname is accented on first syllable; born April 12, 1950, in Brooklyn, N.Y.; daughter of Lawrence (a retail store owner) and Gladys (a bookkeeper; maiden name, Fichtenbaum) Milman; married Stuart Paltrowitz (a writer), August 29, 1971; children: Adam, Darren. *Education:* Hofstra University, B.A., 1971, M.A., 1974. *Home and office:* 2971 Lee Pl., Bellmore, N.Y. 11710.

CAREER: Paltrowitz Productions (writing team), Bellmore, N.Y., partner, 1971—. *Awards, honors:* Music City Song Festival honorable mention, 1984, for song, "Everyone and Everything's for Sale;" *Media & Methods* Awards Portfolio, 1986, for "Mystery Mazes" series.

WRITINGS:

JUVENILE; ALL WITH HUSBAND, STUART PALTROWITZ

Animal Soup (nonfiction short stories) National Educators for Creative Instruction, 1980.
Do You Know Your Boss?, Price, Stern, 1983.
Robotics, Messner, 1983.
The Mystery and Adventure Computer Storybook, Tribeca Communications, 1983.
The Science-Fiction Computer Storybook, Tribeca Communications, 1983.
Computers: Time, Strings, and Pizzas, Banbury, 1984.
More Mystery and Adventure Computer Stories, Tribeca Communications, 1985.
More Science-Fiction Computer Stories, Tribeca Communications, 1985.
Computer Crossroads (software), Educational Activities, 1985.
Springboard, Educational Activities, 1986.
Content Area Reading Skills—Competency Canada: Main Idea, Educational Activities, 1987.
Content Area Reading Skills—Competency Mexico: Locating Details, Educational Activities, 1987.
Content Area Reading Skills—Competency U.S. History: Detecting Sequence, Educational Activities, 1987.
Content Area Reading Skills U.S. Geography: Cause and Effect, Educational Activities, 1987.

"I HATE TO READ" SERIES; JUVENILE; ALL WITH S. PALTROWITZ

Crime and the Sweets, Educational Activities, 1975.
Cheaters Are Losers, Educational Activities, 1975.
Kate You're Late, Educational Activities, 1975.
Nervous Jervis, Educational Activities, 1975.
Kung Fu for Two, Educational Activities, 1977.
No Ifs, Ands, or Butts, Educational Activities, 1977.
Sink the Sub, Educational Activities, 1977.
Sloppy Copy, Educational Activities, 1977.

Stuart and Donna Paltrowitz

Bored of Education, Educational Activities, 1977.
Chicken Delight, Educational Activities, 1977.
Hold Your Fire, Educational Activities, 1977.
Throw It Your Way, Educational Activities, 1977.
Missing the Point, Educational Activities, 1978.
Principal for a Day, Educational Activities, 1978.
Gang Green, Educational Activities, 1978.
Pain and the Class, Educational Activities, 1978.
Break Out, Educational Activities, 1979.
I Can't Believe My Eyes, Educational Activities, 1979.
Crash, Educational Activities, 1979.
Sweet Nothings, Educational Activities, 1979.
Put On, Educational Activities, 1979.
Bits and Pizzas, Educational Activities, 1979.
Food for Thought, Educational Activities, 1979.
Brush Off, Educational Activities, 1979.

"WORK WORLD" SERIES; JUVENILE; ALL WITH S. PALTROWITZ

Workout, Educational Activities, 1977.
Head for Bread, Educational Activities, 1977.
Job Jive, Educational Activities, 1977.
Wonder Worker, Educational Activities, 1977.
Push Button, Educational Activities, 1980.
No Way to Fly, Educational Activities, 1980.
More Than Money, Educational Activities, 1980.
A Tip in Time, Educational Activities, 1980.

"PHONICS" COMPUTER SOFTWARE SERIES; JUVENILE; ALL WITH S. PALTROWITZ

Key to Consonant Sounds, Media Materials, 1984.
Key to Consonant Blends, Media Materials, 1984.
Key to Vowel Digraphs, Media Materials, 1984.
Key to Vowel Diphthongs, Media Materials, 1984.
Key to Word Recognition, Media Materials, 1984.

"MYSTERY MAZES" COMPUTER READING SERIES; JUVENILE; ALL WITH S. PALTROWITZ

The Carnival Caper, Educational Activities, 1985.
Houseboat Hideaway, Educational Activities, 1985.
Castle Clues, Educational Activities, 1986.

OTHER

The Bargain Hunter's Guide to Investing in Real Estate, Liberty House, 1990.

Has also written songs.

ADAPTATIONS:

"I Hate to Read, Series 1" (cassette; includes *Cheaters Are Losers, Kate, You're Late,* and *Crime and the Sweets*), Educational Activities, 1975.
"I Hate to Read, Series 2" (cassette; includes *Gang Green, Pain and the Class, Missing the Point,* and *Principal for a Day*), Educational Activities, 1977.
"I Hate to Read, Series 3" (cassette; includes *Chicken Delight, Hold Your Fire, Throw It Your Way,* and *Bored of Education*), Educational Activities, 1978.
"I Hate to Read, Series 4" (cassette; includes *Sloppy Copy, Kung Fu for Two, Sink the Sub,* and *No If, Ands, or Butts*), Educational Activities, 1979.
"I Hate to Read, Series 5" (cassette; includes *I Can't Believe My Eyes, Break Out,* and *Brush Off*), Educational Activities, 1980.
"I Hate to Read, Series 6" (cassette; includes *Bits and Pizzas, Sweet Nothings, Crash,* and *Food for Thought*), Educational Activities, 1981.
"Work World" (videocassette), Educational Activities, 1987.

WORK IN PROGRESS: How They Met; The Instant Guide to the Stock Market; "Body Buddies" series for young readers, about body parts, written in rhyme in a humorous vein.

PALTROWITZ, Stuart 1946-

PERSONAL: Surname is accented on first syllable; born January 31, 1946, in Brooklyn, N.Y.; son of Maurice (a securities trader) and Alice (Faden) Paltrowitz; married Donna Milman (a writer), August 29, 1971; children: Adam, Darren. *Education:* Nassau Community College, A.A., 1965; Hofstra University, B.A., 1967; Long Island University, M.S., 1975. *Home and office:* 2971 Lee Place, Bellmore, N.Y. 11710.

CAREER: Paltrowitz Productions (writing team), Bellmore, N.Y., partner, 1971—. *Awards, honors:* Music City Song Festival honorable mention, 1984, for song, "Everyone and Everything's for Sale;" *Media & Methods* Awards Portfolio, 1986, for "Mystery Mazes" series.

WRITINGS:

JUVENILE; ALL WITH WIFE, DONNA PALTROWITZ

Animal Soup (nonfiction short stories) National Educators for Creative Instruction, 1980.
Do You Know Your Boss?, Price, Stern, 1983.
Robotics, Messner, 1983.
The Mystery and Adventure Computer Storybook, Tribeca Communications, 1983.
The Science-Fiction Computer Storybook, Tribeca Communications, 1983.
Computers: Time, Strings, and Pizzas, Banbury, 1984.
More Mystery and Adventure Computer Stories, Tribeca Communications, 1985.
More Science-Fiction Computer Stories, Tribeca Communications, 1985.
Computer Crossroads (software), Educational Activities, 1985.
Springboard, Educational Activities, 1986.
Content Area Reading Skills—Competency Canada: Main Idea, Educational Activities, 1987.
Content Area Reading Skills—Competency Mexico: Locating Details, Educational Activities, 1987.
Content Area Reading Skills—Competency U. S. History: Detecting Sequence, Educational Activities, 1987.
Content Area Reading Skills U. S. Geography: Cause and Effect, Educational Activities, 1987.

"I HATE TO READ" SERIES; JUVENILE; ALL WITH D. PALTROWITZ

Crime and the Sweets, Educational Activities, 1975.
Cheaters Are Losers, Educational Activities, 1975.
Kate You're Late, Educational Activities, 1975.
Nervous Jervis, Educational Activities, 1975.
Kung Fu for Two, Educational Activities, 1977.
No Ifs, Ands, or Butts, Educational Activities, 1977.
Sink the Sub, Educational Activities, 1977.
Sloppy Copy, Educational Activities, 1977.
Bored of Education, Educational Activities, 1977.
Chicken Delight, Educational Activities, 1977.
Hold Your Fire, Educational Activities, 1977.
Throw It Your Way, Educational Activities, 1977.
Missing the Point, Educational Activities, 1978.
Principal for a Day, Educational Activities, 1978.
Gang Green, Educational Activities, 1978.
Pain and the Class, Educational Activities, 1978.
Break Out, Educational Activities, 1979.
I Can't Believe My Eyes, Educational Activities, 1979.

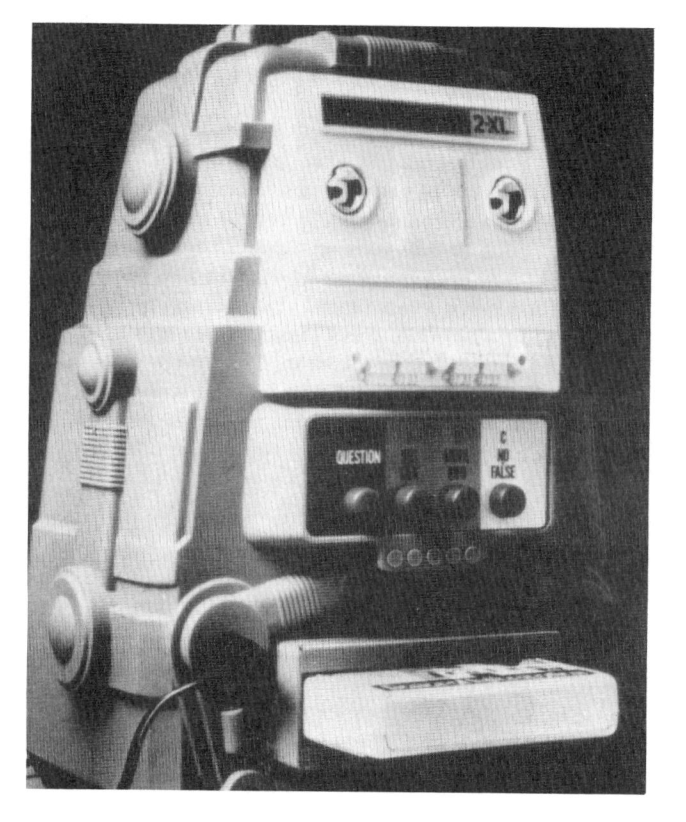

The 2-X-L is a robot that was invented by a teacher to help students learn. (From *Robotics* by Stuart and Donna Paltrowitz.)

Crash, Educational Activities, 1979.
Sweet Nothings, Educational Activities, 1979.
Put On, Educational Activities, 1979.
Bits and Pizzas, Educational Activities, 1979.
Food for Thought, Educational Activities, 1979.
Brush Off, Educational Activities, 1979.

"WORK WORLD" SERIES; JUVENILE; ALL WITH D. PALTROWITZ

Workout, Educational Activities, 1977.
Head for Bread, Educational Activities, 1977.
Job Jive, Educational Activities, 1977.
Wonder Worker, Educational Activities, 1977.
Push Button, Educational Activities, 1980.
No Way to Fly, Educational Activities, 1980.
More Than Money, Educational Activities, 1980.
A Tip in Time, Educational Activities, 1980.

"PHONICS" COMPUTER SOFTWARE SERIES; JUVENILE; ALL WITH D. PALTROWITZ

Key to Consonant Sounds, Media Materials, 1984.
Key to Consonant Blends, Media Materials, 1984.
Key to Vowel Digraphs, Media Materials, 1984.
Key to Vowel Diphthongs, Media Materials, 1984.
Key to Word Recognition, Media Materials, 1984.

"MYSTERY MAZES" COMPUTER READING SERIES; JUVENILE; ALL WITH D. PALTROWITZ

The Carnival Caper, Educational Activities, 1985.
Houseboat Hideaway, Educational Activities, 1985.
Castle Clues, Educational Activities, 1986.

OTHER

The Bargain Hunter's Guide to Investing in Real Estate, Liberty House, 1990.

Has also written songs.

ADAPTATIONS:

"I Hate to Read, Series 1" (cassette; includes *Cheaters Are Losers, Kate, You're Late,* and *Crime and the Sweets*), Educational Activities, 1975.
"I Hate to Read, Series 2" (cassette; includes *Gang Green, Pain and the Class, Missing the Point,* and *Principal for a Day*), Educational Activities, 1977.
"I Hate to Read, Series 3" (cassette; includes *Chicken Delight, Hold Your Fire, Throw It Your Way,* and *Bored of Education*), Educational Activities, 1978.
"I Hate to Read, Series 4" (cassette; includes *Sloppy Copy, Kung Fu for Two, Sink the Sub,* and *No If, Ands, or Butts*), Educational Activities, 1979.
"I Hate to Read, Series 5" (cassette; includes *I Can't Believe My Eyes, Break Out,* and *Brush Off*), Educational Activities, 1980.
"I Hate to Read, Series 6" (cassette; includes *Bits and Pizzas, Sweet Nothings, Crash,* and *Food for Thought*), Educational Activities, 1981.
"Work World" (videocassette), Educational Activities, 1987.

WORK IN PROGRESS: How They Met; The Instant Guide to the Stock Market; "Body Buddies" series of books for young readers, about body parts, written in rhyme in a humorous vein.

PENDER, Lydia (Podger) 1907-

PERSONAL: Born June 29, 1907, in London, England; daughter of George Herbert (a paint factory manager) and Ethel (a homemaker; maiden name, Ward) Podger; married Walter G. B. Pender (a chartered accountant), March 5, 1932; children: John Douglas, Judith Margaret Pender Stehli, Alison Mary Pender Newcombe, William Michael. *Education:* Attended Sydney University, 1925. *Home:* 10 Blenheim Rd., Lindfield, New South Wales 2070, Australia. *Agent:* c/o Curtis Brown Australia Pty Ltd., 27 Union St., Paddington, Sydney, New South Wales 2021, Australia.

CAREER: E. S. Wolfenden (chartered accountant and actuary), Sydney, Australia, typist, audit clerk, and student in accountancy, 1928-32; writer 1943—. *Member:* Australian Society of Authors, Children's Book Council of Australia (New South Wales Branch; past honorary secretary). *Awards, honors:* Highly Commended Book from the Australian Children's Book Council, 1968, for *Sharpur the Carpet Snake,* Commended Book, 1973, for *Barnaby and the Rocket,* and 1980, for *The Useless Donkeys;* Lady Cutler Award from the New South Wales Branch of the Australian Children's Book Council, 1988, for Distinguished Services to Australian Children's Literature.

WRITINGS:

JUVENILE

Marbles in My Pocket (poetry; illustrated by Pixie O'Harris), Writers Press (Sydney), 1957.
Barnaby and the Horses (illustrated by Alie Evers), Abelard, 1961, revised edition (illustrated by Inga Moore), Oxford University Press, 1980.
Dan McDougall and the Bulldozer (illustrated by Gerald Rose), Abelard, 1963, new edition (illustrated by Tony Oliver), Hodder & Stoughton, 1987.
Sharpur the Carpet Snake (illustrated by Josephine Smith), Abelard, 1967, new edition (illustrated by T. Oliver), Hodder & Stoughton, 1982, large print edition, 1983.
(With Mary Gilmore) *Poems to Read to Young Australians,* Paul Hamlyn, 1968.
Brown Paper Leaves (poetry), Wentworth (Sydney), 1971.
Barnaby and the Rocket (illustrated by Judith Cowell), Collins, 1972.
The Useless Donkeys (illustrated by J. Cowell), Methuen, 1979, Warne, 1980.
Morning Magpie: Favorite Verse (illustrated by Noela Young), Angus & Robertson, 1984, Salem House, 1986.
Lydia Pender's Australian Alphabet (verse; illustrated by T. Oliver), Margaret Hamilton Books (Sydney), 1989.

CONTRIBUTOR TO ANTHOLOGIES:

Chosen for Children, Angus & Robertson, 1966.
The Magic of Verse, Angus & Robertson, 1969.
More Poems to Read to Young Australians, Paul Hamlyn, 1971.
Emu Stew, Kestrel, 1976.
Taking the Sun, Logman Cheshire, 1981.
Someone Is Flying Balloons, Omnibus, 1984.
Apples in Hurricane Street, Methuen, 1985.

LYDIA PENDER

ADAPTATIONS:

"Barnaby and the Rocket" (cassette), Sound Information (Sydney).

WORK IN PROGRESS: An autobiography, *I Too Will Something Make*.

SIDELIGHTS: "I was born on the Isle of Dogs, just across the Thames from Greenwich, in England, where I walked to school each day by way of the Millwall Tunnel, a pedestrian tunnel right underneath the river. I had four brothers, and was a real tomboy myself, loving to climb trees and play football in the park. Our mother read us Lewis Carroll's 'Alice' books, and I can still recite 'The Walrus and the Carpenter' right through without any hesitation. The 'Just-So Stories' and the Beatrix Potter tales were other favourites, but we did not have the marvellous choice and variety of children's books that today's youngsters take for granted.

"We all came to Australia in 1920, and I have lived here ever since. I wrote nothing myself till I was married and had three children (another one was to come later). Then I began with poems published one by one in the New South Wales Education Department's *School Magazine,* later collected into my first book, *Marbles in My Pocket,* illustrated by Pixie O'Harris. This was in 1957, after which I set off on a new track with my first picture book, *Barnaby and the Horses,* published in the U.S. by Abelard-Schuman. From then on I have swung back and forth between stories and verse. Each new idea I have seems to choose its own pattern, to grow into a picture book or a poem.

"I have never been a prolific writer. My work is an occasional obsession. Gaps of months or even years alternate with periods of intense concentration, when everything else I do is subordinated to the completion of the work in hand, whether prose or verse. What matters to me most, always, is not the plot, nor even the characters, but making a music with the words, in prose just as much as in poetry. One sentence may well take me days or weeks before it satisfies my own critical ear, and one picture-book story many months.

"Stories can eventually go out of print, which is sad. But poems have a way of popping up here and there in anthologies long after they were first printed, which is a great joy to me.

"Now in my eighties, when I thought my writing days were over, and my principal interest had turned to embroidering dinner cloths for all my granddaughters, I have recently completed a new picture book, *Australian Alphabet,* all in verse. Who knows, there may be more books yet! It is important to go on living and doing and creating, so long as one is alive at all."

HOBBIES AND OTHER INTERESTS: Gardening, local reading circle, family, visiting schools.

FOR MORE INFORMATION SEE:

Martha E. Ward and Dorothy A. Marquardt, *Authors of Books for Young People,* Scarecrow, 1971.

COLLECTIONS

Lu Rees Archives, Canberra College of Advanced Education, Belconnen, Australia.

PEPPER, Frank S. 1910-1988 (Stewart Colwyn, Hal Wilton)

OBITUARY NOTICE: Born February 8, 1910, in Ilford, England; died December 11, 1988. Journalist, comic book writer, and author. Pepper was best known for his contributions to boys' magazines in Britain. After graduation from high school in the 1920s, Pepper joined the staff of the *Children's Newspaper*. In the October, 1938 issue of the boys' weekly *Champion,* Pepper, under the pseudonym Hal Wilton, introduced the hero Rockfist Rogan, a boxing fighter pilot whose adventures in both world wars remained popular with readers until 1961. He later created the comic strip superstar Captain Condor, an outer space warrior who appeared for twelve years in the periodical *Lion*. Pepper used the pseudonym Stewart Colwyn to introduce his longest-running character, soccer star Roy of the Rovers, who has appeared on the cover of the comic book *Tiger* since 1954. A longtime collector of newspaper quotations and clippings, Pepper also compiled several books, including *The Handbook of Twentieth-Century Quotations* and *Contemporary Biographical Quotations*.

FOR MORE INFORMATION SEE:

The Men behind Boys' Fiction, Howard Baker, 1970.

OBITUARIES

Times (London), December 13, 1988.

PETERSEN, Gwenn Boardman 1924- (Gwenn R. Boardman)

PERSONAL: Born November 16, 1924, in London, England; daughter of Edward and Mabel (Ware) White; married Henry Petersen (a U.S. Merchant Marine captain), August 9, 1975. *Education:* University of California, Berkeley, B.A. (with highest honors), 1957; Claremont Graduate School, M.A., 1961, Ph.D., 1963. *Residence:* San Francisco, Calif., and London, England.

CAREER: Worked with South-East European Service of British Broadcasting Corp. during her teens; University of California Medical School, Cancer Research Institute, San Francisco, administrative assistant, 1952-54; kindergarten and elementary teacher in Riverside, Calif., 1957-59; University of California, Riverside, associate in English, 1959-61; Claremont Men's College, Claremont, Calif., instructor in English, 1961-63; Kobe College, Nishinomiya, Japan, professor of English, 1963-65; University of the Pacific, Raymond College, Stockton, Calif., assistant professor of humanities, 1965; returned to Japan to continue research, 1965; part-time professor of English at Osaka City University and English tutor to physicians and surgeons at the medical schools of Kobe and Osaka universities, 1965-67; University of Saigon, Saigon, Vietnam, Fulbright professor of American literature, 1967-68; Immaculate Heart College, Los Angeles, Calif., assistant professor of English literature, 1968- 70; International Christian University, Tokyo, Japan, visiting associate professor, 1970-71; United Nations Centre for Regional Development, Nagoya, Japan, editorial and publications officer, 1972-73; University of San Francisco, San Francisco, lecturer in English, 1973-76; research associate, Institute for Asian and Pacific Studies, 1976-77. Free-lance writer and photographer.

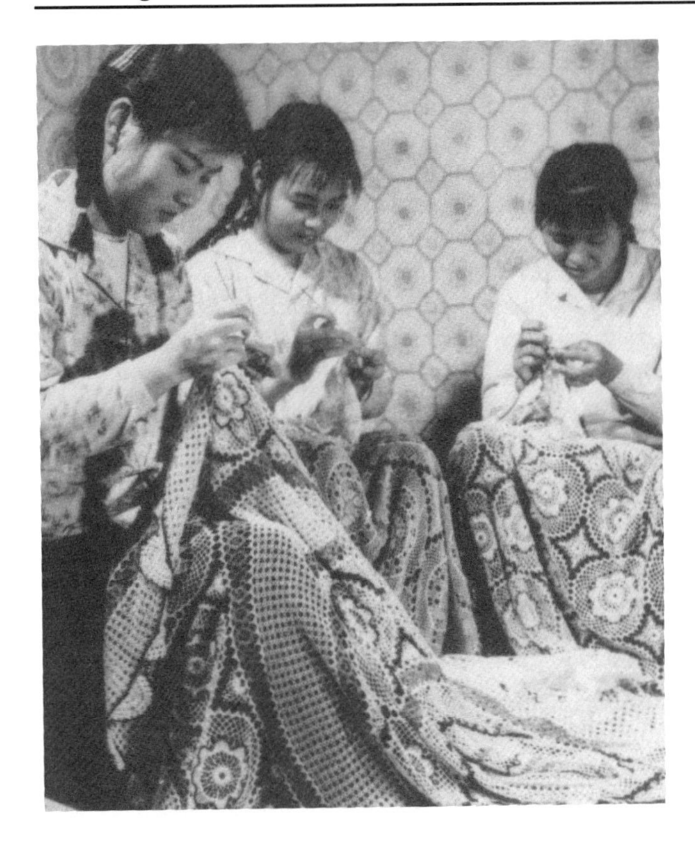

A group of girls work on some of the lace fabrics produced in Soochow and other areas. (From *Across the Bridge to China* by Gwenn Boardman Petersen. Photograph courtesy of China's Foreign Trade.)

Visiting professor at Kwansei Gakuin University, 1965, University of Cape Town, 1968, and World Campus Afloat of Chapman College, 1970; visiting lecturer at universities in South Africa, Japan, and for Far East Division, University of Maryland. *Member:* Authors Guild, Modern Language Association of America, International Platform Association.

WRITINGS:

UNDER NAME GWENN R. BOARDMAN

Carrying Cargo, T. Nelson, 1968.
Living in Tokyo (young adult book; self-illustrated with photographs), T. Nelson, 1970.
Graham Greene: The Aesthetics of Exploration, University of Florida Press, 1971.
Living in Singapore (young adult book; self-illustrated with photographs), T. Nelson, 1971.

UNDER NAME GWENN BOARDMAN PETERSEN

The Moon in the Water: Understanding Tanizaki, Kawabata, and Mishima, [Honolulu], 1979.
Across the Bridge to China (young adult book; self- illustrated with photographs), T. Nelson, 1979.
Careers in the United States Merchant Marine (self- illustrated with photographs), Lodestar, 1983.

Contributor to periodicals, including *Critique, Journal of Modern Literature, Renascence, English Journal, Inside Japan, Queens Quarterly, Modern Fiction Studies, Today's Health, RN, Mademoiselle, Japan Times Weekly,* the bilingual *Student Times* (published by the *Japan Times*), *Medical English, Business View, Fairplay, Shipping Weekly, Shipping and Trade News* (Tokyo; United Kingdom correspondent), and other magazines and newspapers in Japan, the United Kingdom, and the United States.

WORK IN PROGRESS: A study of Japanese women; study of the role of the U.S. Merchant Marines in Vietnam.

HOBBIES AND OTHER INTERESTS: Photography of people and ships.

PUSHKIN, Alexander (Sergeyevich) 1799-1837

PERSONAL: Born June 6, 1799 (some sources say May 26, 1799), in Moscow, Russia, died February 10, 1837 (some sources say January 29, 1837), in St. Petersburg, U.S.S.R.; son of Sergei Lvovich (an army officer) and Nadezhda Osipovna (Hannibal) Pushkin; married Natalia Goncharova, January 19, 1831; children: three. *Education:* Educated at home and at Imperial Lyceum (now called Pushkin), Tsarskoye Selo, 1811-17.

CAREER: Russian poet, novelist, dramatist, and short story writer. Appointed to a clerkship in the Ministry for Foreign Affairs, St. Petersburg, 1817-24. Founder of literary journal, *Sovremennik* (title means "*The Contemporary*"), 1836.

Pushkin in 1822.

WRITINGS:

POETRY

Recollections of Tsarskoe-Selo, [U.S.S.R.], 1815.

Ruslan i Liudmila, [U.S.S.R.], 1820, translation by Walter Arndt published as *Ruslan and Liudmila,* Ardis, 1974, [another edition published as *Ruslan I. Liudmila,* State Mutual Bank, 1985].

The Gavriiliad, [U.S.S.R.], 1821.

Kavkazskii plennik (title means "The Prisoner of the Caucasus"), [U.S.S.R.], 1822.

Bratia razboiniki, (title means "The Robber Brothers"), [U.S.S.R.], 1822.

Evgenii Onegin, [U.S.S.R.], 1823-31, translation by Lieutenant-Colonel Spalding published as *Eugene Oneguine: A Romance of Russian Life in Verse,* Macmillan (London), 1881, translation by Dorothea Prall Radin and George Z. Patrick, published as *Eugene Onegin,* University of California Press, 1937, translation by Babette Deutsch published as *Eugene Onegin: A Novel in Verse* (illustrated with lithographs by Fritz Eichenberg), Limited Editions, 1943, translation by Vladimir Nabokov, Pantheon, 1964, revised edition, Princeton University Press, 1976, translation by Charles Johnston, Viking, 1978.

Bakhchisaraiskii fontan, [U.S.S.R.], 1824, published as *The Bakhchesarian Fountain: A Tale of the Tauride,* Ardis, 1987.

Graf Nulin (title means "Count Nulin"), [U.S.S.R.], 1825.

Stansy, [U.S.S.R.], 1826.

The Prophet, [U.S.S.R.], 1826, translated by Jean Overton Fuller, Fuller d'Arch Smith, 1983.

Stikhotvoreniya, [U.S.S.R.], 1826, revised edition (4 volumes), 1829-35.

Tsygany, [U.S.S.R.], 1827, published as *The Gipsies,* introduction by Peter Henry, Bradda Books, 1968.

Poltava, [U.S.S.R.], 1828.

Angelo, [U.S.S.R.], 1833.

Domik v Kolomne (title means "The Little House in Kolomna"), [U.S.S.R.], 1833.

Mednyi vsadnik, [U.S.S.R.], 1841, translation published as *The Bronze Horseman* (illustrated by Fedor Costantinov), De Tskaya Literature, 1975.

Ivan Panin, translator, *Poems by Alexander Pushkin,* Cupples and Hurd, 1888.

Max Eastman, translator, *Gabriel: A Poem in One Song* (illustrated by Rockwell Kent), Covici-Friede, 1929.

Walter Morison, translator, *Pushkin's Poems,* Allen & Unwin, 1945 [another edition selected and interpreted by Henry Jones published as *Poems,* Citadel, 1965].

Walter Arndt, translator, *Pushkin Threefold; Narrative, Lyric, Polemic, and Ribald Verse,* Dutton, 1972.

Also author of *Vol'nost* (title means "Ode to Liberty"), 1817.

NOVELS

Arap Petra Velikogo (title means "The Negro of Peter the Great"), [U.S.S.R.], 1828.

Kapitanskaia dochka, [U.S.S.R.], 1831, translation by C. G. Hebbe published as *The Captain's Daughter; or, The Generosity of the Russian Usurper Pugatscheff,* C. Muller, 1846, translation by I. Litvinov and T. Litvinov published as *The Captain's Daughter,* Progress Publishers (Moscow), 1965.

Dubrovski, [U.S.S.R.], 1832-33, translation by Ivy Litvinov and Tatyana Litvinov published as *Dubrovsky,* Foreign Languages Publishing House (Moscow), 1955.

Istoriya Pugacheva, [U.S.S.R.], 1835, translation by Earl Sampson published as *The History of Pugachev,* Ardis, 1983.

Istoriya sela Goryukhina, [U.S.S.R.]. 1837, translation by Gillon Aitken and David Budgen published as *History of the Village of Goryukhino,* Angel Classics, 1983.

PROSE

Baryshnia krest 'ianka, [U.S.S.R.], 18(?), published as *An Amateur Peasant Girl* (illustrated by Ian Ribbons), Rodale Press, 1955.

The Snow Storm, [U.S.S.R.], 18(?), edited by Ann Redpath, Creative Education, 1983.

The Postmaster, [U.S.S.R.], 18(?).

SHORT STORIES

Povesti Belkina, [U.S.S.R.], 1831, translation by I. Litvinov and T. Litvinov published as *The Tales of Ivan Belkin,* Foreign Languages Publishing House, 1954, translation by G. Aitken and D. Budgen published as *The Tales of Belkin,* Dufour, 1983.

Pikovaia dama, [U.S.S.R.], 1834, translation by I. Litvinov and T. Litvinov published as *The Queen of Spades* (illustrated by V. Sveshnikov), Foreign Languages Publishing House, 1956.

FOLKTALES

Skazki, [U.S.S.R.], 1831-34, translation by Janet Dalley published as *Pushkin's Fairy Tales,* (illustrated with lithographs by Arthur Boyd), Barrie & Jenkins, 1978.

PLAYS

"Vadim" (unfinished), 1821.

"Skazhi, kakoy sudboy . . . " (unfinished; title means "Say, What Fate"), 1821.

Boris Godunov (produced in St. Petersburg, at Mariinsky Theatre, September 17, 1870, in Moscow, 1880, and at Moscow Art Theatre, 1970) [U.S.S.R.], 1831, translation by Alfred Hayes, Dutton, 1918, translation by Philip L. Barbour, Columbia University Press, 1953, reissued, Greenwood, 1976 [another edition illustrated by Boris Zvorykin, with an introduction by Peter Ustinov, Viking, 1982].

Motsart i Salieri (produced in St. Petersburg at Bolshoi Dramatic Theatre, January 27, 1832, and at Moscow Art Theatre, 1915), [U.S.S.R.], 1832, translation by R. M. Hewitt published as *Mozart and Salieri,* Nottingham University, 1938, translation by Anthony Wood, Dufour, 1982.

Pir vo vryemya chumy (title means "The Feast during the Plague"; based on *The City of the Plague* by John Wilson, pseudonym of Christopher North; produced in St. Petersburg at Alexandrinsky Theatre, 1899, and in Moscow at Moscow Art Theatre, 1915), [U.S.S.R.], 1832.

"Stseny iz rytsarskikh vryemen," (unfinished; title means "Scenes from the Age of Chivalry"), 1835, produced in Leningrad at Bolshoi Dramatic Theatre, 1937.

Skupoi rystar (title means "The Avaricious Knight"; produced in St. Petersburg at Alexandrinsky Theatre, September 23, 1852, in Moscow at Maly Theatre, January 9, 1853), [U.S.S.R.], 1836.

Rusalka (title means "The Water Nymph"; first produced in St. Petersburg at Alexandrinsky Theatre, April 25, 1838), [U.S.S.R.], 1837.

Kamennyi gost (title means "The Stone Guest"; first produced in St. Petersburg at Alexandrinsky Theatre, November 18, 1847, and at Moscow Art Theatre, 1915), [U.S.S.R.], 1839.

Also wrote an outline of a drama, "Papessa Ioanna" (title means "The She-Pope Joan"), 1834-35.

(From "The Tale of the Fisherman and the Fish" by Alexander Pushkin. Illustrated by Ivan Bilibin.)

There, in regal raiments, sate [sic] Tsar Saltan in royal state. (From *The Tale of Tsar Saltan* by Alexander Pushkin. Illustrated by Ivan Bilibin.)

OTHER

The Frog Princess, [St. Petersburg], 1901, Imported, 1979.

Vasilisa prekrasnaia, [St. Petersburg], 1902, published as *Vasilisa the Beautiful,* Imported, 1974, translation and retelling by Irina Zheloznova, published as *Vasilisa the Beautiful,* Central Books, 1976.

Skazka o tsare Saltane, [St. Petersburg], 1831, translation by Louis Zellikoff published as *The Tale of Tsar Saltan, of His Son, the Glorious and Mighty Knight Prince Guidon Saltanovich, and of the Fair Swan-Princess* (illustrated by Ivan Bilibin), Progress, 1968, translation by Patricia Tracey Lowe published as *Tale of Csar Saltan; or, The Prince and the Swan Princess* (illustrated by I. Bilibin), Crowell, 1975.

Skazka o zolotom petushke, [St.Petersburg], 1834, translation by Elaine Pogany published as *The Golden Cockerel* (illustrated by Willy Pogany), T. Nelson, 1938, translation by Elizabeth C. Hulick (illustrated by Rosalie Richards), Astor-Honor, 1962; translation by P. T. Lowe published as *The Tale of the Golden Cockerel* (illustrated by I. Bilibin), Crowell, 1975 [another edition illustrated by Edmund Dulac, Limited Editions, 1950].

Puteshestviye v Arzrum (travel essay), [U.S.S.R.], 1836, translation by Birgitta Ingemanson published as *A Journey to Arzrum,* Ardis, 1974.

Table Talk (essays), [Russia], 1857.

Marie H. de Zierlinska, translator, *Marie: A Story of Russian Love: From the Russian of Alexander Pushkin,* Jansen, McClurg, 1877.

I. P. Foote, editor, *A Pushkin Verse Reader*, Pitman, 1962.

J. Thomas Shaw, editor, *The Letters of Alexander Pushkin,* three volumes, Indiana University and University of Pennsylvania, 1964.

L. Zellikov, translator, *The Fisherman and the Goldfish* (illustrated by B. Dekhteryov), Progress Publishers, 1969.

W. Arndt, translator, *Pushkin Threefold: Narrative, Lyric, Polemic, and Ribald Verse,* Dutton, 1972.

Tales by Alexander Pushkin (illustrated by I. Bilibin), Malysh, 1982.

Tale of the Dead Princess and the Seven Knights, Raduga, 1984.

COLLECTIONS:

J. Buchan Telfer, translator, *Russian Romance* (contains *The Moor of Peter the Great, The Captain's Daughter, The*

Lady-Rustic, The Pistol-Shot, The Snow-Storm, The Station-Master, and *The Undertaker*), H. S. King, 1875.
T. Keane, translator, *The Prose Tales of Alexander Pushkin,* G. Bell & Sons, 1894, Books for Libraries, 1971.
Charles Edward Turner, *Translations from Pushkin in Memory of the Hundredth Anniversary of the Poet's Birthday* (contains *The Gipsies, Boris Godunov, Mozart and Salieri, The Bronze Cavalier,* and *The Statue Guest*), S. Low Marston & Co., 1899.
Natalie Duddington, translator, *The Captain's Daughter and Other Stories,* Dutton, 1933, reissued, 1961.
Avrahm Yarmolinsky, editor, *The Poems, Prose and Plays of Alexander Pushkin,* Random House, 1936, Modern Library, 1962.
Boris Brasol, translator, *The Russian Wonderland,* Paisley Press, 1936.
Mary Kramer Gray, *A Collection of Short Lyrics by Pushkin,* (taken from the literal translation of I. Panin), privately printed, 1936.
R. T. Currall, translator, *Three Tales: The Snow-Storm, The Postmaster, The Undertaker,* Harrap, 1943.
Vladimir Nabokov, translator, *Three Russian Poets: Selections from Pushkin, Lermontov and Tyutchev,* New Directions, 1944, reissued, Folcroft, 1969.
Fruma Gottschalk, reteller, *Two Short Stories: The Stationmaster* [*and*] *A Shot,* D. C. Heath, 1946.
T. X. H. Pantcheff, *Two Fairy Tales* (includes *The Golden Fish* and *The Tales of Tsar Salten;* illustrated by V. Neshumoff), Owl Press, 1947.
Polnoe sobranie sochineniy, 16 volumes, [Moscow], 1948.
Rosemary Edmonds, translator, *The Captain's Daughter* [*and*] *The Negro of Peter the Great,* Spearman, 1958.
I. Litvinov and T. Litvinov, translators, *The Queen of Spades and Other Tales,* New American Library, 1961.
R. Edmonds, translator, *The Queen of Spades and Other Stories,* Penguin, 1962.
I. P. Foote, *A Pushkin Verse Reader,* Allen & Unwin, 1962.
John Fennell, editor, *Pushkin* (prose translations of poems), Penguin, 1964.
E. M. Kayden, translator, *Little Tragedies* (contains *The Covetous Knight, Mozart and Salieri, The Stone Guest,* and *The Feast during the Plague;* illustrated by Vladimir Favorsky), Antioch Press, 1965.
Gillon R. Aitken, translator, *The Complete Prose Tales of Alexander Sergeyevitch Pushkin,* Norton, 1966, revised edition, Michael Russell, 1978.
Carl R. Proffer, editor and translator, *The Critical Prose of Alexander Pushkin,* Indiana University Press, 1969.
James Reeves, *The Golden Cockerel and Other Stories* (illustrated by Jan Lebis), F. Watts, 1969.
G. R. Aitken, translator, *The Queen of Spades* [*and*] *The Captain's Daughter* (illustrated with etchings by Clarke Hutton), Folio Society, 1970.
Kathryn Feuer, author of introduction, *The Captain's Daughter and Other Stories* (illustrated by Charles Mozley), Limited Editions Club, 1971.
Selected Works in Two Volumes, Progress Publishers, 1974.
William E. Harkins, editor and translator, *Three Comic Poems,* Ardis, 1974.
R. Edmonds, *The Queen of Spades* [*and*] *The Negro of Peter the Great* [*and*] *Dubrovsky* [*and*] *The Captain's Daughter,* Penguin, 1978.
Janet Dalley, translator, *Pushkin's Fairy Tales* (illustrated by Arthur Boyd), Barrie & Jenkins, 1978.
C. Johnston, *Poems and Journeys,* Bodley Head, 1979.
Tales by Alexander Pushkin (contains *The Tale of the Golden Cockerel,* and *The Tale of Tsar Salten*; illustrated by I. Bilibin), Imported, 1981.
A. Wood, translator, *Mozart and Salieri: The Little Tragedies,* Angel Books (England), 1982.
D. M. Thomas *The Bronze Horseman: Selected Poems,* Viking, 1982.
The Queen of Spades and Other Tales, Franklin Library, 1983.
Paul Debreczeny, translator, *Alexander Pushkin: Complete Prose Fiction,* Stanford University Press, 1983.
G. Aitken and D. Budgen, *The Tales of Belkin* [*with*] *The History of the Village of Goryukhino,* Angel, 1983.
C. Johnston, translator, *Narrative Poems by Alexander Pushkin and Mikhail Lermontov,* Random House, 1983.
Alexander Pushkin: Collected Narrative and Lyrical Poetry, Ardis, 1984.
Cynthia A. Whittaker, translator, *Alexander Pushkin: Epigrams and Satrical Verse,* Ardis, 1984.
Tale of the Dead Princess and the Seven Knights, Raduga, 1984.
Dramas by Pushkin, Russian Language Publishers, 1985.
Tales (illustrated by Vladimir Konashevich), Raduga Publishers, 1985.
Selections from Pushkin, Russian Language Publishers, 1985.
William Lewis, translator, *The Bakhchesarian Fountain and Other Poems by Various Authors,* Ardis, 1987.

Contributor of poetry to *Vestnik Europy* (title means "The Messenger of Europe").

ADAPTATIONS:

OPERA

"Ruslan i Lyudmila," composed by Mikhail Ivanovich Glinda, first produced in Moscow, 1847.
"Rusalka" (title means "The Nixie"), composed by A. S. Dargomyzhskii, produced in St. Petersburg at Mariinsky Theatre, May 16, 1856.
"Kamennyi gost" (title means "The Stone Guest"), composed by A. S. Dargomyzhsky, performed in St. Petersburg at Mariinsky Theatre, February 28, 1872.
"Boris Godunov," composed by Modest Mussorgsky, performed in St. Petersburg at Mariinsky Theatre, January 27, 1874, performed in U.S.S.R. at the Maly Theater, in honor of "Pushkin Days," 1937, English translation produced on NBC-TV, March 26, 1951.
"Yevegeny Onyegin," composed by Peter Ilych Tchaikovsky, produced in Moscow by the Imperial College of Music at the Little Theatre, January 23, 1881.
"Pikovaya dama," (title means "The Queen of Spades"), composed by P. I. Tchaikovsky, produced in Kiev, Russia, December, 1890.
"Motsart i Salieri," composed by Nikolay Rimsky-Korsakov, produced in Moscow at Moscow Private Russian Opera, December 7, 1898.
"Pir vo vryemya chumy," (title means "The Feast during the Plague"), composed by Cesar Cui, produced in Moscow at Novyy Theatre, 1901.
"Skupoi rytsar" (title means "The Avaricious Knight"), composed by S. V. Rachmaninov, performed in Moscow at Bolshoi Theatre, 1906.
"Dubrovsky," composed by E. Napravnik, performed in Moscow at Bolshoi Theater, April 11, 1936.
"The Stone Guest," "Mozart and Salieri" and "Gypsies," performed at the Nemirovich-Danchenko Theater, U.S.S.R., in honor of "Pushkin Days," 1937.
"The Bumble Bee Prince" (based on *The Tale of Tsar Saltan*), composed by N. Rimsky-Korsakoff, performed in New York City at St. James Theatre, December 27, 1937, and in Brooklyn, N.Y. at Brooklyn Academy of Music, December 30, 1937.

(From *Vasilisa the Beautiful* by Alexander Pushkin. Illustrated by Ivan Bilibin.)

It is impossible to pray for Tsar Herod; the Mother of God forbids it. (From *Boris Godunov* by Alexander Pushkin. Illustrated by Boris Zvorykin.)

PLAYS

"Boris Godunov," "Ruslan and Ludmila," "Eugene Onegin" and "The Queen of Spades," performed at the Bolshoi Theater, in honor of "Pushkin Days", 1936-37.
"The Captain's Daughter," performed at Maly Theater, U.S.S.R., in honor of "Pushkin Days," 1937.
"The Queen of Spades," performed in Cambridge, England at the A.D.C. Theatre, February, 1937.
"A Feast in the Plague-Time" (includes excerpts from *The Miserly Knight, The Stone Guest, Mozart and Saliere,* and *A Feast in the Plague-Time*), performed in Purchase, N.Y. at Pepsico Summerfare, July 23, 1987.

MOTION PICTURES

"Der Postmeister" (title means "The Postmaster"), Wien Films, 1940.
"The Queen of Spades," Associated British Picture Corp., 1949, adaptation by Tom Sterling, Guild Films, 1954.
"The Shot" (based on a story by Alexander Pushkin), Pyramid Productions, 1950.
"The Fish and the Fisherman," Mosfilm (Moscow), 1950, Brandon Films, 1952.
"Tempest" (based on a novel by Alexander Pushkin), Paramount, 1958.

CASSETTES

"Boris Godunov," Caedmon, 1976.
"Eugene Onegin" and "The Tale of the Golden Cockerel," Caedmon, 1978.
"The Shot," Jimcin Records, 1979.

SIDELIGHTS: Alexander Sergeyevich Pushkin is perhaps lesser known to Western readers than other Russian literary giants, but in the Soviet Union he is considered the nation's greatest man of letters by adults and children alike.

Born in Moscow in **1799,** Pushkin's family was both illustrious and eccentric. "My grandfather was a passionate and cruel man. His first wife died in a dungeon in one of his country houses where he had thrown her for an imaginary or real affair with a Frenchman, a former tutor of his sons, whom he very feudally hanged in the backyard. His second wife suffered a great deal at his hands. One day he told her to dress and drive with him on a visit to some neighbouring squires. My grandmother, who was pregnant, did not feel well but she dared not refuse. On the way she felt the pains of childbirth. My grandfather told the coachman to stop and she gave birth in the carriage—to my father, I believe. She was brought back home more dead than alive and put to bed in her finery and wearing her jewels. All this I have learnt in a rather roundabout way. My father never spoke of my grandfather's eccentricities and our old servants died long ago."[1]

"My mother's genealogy is still more curious. Her grandfather was a Negro, the son of a wealthy prince. The Russian ambassador in Constantinople, having gotten him from a seraglio where he was kept as a chieftain, sent him to Peter I together with two other Negroes."[2]

After several generations of nobility, the Pushkins had earned their place in Moscow society, about which the author affectionately wrote when he was a teenager. "A long time ago Moscow was full of retired wealthy noblemen, grandees who had left the court, men of independent means with no care in the world, passionately addicted to harmless gossip and cheap hospitality; a long time ago Moscow was the gathering place of the entire Russian nobility who came from all over Russia to spend the winter there; resplendent young guards officers came flying from Petersburg. Music resounded at every corner of the ancient Russian capital and there were crowds everywhere. In the ballroom of the Noblemen's Assembly there were about five thousand people twice a week. It was there that young people struck up acquaintances and weddings were arranged. Moscow was famous for her marriageable young ladies, like Vyazma for her honey cakes. Moscow dinners were proverbial.

"The innocent eccentricities of Muscovites were regarded merely as a sign of their independence. They lived after their own fashion and amused themselves as they liked, caring little what their neighbours thought of them. Sometimes a wealthy eccentric would build himself, in one of the chief streets, a Chinese palace with green dragons and wooden mandarins under gilt parasols. Another would drive through the Maryinsky Copse in a carriage of pure, hallmarked silver. A third would put five Negroes at the back of his spacious four-seater sledge and drive with his huntsmen and runners along the summer streets, his sledge drawn by half a dozen horses harnessed in single file. Imitating Petersburg fashion, the smart ladies outdid each other in the dresses they wore. Haughty Petersburg laughed from afar and did not interfere with old lady Moscow's fun."[1]

Active members of Moscow's social whirl, Pushkin's parents had little time to devote to their children. His happiest times were spent away from the city, at his grandmother's country estate, Zakharovo: "It is reflected in the mirror of waters, with its fences, its bridge over the river and its shady groves. My house is on a hill; from the balcony I can go down into the gay garden, where Flora and Pomona together offer me their gifts of flowers and fruits, where the dark line of old maple trees rises to the very sky and the poplars rustle mysteriously. There I would hasten at dawn with a humble spade in my hands, or walk across the meadows, along a twisting path, or water the tulips and the roses and—feel happy in this morning's work. There beneath a spreading oak tree, I would become immersed in pleasant dreams with La Fontaine and Horace. Nearby a brook ran along noisily between its moist banks, hiding its bright current vexatiously in the neighbouring woods and meadows. But it is noon. In the light dining room, the round table is gaily laid; there is bread and salt on the clean tablecloth; the steam rises from the cabbage soup; the glasses are filled with wine and a pike lies stretched out on the tablecloth. Breaking the silence, the neighbours enter in a noisy crowd. They sit down; we listen to the tinkling of their glasses; everyone praises Bacchus and Pomona and, with them, the beautiful spring."[1]

Pushkin's formal education began in 1811, when he was accepted into the first class of a special school founded by Tsar Alexander I. "For the school establishment, a whole wing, four stories high, of the Imperial Palace was remodeled, together with all the adjoining buildings. Under the reign of Catherine II this part of the palace had been occupied by the Grand Duchesses, all of whom were married by 1811, with the exception of Anna Pavlovna. On the ground floor were located the bursar's office and the rooms belonging to the inspector, the housemasters, and certain other school officials. On the second floor were the refectory, the infirmary, the pharmacy, lecture room, and offices; on the third were the recreation room, classrooms (two with platforms and one for study hour with a master on duty), a physics laboratory, a reading room with newspapers and periodicals, and a library in the vaulted passageway connecting the school with the palace through the rood-loft of the Imperial Chapel; on the top floor, the dormitories.

"The food was good, but that did not prevent the boys from throwing pastry at the whiskered face of Zolotarev, the steward. For their morning tea they were given a small loaf of white bread, and a half a loaf for their afternoon tea. On Mondays the menu for the week's meals was posted in the refectory, and the boys then arranged to trade dishes with each other, according to their tastes. In the beginning they were served a half-glass of port at lunch, but eventually this English custom was dropped. We had to be satisfied with kwass [a popular soft drink] and water."[3]

Shortly upon entering the Tsar's lyceum, the students were surprised by a rule which forbade them to leave school grounds. "This categorical ruling had doubtless been planned in advance but not mentioned, of course, and it was so unexpected that we were all greatly upset by it."[3]

After five years of this tormenting restriction, Pushkin wrote to a friend: "What is there to say about our isolation? School has never seemed so intolerable as now. I assure you that solitude is really absurd, regardless of what philosophers and poets write about living in the country and loving silence and tranquility. It is true that the time is drawing near for us to go out into the world. We have only one year more. But it means one whole year 'more' or 'less' of rules, discipline, of the lofty and admirable. One more year of dozing in front of the teacher's desk. It is awful. It is wicked to keep a young man under lock and key. As I am bored, I am writing rather boring verses."[3]

Graduation of the first class of the lyceum took place in 1817. "The ceremony had a very special character. The closing exercises were as simple as the opening ones had been pompous.

"Finally, we were all presented to the Emperor, each in accordance with his achievements, with mention made of his record and the honors won.

"The Emperor . . . was touched by the poetry and music; he noticed the tears that came into the eyes of both students and teachers. He said good-bye with his customary kindliness and, taking Prince Golitzin's arm, went off to inspect the student's rooms. Engelhardt warned him that he would find everything in disorder because of the preparations for departure. 'It does not matter,' said the Emperor; 'I am visiting you today.' And, in fact, the dormitories were in a topsy-turvy state. Clothes, valises, and packing-cases were scattered everywhere."[3]

Shortly after graduation, Pushkin went to live in St. Petersburg, where he soon gained a reputation for his wit, his excellent poetry, and his radical opinions. When word of his political beliefs reached the Emperor's palace, he found himself the object of suspicion, and tried to explain his position to the Tsar in a letter that he never mailed. "I was twenty years old in 1820. Hasty remarks, satirical verses [focused the public's attention on me] . . . . The rumor went about that I had been taken to the Secret Police Bureau and given a thrashing. I was the last to hear the report, which had become generally known. I considered myself dishonored, [lowered] in people's opinion. I was discouraged; I fought; I was twenty. I wondered whether I had better commit suicide or assassinate You. In the first case, I should only be confirming the rumor which had disgraced me; in the second, I would not be getting my revenge because no direct injury had been done me. I would be committing a crime and sacrificing to the opinion of a public I scorned a man whom everyone loved . . . and whom I admired in spite of myself. These reflections decided me. That is the way I thought about it. I talked it over with a friend, who entirely agreed with me. He advised me to ask the authorities for redress. But I felt it was useless. I decided to put so much insolence and boasting into my talk and writings that the authorities would be forced to treat me as a criminal: I hoped they would send me to Siberia, or shut me up in prison as a way of rehabilitating me."[3]

Pushkin's irreverence led to his exile in the south of Russia. Far from the excitement of St. Petersburg, he amused himself with love affairs, duels with anyone who challenged his honor, and the writing of some of his best known works. Here he created many epic poems, including *The Prisoner of the Caucasus.* "The faults of this story, or poem, or whatever you want to call it, are so obvious that I hesitated a long time before having it printed. The simplicity of the plot borders on poverty of imagination; the description of the Caucasian customs, not integrated with the action, is hardly more than a geographical sketch or a tourist's report. The character of the chief protagonists (and there are only two) would be more suitable for a novel than for a poem. And what is it as a character? Who can take much interest in a young man who has lost all his finer feelings because of a few vague misfortunes about which the reader knows nothing? . . . So far as *The Prisoner of the Caucasus* is concerned . . . I must confess that I am fond of it, though I don't know exactly why. I suppose it is because the poem contains lines that are dear to my heart."[3]

With many of his works, Pushkin had to deal with government censorship. When *The Prisoner of the Caucasus* was published, portions of it, as well as a portrait of Pushkin himself, had been deleted. His classic humorous fairy tale, *Tsar Nikita and His Daughters* had been dubbed "obscene." "An obscene work is one whose aim or action leads to the undermining of the rules upon which social happiness or human dignity is based. Poems whose aim is to inflame the imagination by lascivious descriptions degrade poetry, transforming its divine nectar into an inflammable substance . . . . But a jest inspired by heartfelt gaiety and a momentary play of imagination can appear immoral only to those who have a childish or obscure idea of immorality confusing it with didacticism and who see in literature only a pedagogic occupation."[1]

1823. Pushkin was allowed to relocate to Odessa through the influence of some powerful friends. In this cosmopolitan new city, he wrote to his brother: "Please explain to Father that I cannot live without money. Because of the present censorship restrictions it is impossible to make a living by my pen. I wasn't taught the carpenter's trade; I can't become a professor even if I do know Bible history and the rules of arithmetic. It isn't my fault that I am a mere petty official and cannot resign. Everything and everybody is against me."[3]

Upon the sale of his poem, *The Bakhchesarian Fountain,* which brought the impressive sum of three thousand rubles, he wrote: "I am beginning to have some respect for publishers, and I have come to the conclusion that our profession is no worse than any other. Luckily for me, I don't belong to the eighteenth-century group of writers. I write for myself and I publish my work to earn money and not for the smiles of the fair sex."[3]

But despite his growing reputation, government officials continued to condemn his poetry as subversive, and thus a threat to the Empire. Pushkin attempted to resign from the bureaucratic position to which he had been named, instead he was dismissed in disgrace because of a remark he had made in defense of atheism. Again he was exiled, this time to his mother's estate at Mikhaylovskoye, in Northern Russia. "His majesty had deigned to send me back to my parents' estate, thinking thus to lighten their sorrow and the fate of their son. But the grave accusations of the Government have deeply shaken my father's heart and aroused in him suspicions which can be accounted for only by his old age and the tender love he has for his other children."[3]

"When I arrived . . . I was met by all as well as could be, but soon everything changed: frightened by my exile, my father kept repeating over and over again that he was expecting the same

A tempest raged over the ocean. (From *The Fisherman and the Goldfish* by Alexander Pushkin. Illustrated by B. Dekhteryov.)

thing to happen to him; Peshchurov, appointed to keep an eye on me, had the effrontery to saddle my father with the duty of opening my letters, in short, of being my spy; my father's hot temper and morbid sensitivity made it impossible for me to talk to him; I decided to be silent. My father began to reproach my brother for allowing me to preach atheism to him. I still kept silent .... Finally, wishing to put an end to this painful situation, I went to my father and asked permission to speak frankly to him .... My father flew into a temper. I bowed, mounted a horse and rode off. My father called my brother and ordered him to have nothing to do *avec ce monstre, ce fils denature* .... I seethed with rage. I went to my father, found him with my mother and told him all I had been keeping back for the last three months. I concluded by saying that I was talking to him for the last time. Taking advantage of the absence of witnesses, my father rushed out of the room and declared to the whole household that *I had struck him, that I wanted to strike him, that I raised my hand to him, that I could have thrashed him*. ... What does he want to achieve by his accusation of a criminal assault? Siberian mines or deprivation of honour? Save me. Let it be a fortress or the Solovetsky Monastery!

"My father's accusation is known to the whole household. Nobody believes it, but everybody repeats it. Our neighbours know. I do not want to offer any explanations to them. You can't imagine what would happen if it were to reach the government."[1]

1825. Two issues consumed Pushkin in exile: escape from Russia and the completion of his first theatrical piece, *Boris Godunov*. "I, of course, despise my country from head to foot .... If the Tsar grants me freedom, I shall not remain here for one month. We live in a sad age, and when I think of London, railways, steamships, English journals or Paris theatres and brothels, my God-forsaken Mikhaylovskoye bores me to death and drives me to distraction. In the fourth Canto of *Onegin* I have described my life."[1]

"I have literally ... no other company than my old servant and my tragedy. The latter is coming along well, and I am pleased. While writing it, I have reflected on the subject of tragedy in general. The classics and the romantics based all their rules on probability, and that is just what they have excluded from their plays.

"The inevitability of the situations and the naturalness of the dialogue are the best rules for tragedy. I have never read Calderon or Vega; but what a man was Shakespeare! I am still amazed by him! And how paltry the tragic Byron is compared to him!

"There is another mania writers have: when they have conceived a character, everything he says, even the strangest sort of thing, must bear the essential stamp of that character .... A conspirator says, 'Give me to drink,' in his role of conspirator, which is only ridiculous .... Is that monotony, that affection of laconic speech and continual rage, true to life? The result is awkwardness and timidity in the dialogue. Read Shakespeare. He is not afraid of compromising a character. He makes him speak with all the abandon of real life, for he is sure of finding at the right time and place the speech appropriate to that character.

"I did my writing in absolute solitude, without being disturbed by any outside influence. I imitated Shakespeare in the broad, free drawing of his characters, in his astonishing choice of stage types, and in his simplicity. I followed Karamzin in my presentation of the methodic march of events, while from the historic documents I tried to form an idea of the mentality and speech of the men of that period. My sources were very rich."[3]

The end of 1825 brought the "Decembrist" uprising in St. Petersburg, a revolution of liberal intellectuals against the newly crowned Tsar Nicholas I. Rumors that Pushkin had been an influence in this movement led him to write the Tsar, repudiating such insinuations. "Your Majesty: Having had, in 1824, the misfortune of drawing down upon myself the displeasure of the late Emperor because of several ill-considered opinions expressed in a letter on the subject of atheism, I was removed from Government service, exiled to the country, and placed under the surveillance of the Governor. Today, having entire confidence in Your Majesty's magnanimity, and being filled with sincere remorse and firmly determined not to disturb the peace by expressing my ideas (I am ready to guarantee my promise both in writing and by my word of honor), I have decided to address the following petition to Your Majesty: My health, which has been undermined from my earliest years, and a sort of aneurysm, both require extensive treatment, as medical certificates will show. In consequence, I am taking the liberty of requesting permission to go to some place for medical care either in Moscow or in a foreign country.

"I, the undersigned, promise never to become a member of any secret society of any kind whatsoever. I testify to this—that I have never belonged, nor do I now belong, to any such secret society, and that I have never had any knowledge of such. Alexander Pushkin Functionary of the 10th class.)"[3]

After being fully investigated, and personally interviewed by Nicholas I, Pushkin was released from exile. But far from being free to travel, he was now prohibited from going abroad, restricted from contributing to any journal, or publishing any of his works, without the express permission of the Tsar, who had appointed himself Pushkin's personal censor. "I am the only one of all our writers . . . . to be subjected to the most cramping censorship, a censorship . . . that regards me with prejudice and finds everywhere all sorts of hidden meanings, allusions and difficulties, and these accusations of hidden meanings and their implications have neither limit nor justification if the word *tree* is taken to stand for constitution and the word *arrow* for autocracy."[1]

By early **1829,** Pushkin was again spending time in both St. Petersburg and Moscow, engaging in the same roguish pastimes as he did before his exile. At a ball in his native city, he caught sight of a sixteen-year-old girl named Natalia Goncharova and soon asked for her hand. He wrote to her mother: "When I saw her for the first time her beauty had hardly begun to be noticed in society. I fell in love with her. My head was in a whirl. I made a proposal, and your answer, vague as it was, nearly made me lose my reason. The same night I departed for the army. You ask me whatever for. I swear to you that I do not know, but a kind of involuntary anguish drove me out of Moscow. I would not have been able to bear either your or her presence there. I wrote to you. I hoped. I waited for an answer. It did not come. The mistakes of my early youth presented themselves to my imagination; they were too violent by themselves and calumny has added to them further; the talk about them has become unfortunately widespread. You might have believed it. I dared not complain, but I was in despair."[1]

In a self-imposed exile, Pushkin traveled east, intending to meet his brother who was stationed with the army in the Caucasus. He became inspired to join the army as well, but was refused. He pined for Natalia, wrote poetry, gambled, and drank. In September he returned to Moscow, and was coldly received by Natalia and her mother. As he felt he had lost his chance to marry her, his outlook became bleak and he worried about his literary reputation. "The ideas and feelings of an eighteen-year-old poet are still near and familiar to everyone. Young readers understand him and recognise excitedly their own feelings and thoughts in his work . . . . But years pass, the young poet matures, his talent grows, his ideas become loftier and his feelings change. His poems are no longer the same, but his readers are sill the same except that, perhaps, they have become colder at heart and more indifferent to life's poetry. The poet separates himself from them and little by little retires completely into his shell. He still creates, but he does so for himself alone and if, occasionally, he publishes his works, their reception is cold, he encounters complete lack of attention, and finds an echo to his sounds only in the hearts of a few admirers of poetry who are as lonely and lost to the world as he is."[1]

Pushkin was finally accepted as a suitor to Natalia, and after much indecision on the part of Madame Goncharova, they became betrothed. A month after his engagement, Pushkin wrote: "I am getting married, that is to say, I am sacrificing my happy-go-lucky existence, my expensive habits, my aimless wanderings . . . . I am about to double a life which is incomplete anyhow. I never worried about happiness. I could do without it. Now I shall have to have enough happiness for two, and where am I to get it? While I am still unmarried what do my obligations amount to? I have an ailing uncle, whom I practically never see. If I visit him, he is very glad, if not, he finds an excuse for me: the rascal is young, he has other things to think of. In the morning I get up when I like . . . I go for a ride on my intelligent, gentle Jennie . . . . When I return home, I look through my books and papers, put my dressing-table in order, dress casually if I am going to see friends or with painstaking care if I am dining at a restaurant where I proceed to read the journals or a new novel; if Walter Scott or Fenimore Cooper have not written anything new and if there is no murder trial in the papers, I order a bottle of champagne on ice, watch my glass go cold, drink slowly, happy in the thought that the dinner only cost me seventeen roubles and that I can permit myself such luxury. I go to the theatre, search for some wonderful dress in a box, for a pair of black eyes, I start a flirtation that keeps me busy till the end of the play. The evenings I pass either in noisy society where the whole town seems to be present, where I can see everyone and everything, where no one pays any attention to me, or in a selected circle of friends where I keep talking about myself and where everyone listens to me. I return home late and doze off reading a good book . . . . That's what my bachelor life is like . . . . At that moment I am handed a note . . . . My proposal has been accepted . . . . All my sad doubts disappear before this heavenly thought.

"The life of a thirty-year-old fiance is worse than thirty years of a gambler's life . . . . Meanwhile I am cooling off. I am thinking of the worries of a married man and of the delights of bachelor life. Besides, Moscow gossip is reaching the ears of my fiancee and her mother, giving rise to tiffs and all sorts of sarcastic insinuations, shortlived reconciliations. In short, if not unhappy, I am not particularly happy, either. Autumn is approaching, my favourite season, when my health usually becomes more robust and the time of my literary labours approaches, but I have to

She scolded him now worse than ever. (From *Tales* by Alexander Pushkin. Illustrated by Vladimir Konashevich.)

worry about the dowry and the wedding, which goodness only knows when we shall celebrate."[1]

During the last, uncertain days before his marriage, Pushkin journeyed to his father's estate at Boldino, in east-central Russia. There he was held in quarantine because of an outbreak of Asiatic cholera. Those three months were among the most productive in his life. "In Boldino I wrote as I have not written for a long time. This is what I have brought back: the two last Cantos of *Onegin,* the eighth and the ninth completely ready for the press, a narrative poem written in octaves about four hundred lines in length [*The Little House in Kolomna*], which will be published anonymously. Several dramatic scenes or little tragedies, namely, *The Covetous Knight, Mozart and Salieri.* . . .

"During the first performance of *Don Giovanni,* when the whole theatre, full of astonished aficionados, were revelling in Mozart's harmony, somebody hissed—everyone turned indignantly to the man—and the famous Salieri left the auditorium in a fit of rage, eaten up by envy. Salieri died eight years ago. Some German journals stated that on his deathbed he confessed to having committed a terrible crime—he had poisoned the great Mozart. An envious person who could hiss *Don Giovanni* could very well have also poisoned its creator."[1]

Pushkin and Natalia Goncharova were married on January 19, 1831. "I have only calmly weighed the advantages and disadvantages of the married state. My youth has passed tempestuously and fruitlessly. Till now I have lived differently from the way people usually live. There has been no happiness for me . . . . I am over thirty. At thirty people usually get married. I do as people usually do and I shall probably not regret it. Besides, I am marrying without rapture, without childish enchantment. The future does not appear in roseate hues to me, but in all its austere nakedness. Misfortunes will not surprise me; they are included in my family budget. Any job will be something I did not expect."[1]

The newlyweds moved to Tsarkoe Selo where Pushkin had lived during his school days. "I feel that I have arranged everything very well, now, and I can live peacefully without a mother-in-law, without luxuries, and in consequence, without excessive expense or gossip."[3]

Unfortunately, the Tsar, eager to keep Pushkin's beautiful wife at court, assigned him to yet another bureaucratic post. The position carried little power, but enough responsibility to keep Pushkin from his writing, and an insufficient salary to meet expenses. Despite her pregnancy, Natalia lived a gay life in St. Petersburg. In letters from Boldino, where he had gone once again to write, Pushkin begged her to be sensible. "Let me repeat to you a little more gentle that flirting leads to nothing good and, though it has its pleasant moments, nothing deprives a young woman so quickly of the things without which there is no family happiness nor tranquility in her relationships to society: *respect*. There is nothing for you to be pleased about in your conquests.

"Think it over carefully and do not worry me needlessly .... My dear, dear, dear wife, I am traveling along highways, living three months in the wilds, stopping in horrible Moscow which I detest, and all for what? For you, darling, so that you should not be worried and shine in society to your heart's content as befits a beautiful woman of your age. But, please, take care of me, too. Do not add to the worries which are inseparable from a man's life, family troubles, jealousy, etc., etc."[1]

On **June 4, 1832,** their first child, Maria Pushkina was born. "Can you imagine my wife being so foolish as to give birth to a little lithograph of myself? I am in despair despite all my conceit."[3]

In **1833,** a son followed, named Alexander for his father, and called Sasha.

1834. Pushkin resigned his government post, hoping to have the freedom to write and have his work published. His request to the Tsar was construed as ungrateful and disrespectful. He wrote to a friend: "I myself truly don't know what's happening to me. What crime—what ingratitude—is there in going into retirement when my circumstances, the future fate of my family, and my own peace of mind demand it? But the Sovereign is nevertheless able to see in this something resembling what I cannot understand. In that case I do not submit my resignation, but I ask to be left in the service .... In the depths of my heart I feel myself in the right toward the Tsar. His wrath grieves me, but the worse my position is, the more tongue-tied and numb-tongued I become. What am I to do? Ask forgiveness? All right. But for what?"[4]

Within a few weeks, the crisis subsided, and once again Pushkin resumed his position. Historians believe it suited the government to keep the poet in this post where his liberal ideas could least influence the populace. Pushkin continued to write, but had difficulties finding publishers for his work. Even his request to publish a journal was denied, prompting him to write the governor: "When I asked for permission to become the publisher of a literary and political gazette, I myself felt all the objections to this undertaking. I was compelled to do so by painful circumstances. Neither I nor my wife, so far, has an estate; that of my father is so disorganized that I have been obliged to take over the direction of it, in order to assure a future to the rest of my family. I wanted to become a journalist only so as not to reproach myself with having neglected a means which, by giving me an income of 40,000, would deliver me from my difficulties. I confess that, my plan not meeting with His Majesty's approval, I was relieved of a great burden."[4]

It was Madame Pushkina's manners at court that were her husband's final undoing. While there she became acquainted with the Baron Georges-Charles d'Anthes, who openly pursued Natalia for nearly two years. D'Anthes' boldness became common knowledge and Pushkin challenged him to a duel.

They met at five o'clock in the afternoon. D'Anthes fired first and badly wounded Pushkin in the stomach. From the ground, Pushkin took his shot; the bullet only grazed d'Anthes. Two days later, on **February 10, 1837,** Pushkin was dead.

Court society sympathized with d'Anthes. But thousands of people of other social classes came to Pushkin's apartment to mourn him and to pay their respects.

In his lifetime, Pushkin had been beset by financial problems, narrow-mindedness and censorship. Translations of his works were not well-received, because of the difficulty of translating his language into foreign idioms.

After his death, he was called the "Byron of Russia." At the unveiling of the Pushkin monument in Moscow in 1880, Dostoevsky said: "He was a Russian in his final stage of development."[5]

He remains the favorite poet and storyteller of the Russian people, for whom, and in whose own language he always wrote. "If science, philosophy, and sociology may change and improve with the passing of time, poetry neither ages nor changes. Its aim remains the same and its means are the same. While the ideas, the works and the discoveries of the great representatives of ancient astronomy, physics, medicine, and philosophy are out of date, the works of true poets remain fresh and eternally young. If a poetic work is weak, unsuccessful and full of faults, it is the talent of the poet that is at fault. It is not the age that has left him behind."[1]

FOOTNOTE SOURCES

[1]David Magarshach, *Pushkin: A Biography,* Grove Press, 1967.
[2]Anna Heifetz, "Pushkin in Self-Portrayal," *Crisis,* May, 1937.
[3]Henri Troyat, *Pushkin: A Biography,* translated by Randolph T. Weaver, Pantheon, 1950.
[4]Thomas Shaw, translator, *The Letters of Alexander Pushkin,* Indiana University and University of Pennsylvania Press, 1963.
[5]Ed Falowski, "Pushkin, Russia's Greatest Poet, Born 137 Years Ago Today," *Moscow Daily News,* June 6, 1936.

FOR MORE INFORMATION SEE:

BOOKS

Maurice Baring, *An Outline of Russian Literature,* Holt, 1915.
Boris Brasol, *The Mighty Three: Poushkin, Gogol, Dostoievsky; A Critical Trilogy,* William Farquhar Payson, 1934.
Samuel H. Cross and Ernest J. Simmons, editors, *Alexander Pushkin 1799-1837: His Life and Literary Heritage,* American Russian Institute, 1937, published as *Centennial Essays for Pushkin,* Russell, 1967.
Beatrice Fleming and Marion Pryde, *Distinguished Negroes Abroad* (juvenile), Associated Publishers, 1946.
Lydia Lambert, *Pushkin: Poet and Lover,* translated from the French by Willard R. Trask, Doubleday, 1946.
Bernard Guilbert Guerney, editor, *Portable Russian Reader,* Viking, 1947.
Janko Lavrin, *Pushkin and Russian Literature,* Macmillan, 1948.
Edmund Wilson, *Triple Thinkers,* Oxford University Press, 1948.
Vladimir Weidle, *Pushkin, 1799-1837,* translated by David Scott, UNESCO, 1949.
Avrahm Yarmolinsky, editor, *Treasury of Russian Verse,* Macmillan, 1949.
J. Lavrin, *Russian Writers: Their Lives and Literature,* Van Nostrand, 1954.
Russell L. Adams, *Great Negroes: Past and Present,* Afro-American Publishing, 1963, 3rd edition, 1969.
Dmitrii Petrovich Mirskii, *Pushkin,* Dutton, 1963.

(From *The Frog Princess* by Alexander Pushkin. Illustrated by Ivan Bilibin.)

Statue of Pushkin.

Stanley J. Kunitz and Vineta Colby, editors, *European Authors, 1000-1900,* H. W. Wilson, 1967.
Walter N. Vickery, *Pushkin: Death of a Poet,* Indiana University Press, 1968.
W. N. Vickery, *Alexander Pushkin,* Twayne, 1970.
Elsa Z. Posell, *Russian Authors* (juvenile), Houghton, 1970.
Tatiana Wolff, editor and translator, *Pushkin on Literature,* Barnes & Noble, 1971, reissued, Stanford University Press, 1986.
Helen Muchnic, *Russian Writers,* Random House, 1971.
Pushkin: A Collection of Articles and Essays on the Great Russian Poet A. S. Pushkin, Books for Libraries, 1971.
Martha Warren Beckwith and others, *Pushkin: The Man and the Artist,* Books for Libraries, 1971.
James Cleugh, *Prelude to Parnassus: Scenes from the Life of Alexander Sergeyevich Pushkin 1799-1837,* R. West, 1973.
D. S. Mirsky, *Pushkin,* Haskell, 1974.
Andrej Kodjak and Kiril Taranovsky, editors, *Alexander Pushkin: A Symposium on the 175th Anniversary of His Birth,* New York University Press, 1976.
Waclaw Lednicki, *Pushkin's Bronze Horseman: The Story of a Masterpiece,* Greenwood, 1978.
A. Kodjak and others, editors, *Alexander Pushkin Symposium II,* Slavica, 1980.
Norman Donaldson and Betty Donaldson, *How Did They Die?,* St. Martin's, 1980.
D. Blagoy, *Sacred Lyre,* Progress Publishers, 1982.
P. Debreczeny, *The Other Pushkin: A Study of Alexander Pushkin's Prose Fiction,* Stanford University Press, 1983.
Abram Lezhnev, *Pushkin's Prose,* translated by Roberta Reeder, Ardis, 1983.
Laurie Lanzen Harris, editor, *Nineteenth-Century Literature Criticism,* Volume 3, Gale, 1983.
Jacques Barzun, editor, *European Writers: The Romantic Century,* Volume 5, Scribner, 1985.
G. P. Balog and A. M. Mukhina, *A. Pushkin and His Time in the Fine Arts of the Early Nineteenth Century,* Collets, 1985.
William M. Todd III, *Fiction and Society in the Age of Pushkin: Ideology, Institutions, Narrative,* Harvard University Press, 1986.

PERIODICALS

Connoisseur, September, 1930.
Moscow Daily News, April 17, 1936, May 12, 1936, February 16, 1937, February 18, 1937, October 26, 1937.
Times, February 12, 1937.
Poetry, March, 1937 (p. 328ff).
Crisis, June, 1937 (p. 175).
New York Times, December 26, 1937, July 25, 1987.
Daily Worker, January 28, 1942.
Negro History Bulletin, March, 1948 (p. 135), July/September, 1982 (p. 81ff).
Time, May 17, 1948 (p. 116ff), February 21, 1969 (p. 86ff).
Modern Language Notes, May, 1950 (p. 300ff).
Russian Review, July, 1958 (p. 183ff).
Times Literary Supplement, April 6, 1962 (p. 226), January 28, 1983 (p. 86), March 6, 1987 (p. 242).
Encounter, July, 1962 (p. 11ff), April, 1978 (p. 42ff).
Newsweek, November 23, 1970 (p. 126ff).
Soviet Literature, number 10, 1975 (p. 23ff).
Encore, June 5, 1978 (p. 39).
History Today, September, 1980 (p. 44ff).
New York Review of Books, February 3, 1983 (p. 35ff).
New York Times Book Review, March 25, 1984 (p. 15).

FILMS

"The Journey to Erzerum," Leningrad Film Studios, 1937.
"Young Pushkin," Lenfilm, Leningrad, 1937.

PUTNAM, Alice (Marie) 1916-

PERSONAL: Born September 14, 1916, in Pittsburgh, Pa.; daughter of Henry Franklin (an engineer) and Gertrude (a homemaker; maiden name, Phillips) Dorr; married Travers D. Putnam (a professor), October 19, 1946; children: Gretchen Putnam Poole, Travers D., Jr. *Education:* Wilson College, A.B., 1937. *Politics:* Republican. *Religion:* Christian Scientist. *Home and office:* 221 21st Ave. N., St. Petersburg, Fla. 33704.

CAREER: Writer, 1970—. Teacher at writers' conferences; member of board of directors of Reading Is Fundamental, 1980—. *Military service:* U.S. Naval Reserve, active duty in Women Accepted for Volunteer Emergency Service (WAVES), 1941-46. *Member:* League of Women Voters (member of board of directors, 1967-72), Society of Children's Book Writers, Sierra Club, National Audubon Society, Cousteau Society, National Wildlife Federation, Defenders of Wildlife.

WRITINGS:

The Spy Doll, Elsevier-Nelson, 1979.
The Whistling Swans (illustrated by Scott Hiestand), Messner, 1981.
That New Guy! (young adult), Willowisp Press, 1987.
The Westering, Dutton, 1990.

Contributor to periodicals, including *Ranger Rick, Child Life, Florida Wildlife, Ford Times, Floridian, Sunshine, Rock & Gem, Tampa Bay, Secretary, Unity, Child Life, Cricket, Highlights for Children, Retired Officer,* and *Christian Science Monitor.*

WORK IN PROGRESS: The Bronze Buffalo, an adult mystery with a western setting; adventure books for boys.

SIDELIGHTS: "As far back as I can remember (which is quite a long time!), I have wanted to be a writer. Even before I started school I 'made up' stories to entertain anyone who would listen. At the age of eight I began to keep a notebook of poems and ideas for more tales (a practice I still follow and that, surprisingly, many of the children in workshops where I have taught use as an important tool in their own writing).

"In high school I edited the yearbook, submitted a regular column to the newspaper, and wrote the senior class play. In college, English courses were my favorite and I decided on journalism as a career. After graduation I even managed a trip to New York and an interview with the city editor of the *New York Times,* who tactfully and wisely advised me to go back to the small town where I lived and get a start with the weekly newspaper there. I wish I could say I followed his advice. Instead, I took a business course, joined the WAVES during World War II, married, had two children, and did nothing at all with writing until they were grown with lives of their own. Then, inspired by an adult course in marketing articles, I went to work determined to become a professional.

"How exciting that first sale was, in spite of the fact that it was to a secretarial magazine and my story, about how President Polk's wife helped him organize his correspondence in the White House, was printed in shorthand, which even I had difficulty reading! But that was only the beginning. Next came acceptances from the Sunday supplement of our local *St. Petersburg Times*—lengthy pieces complete with illustrations. Then *Rock & Gem, Florida Wildlife, Retired Officer,* and *Ford Times.*

ALICE PUTNAM

"All these were for adult readers but I had a real desire to have children as an audience, so now I concentrated on them. Sunday school magazines, *Child Life, Christian Science Monitor,* and finally, biggest thrill of all because of my love for nature and its creatures, an acceptance from *Ranger Rick*. Then two others and, with the encouragement and advice of the editor, several more.

"Now what I really wanted to do was a book for children. An ardent reader and 'clipper' of newspaper items, I had a file bulging with possible subjects. I selected one at random, the true account of a doll used by the Confederates in the Civil War to smuggle medicine, went to the museum in Richmond to actually see the doll, and was off! The editor at Elsevier-Nelson liked the book but thought it too short and doubted whether I could make it longer. I could and did and within a year my first book was in print.

"Then, again digging into my file of clippings, I discovered an item about a wounded swan at our local seabird sanctuary. I went to see the swan, talked with the man in charge of the sanctuary, did more reseach, and the result was *The Whistling Swans*. This time the editor wanted me to furnish the illustrations. I am no artist but I was lucky in finding one in our city who shared my enthusiasm for the subject. The book, although fictional, is based on fact and tells of the many perils wild birds encounter when they migrate. The illustrations, especially the one of the swans flying through a snowstorm, are very realistic. This book, after I had done the basic research, practically wrote itself.

"In *That New Guy!,* once I decided on a theme, the writing was easy. I simply remembered my own high school days and how I felt then. The 'heroine,' who plays flute in the band as I did, is really me.

"My most recent book is *The Westering*. I love the West and this book is based on my research of pioneer days. It is the story of a boy who goes to Oregon with a wagon train in 1850.

"Lately I have had a number of articles on art for young readers published in the *Christian Science Monitor* and am working on more. I am also planning a series of adventure books for boys and want to do some with a western background, which I especially like.

"My advice to young writers who attend my workshops is 'Never give up.' Keep a constant picture before you of the book or story you hope to see in print, accept advice and criticism without becoming discouraged."

HOBBIES AND OTHER INTERESTS: Travel, playing piano and flute (classical and ragtime music).

RAPOSO, Joseph Guilherme 1938-1989

OBITUARY NOTICE: Born February 8, 1938, in Fall River, Mass.; died of complications of lymphoma, February 5, 1989, in Bronxville, N.Y. Educator, music director, composer, and lyricist. Raposo is best remembered for his contributions to the popular children's public television show "Sesame Street." A graduate of Harvard University and former student of renowned French music instructor Nadia Boulanger, Raposo taught music seminars at Harvard and Yale and lectured at Massachusetts Institute of Technology, New York University, and Southern Methodist University. In 1969 Raposo, Jim Henson, and Jon Stone created "Sesame Street." Raposo remained with the series as its music director until 1974, earning four Grammy Awards and several Emmy Awards for his work. Raposo composed numerous songs, including the "Sesame Street" theme song, "It's Not Easy Being Green," "Sing," and "Here's to the Winners," and the music for movies such as "Raggedy Ann and Andy," "The Possession of Joel Delaney," and "The Great Muppet Caper," for which he was nominated for an Academy Award. Many of his songs are represented in *The Sesame Street Songbook* and *It's Not Easy Being Green*.

FOR MORE INFORMATION SEE:

Martin Mayer, *About Television,* Harper, 1972.
Newsweek, August 27, 1973 (p. 85).
New Yorker, March 17, 1975 (p. 32).
Who's Who in America, 43rd edition, Marquis, 1984.

OBITUARIES

New York Times, February 6, 1989 (p. D-12).
Chicago Tribune, February 7, 1989, February 12, 1989.
Time, February 20, 1989 (p. 94).

REDEKOPP, Elsa

PERSONAL: Born in U.S.S.R.; daughter of Jacob and Margaret (Warkentin) Sawatsky; married Jacob P. Redekopp (a professor); children: Karin, Elisabeth, Peter, Reynold, David. *Education:* University of Winnipeg, B.A., 1982. *Home:* 32 Rossmere Crescent, Winnipeg, Manitoba, Canada R2K OE9. *Agent:* G. Brandt, 4-169 Riverton Ave., Winnipeg, Manitoba, Canada R2L 2E5.

CAREER: Teacher of children's literature at Red River Community College; violist for the Winnipeg Symphony, Winnipeg, Manitoba, and Holiday String Quartet; author. Gives readings at schools throughout Manitoba; public speaker. *Member:* Canadian Authors Association, Manitoba Writers Guild.

WRITINGS:

JUVENILE

Wish and Wonder: A Manitoba Village Child (illustrated by Veleda Goulden), Reddell, 1982.
Dream and Wonder: A Child's View of Canadian Village Life (sequel to *Wish and Wonder;* illustrated by Margaret Quiring), Kindred Press, 1986.
Shoes for Michel, Hyperion Press, 1988.

Also author of *Josh Comes to Canada,* 1988. *Wish and Wonder* has been published in German. Contributor of stories to periodicals, including *Mennonite Mirror,* and *Der Bote.*

RYAN, Mary E(lizabeth) 1953-

PERSONAL: Born August 19, 1953, in Manchester, N.H.; daughter of Leo T. (an art teacher) and Lorraine (an English professor; maiden name, Joseph) Ryan; married Brent Youlden (a writer), February 4, 1989. *Education:* London Film School, certificate, 1974; New York University, B.F.A., 1977; University of Washington, M.A., 1987. *Politics:* Democrat. *Religion:* Unitarian. *Home:* 1139 17th Ave., 6, Seattle, Wash. 98122.

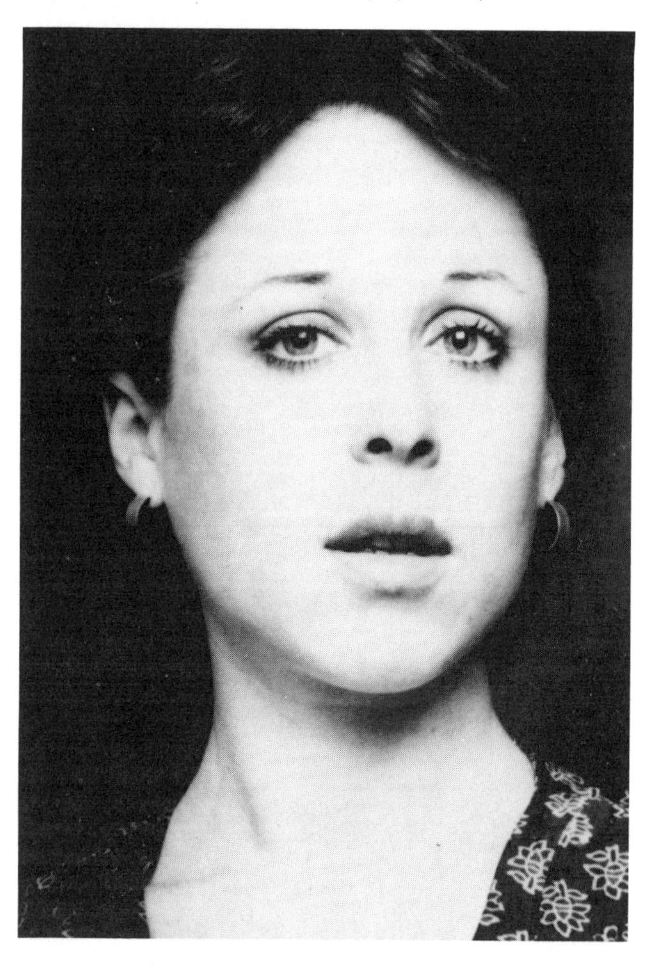

MARY E. RYAN

Agent: Jo Stewart, 201 East 66th St., 18G, New York, N.Y. 10021. *Office:* c/o Delacorte Press, 666 Fifth Ave., New York, N.Y. 10103.

CAREER: New Yorker Magazine, New York, N.Y., administrative assistant, 1978-80; Coldwell Banker, San Francisco, Calif., in real estate, 1980-81; Seattle University, Seattle, Wash., records coordinator, 1984; Northwest Renewable Resources, Seattle, grant writer, 1985; Bogle & Gates (law firm), Seattle, legal secretary, 1985-88; WordCrafters (word processing service), Seattle, owner, 1988—; writer. Speaker in schools and at writing conferences. *Member:* Authors Guild, Poets & Writers, American Federation of Television and Radio Artists. *Awards, honors:* Hoynes Fellowship from the University of Virginia, 1982; Stegner Fellowship from Stanford University, 1982-83; PEN American Grant, 1984; Carnegie Fund Grant, 1984, 1985; *Dance a Step Closer* was named an Outstanding Book of the Year by the University of Iowa, 1985.

WRITINGS:

YOUNG ADULT NOVELS

Dance a Step Closer, Delacorte, 1984.
I'd Rather Be Dancing, Delacorte, 1989.

Contributor of short stories to *Young Miss, Co-Ed, St. Anthony Messenger, McCall's, Face-to-Face,* and *Woman's Own.*

WORK IN PROGRESS: Twice in a Lifetime, for Delacorte; an adult mystery; a sequel to *Twice in a Lifetime* featuring Mattie and Prune, the Darwin twins; a book for younger children about life in Arizona in 1963.

SIDELIGHTS: "My twin sister and I were writing stories, poems, plays, and even novels from the time I can remember. In fact, my first 'book' was an illustrated sequel to *Winnie-the-Pooh,* done around the age of four. In high school and college, I got carried away by thoughts of acting and the theater, and then by film-making. In 1978, having spent three- and-one-half years at schools in Switzerland and England and then graduated from New York University Film School, I decided I would take a stab at making it in the theater. I gave myself a year to 'get somewhere.' But all I got to was a summer stock playhouse in Pennsylvania and a brief stint as a chorus dancer in an off-Broadway musical. The year up, I retired from the stage. But that experience later gave me a lot of material I used in stories about show biz and in *Dance a Step Closer,* in which the mother is a not very successful 'trooper,' much like the actresses I observed while doing auditions and casting rounds.

"Meanwhile, my boyfriend of the time turned out to be a poet, and very serious about writing. This reignited my older ambition, and on a whim, I sent off a novelette to a contest at *Seventeen.* Unlike acting, the doors to publication seemed to open very readily. I was called in for a story conference at *Seventeen*'s offices in early 1980, and began the hard work of revising.

"Ultimately, *Seventeen* didn't take the story, and I moved to San Francisco to sulk. A few months later, however, the editor who'd liked my novelette went over to *Young Miss,* a rival teen magazine, and bought that story and several others.

"During my year in San Francisco (1980-81), I was seized by the need to get my stories published, and they found homes as diverse as national Catholic magazines and Methodist teen publications. I also started reading all the teen (young adult) novels at the local library, with an eye to getting a book written and published in this genre. After absorbing lots of formulas and cliches (and basic structures of novel writing), I wrote a first draft of *Dance a Step Closer* and sent it to an agent whom a New York friend had recommended.

"She took it on, but the first two publishers passed. Then a kindly, sharp-eyed, optimistic editor at Delacorte saw something in it, and a year and four revisions later, Delacorte sent a contract.

"In mid 1981, I'd headed up to Seattle to start graduate school in writing. My relationship with the poet boyfriend foundered, and I took refuge in applications for grants and fellowships. To my surprise, three places—Stanford, Virginia, and Boston University—offered me writing fellowships. In August I went back to California for a year as a fiction fellow at Stanford.

"In 1983 I returned to Seattle without enough money to continue school (I finally completed my master's in writing in 1987). I sold stock, edited manuscripts for a local agent, and began work on the sequel to *Dance a Step Closer*. A much harder book to write, as I had to submit a proposal and outline, and then live up to this blueprint. Also, it was four years after my first encounter with my first-person heroine, and though she was the same person, I wasn't. It was hard to find and recreate her voice.

"In 1984 *Dance, a Step Closer* was published—the story of Katie Kusik from Brooklyn, her desire to attend a top dancing school in Manhattan against her actress-mother's well-meaning wishes—and I decided to go all out to publicize it. I offered my services as a speaker to schools and libraries all over the Northwest, took buses and planes, and got to see kids up close for the first time in years.

"I also got to talk a lot about writing, how and why to do it, how and why I do it. Several issues arose. The first: many kids were surprised to discover that I hadn't made my first novel strictly autobiographical, i.e. I'd never spent much time in Brooklyn, hadn't grown up wanting to be a dancer, etc. Regarding the second, several reviewers disliked the fact that 'too much' was going on in this short novel—Katie has to deal with her parents' divorce, her mother's stuffy boyfriend and failed career, her impossible sister, her rebellious friend Jessica, peer pressure at school, her dancing, a job, a boyfriend.

"My response to the first observation is that as far as plain facts are concerned, I'd much rather make up a character and invent a setting or situation than recycle my own familiar trappings (familiar to me, at any rate). On the other hand, a lot of personal insights and experience naturally become incorporated into a novel. It's balancing one's sense of what's true with the imaginary that makes writing books such fun.

"As to the reviewers' charge that 'too much' takes place in Katie's busy life, I think kids' lives are every bit as hectic and stressful and overflowing with problems and activities and concerns as any adult's. Many young adult books seem to pick *one* problem (divorce, drug addiction, a death in the family) and then, for the sake of drama, truncate everything else in the characters' lives. With Katie, I wanted to show what I thought was a fair representation of a real kid's life—highly problematic and breathtakingly busy. And hopefully dramatic and interesting, as well.

"Finally, many assemblies and library conventions later, my message has become more distilled. Though my first two books are about the world of dance, my theme could very well represent my own career so far: aim for what you want to accomplish, keep

Whenever Richie was around, I froze into unanimated Jell-O. (Jacket illustration by Dan Brown from *Dance a Step Closer* by Mary E. Ryan.)

learning the ropes, and about yourself, your own strengths and weaknesses. Don't confuse the humility of learning something new with the passivity of accepting an unquestioned judgment. Question everything. Nothing's impossible. Writing a book seems like a hard, endless project, but when it gets broken down to its component parts, it becomes quite manageable. (The genesis of my first novel goes back to when I was doing freelance typing for a typing service. One of my jobs was typing from a cassette on which a woman had dictated her not-very-good novel. Still, I was impressed to see 'Chapter One,' 'Chapter Two,' 'Chapter Three' accumulating, page after page, into a tidy pile of words. Aha, I thought. So that's what it looks like when it's taking shape.) Last but not least, don't be afraid to look—or sound—stupid, or to be yourself. Don't worry about the status quo. These are all things I think everyone can stand to hear, but particularly kids, who know enough to take people, and life, as seriously as they ought to be taken. As one reviewer put it, regarding my character Katie's tribulations, 'the best way out is always through.' I think that's true for me, true for my characters, and also true for my readers.

"These days, I have my own business, typing and editing, in Seattle. I share the rest of my time with three cats and my husband, Brent. I'd like to write for television eventually, but for now novel writing seems to be the main activity. I crave baseball games, horse racing, movies and Haagen-Dazs. And so, sooner or later, will Katie."

FOR MORE INFORMATION SEE:

Mary E. Ryan, "My Say," *Publishers Weekly*, April 13, 1984.

SANFORD, Agnes (White) 1897-1976

PERSONAL: Born November 4, 1897, in Kashing, China; died in 1976; daughter of Hugh W. (a Presbyterian missionary) and Augusta (Graves) White; married Edgar L. Sanford (a clergyman), April 2, 1923 (deceased); children: Edgar L., Virginia T. Clark, John A. *Education:* Attended Peace Institute (now Peace College), 1914-18; Agnes Scott College, special courses in literature, 1918-19. *Religion:* Episcopalian. *Residence:* Monrovia, Calif.

CAREER: Writer. Co-founder of School of Pastoral Care, Northborough, Mass., 1955. Lay lecturer on prayer and healing (sponsored only by the inviting churches), in United States, Canada, England, Australia, and New Zealand. *Awards, honors:* Lit.D., Peace College.

WRITINGS:

The Healing Light, Macalester Park, 1946.
Oh, Watchman (novel), Lippincott, 1951.
Lost Shepherd (novel), Lippincott, 1953.
Let's Believe, Harper, 1954.
A Pasture for Peterkin, Macalester Park, 1957.
Behold Your God, Macalester Park, 1958.
Dreams Are for Tomorrow (novel), Lippincott, 1963.
The Second Mrs. Wu (novel), Lippincott, 1965.
The Healing Gifts of the Spirit, Lippincott, 1966.
The Rising River (novel), Lippincott, 1968.
The Healing Power of the Bible, Lippincott, 1969.
Twice Seven Words, Logos International, 1971.
Sealed Orders, Logos International, 1972.
Route One, Logos International, 1975.

Also author of *Melissa and the Little Red Book,* illustrated by Sandy Heinen, published by Macalester Park; *Healing Touch of God*, published by Ballantine; and *Creation Waits.*

SAVAGE, Katharine James 1905-1989

OBITUARY NOTICE: Born August 13, 1905, in Worcester, England; died March 24, 1989. Administrator, editor, and author. Savage wrote nonfiction for children. She worked as a director for Britain's Ministry of Information during World War II and joined the editorial staff of *Economist* afterwards. In 1957, only a few years after leaving the magazine, Savage began producing children's books. Among her works are *The Story of the Second World War,* which received a Carnegie Medal Commendation in 1957, *The Story of Africa South of the Sahara, The Story of the United Nations, The Story of World Religions,* and *The Story of the Common Market.*

FOR MORE INFORMATION SEE:

Doris de Montreville and Elizabeth D. Crawford, *Fourth Book of Junior Authors,* H. W. Wilson, 1978.

OBITUARIES

Times (London), April 5, 1989.

SCHLESINGER, Arthur M(eier), Jr. 1917-

PERSONAL: Name originally Arthur Bancroft Schlesinger, born October 15, 1917, in Columbus, Ohio; son of Arthur M. (a professor of history) and Elizabeth (a writer; maiden name, Bancroft) Schlesinger; married Marian Cannon (an author and artist), August 10, 1940 (divorced, 1970); married Alexandra Emmet (an artist), July 9, 1971; children: (first marriage) Stephen Cannon and Katharine Bancroft (twins), Christina, Andrew Bancroft; (second marriage) Robert Emmet Kennedy. *Education:* Harvard University, A.B. (summa cum laude), 1938. *Politics:* Democrat. *Religion:* Unitarian. *Home:* 171 East 64th St., New York, N.Y. 10021. *Office:* Graduate School and University Center, City University of New York, 33 West 42nd St., New York, N.Y. 10036.

CAREER: Office of War Information, Washington, D.C., 1942-43; Office of Strategic Services, Washington, D.C., England, France, and Germany, 1943-45; free-lance writer, Washington, D.C., 1945- 46; Harvard University, Cambridge, Mass., associate professor, 1946-54, professor of history, 1954-61; special assistant to President John F. Kennedy, 1961-63, and to President Lyndon Johnson, 1963-64; Institute for Advanced Study, Princeton, 1966; City University of New York, New York City, Albert Schweitzer Professor of Humanities, 1966—. Chairman, Franklin and Eleanor Roosevelt Institute (formerly Franklin Delano Roosevelt Four Freedoms Foundation), 1983—. Member of board, Twentieth Century Fund, John Fitzgerald Kennedy Library, Ralph Bunche Institute, and Harriman Institute of Russian Studies. Advisor, Arthur and Elizabeth Schlesinger Library on the History of Women in America, and Library of

ARTHUR M. SCHLESINGER, JR.

America. Consultant, Economic Cooperation Administration, 1948, and Mutual Security Administration, 1951- 52; member, Adlai Stevenson presidential staff, 1952, 1956. *Military service:* U.S. Army, 1945; served in Europe.

MEMBER: American Historical Association, Society of American Historians (president, 1989—), Association for the Study of Afro-American Life and History, Organization of American Historians, Society for Historians of American Foreign Relations, American Academy and Institute of Arts and Letters (president, 1981-84, chancellor of the Academy, 1985-88), American Philosophical Society, Authors League, Center for Inter-American Relations, Council on Foreign Relations, Americans for Democratic Action (national chairman, 1953-54), American Civil Liberties Union (member of national council), Massachusetts Historical Society, Colonial Society of Massachusetts, Phi Beta Kappa.

AWARDS, HONORS: Henry Fellow, Cambridge University (Peterhouse), 1938- 39; Society of Fellows, Harvard, 1939-42; Pulitzer Prize for History, 1946, for *The Age of Jackson,* and for Biography, 1966, for *A Thousand Days;* Guggenheim Fellow, 1946; American Academy and Institute of Arts and Letters Grant for Literature, 1946; voted one of Ten Outstanding Young Americans by the United States Jaycees, 1946; Francis Parkman Prize from the Society of American Historians, 1957, and Frederic Bancroft Prize from Columbia University, 1958, both for *The Age of Roosevelt,* Volume 1: *The Crisis of the Old Order, 1919- 1933;* National Book Award, 1966, for *A Thousand Days,* and 1979, for *Robert Kennedy and His Times;* Gold Medal for History and Biography from the American Academy and Institute of Arts and Letters, 1967, for life achievement; Ohio Governor's Award for History, 1973; Sidney Hillman Foundation Award, 1973, for *The Imperial Presidency;* Eugene V. Debs Award in Education, 1974; Literary Lions Award from the New York Public Library, 1981; Fregene Prize for Literature, Italy, 1983; Commander in the Order of Orange-Nassau (Netherlands), 1987.

Honorary degrees from Muhlenberg College, 1950, Bethany College, 1956, New School for Social Research, 1966, Tusculum College, 1966, University of New Brunswick, 1966, Rhode Island College, 1969, Aquinas College, 1971, Western New England College, 1974, Ripon College, 1976, Iona College, 1977, Utah State University, 1978, University of Louisville, 1978, Northeastern University, 1981, Rutgers University, 1982, State University of New York—Albany, 1984, University of New Hampshire, 1985, Akron University, 1987, University of Oxford (England), 1987, Brandeis University, 1988, and University of Massachusetts, 1990.

WRITINGS:

Orestes A. Brownson: A Pilgrim's Progress, Little, Brown, 1939, published as *A Pilgrim's Progress: Orestes A. Brownson,* 1966.

The Age of Jackson, Little, Brown, 1945, reissued, 1968, abridged edition, New American Library, 1962.

The Vital Center: The Politics of Freedom, Houghton, 1949 (published in England as *The Politics of Freedom,* Heinemann, 1950).

(With Richard H. Rovere) *The General and the President and the Future of American Foreign Policy,* Farrar, Straus, 1951, revised edition published as *The MacArthur Controversy and American Foreign Policy,* 1965.

The Age of Roosevelt, Volume I: *The Crisis of the Old Order, 1919-1933,* Houghton, 1957, reissued, 1988, Volume II: *The Coming of the New Deal,* Houghton, 1959, reissued,

This sense of wholeness and freedom gave him an extraordinary appeal. (Jacket photograph by Thomas N. Bethell from *A Thousand Days: John F. Kennedy in the White House* by Arthur M. Schlesinger, Jr.)

1988, Volume III: *The Politics of Upheaval,* Houghton, 1960, reissued, 1988.

Kennedy or Nixon: Does It Make Any Difference?, Macmillan, 1960.

The Politics of Hope (essays), Houghton, 1963.

(With John M. Blum and others) *The National Experience,* Harcourt, 1963, 7th edition, 1989.

A Thousand Days: John F. Kennedy in the White House, Houghton, 1965, reissued, Greenwich House, 1983.

The Bitter Heritage: Vietnam and American Democracy, 1941-1966, Houghton, 1967.

(With Alfred De Grazia) *Congress and the Presidency: Their Role in Modern Times,* American Enterprise Institute for Public Policy Research, 1967.

Violence: America in the Sixties, New American Library, 1968.

The Crisis of Confidence: Ideas, Power, and Violence in America, Houghton, 1969.

(With Lloyd C. Gardner and Hans J. Morgenthau) *The Origins of the Cold War,* Ginn-Blaisdell, 1970.

The Imperial Presidency, Houghton, 1973.

Robert Kennedy and His Times (ALA Notable Book), Houghton, 1978.

The Cycles of American History, Houghton, 1986.

EDITOR

(With others) *Harvard Guide to American History,* Harvard University Press, 1954.

(With Quincy Howe) *Guide to Politics,* Dial, 1954.

(With Morton White) *Paths of American Thought,* Houghton, 1963.

Herbert Croly, *The Promise of American Life,* Belknap, 1967.

Edwin O'Connor, *The Best and the Last of Edwin O'Connor,* Little, Brown, 1970.

(With Fred L. Israel and William P. Hansen) *History of American Presidential Elections, 1789-1972,* four volumes, Chelsea House, 1971, supplemental volume, *History of American Presidential Elections, 1972-1984,* 1986.

The Coming to Power: Critical Presidential Elections in American History, Chelsea House, 1972.

The Dynamics of World Power: A Documentary History of United States Foreign Policy, 1945-1973, Chelsea House, 1973, Volume 1: *Western Europe,* Volume 2: *Eastern Europe and the Soviet Union,* Volume 3: *Latin America,* Volume 4: *Far East,* Volume 5: *United Nations, Middle East, Subsaharan Africa.*

History of U. S. Political Parties, Chelsea House, 1973, Volume 1: *1789-1860: From Factions to Parties,* Volume 2: *1860-1910: The Gilded Age of Politics,* Volume 3: *1910-1945: From Square Deal to New Deal,* Volume 4: *1945-1972: The Politics of Change.*

(With Roger Bruns) *Congress Investigates: A Documented History, 1792-1974,* five volumes, Chelsea House, 1975.

(With John S. Bowman) *The Almanac of American History,* Putnam, 1983.

(From *Robert Kennedy and His Times* by Arthur M. Schlesinger, Jr. Jacket design by Louise Noble. Photograph by Paul Slade.)

OTHER

(Contributor) *Four Portraits and One Subject: Bernard DeVoto,* Houghton, 1963.

(Author of foreword) Arthur M. Schlesinger [Sr.], *Paths to the Present,* revised and enlarged edition, Houghton, 1964.

(Author of preface) A. M. Schlesinger [Sr.], *The American as Reformer,* Harvard University Press, 1968.

(Author of introduction) *The Birth of the Nation: A Portrait of the American People on the Eve of Independence,* Knopf, 1968.

(Author of introduction) A. M. Schlesinger [Sr.], *Nothing Stands Still: Essays,* Belknap Press, 1969.

Also author of television screenplay, "The Journey of Robert F. Kennedy." Author of pamphlets on political subjects. Author of introductions for "American Statesmen" series, 45 volumes, "World Leaders Past and Present" series, 56 volumes, and "Know Your Government" series, all for Chelsea House. Movie reviewer for *Show,* 1962-64, *Vogue,* 1966-72, *Saturday Review,* 1977-80, and *American Heritage,* 1981-82; member of jury, Cannes Film Festival, 1964. Contributor to magazines and newspapers, including *Atlantic, Fortune, Wall Street Journal, New York Times, Life, New Republic, American Sociological Review, Foreign Affairs,* and *Encounter.*

ADAPTATIONS:

"The Imperial Presidency" (cassette), J. Norton.

WORK IN PROGRESS: Volume 4 of *The Age of Roosevelt.*

SIDELIGHTS: "The son of a historian, I grew up in a household alive with the fascinations and perplexities of history. As a boy, I first began to learn history from historical novels— Dumas, Scott, Cooper, as well as the once popular but now forgotten British writer of boy's books G. A. Henty. In college I concentrated in history and literature. Ever since, writing history—trying to reimagine the past in its own terms, not in ours—has always seemed to me more fun than almost anything else.

"I regret what has sometimes seemed an ebbing of popular interest in history. For history is to the nation what memory is to the individual. An individual deprived of memory becomes disoriented, confused, helpless, incapable of knowing where he has been or where he wants to go. A nation that forgets its history will lose its capacity for judgment in the present and foresight in the future."

"It is sometimes said that a knowledge of history enables the policy maker to foretell the future. I think the exact opposite is nearer the case: the knowledge of history should remind the statesman of the extreme difficulty of foretelling the future. If anything is evident, it is that history is full of surprises and that the historical process, far from being a means of clairvoyance, is inherently inscrutable. So I'd say the wise statesman learns from history that he should not base his policy on personal guesses as to what the behaviour of nations is going to be ten or fifteen years from now.

"What a knowledge of history does, it seems to me, is to encourage in the statesman a sense of human frailty, and to encourage a certain humility about the future. In a world where enemies become allies and allies become enemies, in a world where events of a completely unpredictable, or at least non-predicted sort, transform the whole situation of nations, . . . I think it's clear that the possibilities of history are far richer and

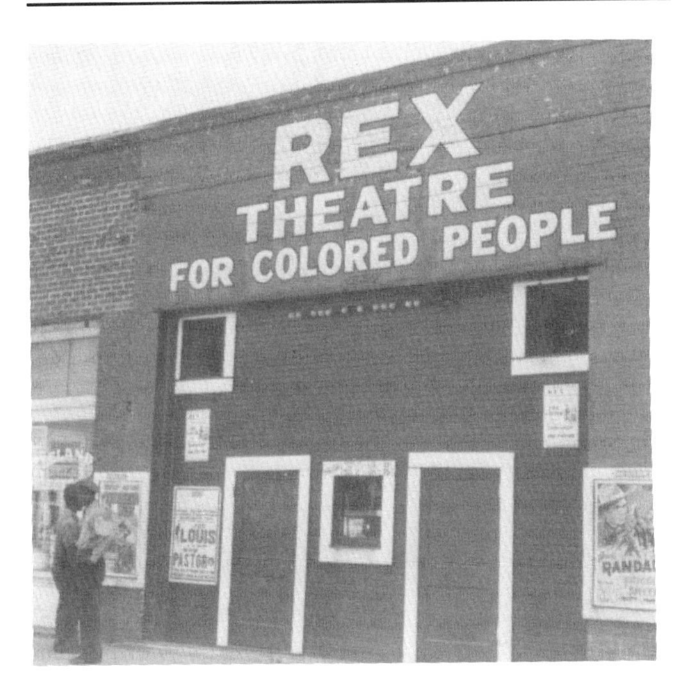

The Supreme Court ruled in 1954 . . . that segregation was unconstitutional. (From *The Department of Justice* by Lynne Dunn. Introduction by Arthur M. Schlesinger, Jr.)

more various than the human intellect is likely to see. This should lead statesmen not to make drastic and terrible decisions—like picking a war with Communist China now on the theory that, if we don't, China ten years from now may be doing something we don't like. This doesn't mean that the statesman cannot and must not have some vision of the broad direction in which the world is moving and have his policies derive from that vision; the great statesmen are those whose vision corresponds to the actual drift or possibility of affairs. That longer perspective which history offers is indispensable."[1]

"Writing history requires, first, extensive reading and research and careful note-taking. It next requires reflection and analysis in order to tease out the patterns of the past. Finally it requires literary skill to make the past live for the present. I work whenever and wherever I can. Having recently accomplished the technological leap to a word processor, I think ruefully of all the years I have wasted in typing and retyping the same page—and then I wonder how the great nineteenth-century historians wrote as much as they did without any mechanical aids beyond a pen."

"Dealing with *The Age of Jackson,* one was entirely dependent upon documentary remains: on . . . newspapers, magazines, letters, journals and so on. Obviously it was no longer possible to talk to people who had known Jackson or had worked in the Jackson Administration. The Roosevelt Administration was, so to speak, at a middle distance, where one found both a fairly wide range of documentary material and at the same time a considerable number of participants still available and ready to talk. In the case of the Kennedy book, this was not, as I saw it, a history in the same sense that the other two efforts were, but rather, a personal memoir by a participant—testimony hopefully for some future historian. In that case I was dependent on my own papers; I had and sought no access to anything beyond that. In addition, I had the benefits of personal experience, as well as the opportunity to talk to a large number of other participants.

"The historian can never recapture the totality of a situation; all he can do is give his own best understanding of the sequence and colour of events and what the major determining factors were. The sense of what is a determining factor is likely to vary from one period to another. At one time historians felt that religious motives were dominant; and later generations of historians, looking at the same problem, would assume economic motives to be dominant. So that in the large sense there is never any definitive historical truth. Once an event has happened, it disappears into the mists of the past and can never be replayed. The totality of the events, particularly the problems of motivation, are mysterious when they happen; and, after they've happened, they're gone, and the mystery is, I believe, permanent and irreducible. So that the trauma of choice is the problem—given the welter of events, given the impossibilities of total reconstruction—of the historian seeking to select out the features which count. Because of the essentially mysterious character of something that is irretrievably gone, this is not an easy thing for the historian to do."[1]

"My field is American history, and my particular interest has always been the area where ideas and politics intersect. Change is the one constant in history, and peaceful change is the means by which democracy endures and prospers. I have been especially concerned as a historian with presidents like Jackson, Franklin, Roosevelt, and Kennedy who by understanding the necessities of change have strengthened the idea of self-government in turbulent times."

"It has always seemed to me that the trick of writing history is to fuse narrative and analysis in a consistent literary texture. The history which is purely narrative history has its qualities, but I find it ultimately unsatisfactory. It's not enough to describe the events, however superbly they may be described, without giving some indication why they were happening and what the problems were, and so on. Purely analytical history has its disadvantages because by leaving out the emotions and the colour and the atmosphere, it is dehydrated history and tends to be sterile and doesn't do full justice to the period discussed; it doesn't re-create the mood in which choices were made at the time. I think what one must try to do, as I say, is to write a combination of narrative and analytical history, in which you describe as vividly as seems appropriate what happened; at the same time you try to indicate what the problems were and why they occurred and what the social or political or intellectual forces were that were operating upon the actors and the events.

"I myself am among those who tend to see all history through the lens of intellectual history.

"Intellectual history, as I understand it, deals with the interaction between ideas and social structure; it approaches politics, institutions, wars and so on from the perspective of ideas."[1]

"I have also felt that participation in events is a considerable aid to a historian. As Edward Gibbon observed, reflecting on his own military service, 'The captain of the Hampshire grenadiers . . . has not been useless to the historian of the Roman empire.' When President Kennedy asked me to come to the White House as one of his special assistants, I seized an opportunity to watch the making of history at first hand that few American historians have ever enjoyed (excepting Theodore Roosevelt and Woodrow Wilson, who were historians themselves.)"

"What the person who writes history is going to be interested in is governed by the preoccupations of his time. Women always had a role in history, so did Blacks, so did Indians; but it took the raising of consciousness created in our own time by the women's liberation movement, by the racial justice efforts, and so on, to make historians recognize that role, to make them realize that all these things *were* in fact there in the past, and belatedly to bring them forward . . . . As Oscar Wilde said, 'The one duty we owe to history is to rewrite it.' What the archivists and the oral historians can do is to make sure that a much wider range of evidence is available, so that when the flickering spotlight of the historian searches the darkness of the past, it will find things to illuminate. For a long time the historian just picked out a few things over here—now they're under the influence of Women's Liberation, and the spotlight goes over there and discovers women; but God knows what is left which is yet to be discovered. What the archivists and the oral historians can do is to make sure that, when the spotlight moves, there'll be some evidence to nourish the writer of history.

"When I embarked on *The Age of Roosevelt,* I . . . heard about the establishment of the Oral History Project at Columbia, the result of the imagination and energy of Allan Nevins, and I welcomed that. I did quite a lot of interviewing for the three volumes of the Roosevelt book, and I wish I had done more . . . . I did not, however, use a recorder. I took notes. I don't suppose that technology really became manageable for a totally non-technological person until the last ten years or so. It's only with the small cassette recorder that I've been able to master the art; and by this time I no longer believe in transcribing entire interviews, because once you've put something on tape, you have to hire someone to copy it. Then you have to take notes on that. So I prefer to take notes as I go on the salient things, and then to check exact quotations back with the source. That's what I did with the Robert Kennedy book. I interviewed quite a number of people, took notes on interviews, and cleared the quotations with the interviewees.

"Schlesinger is learned, thoughtful, occasionally outrageous, and always, with his fine literary style, a delight to read."
—Ronald Steel

Arthur M. Schlesinger, Jr.

THE CYCLES OF AMERICAN HISTORY

(Cover illustration "Three Flags" by Jasper Johns from *The Cycles of American History* by Arthur M. Schlesinger, Jr. Jacket design by Robert Anthony, Inc.)

"My father, in fact, *did* very much approve of oral history. He died in 1965, by which time the Columbia project was well underway. He thought that interviewing provided a valuable means of rescuing testimony that otherwise would perish so far as the historical record is concerned. There had been precedents, such as the WPA narratives of people who were born in slavery. My father thought such things extremely useful, as supplementary evidence perhaps, rather than as primary evidence."[2]

"I think the value is self-evident; that is, that you rescue a great mass of material that would not otherwise be available to historians. The preservation of any form of historical evidence is important; the preservation of the testimony of eye witnesses is peculiarly important. One has only to imagine how much our knowledge of the past would be enriched had there been oral history projects on the fall of the Roman Republic, for example, or the Peloponnesian wars, or the impact of William Shakespeare on the London theater. There is absolutely no question about it. It's of immense value.

"The limitations of oral history are limitations of human memory; those are very considerable limitations. Memory shapes things to make the past more attractive to us, or more dramatic, or a better story.

"I . . . kept an intermittent journal for many years. When I was working on the Robert Kennedy book, I went through the journal. I was astonished and chagrined to discover not only how many things I had forgotten, but also how many things I have misremembered. As you think about it, or talk about it, or tell it, the past subtly and imperceptibly changes shape.

"I think the great thing that made oral history possible was the invention of easy means of transcription. In one sense, oral history is quite old. I suppose the first and greatest historian, Thucydides, did a great deal of interviewing. He was writing about events which took place in his own time, and he describes in his *History of the Peloponnesian Wars* the effort he made to verify facts through interviews. So historians, particularly and above all historians writing about contemporaneous events, have always used interviews as a technique. Now the tape recorder gives the interview fidelity and permanence.

"I got very much interested in the idea of oral history, as a result of working in the Jackson period. James Parton, in the preface to his biography of Jackson, explains how he began writing the biography by immersion in documents. He read pamphlets, speeches, campaign biographies, pro and con, and all the rest; and at the end found himself in total confusion. If he had been asked to sum up the view of Jackson emerging from the documentation, he would have had to say, 'Andrew Jackson is a hero and a monster, Andrew Jackson is a patriot and a traitor,' and so on. He was left with a chaos of contradictions. Then he spent several months going around and talking to people, a great number of people. He said, 'I talked to politicians of the last generation who no longer had any interest in concealing the truth,' and so on. In the three volumes of his biography he quotes quite a lot from these interviews. I thought, 'My God, what a great thing to have done' and at the same time, 'What a shame that he did not ask the kind of questions that I, as a young historian working in 1940-42 on *The Age of Jackson,* wished he'd asked.'

"But I think the more you can enrich the evidence by getting other views on some of these controversies, the better."[2]

"The United States will be measured in the years of posterity not by its economic power nor by its military might, not by the territories it has annexed nor by the battles it has won, but by its character and achievement as a civilization."[3]

FOOTNOTE SOURCES:

[1]Henry Brandon, *Conversations with Henry Brandon,* Andre Deutsch, 1966.
[2]Lynn A. Bonfield, "Conversation with Arthur M. Schlesinger, Jr.: The Use of Oral History," *American Archivist,* fall, 1980.
[3]Milton Rhodes, "ACA: A View from the Field, the Arts and Public Policy," *Horizon,* July/August, 1988.

FOR MORE INFORMATION SEE:

New York Times, April 23, 1939, September 16, 1945, March 3, 1957, January 4, 1959, November 24, 1965, January 16, 1967, October 31, 1985, November 13, 1986, September 16, 1987, April 14, 1988.
Saturday Review, March 2, 1957, September 18, 1971.
New Republic, October 27, 1958, November 10, 1958, January 12, 1959, September 26, 1960, December 4, 1965, February 11, 1967, November 26, 1977 (p. 16ff), September 9, 1978, December 1, 1986.
American Historical Review, October, 1959, April, 1961.
New Yorker, September 10, 1960, December 10, 1973, November 17, 1986.
Deane Heller and David Heller, *Kennedy Cabinet,* Monarch, 1961.
New York Post, April 3, 1961 (p.25), April 4, 1961 (p. 25), April 5, 1961 (p. 39), April 6, 1961 (p. 25), April 7, 1961 (p. 37), December 5, 1965 (p. 28).
Arthur Meier Schlesinger [Sr.], *In Retrospect: The History of a Historian,* Harcourt, 1963.
Life, July 16, 1965.
New York Times Magazine, November 21, 1965 (p. 30ff).
Time, December 17, 1965 (p. 54ff), September 4, 1978, December 1, 1986.
Playboy, May, 1966 (p. 75ff), March, 1988.
Atlantic, March, 1967.
New Leader, May 8, 1967, November 17, 1986 (p. 12ff).
Marcus Cunliffe and Robin W. Winks, editors, *Pastmasters: Some Essays on American Historians,* Harper, 1969.
John A. Garraty, *Interpreting American History: Conversations with Historians,* Macmillan, 1970.
Washington Post, February 18, 1970, October 20, 1978 (p. 1ff), November 30, 1986, September 18, 1987.
American Political Science Review, December, 1972.
America, October 6, 1973, August 12, 1989.
Newsweek, November 19, 1973, September 4, 1978, October 27, 1986.
Village Voice, December 20, 1973, September 11, 1978.
Akron Beacon Journal, December 30, 1973.
Modern Age, winter, 1975.
Authors in the News, Volume I, Gale, 1976.
Review of Politics, January, 1977 (p. 3ff).
Mitchell S. Ross, *The Literary Politicians,* Doubleday, 1978.
Harper's, September, 1978.
Wall Street Journal, September 8, 1978, November 19, 1986.
Esquire, September 26, 1978, December, 1983.
American Heritage, October, 1978.
Los Angeles Times, March 22, 1979.
Political Science Quarterly, summer, 1979.
Current Biography, H. W. Wilson, 1979.

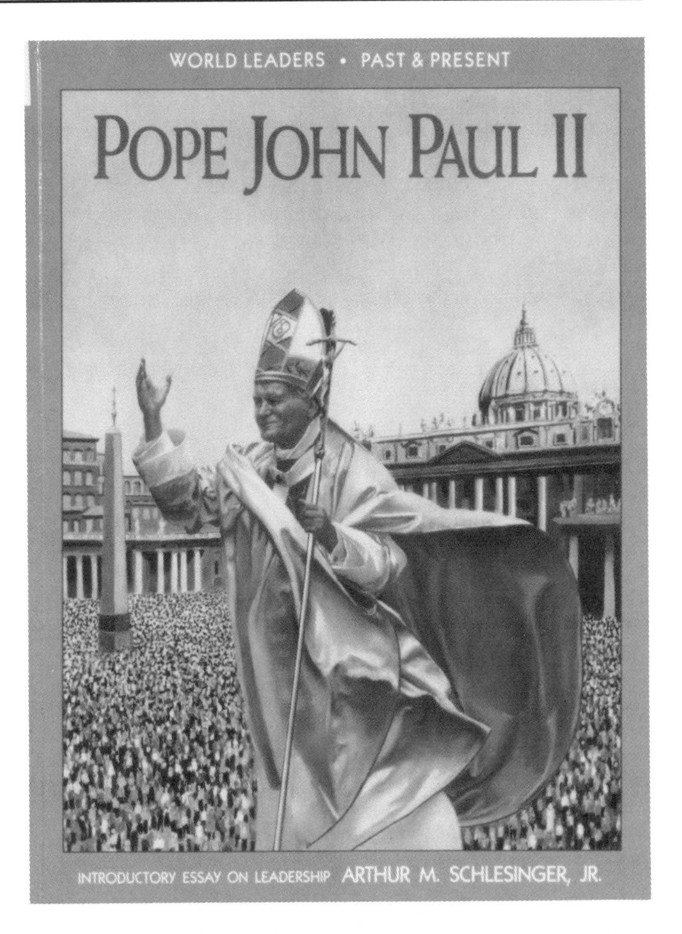

The cardinals had broken with tradition by electing a pope from Poland. (From *Pope John Paul II* by Timothy Walch. Introductory essay on "Leadership" by Arthur M. Schlesinger, Jr.)

Journal of American Culture, winter, 1982 (p. 96).
Dictionary of Literary Biography, Volume 17, *Twentieth-Century American Historians,* Gale, 1983.
Carol Fitzgerald, editor, *American History: A Bibliographic Review,* Volume 1, Meckler, 1985.
U.S. News & World Report, December 1, 1986 (p. 68).

COLLECTIONS

Schlesinger's White House staff papers are in the John F. Kennedy Library, Boston, Massachusetts.

SCHWANDT, Stephen (William) 1947-

PERSONAL: Born April 5, 1947, in Chippewa Falls, Wis.; son of Roland Lawrence (a Lutheran minister) and Mildred (a homemaker; maiden name, Ulvestad) Schwandt; married Karen Sambo (a teacher), June 13, 1970; children: Reed, Andrew. *Education:* Valparaiso University, B.A., 1969; St. Cloud State University, B.S., 1972; University of Minnesota—Twin Cities, M.A., 1972. *Religion:* Lutheran. *Home and office:* 12430 48th Ave. N., Minneapolis, Minn. 55442. *Agent:* Marilyn Marlow, Curtis Brown Ltd., 10 Astor Pl., New York, N.Y. 10003.

CAREER: Irondale High School, New Brighton, Minn., teacher of English and American literature, 1974—; Concordia College, St. Paul, Minn., part-time instructor, 1975-80; Normandale Community College, Bloomington, Minn., part-time instructor, 1982—. *Member:* National Education Association, Authors Guild, Book Critics Circle, National Council of Teachers of English, The Loft, Minnesota Community College Faculty Association. *Awards, honors: The Last Goodie* was selected one of New York Public Library's Best Books, and one of Philadelphia Public Library's Best Books, both 1985, one of Child Study Association of America's Children's Books of the Year, and nominated for the Edgar Allan Poe Award by the Mystery Writers of America, both 1986; *Holding Steady* was selected one of "Youth to Youth Books: A List for Imagination and Survival" by the Young Adult Advisory Board of the Baltimore Public Library, 1989.

WRITINGS:

YOUNG ADULT NOVELS

The Last Goodie, Holt, 1985.
A Risky Game, Holt, 1986.
Holding Steady, Holt, 1988.
Guilt Trip, Atheneum, 1990.

Book reviewer and young adult columnist, *Minneapolis Star Tribune,* 1983—.

WORK IN PROGRESS: Funnybone, a young adult novel with William E. Coles, Jr., for Atheneum.

SIDELIGHTS: "My family, teaching career, and athletic experiences have inspired or motivated me to write. So has my major-league debt service. My first two young adult novels, *The Last Goodie* and *A Risky Game,* were clearly products or conse-

STEPHEN SCHWANDT

It wasn't long before he found out that what everyone feared actually had happened. (Jacket illustration by Eric Jon Nones from *The Last Goodie* by Stephen Schwandt.)

quences of my many days in the classroom teaching writing to college prep seniors. And the first book pays particular homage to the notion that in sports (as in any highly competitive and intense activity) one can find one's *self,* that part which enables a performer to do for pride what should be impossible.

"Personally . . . as an undergraduate at Valparaiso University, which I attended on a basketball scholarship, my only remarkable performance was to be a starter on both the 1966-67 team that appeared in the NCAA College Division Finals, and on the 1967-68 team which helped set the existing NCAA record for the most points scored in a major college game: On February 24, 1968, my Valparaiso Crusader teammates and I fell to the University of Houston Cougars by the score of 158-81. And I'm proud to admit being a part of the 'swarming defense' that held the great Elvin 'Big E' Hayes to only sixty-two points in thirty-eight minutes.

"Besides teaching and sports, the other big influence on my writing has been the lifestyle my family enjoys on Washington Island, Wisconsin, where we are summer residents. Washington Island is also the setting of my latest novel (and my sentimental favorite), *Holding Steady.*

"That book, like my others, attempts to explore the themes of freedom and confinement, particularly the limitations people impose on themselves by addictive dependence on certain roles or perspectives, and the empowerment that can accompany the shedding of such dependencies. My lead characters, then, don't experience much success until they decide to *do* something, take an active role in winning the freedom to invent their own lives and see with their own eyes.

"In all of my books it is my primary assumption that young adult (and adult) readers are genuinely interested in puzzling, even troubling explorations of significant subjects. Such readers are looking for workable definitions of merit regarding values and behavior. My books attempt to pursue such definitions.

"I place a great deal of emphasis on voice in my writing, and I work especially hard to create believable, energetic dialogue. When one reviewer (*School Library Journal*) called me 'a master of conversation,' I took it as a supreme compliment.

"My career, then, should be an inspiration to others, for as one student said after my first novel appeared, 'This must be fun . . . and easy. I mean if *you* can do it, anybody in America can do it.'"

HOBBIES AND OTHER INTERESTS: Sailing, fishing, cross-country skiing.

FOR MORE INFORMATION SEE:

Golden Valley Post, February 13, 1986.
Minneapolis Star Tribune Sunday Magazine, November 30, 1986.
"Northern Lights and Insights" (cable TV interview), February 6, 1988.
Star Tribune, July 10, 1988 (p. 12F).

SEGAR, E(lzie) C(risler) 1894-1938

PERSONAL: Born December 8, 1894, in Chester, Ill.; died October 13, 1938, in Santa Monica, Calif; son of Amzi Andrews (a house painter and paper hanger) and Erma Irene (Crisler) Segar; married Myrtle Johnson; children: Marie Clausen, Thomas. *Education:* Evans Correspondence Course in Cartooning.

CAREER: Chicago Herald, Chicago, Ill., cartoonist, drawing "Charlie Chaplin's Comic Capers," 1916-18; *Chicago Evening American,* Chicago, Ill., reporter and cartoonist, drawing comic strip "Looping the Loop," 1918-19; King Feature Syndicate, New York, N.Y., creator of comic strip "Thimble Theatre," later renamed "Popeye," 1919-38. *Member:* Santa Monica Rod and Reel Club.

WRITINGS:

Thimble Theatre Starring Popeye, Sonnet, 1931, published as *Thimble Theater Starring: Popeye the Sailor,* Nostalgia Press, 1971.
Popeye among the White Savages with "Pop-up" Picture, Blue Ribbon Press, 1934.
Popeye Cartoon Book, Saalfield, 1934.
Popeye, the Sailor Man, Grosset, 1937.
Popeye and the Pirates (animated by Julian Wehr), Duenewald Printing, 1945.

COLLECTIONS

Thimble Theatre: An Original Compilation—First Collection of the Rare Daily Strips in Which Popeye Appears for the First Time; Complete Run from 1928 to 1930, introduction by Bill Blackbeard, Hyperion, 1977.
Prophetic Allegory: Popeye and the American Dream: Two Classics by E. C. Segar, introduction and annotated by Alan Gowans, American Life Books, 1983.

The "Popeye" strip appears in about 200 newspapers around the world, and is translated into twelve languages, including Greek, Italian, Danish, Spanish, and Norwegian. More than 1,000 products based on Popeye are licensed by King Features.

ADAPTATIONS:

"Popeye the Sailor" (animated film) Fleischer Studios, 1933, (radio program), WABC radio, September 8, 1936, May 4, 1938.
"Popeye the Sailor Meets Sinbad the Sailor" (animated film), Fleischer Studios, 1936.
"Popeye the Sailor Meets Ali Baba's Forty Thieves" (animated cartoon), Fleischer Studios, 1937.
"Popeye the Sailor Meets Aladdin and His Wonderful Lamp" (animated cartoon), Fleischer Studios, 1939.
"Popeye and Friends in the South Seas" (videocassette), King Features/Media Home, 1961.
"Popeye" (animated cartoon; four half-hour episodes), King Features, 1961-63.
"Thimble Theatre Starring Popeye" (record), Mark 56 Records 715, 1976.
"Popeye" (record), Mark 56 Records 715, 1976.
"The All-New Popeye Hour" (television series), Hanna Barbera Productions, premiered on CBS-TV, September 9, 1978.
"Popeye" (motion picture), starring Robin Williams and Shelley Duvall, Paramount, 1980.
"Popeye: Travelin' on about Travel" (videocassette), Media Home, 1984.

Also "Popeye's Mirthday," 1953, and a videocassette of "Popeye and Friends in Outer Space," produced by Paramount/Media Home.

SIDELIGHTS: Born in Chester, Illinois on **December 8, 1894,** into a family of five sons and three daughters. Many of Segar's childhood activities centered around the Chester Opera House. Jessie Lee Huffstutler wrote an article entitled "I Remember: Early Memories of Chester, Illinois," in which she shares her childhood memories of Segar: "Elzie Crisler Segar lived with his parents, Mr. and Mrs. Amzi Segar, near the City Steps at the north end of Harrison Street, having moved there from the farm. His father was an interior decorator and was anxious for Elzie to help him and to follow this vocation. But Elzie would have none of that. As a lad he was shy, very quiet and frail. His eyes were large but very soft and I could see kindness in them. He often smiled quietly when we played soft music. His spare time was spent in drawing and I shall always remember the wide brimmed straw hat he wore in summer."[1]

Mrs. Huffstutler played the piano at the Opera House, and was often accompanied by Segar on the drums. The Opera House was owned and operated by Bill Schuchert, who proved to be influential in Segar's life.

1907-1914. Schuchert hired the thirteen-year-old Segar to put up posters for upcoming attractions, and soon Segar was designing the posters and drawing on the sidewalk outside the theatre to

E. C. SEGAR

attract customers. He loved to hang around the projection booth with Red Faverty, the projectionist, who sometimes allowed him to work the projector. Mrs. Huffstutler recalled: "At that time the reel had to be rewound before the next picture could be shown. Elzie used his creative ability by making slides to be thrown on the screen during this period. Often he used local people and events for this cartoon. For one such slide he used a local young man knocking on the door, calling on his girlfriend. Of course, everyone knew who the young man was because he made the face to look just like him.

"After the evening performance it was Elzie's duty to go to the several bulletin boards located at various places in the area and change the poster for the next performance. He had as his assistant a small neighborhood boy with a little red wagon to haul the posters. This boy was Brother Gollon."[1]

He was so proud of becoming a projectionist that he had the letters M.P.O. tattooed on his arm, for Motion Picture Operator.

Schuchert took a liking to Segar and encouraged his cartooning by buying him a camera. The boy would photograph local characters and then draw on the negatives, using the original face and adding grotesque bodies to make them funny. These were the slides he projected while the reel was being rewound, and they delighted his audiences.

He also dubbed in commercial art. He was once hired by the local hardware store to paint a billboard on the side of a barn. The whole town came out to see it, but unfortunately he had used water-based paint and it dissolved in the first rain. Bud Sagendorf, in later years Segar's assistant, recalls Segar saying: "They were very pretty puddles, but you couldn't read 'em."[2]

In addition to art, Segar, fascinated by inventions and electricity, attempted to electrify the movie projector so the reels wouldn't have to be hand wound or the projector hand cranked.

As he became more serious about commercial art, he enrolled in the Evans Correspondence Course in Cartooning, paid for by Schuchert. His boss allowed him to set up a studio on the Opera House stage, but Segar had to vacate it whenever a vaudeville troupe was in town.

1915. After working for eighteen months on the correspondence course, Segar moved to Chicago. With the help of R. F. Outcalt, the creator of the comic strip "Buster Brown and Tige," he found a job with the *Chicago Herald*. His assignment was to work on "Charlie Chaplin's Comic Capers," a well-known feature strip. Recalled Sagendorf, "At that time he wasn't married and he was living in a boarding house in a tough section of the city. Since he was a darn good billiard player, he had formed the habit of eating in a little place which was a combination pool hall and restaurant. And there was this fellow he struck up an acquaintance with, and with whom he used to eat occasionally. The fellow taught Segar how to twirl spaghetti on a fork and the two became good friends. Anyhow, Segar would work late at night at the newspaper office doing his strip (until 2 or 3 A.M.) and then walk the ten or eleven blocks to his rooming house without ever being bothered by any of the tough characters in the area. Everyone told him he was crazy to take these wee-hour walks. Not until he had moved to New York and chanced one day to see a picture of his pool hall-lunch-room friend in the newspaper, did he realize that the friend was Al Capone—and that Al had passed the word, 'this is a friend of mine—hands off!'"[3]

During this period Segar met and married Myrtle Johnson of Chicago. He also started his own strip, "Barry the Boob," about a young nitwit soldier.

1917-1919. When the *Chicago Herald* ceased publication, Segar went to work for the *Chicago Evening American*, creating his own column, "Looping the Loop." In it he illustrated special events and featured his own reviews of night clubs and theaters, satirizing downtown Chicago and its "loop" district.

His work drew the attention of Arthur Brisbane of the Hearst Corporation, who recruited Segar for King Features Syndicate, requiring him to move to New York City. Here he began work on a strip titled "Thimble Theatre." Segar loved to tell the story of his first day on the job. To make a good impression, he decided to buy a new suit, but his money was limited. He was delighted to find a dimly-lit bargain basement with suits on sale, and promptly bought what he thought was a conservative tan suit. In the daylight, however, it proved to be bright orange. Sagendorf recalled him saying: "I was dressed like a short, thin pumpkin whose light had gone out."[2]

Another surprise was Segar's office. The comic art department was in a leased room on the fourth floor next to the main Hearst building. Instead of going up and down stairs, the cartoonists crawled on a narrow plank from window to window.

December 27, 1919. The first of Segar's episodes of "Thimble Theatre" ran in the *New York Journal*. Segar began to develop a cast of characters known as the Oyl family: Caster Oyl and Ma Oyl, Olive Oyl, and her beau, Ham Gravy, populated the "Thimble Theatre" strip without Popeye for many years.

December 24, 1920. Segar launched a new strip "The Five-Fifteen." Bud Sagendorf in his memoir, *Popeye: The First Fifty Years,* described how it began. "Walter Berndt, creator of the unique 'Smitty' comic strip, has described how Segar came to introduce the well-known 'Five-Fifteen' feature. Though Segar grew up along the Mississippi and Berndt was born in Brooklyn, they were both avid fishermen. Several days a week, the two cartoonists sneaked out of their offices and took the ferry to New Jersey, where they fished along the Hudson River.

"King Features' comic art director at the time became aware that one of his flock (the cartoonists all sat together in a large room under his eagle eye) was rushing through his work and then playing hooky. Undoubtedly a man who preferred poker and golf to angling, he took Segar to task—if there was time to waste on fishing, there was time to produce yet another comic strip for the company. 'The Five-Fifteen' was thus forced onto the pages of American newspapers.

"The feature . . . centered on a short character named John Sappo and his large wife Myrtle (named after Segar's own wife). It was a gag-a-day strip about the suburbs and the commuter's way of life.

"For several years, 'Five-Fifteen' flourished in its original format. Then, in the late twenties, Segar redesigned the strip. It was customary at this time for newspapers to divide the Sunday comics page into two sections—the main feature taking up about three-fourths of the lower portion, another feature by the same cartoonist occupying the top. When Segar needed to create a 'top piece' for his 'Thimble Theatre' Sunday page, he converted 'Sappo' and added a character named Professor O. G. Watasnozzle, a brilliant scientist and mad inventor.

"Segar had always loved science fiction, using it frequently even in pre-Popeye 'Thimble Theatre' strips. But with Sappo

Segar's strip for January 17, 1929. (Copyright © by King Features Syndicate, Inc.)

and Watasnozzle at his command, he moved full force into the world of the future. Watasnozzle, in the early thirties, was splitting atoms as easily as walnuts. Sappo and the professor visited distant planets with ease. Whenever the spirit moved them to travel, Segar simply inked them a spaceship and off they went. When the first walks in space astonished the world, Sappo and Watasnozzle only yawned. It was old hat to them—Sappo's wife Myrtle had space-walked in 1937.

"In the real world, Segar was an inventive amateur engineer. A master with tools, he designed much of the equipment used in his photography studio. One of his creations was a camera and enlarger to reproduce thousands of special drawings to mail to fans who wrote him. Though it looked like a project from O. G. Watasnozzle's mind, it worked flawlessly. As his assistant, it was my job to operate the machine. There was only one minor problem—Segar's favorite building material was wood yard-sticks, and when operating the camera it was sometimes difficult to tell which of the many scales to use."[2]

April 18, 1925. The first full-color page of "Thimble Theatre" appeared in the *New York Journal*. The "Five-Fifteen," renamed "Sappo," was added to the color page a year later and was increased to one-third of a page. With this success as a cartoonist, Segar decided to move to Santa Monica, California, where he would meet Bud Sagendorf, his assistant and successor. Sagendorf recalled the move: "After New York City, a very short stay in Florida and a few years in Hollywood, Santa Monica was finally selected as a permanent homesite. The location was chosen for its pleasant surroundings, but I have always thought its proximity to the ocean and its fine fishing pier were the reasons. Segar had three loves, his family, his work and fishing. He didn't care for sport fishing, as such, and didn't go after the big ones. He liked to eat what he caught, so nearly all his angling from the pier was for pan fish. Between the ages of eight and twelve, I haunted the same pier, fished with a drop line and mooched bait from fellow fishermen. Segar and I wondered how many times we had stood side by side, fishing."[2]

Years later, they discovered they *had* met, when Sagendorf was a young boy. Sagendorf explains: "One morning . . . Segar and I were eating dinner and watching the sun come up when he began to reminisce about those days in the office where he created Popeye. He told about a funny little kid who had sold him his evening papers. This small boy in overalls would be waiting for him, rain or shine, each evening. Segar stopped speaking when he saw the startled expression on my face. He asked me what was wrong, and I said, 'Nothing.' But I asked him a few questions, and sure enough: *I* was that paper boy. It was my first job, and where I was assigned to sell my papers was the least choice corner in the city. I stuck it out because I had one steady customer, a kind man who'd give me a nickel or a dime for a three-cent copy of the Los Angeles *Hearld-Express* and never wait for change. Of course, I didn't realize my steady customer drew 'Thimble Theatre,' the comic strip, that ran in the paper he bought from me day after day."[2]

Little did either man know that Segar would hire the newspaper boy as a teenager to become his assistant. Sagendorf became a member of Segar's family, much as Segar had been taken in by the Schucherts. Sagendorf recalled, "During the seven years I lived with him, I learned what a great teacher he was.

"Incidentally, the reason he seemed to like me right off the bat as a punk kid was that I said 'yes' when he asked me if I liked fishing. When he asked me what I read, and I answered 'Science Fiction,' he said, 'You're hired!' Science Fiction, needless to say, was one of his great loves."[3]

"Short of stature, slight of frame, mild-mannered and somewhat introverted, Segar was the complete opposite of his spinach-eating creation—with one exception. For a small man, his strength was phenomenal. As his assistant, I would be given a job requiring muscles, and many times I had to ask for his help. Maybe I wasn't eating enough spinach.

"In his few social activities, he was reserved and uncomfortable—especially with people he didn't know. Many times, when large functions were planned, he would make what to him was the logical excuse that we were going fishing to work on an idea. An excellent billiards player, he had played many of the top professionals and for an 'amateur' had won more than his share of the matches. Like most boys growing up in small towns, he had spent much of his spare time in the only available recreation establishment—the pool hall. His dream was to make enough money to afford billiard tables of his own. When the Segars built their home in Santa Moncia, California, a room was constructed off the studio just for the pool and billiard tables.

"Segar was a night worker, and this meant his assistant was, too. Our usual hours were from seven or eight at night till four or five in the morning. This was tough on a high school student. It wasn't that I worried about my school work; it was that I didn't have the time to pursue the girl I had chosen to be my wife. Fortunately, Segar was most understanding, and between pages or strips I was allowed to dash off for a date with the young lady. Few mothers would understand a boy picking up her daughter at three in the morning for a fast hamburger.

"At least once a week, usually on my night off, Segar would call around midnight to tell me it was time to work on ideas. This meant I was to call the pier, have the boat put in the water, gather the fishing gear and pick him up. Much of the basic, creative thinking was done in this boat, tied to what was then the new Santa Monica breakwater. With fishhooks baited and lines in the water, we would settle down to discuss the next week's work. I always had a pad illuminated by a gasoline lantern to make notes.

"A great part of creating humor is getting into the mood. The more outlandish and bizarre the ideas, the better. When the point is reached where you're laughing at anything, you can settle down to the selection of workable segments. During these warmups, we'd explode into wild bursts of laughter. People trying to sleep on nearby boats must have thought there was a drunken brawl going on. If they yelled and cursed at us, we never knew it; we were too involved to notice. Of course, when either of us hooked a fish, the laughter would cease—pulling in a fish is serious business and no time for levity."[2]

January 17, 1929. Segar was experimenting with some invented animals, including Blizzard the Gamecock and Bernice the Whiffle Hen who had good luck. Sagendorf recounts how Popeye came on the scene: "When Castor Oyl and Ham Gravy gained possession of Bernice the Whiffle Hen, they thought their future was secure. They had discovered Bernice was a 'lucky hen,' and they were determined to use this knowledge to their financial advantage. The plan was to take the hen to Mr. Fadewell's gambling casino on Dice Island. With their mascot, they couldn't lose at any game of chance.

"For six thousand dollars, the would-be sports purchased a splendid sailing ship for their voyage to wealth. The vessel was a real buy: as Castor told Ham Gravy, she had only a few holes in her hull—luckily, all below the waterline, where they wouldn't show.

"With provisions aboard—one thousand cans of beans, three dill pickles and one bar of soap—the two men were ready to sail when they realized neither had the slightest knowledge of how to 'drive a boat.' They would have to find an experienced sailor to see them safely to Dice Island and the gaming tables.

"As logical adventurers would, they searched the waterfront. Seafaring jobs must have been plentiful, for they found only one man in need of employment—a strange-looking character with a jutting chin and one eye. After assuring himself that this odd figure was indeed a sailor, Castor hired him on the spot.

"Readers of 'Thimble Theatre' that day could not know they had witnessed the birth of a legend and folk hero.

"Many of the citizens of Chester, Illinois, Segar's hometown, are convinced that his famous sailor was inspired by a local character named Rocky Feigle. Rocky, a thin, wiry man, was employed part-time to sweep and clean up in the local saloon. His afternoons were spent leaning back in a chair in front of his

Bud Sagendorf's tribute to Segar.

Segar's April 12, 1936 strip. (Copyright © by King Features Syndicate, Inc.)

SEGAR: NOVEMBER 4, 1936

At last, Popeye finds one rewarding virtue in his father

(From *Popeye: The First Fifty Years* by Bud Sagendorf.)

place of work. Known as the town's cock of the walk, Rocky was famous for never having lost a fight, and it was a challenge for small boys—Segar included—to tease him with the hope he would give chase. On one occasion, three local toughs lured Rocky out into the woods where they planned to rob him. A short time later, Rocky, in true Popeye style, nonchalantly strolled back into town and resumed his customary seat in front of the saloon. Meanwhile, the three would-be muggers sought medical aid for injuries received in their robbery attempt.

"It is also a common belief in Chester that Rocky Feigle, in his later years, received a weekly check from Popeye's creator.

"Whether these beliefs are fact or fiction, Popeye was waiting backstage for the opportunity to step into the limelight.

"Bernice the Whiffle Hen was certainly a 'lucky hen' for Segar and 'Thimble Theatre,' but not for Castor Oyl and Ham Gravy. True, they made a fortune on Dice Island, but they paid a tremendous price. Popeye, the sailor they hired, would soon outshine them."[2]

August 27, 1929. Olive Oyl, imagining she was kissing her new beau, Julius J. Herringbone, kissed Popeye by mistake and a great romance was born. Sagendorf commented on their love affair: "Popeye is a perfect example of a creative person's brainchild taking over and controlling the actions of its creator . . . . In his first few months of existence, the new character showed little evidence of the strong, fist-swinging fighter he was to become. On the contrary, during this period, Popeye indicated a tendency to act on the cautious, if not cowardly side. He was nothing but a hired hand, working for the stars of the feature.

Olive Oyl was the first female balloon in the Macy's Thanksgiving Day Parade, 1985.

"Segar often said it was Popeye's first attempt to fend off a monster that began his metamorphosis. The humor and action of the fat arms swinging and landing thunderous blows brought to his creator's awareness the fact that he had inadvertently added a natural fighter to the strip.

"Even with this knowledge, there was still no intention of permitting Popeye to stay in the feature—the strip was doing fine with the stars it had. Segar had just signed a contract with a substantial increase in salary, so why complicate a good thing? A new major character might upset the already well-established theme so solidly set by Castor Oyl, Ham Gravy and Olive Oyl.

"But Segar had underestimated his own instinct. He had accidentally produced an element that wouldn't stay dropped, and a new story had barely begun to develop when he found himself reinserting the sailor into the strip. This time Popeye was there to stay, and 'Thimble Theatre' had a new star in its cast.

"Associating so closely with Popeye and his creator, learning to know and understand them both, I gradually became aware that philosophically the character and the man were one. Popeye's fundamental honesty and loyalty—his absolute belief in right and wrong, with no grays—were but reflections of Segar. All creative people put a part of themselves into their work; it would be difficult not to. With Popeye, Segar continually expressed his own feelings about villains, crooked politicians, dictators and skulduggery in any form opposed to his standards.

"Few characters in real life or literature have loved with such fierce devotion as Popeye. For fifty years, his overwhelming protective feeling for his pickle-nosed sweety, backed by his famous 'twisker sock,' has provided readers around the world with a model of true affection. At times, Popeye may seem neglectful of Olive, and with his tunnel vision these are normal, human interruptions with no bearing on his love. Boats do need to be painted; new monsters must be destroyed and the downtrodden championed. But Olive is never out of Popeye's thoughts.

"The sailor isn't always as secure in Olive's love as he'd like to be. He is capable of jealousy, and the results are physical—a typhoon is a gentle summer breeze compared to the total destruction he wreaks on anyone foolish enough to woo his sweety.

"The decision to make Popeye a professional fighter was a natural step in his development as a character. Segar was a fight fan, and the late twenties and thirties were a period of important heavyweight contests. When Segar discovered he had a great natural fighter, the logical step was to have him turn professional."[2]

By **1932** Popeye was the star of the strip, and clothing, toys, games, and novelties bore his picture. An animated film was produced by Fleischer Studios, accompanied by the famous song by Sammy Lerner, "I'm Popeye the Sailor Man." Popeye's promotion of spinach increased the U.S. consumption of spinach by thirty-three per cent. Every few days crates of spinach arrived at Segar's door from the spinach growers of America. He had so much he had to give it away.

A 1930s Sunday strip. (Copyright © by King Features Syndicate, Inc.)

"In the mid-thirties," recalled Sagendorf, "Segar discovered there was a skeet club in Santa Monica. If fishing was his first love as a sport, shooting was the second. In a short time, he was a member of the club, and a new life style evolved. An excellent shot, he was soon club champion and captain of the skeet team. Suddenly, the boy from the small river town in Illinois found himself in the company—and a teammate—of Eugene Pallette, Clark Gable and Gary Cooper. Segar and Pallette became good friends and spent many afternoons, with me as an awed observer, teaching 'The King' the fine art of bird shooting. Most of these men belonged to a duck club up the coast at Oxnard. Eugene Pallette had a cabin there, and Segar was easily convinced it would be a nice place for his family and a quiet place for us to work. So a cabin was built (they called them cabins, but they were really very comfortable homes). In several Popeye Sunday pages, there are references to the Santa Monica Rod and Reel Club, and many ideas came from the hours spent here and at the skeet club.

"Though Segar was uncomfortable at social events, he was always at home seated at a lunch counter, drugstore or roadside diner. He was at ease with everyday people and never hesitated to start a conversation with the man next to him. He did have one pet peeve. The question of occupation would come up, and after the stranger's business was discussed, Segar would be asked about his work. When he answered that he wrote and drew a comic strip, the stranger would invariably laugh and say, 'That's great, but what do you do for a living?' Segar would boil inside, his face would turn red, and I'd know it was time to go even though neither of us had finished lunch. It was one of the few things that would upset him. He was proud of his profession, and though he never mentioned it to the offending stranger, he and I knew his drawing of funny pictures was giving him a yearly income high in six figures."[2]

From "Thimble Theatre" came other great characters like Brutus, Popeye's sparring partner, Swee'pea, his adopted son, Poopdeck Pappy, his father, and J. Wellington Wimpy, his best friend. Sagendorf explained how Wimpy developed from a character in the "Five-Fifteen" into a regular on "Thimble Theatre." "When Popeye began to fight professionally in the early thirties, it became necessary to create a referee. Segar brought the fat man's image forward from the 'Five-Fifteen,' gave him a personality and a name, and introduced him as the referee in Popeye's fights.

"Many citizens of Segar's birthplace believe that Wimpy's outward appearance was modeled after Bill Schuchert, Segar's

(From the 1980 movie "Popeye," based on Segar's cartoon characters, starring Shelley Duvall and Robin Williams.)

kind boss at the Chester Opera House .... Huffstutler ... recalls Schuchert's love of hamburgers and that he would send young Segar to get them.

"Wimpy's reflection of Segar's boss ends with his physical likeness and his love of hamburgers. His basic character was taken from a prizefight referee seen weekly at the Ocean Park, California, sports arena. This obnoxious man would enter the ring to the sound of boos and catcalls. Ducking flying objects (he once dodged a ladies' shoe thrown by an angry Mrs. Segar), he would introduce himself in a voice much louder and clearer than his mild, delayed introduction of the contestants. There were rumors that his income was greatly increased by his prefight knowledge of contest results. These characteristics are, and have always been, part of J. Wellington Wimpy's behavior when refereeing Popeye's battles in the ring.

"From a creative point of view, Wimpy has always been a problem. Segar often tried to write Sunday gags in which the sailor would get the best of the moocher. Many nights, we'd think we had laid out a page where this would happen, but the next day, starting to work on the penciled Sunday page, I would find that Wimpy had again foxed Popeye. When questioned, Segar's answer was always the same: 'It just happened. Wimpy is smarter than Popeye—he has to win.'

"Popeye's attitude toward his fat pal is simple. Wimpy's mooching may drive the sailor 'nerts,' but in his own words,

'Frien's is the mos' importink thing on eart', even if ya can't stan' 'em!'''[2]

Sagendorf also remembered when Segar was ordered to soften Popeye's image because of his influence over children: "It was my habit as Segar's assistant to arrive at his home about noon, in time for a quiet breakfast and a leisurely discussion of the day's work. Never having seen him angry or violently upset, I was startled one day in 1934 to encounter a black atmosphere and my employer in an even darker mood. He had just received a telegram from the president of King Features. Segar stopped his pacing long enough to shake the yellow paper under my nose. 'Read it!' he ordered.

"The wire is long-lost, but in essence it read: 'Hearst says Popeye is loved by the children of America .... Stop his swearing .... Stop his brutality .... Make him respectable.' These commands could not have been more unexpected or harder to take than if the syndicate had given orders to make Olive a sex symbol. 'The fun will be gone,' Segar muttered. 'There's nothing funny about a sissy sailor!'

"A decree from 'the Chief' was not to be ignored—so Popeye's language was softened and his random smacking without a cause was modified. He was almost made a gentleman."[2]

Segar is credited with adding several new words to the English language: "jeep" and "goon." Alice the Goon inspired the second word; Sagendorf explained how "jeep" came into being: "The small yellow animal Olive received from her Uncle Ben ... has proven through the years to be universally the most popular of 'Thimble Theatre's' menagerie. Eugene the Jeep was a departure from Segar's usual creatures. Most of the side beasts were anything but pleasant in physical appearance. Added as heavies, their purpose was to challenge Popeye and put fear in the hearts of readers. With the Jeep, Segar took the opposite direction. He wanted—and created—an animal that was charming in looks and pleasant in personality. Only villains have anything to fear from Eugene.

"The creation of this appealing animal was the most exciting and pleasing experience of my years with Segar. The Jeep was magic. From the first rough sketches through to the naming, the small creature insisted on being born.

"After settling on the physical design of the new character, we had to decide what to call him. At breakfast one morning, as we were mulling over possible names, one entry on Segar's list stood out like a neon sign: 'Jeep.' There was no doubt; that was it, instantly as natural as calling a dog a dog. We checked English and foreign dictionaries to be sure it wasn't in use, then chose the name once and for all—and added a new word to the language."[2]

In addition to creating new words, Segar was often accused of mutilating the language with Popeye's expressions: "sandrich," "suspose," "forget-me-don'ts," "I yam what I yam an' tha's all I yam," and "I am disgustipated."

October 13, 1938. Segar died at the age of forty-three after a six-month illness.

(The movie "Popeye" co-starred the magnificent setting of Sweethaven.)

(From the animated cartoon "Popeye the Sailor Meets Ali Baba's Forty Thieves," produced by Fleischer Studios, 1937.)

It took several people to replace him. Tom Sims and Ralph Stein wrote the column while Doc Winner and Bill Zaboly did the artwork. Joe Musial and Bud Sagendorf designed Popeye-related novelties, books, and toys, until 1958 when Bud Sagendorf took over all responsibilities relating to the cartoon.

June 25, 1977. In remembrance of Segar, his hometown of Chester, Illinois erected a bronze statue of Popeye.

December 12, 1980. Disney Productions and Paramount Pictures released a non-animated film version of "Popeye," directed by Robert Altman and starring Robin Williams and Shelley Duvall. Jules Feiffer, who wrote the screenplay, commented on the film version: "Right from the beginning, I saw myself as being Segar's agent on this picture. To have this come out of the blue—to allow me to pay homage to this great talent whom practically nobody has heard of anymore, except cartoonists—was like a boon to me. Also, the idea of giving me the opportunity to write in someone else's voice—someone with whom I felt compatible—and to do what I wanted to do with his characters, seemed very exciting.

"What I loved about the tone of Segar's 'Popeye' is how civil he was about the awfulness of everybody. He lived in a world in which every character was corrupt, jealous, greedy and did terrible things to each other—all except Popeye. And somehow he was not mean-spirited. It was not the world of Al Capp where ugliness really seemed ugly. There was genuine charm, and a word that keeps coming back to me, a *civility* toward his view of the universe."[4]

FOOTNOTE SOURCES

[1]Jessie Lee Huffstutler, *Early Memories of Chester, Illinois,* privately printed (Jiffy Printers, Chester, Ill.), 1976.
[2]Bud Sagendorf, *Popeye: The First Fifty Years,* King Features Syndicate and Workman Publishing, 1979.
[3]"Popeye," *Cartoonist Profile,* March, 1972.
[4]Pat McGilligan, "Feiffer and Popeye," *Focus on Film 37,* March, 1981.

FOR MORE INFORMATION SEE:

Chester Herald Tribune (Chester, Ill.), June 23, 1977; October 12, 1978.
Cartoonist Profile, September, 1977 (p. 84ff).
"Fifty Years of Popeye Remembered in Chester, Illinois," *Family* (Illinois Farm Bureau), December, 1979.
Herald and Review (Decatur, Ill.), January 11, 1981 (section C).
Rick Marschall, editor, *The Complete E. D. Segar: Popeye, Sundays 1932-34,* Fantagraphics, 1985.

OBITUARIES

New York Herald Tribune, October 14, 1938.
New York Times, October 14, 1938 (p. 25).

SELDEN, Neil R(oy) 1931-
(Anna Aaron)

PERSONAL: Born March 20, 1931, in New York, N.Y.; son of Joseph (a grocer) and Ann (a saleswoman; maiden name, Sirota) Selden; married Lee Imbrie, July 21, 1960; children: Michael. *Education:* New York University, B.A., 1952. *Home:* 21 Harrison St., 1, New York, N.Y. 10013. *Agent:* William Morris Agency, 1350 Avenue of the Americas, New York, N.Y. 10019.

CAREER: Writer. Member of board of directors of Encounter, Inc. (drug rehabilitation organization); consultant to New York City Addiction Services Agency. *Military service:* U.S. Army, Military Police, 1954-56. *Member:* Dramatists Guild. *Awards, honors:* Poetry Award from the Wisconsin Library, 1953, for poem "Cassandra's Eye"; Audrey Wood Award, 1972, for play "CAR."

WRITINGS:

YOUNG ADULT

Flood, Scholastic Book Services, 1973.
Night Driver, Scholastic Book Services, 1978.
The Great Lakeside High Experiment, Scholastic Book Services, 1982.
Drawing the Dead, Dell, 1983.
(Under pseudonym, Anna Aaron) *Secrets,* Bantam, 1983.
Last Kiss in April, Berkley, 1984.

PLAYS

(With brother-in-law, McCrea Imbrie) "Someone's Comin' Hungry" (three-act), first produced Off-Broadway at Pocket Theater, March 31, 1969.
(With M. Imbrie) "Mr. Shandy" (one-act), first produced Off-Broadway at Roundabout Theatre, 1972.
(With M. Imbrie) "CAR" (one-act), first produced in Berlin, West Germany, at Berlin Festival, 1973.
"Sam Dead" (three-act), first produced in New York, N.Y. at American Theatre of Actors, 1988.
"CAR," "Raincheck" and "Mister Shandy," were performed together in New York, N.Y. at American Theatre of Actors, 1988.
"Ocean in a Teacup" (musical), first produced in New York, N.Y., at Chernuchin Theatre, April, 1989.

Also author with M. Imbrie of plays "Raincheck," first produced in Berlin at Berlin Festival; "The Feeling Shop," first produced in New York, N.Y. at Actor's Studio; "Clearing," first produced at Huntington Theatre Workshop; and "Gino," first produced in New York, N.Y. at Journey Theatre. Also author with M. Imbrie of screenplays "Someone's Comin' Hungry," "Roll, China, Roll," "Finders Keepers," and "A Girl Like Norman Mailer."

WORK IN PROGRESS: "Nights in a Place of No Tears," a musical drama; "Probable Autumn," a two-character musical.

SIDELIGHTS: "My major effort has been directed toward creating works for the theater. I have also continued to write poems for the past twenty-seven years as acts of love and meditation, and I hope to persist in such divine madness even into the last moment of my departure.

"I write for the joy and I write for the money, in that order. Of joy there has been more than I dreamed possible; of money far, far less. I love actors and I love theatres, especially when they are bare, transfixed perhaps by one bright light, awaiting a word or a gesture or a note of music to make love alive in its many disguises.

"I write for people who want to live in the land of love, a land where we must laugh all of our laughter and cry all of our tears. What I seek from plays and books is the inspiration to make each moment of life a giving and receiving of wonder, compassion, mercy and creativity. I've lived in big cities and little towns, in New York, New Jersey, Massachusetts, Wisconsin, California, Illinois, Germany, Greece, India; I've worked as a teacher, a military policeman, a taxi driver, a journalist, a therapist with drug addicts and with schizophrenics, and in every man and woman I have ever met I have seen a completely unique universe and a potential for living life joyously and gratefully. To point at and help manifest this potential is one of the reasons I write."

SHAPP, Charles M(orris) 1906-1989

OBITUARY NOTICE: Born February 13, 1906, in New York, N.Y.; died of a heart attack, January 3, 1989, in Marbella, Spain. Educator, administrator, and author, Shapp retired in 1973 after forty years of service with the New York City school system. An assistant superintendent when he retired, Shapp previously was a teacher and principal who served primarily in the Harlem and Bronx districts. After his retirement he joined the faculty of education at Pace University. He and his wife, Martha Glauber Shapp, together wrote forty-two books for juvenile readers, including *Let's Find Out What Electricity Does, Let's Find Out about the Moon,* and *Let's Find Out about Cavemen,* as well as educational filmstrips and teaching guides.

FOR MORE INFORMATION SEE:

OBITUARIES

New York Times, January 5, 1989 (p. B-11).

SHAW, Janet 1937-
(Janet Beeler, Janet Beeler Shaw)

PERSONAL: Born September 30, 1937, in Springfield, Ill.; daughter of Russel Henry (a teacher) and Nadina (a homemaker; maiden name, Boardman) Fowler; married Thomas Beeler, August 22, 1959 (divorced); married Robert C. Shaw (a counselor), September 12, 1978; children: (first marriage) Kristin, Mark, Laura. *Education:* Stephens College, A.A., 1957; Goucher College, B.A., 1959; Cleveland State University, M.A., 1975. *Home and office:* Route 1, Box 134, Ridgeway, Wis. 53582. *Agent:* Ned Leavitt, William Morris Agency, 1350 Avenue of the Americas, New York, N.Y. 10019.

CAREER: Free-lance writer, 1959-80, 1986—; University of Wisconsin—Madison, lecturer, 1980—; Edgewood College, Madison, lecturer, 1985. Writer-in-residence, Associated Colleges of the Twin Cities, 1983; visiting writer, Florida State University, spring, 1986. Administrator for South Dakota Arts Board, 1981, Wisconsin Arts Board, 1981-83, Illinois Arts Board, 1985, National Endowment for the Arts, 1987-88. Member of Dane County Cultural Affairs Commission, 1983-86. *Member:* Phi Beta Kappa. *Awards, honors:* Short Story Award from *Mademoiselle,* 1958, for "A Day for Fishing"; *Seventeen* magazine's Poetry Contest Award, 1985, for "Conversation in Eden"; Devins Award for Poetry from the Devins

JANET SHAW

Foundation, 1978, for *Dowry;* fellow, Wisconsin Arts Board, 1981-1982; cited for Outstanding Literary Achievement by the Wisconsin Library Association, 1987, for *Taking Leave.*

WRITINGS:

JUVENILE

Meet Kirsten: An American Girl (illustrated by Renee Graef), Pleasant, 1986.
Kirsten Learns a Lesson: A School Story (illustrated by R. Graef), Pleasant, 1986.
Kirsten's Surprise: A Christmas Story (illustrated by R. Graef), Pleasant, 1986.
My Hiding Place, Salem House, 1986.
Happy Birthday, Kirsten! A Springtime Story (illustrated by R. Graef), Pleasant, 1987.
Changes for Kirsten: A Winter Story (illustrated by R. Graef), Pleasant, 1988.
Kirsten Saves the Day: A Summer Story (illustrated by R. Graef), Pleasant, 1988.
Kirsten's Keepsake Edition (six books; illustrated by R. Graef), Pleasant, 1988.

OTHER

(Under name Janet Beeler) *How to Walk on Water* (poems), Cleveland State University Poetry Forum, 1973.
(Under name Janet Beeler) *Dowry* (poems), University of Missouri Press, 1978.
(Under name Janet Beeler Shaw) *Some of the Things I Did Not Do* (short stories), University of Illinois Press, 1984.
Taking Leave (novel), Viking, 1987.

Short stories represented in anthologies, including *Prize Stories of 1960: The O. Henry Awards,* 1960; *The Mademoiselle Prize Stories,* 1975; *The Editors' Choice: New American Stories,* Bantam, 1985; *Family: Stories from the Interior,* Grey Wolf Press, 1987; *The Norton Anthology of Short Fiction,* 1988; *Stiller's Pond,* New Rivers Press, 1988; *Prime Number,* University of Illinois Press, 1988. Poetry represented in anthologies, including *Bear Crossings: An Anthology of North American Poets,* 1978; *Poems out of Wisconsin V,* 1980; *In the Middle: Ten Midwestern Women Poets,* 1985.

Contributor of stories to periodicals, including *American Voice, Atlantic, Denver Quarterly, Family Circle, Fiction Network, Indiana Review, Mademoiselle, McCall's, Milwaukee Journal, Missouri Review, Redbook, Sewanee Review, Southwest Review, Triquarterly,* and *Wisconsin Academy Review.* Contributor of poems to periodicals, including *American Poetry Review, Antaeus, Esquire, New Catholic World, New Orleans Review, Open Places, Perspective, Poet Lore,* and *Primavera.* Reader and editor, University of Illinois fiction series, 1986-88. Also writer and editor for Frank Lloyd Wright exhibition catalogue.

ADAPTATIONS:

CASSETTES

"Kirsten Learns a Lesson: A School Story," Pleasant, 1986.
"Kirsten's Surprise: A Christmas Story," Pleasant, 1986.
"Meet Kirsten: An American Girl," Pleasant, 1986.

WORK IN PROGRESS: Six novels about a contemporary girl in Seattle in which the character is a Korean-American adopted child; a novel; children's novels; short stories.

(From *Meet Kirsten* by Janet Shaw. Illustrated by Renee Graef.)

SIDELIGHTS: "In the 'American Girl' series Kirsten and her family experience the loss of their homeland and all that is familiar to them when they immigrate to the United States in 1854. In their new home on the frontier in Minnesota they search for new identities as Americans. The bond of love in their family stretches to include the new teacher, an Indian friend, and the children and adults they meet in the harsh world they've come to. These books are as unsentimental as possible about the conditions in which the new settlers find themselves.

"Kirsten is a resourceful girl with heart. She shows real courage when she saves her father in the blizzard and also makes real mistakes when she thinks she can outsmart the bears. She faces her fears and forms deep bonds of love and friendship—qualities I'd certainly wish for all of us.

"The skills in writing for children are much the same as in writing for adults: the story has to have drive and a dramatic question to be resolved; the characters must be believable and empathetic and the source for the conflict within the story; dialogue must be natural. Of course you must write in shorter sentences, but my husband pointed out to me that I write in short sentences anyway! My pleasure in writing the children's books has been to create stories I'd like my own daughters to read."

HOBBIES AND OTHER INTERESTS: Teaching children and adults, reading, gardening, biking, hiking, her dogs.

SILLITOE, Alan 1928-

PERSONAL: Born March 4, 1928, in Nottingham, England; son of Christopher Archibald (a tannery laborer) and Sylvina (a mill worker, homemaker; maiden name, Burton) Sillitoe; married Ruth Fainlight (a poet, writer, and translator), November 19, 1959; children: David Nimrod, Susan Dawn (adopted). *Education:* Left school at the age of fourteen. *Religion:* "Generally inclined towards Judaism." *Home:* c/o Savage Club, 9 Fitzmaurice Place, London SW1, England. *Agent:* Tessa Sayle, 11 Jubilee Pl., London SW3 3TE, England.

CAREER: Worked in a bicycle plant, in a plywood mill, and as a capstan-lathe operator; air traffic control assistant, 1945-46; free-lance writer, 1948—. *Military service:* Royal Air Force, wireless telegraph operator in Malaya, 1946-49. *Member:* Society of Authors, Royal Geographical Society (fellow), Writers Action Group, Savage Club. *Awards, honors:* Author's Club Prize, 1958, for *Saturday Night and Sunday Morning;* Hawthornden Prize for Literature, 1960, for *The Loneliness of the Long-Distance Runner;* honorary fellow, Manchester Polytechnic, 1977.

WRITINGS:

JUVENILE

The City Adventures of Marmalade Jim (illustrated by Shelagh McGee), Macmillan (London), 1967.
Big John and the Stars, Robson, 1977.
The Incredible Fencing Fleas, Robson, 1978.
Marmalade Jim at the Farm (illustrated by S. McGee), Robson, 1980.
Marmalade Jim and the Fox (illustrated by Tony Ross), Robson, 1984.

POEMS

Without Beer or Bread, Outposts (London), 1957.
The Rats and Other Poems, W. H. Allen, 1960.

ALAN SILLITOE

A Falling Out of Love and Other Poems, W. H. Allen, 1964.
Shaman and Other Poems, Turret Books, 1968.
Love in the Environs of Voronezh and Other Poems, Macmillan (London), 1968, Doubleday, 1969.
(Contributor) *Poems* [by] *Ruth Fainlight, Ted Hughes, Alan Sillitoe,* Rainbow Press, 1971.
Storm: New Poems, W. H. Allen, 1974.
Barbarians and Other Poems, Turret Books, 1974.
Snow on the North Side of Lucifer, W. H. Allen, 1979.
Sun Before Departure, Grafton, 1984.
Tides and Stone Walls, Grafton, 1986.

NOVELS

Saturday Night and Sunday Morning, W. H. Allen, 1958, Knopf, 1959, new edition, with an introduction by the author and commentary and notes by David Craig, Longmans, Green, 1968.
The General, W. H. Allen, 1960, Knopf, 1961, published as *Counterpoint,* Avon, 1968.
Key to the Door, W. H. Allen, 1961, Knopf, 1962.
The Death of William Posters, Knopf, 1965.
A Tree on Fire, Macmillan (London), 1967, Doubleday, 1968.
A Start in Life, W. H. Allen, 1970, Scribner, 1971.
Travels in Nihilon, W. H. Allen, 1971, Scribner, 1972.
The Flame of Life, W. H. Allen, 1974.
The Widower's Son, W. H. Allen, 1976, Harper, 1977.
The Storyteller, W. H. Allen, 1979, Simon & Schuster, 1980.
Her Victory, F. Watts, 1982.
The Lost Flying Boat, Granada, 1983, Little, Brown, 1984.
Down from the Hill, Granada, 1984.
Life Goes On (sequel to *A Start in Life*), Grafton, 1985.
Out of the Whirlpool, Harper, 1988.
The Open Door, Grafton, 1989.
Last Loves, Grafton, 1990.

(From the movie "The Loneliness of the Long-Distance Runner," starring Tom Courtenay. Copyright © by Continental Distributing Inc., 1963.)

SHORT STORIES

The Loneliness of the Long-Distance Runner, W. H. Allen, 1959, Knopf, 1960, bound with *Sanctuary* by Theodore Dreiser, and related poems, edited by Roy Bentley, Book Society of Canada, 1967.

The Ragman's Daughter and Other Stories, W. H. Allen, 1963, Knopf, 1964.

Guzman Go Home and Other Stories, Macmillan (London), 1968, Doubleday, 1969.

A Sillitoe Selection, edited by Michael Marland, Longmans, Green, 1968.

Men, Women and Children, W. H. Allen, 1973, Scribner, 1974.

The Second Chance and Other Stories, Simon & Schuster, 1981.

PLAYS

(Translator and adapter with Ruth Fainlight) Lope de Vega, *All Citizens Are Soldiers* (two-act; first produced in Stratford, England, at Theatre Royal, June 20, 1967), Macmillan (London), 1969, Dufour, 1970.

Three Plays: The Slot Machine, The Interview, Pit Strike ("The Slot Machine," first produced as "This Foreign Field," in London, England at Round House, March, 1970; "Pit Strike," produced by British Broadcasting Corporation, 1977; "The Interview," first produced in St. Martin's-in-the-Fields, England, September 16, 1976), W. H. Allen, 1978.

OTHER

Road to Volgograd (travel), Knopf, 1964.

(Author of introduction) Arnold Bennett, *Riceyman Steps,* Pan Books, 1964.

(Author of introduction) A. Bennett, *The Old Wives' Tale,* Pan Books, 1964.

Raw Material (memoir), W. H. Allen, 1972, Scribner, 1973.

Mountains and Caverns: Selected Essays, W. H. Allen, 1975.

The Saxon Shore Way (travel), Hutchinson, 1983.

Nottinghamshire (travel; illustrated with photographs by David Sillitoe), Grafton, 1987.

Author of film script "Che Guevara," 1968; author of television script "Pit Strike," BBC-TV, 1977.

ADAPTATIONS:

MOTION PICTURES

(Also author of screenplay) "Saturday Night and Sunday Morning," Continental, 1960.

(Also author of screenplay) "The Loneliness of the Long-Distance Runner," Continental, 1963.

"Counterpoint" (based on the novel *The General*), Universal, 1968.

(Also author of screenplay) "The Ragman's Daughter," Penelope, 1972.

(From the movie "Counterpoint," starring Maximillian Schell. Based on the novel *The General.*)

CASSETTES

"The Loneliness of the Long-Distance Runner," Listen for Pleasure, 1981.
"Raw Material," Books on Tape, 1984.
"The Death of William Posters," Books on Tape.
"A Start in Life," Books on Tape.
"The Widower's Son," Books on Tape.
"Her Victory," Books on Tape.

WORK IN PROGRESS: "*Leonard's War* which takes place in Nottingham between 1939 and 1945. Leonard is a widower and works on the railways as a shunter. He meets a woman who comes to live with him. He finds out that she is a prostitute, and all the battles that go on do so in the shadows of the greater military encounters of the war itself; another novel planned, *Snowstop;* a volume of my collected poems to be published by Grafton Books."

SIDELIGHTS: "As an artist I write from the centre of my experience—the experience which began immediately after I came out of my mother. Therefore, I believe that a writer is born rather than made. Yet, the making of a writer involves much observation and learning. It took me ten years to learn how to write properly, that is to say, how to find the voice that was unique to myself. I read every *important* book of world literature, and also learned French and Spanish. I read Shakespeare and the Hebrew Bible many times, because there is no such thing as an uneducated writer, even though my formal education stopped at fourteen.

"I write and rewrite every book up to eight times, the first draft, always with pen and ink. The qualities one needs are: patience, experience, imagination, pertinacity, knowledge, and absolute dedication. There is no other way. You choose either to write or to live. Observation, memory, and what experiences you have had provide the material. You aim for the highest quality of writing, but never lay it out in such a way as to make it unnecessarily difficult for the reader. The reader is finally yourself, and you must be treated with the respect you deserve.

"I often write about people who would not normally, it seems, be dealt with, those who may never actually read a book in their lives. But they are the unsung kings and queens of the world and deserve all that my art can reproduce of their anguished activities.

"Every story or novel comes out of its separate compartment of the subconscious, and by a different mechanism any poems that I write. When writing for children I am also a child, yet with an adult knowledge of the craft.

"My latest book, *Last Loves,* takes place in Malaya and is about two old soldiers who go on holiday to visit the place forty years after they had been there fighting the terrorists from 1947 to 1949."

HOBBIES AND OTHER INTERESTS: Studying cartography and collecting interesting topographical maps, travel, listening to morse code messages on short-wave radio.

FOR MORE INFORMATION SEE:

BOOKS

James Gindin, *Postwar British Fiction: New Accents and Attitudes,* University of California Press, 1962.
Charles Shapiro, editor, *Contemporary British Novelists,* Southern Illinois University Press, 1965.
John W. Aldridge, *Time to Murder and Create: The Contemporary Novel in Crisis,* McKay, 1966.
Allen Richard Penner, *Alan Sillitoe,* Twayne, 1972.
Contemporary Literary Criticism, Gale, Volume I, 1973, Volume III, 1975, Volume VI, 1976, Volume X, 1979, Volume XIX, 1981.
Authors in the News, Volume I, Gale, 1976.
Dictionary of Literary Biography, Volume 14, Gale, 1983.
F. Grellot and M. H. Valentin, *From Sidney to Sillitoe: An Introduction to English Literature,* Hachette, 1984.
Contemporary Authors Autobiography Series, Volume 2, Gale, 1985.
David Gerard, *Alan Sillitoe: A Bibliography,* Mansell/Meckler, 1988.

PERIODICALS

Times Literary Supplement, October 2, 1959, September 17, 1971 (p. 1105), November 3, 1972 (p. 1305), October 19, 1973 (p. 1269), January 4, 1980 (p. 9), January 15, 1981, January 23, 1981, October 15, 1982, November 11, 1983, June 7, 1985.
New Statesman, October 3, 1959, November 22, 1974 (p. 749), January 16, 1981 (p. 20ff).
San Francisco Chronicle, November 29, 1959, May 1, 1960.
Time, April 18, 1960.
Nation, January 27, 1969 (p. 122ff).
Books and Bookmen, June 1969 (p. 21ff), December, 1973 (p. 42ff).
Contemporary Literature, Volume 10, number 2, 1969 (p. 253ff).
Prairie Schooner, summer, 1971 (p. 178ff), winter, 1974/75 (p. 351ff).
Transatlantic Review, winter-spring, 1972 (p. 108ff).
Milwaukee Journal, November 10, 1974.
Modern Fiction Studies, summer, 1979 (p. 175ff).
Los Angeles Times, October 1, 1980, April 21, 1981.
Chicago Tribune Book World, October 26, 1980, August 31, 1981.
Washington Post Book World, October 26, 1980 (p. 4).
Washington Post, June 2, 1981, December 10, 1982.
London Review of Books, April, 1982 (p. 8ff).
Los Angeles Times Book Review, November 21, 1982.
Globe & Mail (Toronto), September 7, 1985.

SMITH, Jim 1920-

CAREER: Author and illustrator of books for children; owner of a curio shop, Salisbury, England. *Military service:* Was a Japanese prisoner of war during World War II. *Awards, honors:* Children's Choice from the International Reading Association, 1979, for *The Frog Band and Durrington Dormouse,* and 1982, for *The Frog Band and the Owlnapper.*

WRITINGS:

SELF-ILLUSTRATED

The Frog Band and the Onion Seller, Little, Brown, 1976.
The Frog Band and Durrington Dormouse, World's Work, 1977, Little, Brown, 1978.
The Frog Band and the Mystery of Lion Castle, Little, Brown, 1978.
Alphonse and the Stonehenge Mystery, World's Work, 1979, Little, Brown, 1980.
The Frog Band and the Owlnapper, Little, Brown, 1980.
Nimbus and the Crown Jewels, World's Work, 1981, Little, Brown, 1982.
Nimbus the Explorer, World's Work, 1981, Little, Brown, 1982.

STEPTO, Michele 1946-

PERSONAL: Born July 14, 1946, in Santa Monica, Calif.; daughter of Archie Patrick (an automotive parts man) and Rose Helen (a registered nurse and school nurse; maiden name, Paul) Leiss; married Robert Burns Stepto (a professor of English), June 21, 1967; children: Gabriel, Rafael. *Education:* Stanford University, B.A., 1967; San Francisco State College (now University), M.A., 1969; University of Massachusetts at Amherst, Ph.D., 1978. *Politics:* Democrat. *Religion:* None. *Home:* 80 Rimmon Rd., Woodbridge, Conn. 06525. *Office:* Department of English, Yale University, New Haven, Conn. 06520.

CAREER: Yale University, New Haven, Conn., lecturer in English, 1976—. Volunteer literacy worker. *Member:* American Studies Association, Authors Guild.

WRITINGS:

Snuggle Piggy and the Magic Blanket (juvenile; illustrated by John Himmelman), Dutton, 1987.

Contributor to *Cambridge History of American Literature.*

WORK IN PROGRESS: Research on fantasy and subversion in the teaching of children's literature.

UNTERMEYER, Bryna Ivens 1909-1985

PERSONAL: Born April 27, 1909, in New York, N.Y.; died August 30, 1985; daughter of Benjamin F. (a laywer) and Millie (Drescher) Isaacs; married Louis Untermeyer (an author and editor), July 23, 1948 (died December 19, 1977); married Emanuel E. Raices, June 9, 1979. *Education:* Hunter College (now Hunter College of the City University of New York), B.A., 1930. *Residence:* Newtown, Conn. *Agent:* McIntosh & Otis, Inc., 475 Fifth Ave., New York, N.Y. 10017.

CAREER: Old Mr. Boston Liquors, New York City, house organ editor, 1941; *She,* New York City, editor, 1942-46; *Seventeen,* New York City, fiction editor, 1946-57; free-lance writer and editor, 1957-85.

WRITINGS:

(Editor) *The Seventeen Reader,* Lippincott, 1951.
(Editor) *Nineteen from "Seventeen,"* Lippincott, 1952.
(Editor) *Stories from "Seventeen,"* Lippincott, 1954.
(Editor with husband, Louis Untermeyer) Jakob Ludwig Grimm and Wilhelm Karl Grimm, *Fairy Tales: The Complete Household Tales of Jakob and Wilhelm Grimm* (illustrated by Lucille Corcos), Limited Editions Club, 1962.
Memoir for Mrs. Sullavan, Simon & Schuster, 1966.
(Editor) *Sorry, Dear,* Golden Press, 1968.
(Editor with L. Untermeyer) *A Galaxy of Verse,* M. Evans, 1978.

EDITOR WITH L. UNTERMEYER; "GOLDEN TREASURY OF CHILDREN'S LITERATURE" SERIES

Big and Little Creatures (illustrated by Elizabeth Jones and others), Golden Press, 1961.
Beloved Tales (illustrated by Lilian Obligado and others), Golden Press, 1962.
Fun and Fancy (illustrated by L. Obligado and others), Golden Press, 1962.
Old Friends and Lasting Favorites (illustrated by William Dugan and others), Golden Press, 1962.
Wonderlands (illustrated by Joan Winslow and others), Golden Press, 1962.
Creatures All, Golden Press, 1963.
Unfamiliar Marvels (illustrated by Hans Helweg and others), Golden Press, 1963.
Creatures Wild and Tame (illustrated by Charles Harper and others), Golden Press, 1963.
Adventurers All (illustrated by Gordon Laite and others), Golden Press, 1963.
Legendary Animals (illustrated by Alice Provensen, Martin Provensen and others), Golden Press, 1963.
Tall Tales (illustrated by Charles Dolesch and others), Golden Press, 1963.
The Golden Treasury of Children's Literature, Golden Press, 1966, reissued, 1985 (published in England as *The Children's Treasury of Literature in Colour,* Hamlyn, 1966).
Animal Stories, Golden Press, 1968.
Words of Wisdom, Golden Press, 1968.
Stories and Poems for the Very Young, Golden Press, 1973.

VENTURA, Piero (Luigi) 1937-

PERSONAL: Born December 3, 1937, in Milan, Italy; son of Piero (a butcher) and Angela (a homemaker; maiden name, Bernasconi) Ventura; married Marisa Murgo (a writer), May 21, 1962; children: Marco Jacopo, Paolo and Andrea (twins). *Education:* Attended Art School of Castello Sforzesco, 1956-57, and Architecture University, 1958. *Religion:* Roman Catholic. *Home and office:* Via Domenichino 27, Milan 20149, Italy.

CAREER: Associated with Lambert (an advertising agency), 1959-65; P & T of Milan, Italy, art director, 1965-78; author and illustrator of children's books, 1975—; free-lance illustrator, 1978-82. *Military service:* Italian Army, Artillery, 1958-59; became sergeant. *Member:* Illustrators Society of Italy, Society of Illustrators (United States).

PIERO VENTURA

AWARDS, HONORS: Award of Excellence from the Society of Illustrators, and included in the American Institute of Graphic Arts Book Show, both 1976, named book of the year by American Institute of Graphic Arts, 1977, and received Art Books for Children Citation from the Brooklyn Museum and the Brooklyn Public Library, 1977, 1978, and 1979, all for *Piero Ventura's Book of Cities; Christopher Columbus* was selected one of *School Library Journal*'s Best Books for Spring, 1979; Prix de Treize from the Office Chretien du Livre, 1979, and Award from Ministero Spagnolo della Cultura, 1980, both for *Il viaggio di Colombo;* Art Citation from the Fiera of Bologna, 1980, for *I viaggi al Polo Nord;* Honorable Mention from the Biennale of Illustration Bratislava, 1983, for *Pompei; Grand Constructions* was chosen one of *School Library Journal*'s Best Books, 1983; Pier Paolo Vergerio Honor Prize, 1989, for *Venice,* and *Anna dei porci.*

WRITINGS:

SELF-ILLUSTRATED CHILDREN'S BOOKS, EXCEPT AS INDICATED

Piero Ventura's Book of Cities, Random House, 1975.
The Magic Well, Random House, 1976.
(With wife, Marisa Ventura) *The Painter's Trick,* Random House, 1977.
L'uomo a cavallo, Mondadori, 1980, published as *Man and the Horse* (young adult), Putnam, 1982.
I grandi pittori, Mondadori, 1983, translation by Geoffrey Culverwell, published as *Great Painters,* Putnam, 1984.
Com'era una volta, Mondadori, 1986, published as *There Once Was a Time,* Putnam, 1986.
Journey to Egypt, Viking, 1986.
Anna dei porci (title means "Anne of the Swines"), Mondadori, 1987.
Venice: Birth of a City, Putnam, 1988.
Michelangelo's World, Putnam, 1989.
Great Composers, Mondadori, 1988, Putnam, 1989.

ILLUSTRATOR

Guido Sperandio, *Vanuk, Vanuk,* translation by Jane Murgo, Doubleday, 1973.
Gladys Yessayan Cretan, *Ten Brothers with Camels,* Golden Press, 1975.

Canaletto has just finished The Grand Canal and the Bembo Palace, a scene from mid-eighteenth-century Venice. (From *Great Painters* by Piero Ventura. Illustrated by the author.)

Stories from the Bible, Mondadori, 1989.

ILLUSTRATOR; ALL WRITTEN BY G. P. CESERANI

Il viaggio di Colombo, Mondadori, 1977, published as *Christopher Columbus,* Random House, 1978.
Il viaggio di Marco Polo, Mondadori, 1977, published as *Marco Polo,* Putnam, 1982.
Il viaggi di Cook (title means "The Voyages of Cook"), Mondadori, 1978.
Il viaggio di Livingstone, Mondadori, 1978, published in England as *The Travels of Livingstone,* Kestrel, 1979.
I viaggi al Polo Nord (title means "The Voyages to the North Pole"), Mondadori, 1979.
Il viaggio di Magellano (title means "The Voyage of Magellan"), Mondadori, 1979.
Atlante vivo del mare (title means "Great Book of the Sea"), Mondadori, 1979.
Un anno nel bosco (title means "A Year of the Wood"), Mondadori, 1980.
La rivolta dei cinghiali, Mondadori, 1981.
Le grandi costruzioni, Mondadori, 1983, published as *Grand Constructions,* Putnam, 1983.

ILLUSTRATOR; "LA SCOPERTA DI UN MONDO" (TITLE MEANS "IN SEARCH OF" SERIES; ALL WRITTEN BY GIAN P. CESERANI

La scoperta di un mondo: Troia, Mondadori, 1981, translated by Pamela Swinglehurst, published as *In Search of Troy,* Silver, 1985.
La scoperta di un mondo: I Maya, Mondadori, 1982.
La scoperta di un mondo: Tutankhamon, Mondadori, 1983, translated by P. Swinglehurst, published as *In Search of Tutankhamun,* Silver, 1985.
La scoperta di un mondo: Pompei, Mondadori, 1983.
La scoperta di un mondo: Creta, Mondadori, 1984, translation by Michael Shaw, published as *In Search of Ancient Crete,* Silver, 1985.

SIDELIGHTS: Born on December 3, 1937, in Milan, Italy. A free-lance illustrator since 1978, Ventura has won reviewers' praise as an author/illustrator of books for children. As *Publishers Weekly* noted: "Precision plus imagination (to say nothing of an acute sense of color) are the hallmarks of . . . [his] works."

Ventura gained immediate attention with his first book, *Piero Ventura's Book of Cities,* which presented an international selection of well-known cities and towns. "In recreating scenes from cities that I have visited and tried to describe to my sons in words and sketches, I should like to ask a certain artist's license. These illustrations are not exact reproductions—a camera could do that better than I! They are instead an attempt to combine the special elements and colorful impressions that made each city a unique experience for me."[1]

The artist takes his young readers on a trip around the world as he explores the uniqueness of places like London, Moscow, New York, Paris, Tokyo, Rome, and more. "The overall effect of so many city sights and people, even if rose-colored, is exhilarating," observed New York Times Book Review. "Precise, intricate drawings," added *Booklist,* "feature an array of bright colors and an amazing variety of life-goes-on details."

Ventura displayed the same adeptness for detail in his next book, *The Magic Well,* described by *Horn Book* as "a marvelously comic fantasy in picture-book form . . . imbued with typically

The Beatles arrive in their yellow Rolls-Royce at Buckingham Palace to receive honors from the Queen of England. (From *Great Composers* by Piero Ventura. Illustrated by the author.)

European satire.'' It is a fantasy for children set in a medieval village.

Another book for children followed, *The Painter's Trick.* Written with his artist/wife Marisa, the book is a comic tale about vanity and greed. Jon C. Stott, in a review for *World of Children's Books,* called the illustrations ''accurate in both detail and mood in depiction of medieval life. The cartoon-like faces capture character, and the added element of a duck who is an onlooker in nearly every picture seems to express the animal's wonderment over the strange ways of humankind.''

For young adults and up, Ventura wrote and illustrated *Man and the Horse,* a history of the relationship that has existed from cave days to modern times. *Publishers Weekly* commended the ''smooth, readily comprehended writing'' and the paintings that ''are hard to surpass in grandeur, beauty and animation.'' Among his other works for children is *Great Painters* in which he creates what *School Library Journal* called ''an unusual dimension'' as he combines his own paintings with reproductions of master artists. ''A wealth of accurate material is presented,'' added the same reviewer, ''in a readable and spirited style.''

Ventura's nonfiction includes biographies of popular figures, famous archaeologists and their discoveries, and cultural or historical looks at cities, architecture, and Western civilization. *There Once Was a Time,* for instance, gives readers information about how common people lived during various historical periods. In 150 heavily illustrated pages, Ventura explains the history of Western civilization, which he organizes into eight eras. ''In history books we read about wars and battles, peoples and kings, great artists, and famous cities. But we rarely hear about the details that make these things seem real—what people wore, how they traveled, where they lived, and how they earned a living. If we had a more complete picture, perhaps we would be able to understand better why things happened the way they did, and what influenced leaders in making their decisions.

"Imagine that history is like a giant knapsack that could be carried around. Each period of time, group of people, or place on the globe could be taken out and laid on the table. This is what this book is all about—a sample of the stories history has to offer, waiting for the reader to choose.

"Each chapter covers nine aspects of a particular era, which can be read together for an overview of how life was at the time. Or the reader can choose particular subjects such as society, fashion, art, and agriculture, and look at how they differ over time and how important they were at every stage in history. This book can, therefore, be read in two ways: first as a guide to different periods in history, and second as an introduction to various aspects of life through the ages."[2]

FOOTNOTE SOURCES

[1]Piero Ventura, "Author's Note," *Piero Ventura's Book of Cities,* Random House, 1975.

[2]P. Ventura, "Introduction," *There Once Was a Time,* Putnam, 1986.

FOR MORE INFORMATION SEE:

Martha E. Ward and Dorothy A. Marquardt, *Illustrators of Books for Young People,* Scarecrow, 1975.

Bookbird, number 2, 1986 (p. 59).

VINCENT, Gabrielle

PERSONAL: Born in Brussels, Belgium. *Home:* Brussels, Belgium.

CAREER: Illustrator and author of children's books, 1980—. *Awards, honors: Ernest and Celestine, Ernest and Celestine's Picnic,* and *Smile, Ernest and Celestine* were all named *School Library Journal*'s Best Books, 1982; *Smile, Ernest and Celestine* was selected one of *New York Times* Best Illustrated Children's Books of the Year, 1982; *Breakfast Time, Ernest and Celestine,* and *Ernest and Celestine's Patchwork Quilt* were each selected one of Child Study Association of America's Children's Books of the Year, 1986.

GABRIELLE VINCENT

WRITINGS:

SELF-ILLUSTRATED CHILDREN'S BOOKS IN ENGLISH TRANSLATION

Ernest and Celestine (ALA Notable Book), Greenwillow, 1982, large print edition, 1982.

Bravo, Ernest and Celestine!, Greenwillow, 1982, large print edition, 1982.

Ernest and Celestine's Picnic (ALA Notable Book), Greenwillow, 1982.

Smile, Ernest and Celestine (ALA Notable Book), Greenwillow, 1982.

Merry Christmas, Ernest and Celestine, Greenwillow, 1984, large print edition, 1984.

Ernest and Celestine's Patchwork Quilt, Greenwillow, 1985.

Breakfast Time, Ernest and Celestine, Greenwillow, 1985.

Where Are You, Ernest and Celestine?, Greenwillow, 1986.

Feel Better, Ernest!, Greenwillow, 1988.

Ernest and Celestine at the Circus, Greenwillow, 1989.

ADAPTATIONS:

"Ernest and Celestine's Picnic" (filmstrip with cassette), Weston Woods, 1984.

"Ernest and Celestine" (filmstrip), Weston Woods.

Ernest and Celestine is available in Braille.

SIDELIGHTS: Vincent, a painter, illustrator, and author, decided as a child that she would be an artist, but did not pursue that career until 1980. In 1981 her characters Ernest and Celestine were presented at the Bologna Book Fair, and the bear and mouse have been popular in Europe ever since. Vincent's books are published in French by the Belgian publisher Duculot, and have been translated and published in at least a dozen other countries as well.

FOR MORE INFORMATION SEE:

New York Times Book Review, March 30, 1986.

Children's Literature Review, Volume 13, Gale, 1987.

WACHTER, Oralee (Roberts) 1935-

PERSONAL: Born April 16, 1935, in Los Angeles, Calif.; daughter of Bob and Florence G. (Lederer) Roberts; married Mark R. Wachter, August 12, 1955; children: Stephen, Paul, Beth. *Education:* University of California, B.A., 1958; San Francisco State University, M.A., 1978. *Office:* 74 Varick St., New York, N.Y. 10013.

CAREER: Brandeis Day School, San Francisco, Calif., director of general education, 1965-67; University of California, Berkeley, extension instructor, 1969-72; Berkeley Unified Schools, Berkeley, Calif., communications specialist, 1969-75; O.D.N. Productions, Inc., president and creative director of films, 1974—; California Institution for Women, Frontera, Calif., instructor 1975; author. *Member:* Authors Guild, New York Women in Film.

WRITINGS:

No More Secrets for Me (juvenile; with parents' guide; illustrated by Jane Aaron), Little, Brown, 1983, published in England (illustrated by Caroline Binch), Puffin, 1986.
Close to Home (juvenile; illustrated by J. Aaron), Scholastic, 1986.
Sex, Drugs, and AIDS (young adult), Bantam, 1987.

Also author of *Acquaintance Rape Prevention,* 1978; *Spouse Abuse Handbook,* 1981; *The Abusive Partner,* 1982; and *Talking Helps,* 1983.

FOR MORE INFORMATION SEE:

Los Angeles Times Book Review, August 9, 1987.

WALKER, Mary Alexander 1927-

PERSONAL: Born September 24, 1927, in Beaumont, Tex.; daughter of James Cosper (a mechanic and pilot) and Mary Helen (a painter; maiden name, Johnson) Alexander; married Tom Ross Walker (a physician), December 23, 1952; children: Timothy Ross, Mark Thomas, Miles Stephen. *Education:* Lamar Technological College, A.A., 1947; Texas Woman's University, B.A., 1950; San Francisco State University, M.A., 1981; further graduate study at Academy of Art College, San Francisco. *Home:* 22 Corte Lodato, Greenbrae, Calif. 94904. *Agent:* Anita Diamant Literary Agency, 310 Madison Ave., New York, N.Y. 10017. *Office:* 59 Crescente, Bolinas, Calif. 94924.

CAREER: Teacher at public schools in Texas, Washington, Ohio, Arkansas, and Iowa, 1947-57; Marin Country Day School, Corte Madera, Calif., teacher, 1967-68; Dominican College, San Rafael, part-time instructor in writing, 1972-80, director of writer's conference, 1978-80; A Joy Forever (design business), San Rafael, Calif., owner, 1973-76. Instructor of class on writing children's literature at Lone Mountain College, San Francisco, Calif., spring, 1976, and Indian Valley College, Novato, Calif., fall, 1978; lecturer in writing, University of San Francisco, 1983-87. *Member:* American Association of University Women, Society of Children's Book Writers, Mystery Writers of America, American PEN, Western Writers of America.

AWARDS, HONORS: First prize from the Pacific Northwest Writers Conference, 1971, for story "Les Ailes du Papillon," 1973, for story "Brimstone," and 1979, for *To Catch a Zombie; Weekly Reader* Fellowship for Bread Loaf Writers Conference, 1972; Dorothy Canfield Fisher Award Nomination from the Vermont State Parent Teachers' Association and the State Department of Libraries, 1972, for *The Year of the Cafeteria;* Award from Santa Rosa Actors' Theatre, 1977, for adaptation of "Ozma and the Nome King's Palace"; *To Catch a Zombi* was selected one of New York Public Library's Books for the Teen Age, 1980, 1981, and 1982, and *Maggot,* 1981; Arizona Authors Award, 1985, for story "The Bicycle Lock"; juror for Texas Circuit for Austin Author's Award, 1986, and for Edgar Allan Poe Juvenile Awards of the Mystery Writers of America, 1987; Distinguished Alumnae Award from Texas Woman's University, 1988.

MARY ALEXANDER WALKER

WRITINGS:

JUVENILE

The Year of the Cafeteria, Bobbs-Merrill, 1971, reissued as *Bread and Roses,* Grosset, 1972.
To Catch a Zombi, Atheneum, 1979.
Maggot, Atheneum, 1980.
Brad's Box, Atheneum, 1988.
Scathach and Maeve's Daughters, Atheneum, in press.

OTHER

(With Peggy Ford) "Ozma and the Nome King's Palace" (musical play for children; adaptation), first produced in San Leandro, Calif. at Lilliput Theatre, 1982.
(With P. Ford) "Princess with Twenty-eight Heads" (adaptation), first produced at Lilliput Theatre, 1983-84.
(With P. Ford) "The Pied Piper" (adaptation), first produced at Lilliput Theatre, 1983-84.

Work represented in anthologies, including *Awards,* edited by William K. Durr, Rita M. Beau, and others, Houghton, 1981. Author of "College Column," *Beaumont Journal,* 1943-47, and "Children and Books," *Pacific Sun,* 1965. Contributor of stories, articles, and reviews to magazines and newspapers, including *American Girl, In,* and *Extension.*

WORK IN PROGRESS: Screenplays based on her books; research on Celtic legends and designs, early medicine in America, and the history of law in the United States.

SIDELIGHTS: "As a child, I lived with my grandmother on the Gulf Coast of Texas. I think that fruitful and loving experience had much to do with my writing of *The Year of the Cafeteria.* Though the characters in *Year* are black, and we are Caucasian, my feeling is that we are all very similar under the skin. The black grandmother in *Year* is not my grandmother and I am not Azure, but our relationship helped me understand how those two characters might feel about each other. Ray John, another character in *Year* was based on one of my sons who excelled in track and is a very heartful person, as Ray John is.

"At the time *The Year of the Cafeteria* was written, I did not find many books which showed black youngsters as *winners.* I wanted to have a character who was a real winner as I knew some splendid talented and successful black children. I wanted to make Azure that kind of person.

"As for *Maggot,* I had two points of inspiration. One was my genuine interest in dance and the other was a young girl I knew who was an actress. The actress part of her *never turned off.* She worked at it every moment no matter where she was—in restaurants, at school, wherever. Watching her, often outrageous as she was, the character of a dancer who is totally immersed in her art became a challenge to me.

"I often use my own experiences or those of my friends or family as happenings in my books. I find it easier to understand the motives of actions in that way rather than writing about people whose actions or lifestyles are a puzzle. I also write about places I have been or lived. That is true of *Brad's Box.* One of my sons was born in Iowa, and I taught school there. I had never lived where snow fell and the experience had a profound effect on me. I thought Iowa, which I considered the heartland, had a different flavor from Texas.

I found myself staring at a young man with a determined jaw. (Jacket illustration by Phyllis Tarlow from *Brad's Box* by Mary Alexander Walker.)

"I like research and love reading history. There is so much of it and there seems to be a new story popping up with every twist and turn through the centuries. When I read the history of early Louisiana, the story of Vance in *To Catch a Zombi* came out of it. *The Scathach and Maeve's Daughters,* which I have just finished, covers a thousand years from the eighth century almost to the year 2000. The most difficult part was choosing from the many ideas that were available. I feel I will never run out of characters and stories as long as humans and their events continue to fascinate me."

HOBBIES AND OTHER INTERESTS: Tennis, visual and three-dimensional arts.

FOR MORE INFORMATION SEE:

Wilson Library Bulletin, February, 1981.

WHALLEY, Joyce Irene 1923-

PERSONAL: Born August 5, 1923, in Essex, England; daughter of Ernest A. (in government service) and Ellen Louise (a homemaker; maiden name, Brown) Whalley. *Education:* University of Wales, B.A. (with honors), 1944; University of London, diploma in librarianship, 1949; attended Warburg Institute, London, 1952-56. *Religion:* Church of England. *Home:* High Banks, 26 Stoneborough Lane, Budleigh Salterton, Devon EX9 6HL, England.

CAREER: Victoria and Albert Museum, London, England, assistant keeper of library, 1950-81. *Military service:* British Army, 1945- 47. *Member:* Art Libraries Society, National Art Collections Fund, National Trust (life member), Children's Books History Society, Beatrix Potter Society (founding member), Royal Society for the Protection of Birds, Inland Waterways Association.

WRITINGS:

English Handwriting, 1540-1843, H.M.S.O., 1969.

Cobwebs to Catch Flies: Illustrated Books for the Nursery and Schoolroom, 1700-1900, University of California Press, 1974.

Writing Implements and Accessories, David & Charles, 1975.

The Pen's Excellencie: Calligraphy in Western Europe and America, Pentelic, 1980.

(Commentary with Wynne Bartlett) *Facsimile of Beatrix Potter's Derwentwater Sketch Book,* Warne, 1984.

(Compiler with Anne Hobbs) *Catalogue of Beatrix Potter Collections of the Victoria and Albert Museum,* Victoria and Albert Museum/Warne, 1985.

(With Judy Taylor, A. Hobbs, and Elizabeth Battrick) *Beatrix Potter, 1866-1943: The Artist and Her World,* National Trust/Warne, 1987.

(With W. Bartlett) *Beatrix Potter's Derwentwater,* Warne, 1988.

(With Tessa Rose Chester) *The Bright Streams: A History of Children's Book Illustration,* Victoria and Albert Museum/John Murray, 1988, published in the United States as *A History of Children's Book Illustration,* Godine, 1990.

(Contributor) *Catalogue of the Pepys Library at Magdalene College, Cambridge,* Volume IV: *Music, Maps, Calligraphy,* Boydell & Brewer, 1989.

JOYCE IRENE WHALLEY

Contributor of articles and reviews to journals, including *Times Literary Supplement, Journal of Librarianship,* and *Beatrix Potter Society Newsletter.*

WORK IN PROGRESS: A Victorian Keepsake of Flowers and *The Grotesque Alphabet of Marcus van Ypres,* both with the Victoria and Albert Museum.

SIDELIGHTS: "Handwriting and writing implements have for so long been accepted as everyday things that many people have been surprised to find that even handwriting has a history. It is, however, something that everyone does, even if only in signing his name. But because everyone can do it and because it needs little equipment, calligraphy, or the art of fine writing, has become very popular in recent years; some of my publications have intended to provide patterns for would-be exponents as well as indicating the long tradition of fine writing in western Europe and in America. Equally interesting, historically, has been the shared heritage of children's books, the memory of which often remains with people throughout their lives; some of my books have, therefore, dealt with the background to this aspect of early reading among western people.

"Most of my publications have been commissioned as a result of my work at the Victoria and Albert Museum, the national art library where I was in charge of manuscripts and illustrated books of all periods and countries. As an art historian, my travels are inevitably art oriented.

"My work in recent years has been dominated by Beatrix Potter. As a founding member of the Beatrix Potter Society I have made international contacts, half our members coming from the United States, others from Japan, Canada, and Australia. I have also been involved in several books and a major exhibition on aspects of the life and work of this author/artist. Her popularity among children of all ages and countries shows no sign of diminishing and the increasing knowledge about Beatrix Potter and her work brings together people with a variety of different interests, according to whether they think of her as a writer, illustrator, natural historian, diarist, farmer or conservationist. The feedback on the use of her books in schools and among the young shows that good writing and illustration do not date."

HOBBIES AND OTHER INTERESTS: Walking in and exploring the countryside, birdwatching, book and print collecting (especially early children's books), looking at old buildings.

WILLIS, Jeanne (Mary) 1959-

PERSONAL: Born May 11, 1959, in St. Albans, Hertfordshire, England; daughter of David Alfred (a language teacher) and Dorothy Hilda Celia (a teacher of domestic science; maiden name, Avger) Willis; married Ian James Wilcock (an animator), May 26, 1989. *Education:* Watford College of Art, Diploma in Advertising Writing, 1979. *Politics:* "I don't support any of the parties." *Religion:* "I have my own beliefs." *Home:* 63 Crouch Hill, London N.4, England. *Office:* Creative Department, Young & Rubicam Ltd., Greater London House, Hampstead Rd., London N.W.1, England.

CAREER: Doyle, Dane, Bernbach, London, England, advertising copywriter, 1979-81; Young & Rubicam Ltd., London, senior writer, group head, and member of board of directors, 1981—. *Member:* British Herpetological Association. *Awards, honors: The Monster Bed* was named one of *Redbook*'s Top Ten Children's Picture Books, 1987; Gold Clio Award, 1988, for press advertisement for Mansfield Clothes; D & AD Award for excellence in advertising.

WRITINGS:

JUVENILE

The Tale of Georgie Grub (illustrated by Margaret Chamberlain), Andersen Press, 1981, Holt, 1982.

The Tale of Fearsome Fritz (illustrated by M. Chamberlain), Andersen Press, 1982, Holt, 1983.

"The humans will get me," cried Dennis. (From *The Monster Bed* by Jeanne Willis. Illustrated by Susan Varley.)

The Tale of Mucky Mabel (illustrated by M. Chamberlain), Andersen Press, 1984.
The Monster Bed (illustrated by Susan Varley), Andersen Press, 1986, Lothrop, 1987.
The Long, Blue Blazer (illustrated by S. Varley), Andersen Press, 1987, Dutton, 1988.
Earthlets: As Explained by Professor Xargle (illustrated by Tony Ross), Dutton, 1989.
Dr. Xargle's Book of Earthhounds (illustrated by T. Ross), Anderson Press, 1989.
Dr. Xargle's Book of Earthtiggers (illustrated by T. Ross), Anderson Press, 1990.

SIDELIGHTS: "I had a very vivid imagination as a child. I think I felt everything deeply, and in many respects that was good. My happiness, my excitements seemed to be bigger emotions than other children felt. The bad side of the coin is obvious: deep hurt, dreadful fears. Fear is the downside of having an active imagination. Because I was not confidently articulate, I exorcised these intense feelings on paper. I still do. One day somebody pointed out that such things were commercially viable, so they found their way into stories. One day I shall publish my poetry—my adult poetry.

"In the meantime, I have to go and feed my toads. Reptiles and amphibians are dear to my heart. D. H. Lawrence sums it up in 'Lizard': 'If men were as much men as lizards are lizards, they'd be worth looking at.'

"I grew up in a very safe, suburban environment. I went to a wonderful school which had a huge wheatfield growing next to our playground. I was a useless mathematician, but was one of the first to read and write creatively. My grandparents still have several of my 'books,' some poetry which I wrote and stitched together with cotton. I illustrated them with felt pen or with my John Bull printing outfit. When I was nine, my sister and I produced a 'comic' for five of the neighbor kids. Everything was handwritten on cartridge paper. (My dad was in charge of the stationery cupboard at school!) My sister did most of the illustrations. We had drawing competitions. The kids used wax crayons and we were able to 'print' these using an ingenious method with a warm kitchen spoon.

"My other key interests apart from writing were sports and animals. At the grand age of ten, I was made Blue Team captain and I won every race on sports day. I used to run and high and long jump for the county.

"I belonged to the World Wildlife Guard (now the Worldwide Guard for Wildlife) and had a bedroom full of strange creatures—locusts, stick insects, newts, caterpillars, etc. The fascination with these beasts has remained with me all my life. Indeed when I got married our blessing was held in the Aquarium at the London Zoo in front of the shark tank.

"At senior school, I was still very keen on English, biology, and sport. I became quite a good gymnast, but by the fifth year I had become the wrong shape to continue on. I still sprinted for the county—one hundred or two hundred yards. I am no good at long distance—I think that's why I'm so slow in writing the first novel. I'm good for short bursts. That's why I suppose I ended up writing children's stories—plus the fact that as I am a professional copywriter, the discipline of having to get an idea across in thirty seconds comes into play.

"I think the ideas for my books are usually based on fear or mystery. Fear, perhaps, comes out most strongly in *The Monster Bed*. I was terrified of the dark as a child and still am. I check under the bed for monsters, you never know.

"The 'Dr. Xargle's' series is simply the result of realizing how absurd human and animal behaviour is, and also a desire to believe in 'the alien.' I'm sure they exist. In fact, I'm sure they're here already. I often get the feeling I'm on the wrong planet, so perhaps I'm one.

"*The Long, Blue Blazer* is about an alien who is very lonely on planet Earth. I think a lot of children can identify with that loneliness. Childhood is so confusing. I think I may have taken that confusion into my adulthood. Writing is an excellent purge. I do not do it wittingly or deliberately. I cannot sit down and say, 'Now I will write a book.' The books arrive in my head when they're ready, sometimes they write themselves. I did start a novel, but suddenly the characters started to misbehave and I lost control of them. It was quite frightening, it was a little like dabbling with the occult. If they were alter-ego's, then they were better destroyed. I didn't want to be a part of their world."

WILSON, Jacqueline 1945-

PERSONAL: Born December 17, 1945, in Bath, England; daughter of Harry Albert (a civil servant) and Margaret (a local government officer; maiden name, Clibbens) Aitken; married William Millar Wilson (a police superintendent), August 28, 1965; children: Emma Fiona. *Home:* 1B Beaufort Rd., Kingston-on-Thames, Surrey KT1 2TH, England. *Agent:* Gina and Murray Pollinger, 4 Garrick St., London WCZE 9BH, England.

CAREER: Journalist, free-lance magazine writer, and author of books and radio plays. Employed by D. C. Thomsons, Dundee, Scotland, 1963-65. *Awards, honors:* Young Observer/Rank Organization Fiction Prize Runner-up, 1982, for *Nobody's Perfect*, and 1984, for *The Other Side*.

WRITINGS:

JUVENILE

Nobody's Perfect, Oxford University Press, 1982.
Waiting for the Sky to Fall, Oxford University Press, 1983.
The Other Side, Oxford University Press, 1984.
The School Trip (illustrated by Sally Holmes), Hamilton, 1984.
The Killer Tadpole, Hamilton, 1984.
How to Survive Summer Camp (illustrated by Bob Dewar), Oxford University Press, 1985.
Amber, Oxford University Press, 1986.
The Monster in the Cupboard, Blackie Bear Cubs, 1986.
Glubbslyme (illustrated by Jane Cope), Oxford University Press, 1987.
The Power of the Shade, Oxford University Press, 1987.
This Girl, Oxford University Press, 1988.
Falling Apart, Oxford University Press, 1989.
Is There Anybody There? Armada, 1990, Book One: *Spirit Raising*, Book Two: *Crystal Gazing*.

"STEVIE DAY" SERIES

Supersleuth, Armada, 1987.
Lonelyhearts, Armada, 1987.
Rat Race, Armada, 1988.
Vampire, Armada, 1988, large print edition, Chivers Press, 1989.
The Party in the Lift, Blackie, 1989.
The Left-Outs, Blackie, 1989.

JACQUELINE WILSON

ADULT SUSPENSE NOVELS

Hide and Seek, Macmillan (London), 1972, Doubleday, 1973.
Truth or Dare, Doubleday, 1973.
(Contributor) Virginia Whitaker, editor, *Winter's Crimes,* Macmillan (London), 1973.
Snap, Macmillan (London), 1974.
Let's Pretend, Macmillan (London), 1976.
Making Hate, Macmillan (London), 1977, St. Martin's, 1978.

Also author of radio plays "Are You Listening," "It's Disgusting at Your Age," and "Ask a Silly Question," British Broadcasting Corp. (BBC), 1982-84.

SIDELIGHTS: "I wrote my first novel when I was nine years old. It was called 'Meet the Maggots' and it had a lot of chapters and nearly filled a school exercise book so I felt I'd written an impressive tome. The Maggots were a very large and lively family (I was a very solitary only child). I can't remember all the brothers and sisters now, but I know the eldest Maggot girl was a bouncy blonde who bossed everyone around. My favourite character was the second sister who was plain and sharp and imaginative. Then there was a soft shy dreamy sister and an angelic looking baby brother who behaved like a demon and a handful of other assorted siblings who have now slipped my memory.

"I went on writing throughout my childhood, scribbling in shiney red sixpenny notebooks (I didn't dare filch any more from school). Each story generally fizzled out after a few chapters, but I suppose it was all good practise. By the time I was seventeen I was earning my own living by writing short stories for teenage magazines. I was thrilled to see my stories in print (though the magazine editors cut out my finest descriptive passages and pared each character down to a sad stereotype) but it wasn't the sort of fiction I really wanted to write. I wasn't interested in the glossy fantasy world of the magazines. I wanted to write about young people and their problems but I didn't want to pretend there were the easy solutions offered in the magazine stories.

"I wrote five crime novels for adults but each one had a child as one of the major characters, and I knew I didn't really want to write about crime at all, I wanted to write about children. One day I read a newspaper article about adopted children trying to trace their real mothers and I started wondering how it would feel not to have any idea what your own mother is like. I thought someone had already written a book with that theme, so I tried to change the idea around a bit. I started thinking about a girl who searches for her unknown father—and I started writing my first book for young people, *Nobody's Perfect.* Sandra wants to be a writer and her early writing attempts are rather similar to my own. But of course Sandra isn't me, she's an entirely imaginary character—although when I get letters about that book people often assume I'm 'Sandra' grown-up.

"I think it's less likely anyone confuses me with Katherine, the girl in my next novel *Waiting for the Sky to Fall,* as she's very highly gifted and expected to get outstanding results in all her exams. No one ever expected me to do likewise! Even Katherine finds these expectations a great strain and gets very spiteful and irritable and says hurtful things. I don't see why heroines always have to be perfectly behaved. The one thing I do have in common with Katherine is a great weakness for pretend games. When I was young I used to keep quiet about my imaginary games to my friends because I knew they'd think I was crazy—some of them seemed to think that anyway—but now that I'm grown up and a writer, I can play pretend games all the time so long as I write them down on paper and turn them into novels.

"I used to spend hours as a child lying in bed staring at the ceiling, willing myself to levitate right up out of my blankets until I hovered in thin air. I never had any success of course—but in my book, *The Other Side,* Alison finds she can levitate. She learns how to fly around her bedroom, out of the window and around the neighbourhood—eventually into another dimension altogether. Or is it all a dream or delusion because Alison is

"What do you want?" Rebecca asked gruffly. (From *Glubbslyme* by Jacqueline Wilson. Illustrated by Jane Cope.)

going through such a tough time since her parents divorced? The book's called *The Other Side* because Alison learns the other side of her parents' situation, and she also has occult experiences on the 'Other Side.'

"I don't just write books. I read them compulsively and I collect books with manic enthusiasm. I have 10,000 volumes in huge untidy piles all over our very small house. One of my favorite haunts is Hay-On-Wye in the Black Mountains—it has twenty second-hand bookshops. It also has an itinerant population of hippies camping in the mountains. I watched the hippy children wandering around Hay, looking dirty and decorative, and I wondered what it would be like to know no other way of life. What if a hippy teenager wanted to rebel? What if she longed for a conventional clean ordinary sort of life, with the chain-store clothes and constant hot water most teenagers take for granted. So I invented a hippy heroine for my next book *Amber*.

"Sometimes I see real people who remind me of my own inventions. I once saw a very romantic looking busker playing a penny whistle who was exactly the way I imagined Davie, the man who's such a gentle friend to Amber. It gives me an odd little shiver because it's almost like magic. In my book *The Power of the Shade,* May starts to believe she really can make magic when her friend Selina initiates her into witchcraft. Selina is probably only playing games with her, but May believes in her new powers and is terrified. She spends a long time staring at a Salvator Rosa painting of witches in the National Gallery in London. I love putting my favourite galleries and museums and bookshops into my novels. One of my stories for much younger children *The School Trip* is actually set in the National Gallery and I sometimes wonder if any children follow Lisa's frantic flight through the gallery when she gets lost.

"It's fun to have a change writing for young children. I've got a boys' only cast in *The Killer Tadpole,* which contains the most disgusting scene in all my books: imagine eating frog spawn! *The Monster in the Cupboard* is about two sisters frightened by an imaginary lurking beast in the cupboard under the stairs—I had many similar fears as a child. But what I hated most as a little girl was having to join in at school, especially sporty games. I wrote *How to Survive Summer Camp* to comfort all the shy subversive children who find the whole idea of summer camp sheer hell. I touch on the witchcraft theme again in *Glubbslyme,* who is a long-lived talking toad who was once a witch's familiar. I've tried to make him behave like a seventeenth-century character who is utterly appalled by the noisy new inventions of the modern world.

"I like to write different types of books too. The 'Stevie Day' series are quick easy reads about a funny fourteen-year-old feminist who wants to be a detective. Stevie is far bolder and bossier than I'd ever dare to be, and it's wonderfully liberating for me when I'm writing one of her adventures.

"It's strange the way I identify with all my different girls. If I were looking for a mother's helper I'd never risk employing a dreamy difficult girl like Coral in *This Girl,* but all the time I was writing the book I felt I *was* Coral and I first liked and then loathed the family she works for. And I loved Deb too, of course. There's a special block of flats for young single parents across the way from me and I see lots of Debs trailing up and down the road with their prams.

"Coral and I happily share a great interest in all things Victorian—which came in handy for the book *Is There Anybody There?,* a time-slip novel about a Victorian girl who materialises during an amateur seance and keeps taking over her modern counterpart Vicky Smith. She's a plain sharp imaginative girl, part of a large and lively family. She's got a bossy bouncy elder sister, a shy soft dreamy younger sister, and an angelic looking brother who behaves like a demon . . . . Does that sound familiar? It looks as if I've come full circle!"

HOBBIES AND OTHER INTERESTS: Browsing in bookshops, visiting art galleries, watching the deer in the park, afternoon tea, walking along the riverside at sunset, chatting with friends in the local pub.

FOR MORE INFORMATION SEE:

Times Literary Supplement, July 23, 1982.

WINKS, Robin W(illiam) 1930-

PERSONAL: Born December 5, 1930, in West Lafayette, Ind.; son of Evert M. (a teacher and coach) and Jewell (a teacher and administrator; maiden name, Sampson) Winks; married Avril Flockton (a social coordinator and fellowship administrator), September 27, 1952; children: Honor Leigh, Eliot Myles. *Education:* University of Colorado, B.A. (magna cum laude), 1952, M.A., 1953; University of New Zealand, M.A., 1952; Johns Hopkins University, Ph.D. (with distinction), 1957. *Home:* 125 High St., New Haven, Conn. 06510. *Agent:* Julian S. Bach, Jr., Julian Bach Literary Agency, 747 Third Ave., New York, N.Y. 10017. *Office:* Department of History, Yale University, New Haven, Conn. 06520.

CAREER: University of Colorado, Boulder, instructor, 1953; Connecticut College for Women (now Connecticut College), New London, instructor, 1956-57; Yale University, New Haven, Conn., instructor, 1957, assistant professor, 1958-60, associate professor, 1960-67, professor of history, 1967—, master of Berkeley College, 1977-90, Randolph Townsend Jr. Professor, 1984, John B. Madden Master, 1989. Lecturer. Visiting professor, University of Alberta, Edmonton, University of Malaya, University of London, University of Washington, Victoria University (British Columbia), American University (Beirut), University of Sydney, Oxford University, and University of Stellenbosch (South Africa). Cultural attache, American Embassy, London, England, 1969-71. Past chairman, U.S. National Park System Advisory Board; trustee, National Parks and Conservation Association. Director of Yale conference on the teaching of the social studies. Advisor, Department of State, U.S. Information Agency, National Park Sevice.

MEMBER: American Historical Association, Organization of American Historians, Canadian Historical Association, Royal Historical Society (fellow), Royal Asiatic Society (life member), Society of American Historians (fellow), Canadian Historical Association, American Studies Association, Athenaeum (life member), Explorer's Club (fellow), Royal Commonwealth Society (life member), Yale Club.

AWARDS, HONORS: Fulbright Award, 1952, 1962; Morse Fellow, 1959-60; Social Science Research Council Award, 1959-60; Eisenhower Award, for *Canada and the United States;* Smith-Mundt Fellow, 1962-63; Senior Faculty Fellowship from Yale University, 1965-66; Pulitzer Prize nomination, 1971, for *Blacks in Canada,* and 1988, for *Cloak and Gown;* Guggenheim Fellowship, 1976-77; Edgar Allan Poe Award from the Mystery Writers of America, 1982, for *Modus Operandi;* Resident Scholar, School of American Research, 1985; National Intelligence Study Center Prize for the Best Book on Intelligence,

ROBIN W. WINKS

1987, for *Cloak and Gown;* Conservationist of the Year Award from the Department of the Interior, 1988, for his work with the U.S. National Park System Advisory Board; Donner Medal from the Association for Canadian Studies in the United States, 1989, for his contributions to the study of Canada; has also received numerous honorary degrees, including honorary masters degree, Yale University, and honorary doctorate, University of Nebraska, 1977, and University of Colorado, 1987.

WRITINGS:

JUVENILE

(With Honor L. Winks) *The St. Lawrence,* Silver, 1980.
(With H. L. Winks), *The Colorado,* Silver, 1980.

OTHER

These New Zealanders!, Whitcombe, 1953.
New Trends and Recent Literature in Canadian History, American Historical Association, 1959.
Marshall Plan and the American Economy, Holt, 1960.
Canada and the United States: The Civil War Years, Johns Hopkins University Press, 1960, 3rd edition, 1988.
British Imperialism: Gold, God or Glory?, Holt, 1963.
The Cold War, Macmillan, 1964, revised edition (with Dan Yergin), 1978.
(Editor) *British Empire-Commonwealth: Historiographical Re-Assessments,* Duke University Press, 1966.
(Compiler with John Bastin) *Malaysia: Selected Historical Readings,* Oxford University Press, 1967, revised edition, 1979.
The Historian as Detective, Harper, 1969.
(With Marcus Cunliffe) *Pastmasters,* Harper, 1969.
Canadian-West Indian Union, Athlone, 1970.
Blacks in Canada, Yale University Press, 1971.
Slavery: A Comparative Perspective, New York University Press, 1972.
(With others) *The American Experience,* Addison-Wesley, 1972, 3rd edition, 1979.
(Editor) *Other Voices, Other Views,* Greenwood Press, 1978.
The Relevance of Canadian History: U.S. and Imperial Perspectives, Macmillan, 1979, 2nd edition, 1988.
An American's Guide to Britain, Scribner, 1979, 3rd edition, 1987.
Western Civilization: A Brief History, Prentice-Hall, 1979, 2nd edition, Collegiate Press, 1988.
(Editor) *Detective Fiction,* Prentice-Hall, 1980, expanded edition, Countryman Press, 1988.
Modus Operandi, Godine, 1982, 2nd edition, 1990.
(With others) *A History of Civilization: Prehistory to the Present,* Prentice-Hall, 1982, new edition, 1988.
Colloquium on Crime: Eleven Renowned Mystery Writers Discuss Their Work, Scribner, 1986.
Cloak and Gown: Scholars in the Secret War, 1939-1961, Morrow, 1987.
(With James Rush) *Asia in Western Fiction,* Manchester University Press, 1990.
Frederick Billings: A Biography, Oxford University Press, 1990.

Also author of sixteen-part television series "Between the Wars," and of two series for the British Broadcasting Corp. General editor of "The Modern Nations in Historical Perspective" series, Prentice-Hall, 1963. Contributor of articles to periodicals. Author of column on mystery fiction, *Boston Globe.*

WORK IN PROGRESS: The Idea of an American Imperialism; a history of mystery and detective fiction; a book on the writing of history.

SIDELIGHTS: "Historians are the best detectives there are, because they know how to ask good questions and how to dig for the answers. Teachers of history need, when teaching and writing, to demonstrate the enormous applicability of their discipline, to show young people how training in history may prepare them for careers in government, business, education, and research. The historian must reach out to audiences, writing both scholarly and general works, the specialized monograph and the general text. Writers must also grow, by trying their hand at biography, fiction, essays, whatever appeals to them. Above all, we must remember that writing (and reading) are fun.

"Anyone who thinks he consciously and carefully 'chose' an academic field for study is probably misleading himself, for it seems to me that 'choice' is a cover word for what Lippman once called 'drift and mastery.' Looking back, I *can* see certain clear influences in the direction of studying and teaching history. Both my parents were teachers, and to teach seemed an honorable thing to do. An eighth grade teacher made the study of American history through David S. Muzzey [author of history textbooks] seem the most exciting thing in my life for a year. My father introduced me to the boys' books written by Joseph Altsheler (who wrote two distinctly separate accounts of each major Civil War battle, one from the perspective of Johnny Reb and the other from that of Billy Yank), and this led to a fascination with the problem of how people perceive the truth on the basis of different experiences. Much early travel created a greediness for experience, until travel has become my drink. And above all, I knew that I enjoyed words.

(From *The St. Lawrence* by Honor Leigh Winks and Robin W. Winks. Photograph by Roland Weber.)

"So I began as a journalism major, until I discovered that writing sports articles was boring; then a geology major because of my interest in landscape and what happened to it, until I discovered that I preferred to put people on my landscapes; and after a history degree I took a master's in anthropology before I decided that I rested uncomfortably with the canons of evidence then used in that discipline. There was also a near- semester in law school, which proved that one can enjoy an adversary relationship with one's environments (as I like to) without making a career of it. At the time history seemed to win by default, and British Imperial history grew to take central focus in my interests partially on the Ozmandias principle, partially out of an interest in how power was exercised, and above all out of the twin interests in travel—the Empire did reach around the globe—and in how people could view the same subject from different perspectives, as between colonizer and the colonized, the exploiter and the exploited (an interest which also erupts in frequent historiographical essays).

"Still, I suspect that certain personality characteristics led me toward history, and that individual teachers, books, and incidents were meaningful only because those characteristics were already present. Indeed, academia consists of self-selected personality types, and historians in particular are made up of people who want to embrace the world closely by holding it at arm's length. As for myself, I know that I enjoy ambivalence, in human relations as well as professional, and ambivalence is what history is all about."

HOBBIES AND OTHER INTERESTS: Travel, wine, detective fiction, conservation.

FOR MORE INFORMATION SEE:

Yale Alumni Magazine and Journal, December, 1983.

ZUDECK, Darryl 1961-

PERSONAL: Born October 22, 1961, in New York, N.Y.; son of Irving and Elinor Zudeck. *Education:* School of Visual Arts, B.F.A., 1983; attended Art Students League, Brooklyn Museum Art School, and Pels School of Art. *Home:* 35 West 92nd St., New York, N.Y. 10025.

CAREER: Illustrator for magazines, book publishers, and advertising. *Exhibitions:* Kinney Gallery, New York City, 1979; Master Eagle Gallery, New York City, 1982; Art Directors Club, New York City, 1982; exhibition sponsored by *Raw* Magazine, Tokyo, Japan, 1983; RSVP Show, Warner Communications Gallery, New York City, 1983; Society of Illustrators, New York City, 1984, 1985, 1986; Portfolio Show, Society of Publication Designers, New York City, 1985; Society of Illustrators 27, Traveling Show, 1986. *Member:* Graphics Artists Guild. *Awards, honors:* Star Foundation Award, 1982; Rhodes Family Award, 1983; RSVP Award of Excellence, 1983; Creativity Award from *Art Direction,* 1984; Notable Children's Trade Book in the Field of Social Studies from the National Council for Social Studies and the Children's Book Council, 1985, and one of Child Study Association of America's Children's Books of the Year, Western Writers Association Best Cover Art, and Western Heritage Award, all 1986, all for *Prairie Songs*.

ILLUSTRATOR:

Pam Conrad, *Prairie Songs,* Harper, 1985.

Also illustrator of numerous book jackets. Contributor of illustrations to periodicals, including *New York Times, Archeology, Boston Globe, Financial World, Forbes, Global Finance, Harper's, New York, Redbook, Scholastic, Success, Working Woman* and *Avenue*.

DARRYL ZUDECK

WORK IN PROGRESS: Numerous illustrations for magazines such as *Wigwag;* covers for Random House and Harper; annual report covers.

HOBBIES AND OTHER INTERESTS: Collecting and restoring arts and crafts and furniture; restoring antique lights; collecting art and photography.

Cumulative Indexes

Illustrations Index

(In the following index, the number of the volume in which an illustrator's work appears is given *before* the colon, and the page number on which it appears is given *after* the colon. For example, a drawing by Adams, Adrienne appears in Volume 2 on page 6, another drawing by her appears in Volume 3 on page 80, another drawing in Volume 8 on page 1, and another drawing in Volume 15 on page 107.)

YABC

Index citations including this abbreviation refer to listings appearing in *Yesterday's Authors of Books for Children,* also published by Gale Research Inc., which covers authors who died prior to 1960.

A

B

C

D

E

F

G

H

I

J

K

L

M

N

O

P

Q

R

T

U

V

W

Y

Z

Author Index

The following index gives the number of the volume in which an author's biographical sketch, Brief Entry, or Obituary appears.

This index includes references to all entries in the following series, which are also published by Gale Research Inc.

YABC—*Yesterday's Authors of Books for Children: Facts and Pictures about Authors and Illustrators of Books for Young People from Early Times to 1960,* Volumes 1-2
CLR—*Children's Literature Review: Excerpts from Reviews, Criticism, and Commentary on Books for Children,* Volumes 1-19
SAAS—*Something about the Author Autobiography Series,* Volumes 1-9

A

B

C

D

F

G

Author Index

I

J

K

L

M

Q

R

S

T

W

Y

Z